**BARRON'S**

# SPANISH GRAMMAR

**Boris Corredor**

# THE EASY WAY

**BARRON'S**

© Copyright 2004 by Barron's Educational Series, Inc.

**Illustrations: Dre Design**

All rights reserved. No part of this book may be reproduced in any form, by photostat, microfilm, xerography, or any other means, or incorporated into any information retrieval system, electronic or mechanical, without the written permission of the copyright owner.

*All inquiries should be addressed to:*
Barron's Educational Series, Inc.
250 Wireless Boulevard
Hauppauge, New York 11788
*http://www.barronseduc.com*

**Library of Congress Cataloging-in-Publication Data**

Corredor, Boris
    Spanish Grammar the Easy Way / by Boris Corredor.
        p. cm.
    ISBN 0-7641-2263-0 (alk. paper)
    1. Spanish language—Grammar.    I. Title.

PC4105.C67 2003
468.2'421—dc21

                                    2003043540

International Standard Book Number 0-7641-2263-0
Library of Congress Control Number 2003043540

Printed in the United States of America
9 8 7 6 5 4 3

# CONTENTS

# INTRODUCTION

*S*panish Grammar the Easy Way is intended for individual learners who need essential information on the structure of the Spanish language or for students enrolled in a formal language course. It will also be useful to anybody who is planning a trip to Latin America or Spain and wishes to go beyond a basic level.

This book is designed to give students a clear picture of the form and function of Spanish, and to help them develop comprehension and vocabulary skills in a user-friendly and interesting way.

*Spanish Grammar the Easy Way* is organized into 18 chapters that cover pronunciation, parts of speech, and specific features of Spanish grammar that students often find daunting or, at the very least, confusing. In order to further assist the learner, contrasts are made between English and Spanish so as to highlight similarities and differences in grammatical concepts, syntax, and vocabulary. Every topic is immediately followed by practice exercises designed to increase comprehension and to develop vocabulary. After completing these exercises, students should check their answers using the Answer Keys found in Appendix A.

All questions and answers should be read aloud in order to practice pronunciation and to improve comprehension. The glossary at the end of the text (Appendix B) offers the meaning of each word as well as its grammatical function; it should be consulted often. Throughout the book, students will encounter "Tip Boxes" that clarify aspects of grammar that often are confusing or difficult.

The organization of the book by grammar topics allows for flexible use. The learner may go through it sequentially or choose to focus on a particular area where he or she needs more reinforcement.

Boris Corredor
Boston, November 2003

# Chapter 1

# PRONUNCIATION

**T**his chapter focuses on Spanish pronunciation. We will compare the "sounds" in Spanish and English as well as compare their written forms related to pronunciation (i.e. accent marks).

---

**TIP BOX**

Speech sounds are called *phonemes*; these phoneme symbols are written in slant brackets.

> **TIP BOX**
> American Spanish has eighteen consonant phonemes and ten vowel phonemes; Castilian Spanish, which is mainly spoken in Northern Spain, has two more consonant phonemes. These regional distinctions, however, will not be treated in this book.

# I. Vowels

## A. Vowel Sounds

The phoneme /**a**/ in Spanish is represented by the letter <a> and it is pronounced like the English <a> in the words "f**a**r," "f**a**ther," "p**a**lm." The phoneme /**a**/ is also pronounced in Spanish as the letter <o> in English, as in the words "l**o**ck," "h**o**t," "r**o**t," "c**o**t," "t**o**p."

**Example**

   <m**a**-s**a**>   (*dough*)

The phoneme /**e**/ in Spanish is represented by the letter <e>. The closest pronunciation is the English <e> in the word "**e**gg" or the <a> in the word "l**a**te." In Spanish, this sound is shorter and crisper than the sound in English.

**Example**

   <b**e**-b**é**>   (*baby*)

The phoneme /**i**/ in Spanish is represented by the letter <i>. The Spanish <i> is pronounced like the <ea> in the word "l**ea**k" or the <e> in the word "b**e**" or <ee> in the word "b**ee**," or <ea> in the word "b**ea**t." In Spanish, the sound is shorter than the sound in English.

**Example**

   <s**í**>     (*yes*)

The phoneme /**o**/ in Spanish is represented by the letter <o>. The Spanish <o> is pronounced like the <o> in the words "l**o**cation," "b**o**w," or "b**o**at," except that the sound is shorter.

**Example**

   <b**o**-b**o**>   (*dumb*)

The phoneme /**u**/ in Spanish is represented by the letter <u>. The Spanish <u> is pronounced like the <u> in the word "L**u**ke" or the <oo> in the word "l**oo**k." Again, the difference is that in Spanish the sound is shorter.

### Example

   <b**us**>      (*bus*)

## B. Semivowel Diphthong Sounds

The phoneme /**aw**/ in Spanish is represented by the combination letters <au>. This phoneme is composed of the phonemes /a/ and /u/ and it is pronounced as one syllable. The closest like pronunciation is the English <o> in the words "c**o**w," "h**o**w." In Spanish, however, the final /u/ sound is longer.

### Example

   <**au**-la>     (*classroom*)

The phoneme /**ay**/ in Spanish is represented by the combination letters <ai> and <ay>. This phoneme is composed of the phonemes /a/ and /i/ and it is pronounced as one syllable. The closest pronunciation is the <i> in the word "h**i**gh." In Spanish, the final /i/ sound is longer.

### Example

   <**ai**-re>     (*air*)
   <h**ay**>      (*there is*)

The phoneme /**ew**/ in Spanish is represented by the combination letters <eu>. This phoneme is composed of the phonemes /e/ and /u/ and it is pronounced as one syllable. There is no close pronunciation in English.

### Example

   <**Eu**ropa>   (*Europe*)

The phoneme /**ey**/ in Spanish is represented by the combination letters <ei> and <ey>. This phoneme is composed of the phonemes /e/ and /i/ and it is pronounced as one syllable. The closest pronunciation is the <ay> in the words "b**ay**" and "l**ay**." In Spanish, the final /i/ sound is longer.

### Example

   <**rei**-na>   (*queen*)
   <**rey**>     (*king*)

The phoneme /**oy**/ in Spanish is represented by the combination letters <oi> and <oy>. This phoneme is composed of the phonemes /o/ and /i/ and it is pronounced as one syllable. The closest pronunciation is the <oy> in the word "b**oy**." The difference is that in Spanish the final /i/ sound is longer.

**Example**

   &lt;b**oi**-na&gt;    (*beret*)
   &lt;h**oy**&gt;       (*today*)

# II. Consonants

## A. Consonant Sounds

The phoneme /**b**/ in Spanish is represented by the letters <b> and <v>. If either is at the beginning of a word or follows a consonant, it is pronounced like an English <b>. Otherwise, they have a sound that falls somewhere in between the <b> and the <v>.

**Example**

   &lt;**b**ar-co&gt;      (*boat*)
   &lt;**va**-ca&gt;       (*cow*)
   &lt;a**b**-so-lu-to&gt;  (*absolute*)
   &lt;á-**b**a-co&gt;    (*abacus* )
   &lt;a-**ve**&gt;        (*bird*)

The phoneme /**č**/ in Spanish is represented by the letter <ch> and it is pronounced like the <ch> in "**ch**ocolate."

**Example**

   &lt;**ch**i-**ch**a&gt; (South American indigenous drink made from corn)

The phoneme /**d**/ in Spanish is represented by the letter <d> and it is pronounced like the <d> in English. However, when it falls between vowels and follows <l> or <n>, it is pronounced like the <th> in "**th**e."

**Example**

   &lt;**d**os&gt;       (*two*)
   &lt;ha-**d**a&gt;    (*fairy*)
   &lt;cal-**d**o&gt;   (*broth*)
   &lt;ven-**d**er&gt;  (*to sell*)

The phoneme /f/ in Spanish is represented by the letter <f> and it is pronounced like <f> in the word "**f**ather."

### Example

    <**f**a-mi-lia> *(family)*
    <**f**a-ma>     *(fame)*

The phoneme /g/ in Spanish is represented by the letter <g>. It is pronounced /g/ only when followed by <a, o, u>, like the letter <g> in the word "**g**et."

### Example

    <**g**a-to>     *(cat)*
    <**g**o-rra>     *(cap)*
    <**g**u-sa-no> *(worm)*

The phoneme /h/ in Spanish is represented by the letter <j>, and by <g> when the latter is followed by <e, i>. It is pronounced like the English <h>, but stronger.

### Example

    <**j**i-ra-fa>     *(giraffe)*
    <**G**e-rar-do>   *(Gerard)*
    <**g**i-rar>     *(to spin)*

The phoneme /k/ in Spanish is represented by the letter <c> when it is followed by <a, o, u>. Similarly, the letter <q>, when followed by <ue, ui>, is pronounced /ke/ and /ki/. The letter <k>, as in the example "*kilogramo*," is pronounced like the <c> in the word "**c**at."

### Example

    <**c**a-sa>     *(house)*
    <**c**o-mi-da>   *(food)*
    <**c**u-ra>     *(priest)*
    <bu-**q**ue>     *(ship)*
    <**q**uin-to>   *(fifth)*
    <**k**i-lo>     *(kilogram)*

The phoneme /l/ in Spanish is represented by the letter <l> and it is pronounced like an English <l>.

### Example

    <**l**o-bo>     *(wolf)*

The phoneme /**m**/ in Spanish is represented by the letter <m> and it is pronounced like an English <m>.

### Example

<**m**a-**m**á>    (*mother*)

The phoneme /**n**/ in Spanish is represented by the letter <n> and it is pronounced like an English <n>.

### Example

<**n**o>        (*no*)

The phoneme /**ñ**/ in Spanish is represented by the letter <ñ> and it is pronounced like the <n> in the word "can**y**on."

### Example

<ca-**ñ**ón>    (*cannon*)

The phoneme /**p**/ in Spanish is represented by the letter <p> and it is pronounced like an English <p>.

### Example

<**p**e-lo>      (*hair*)

The phoneme /**r**/ in Spanish is represented by the letter <r>. When a word does **not** begin with an initial <r> or is preceded by <l, n, s>, the <r> is pronounced like the English <r> in "**r**ain."

### Example

<a-**r**o>        (*hoop*)

The phoneme /**rr**/ in Spanish is represented by the letter <r> when a word begins with <r> or the letter <r> is preceded by <l, n, s> or by the letters <rr> in the middle of a word. The /rr/ phoneme is pronounced as an English <r> but stronger, which in Spanish is done by trilling the tongue.

### Example

<**r**a-tón>        (*mouse*)
<a**l**-**r**e-de-dor>    (*around*)
<I**s**-**r**a-el>        (*Israel*)

The phoneme /**s**/ in Latin American Spanish is represented by the letter <s>, the letter <c> when followed by <e, i>, or the letter <z>. It is pronounced like the English <s> in the word "**s**un."

## Example

| | |
|---|---|
| <ab-**s**ur-do> | (*absurd*) |
| <**c**elos> | (*jealousy*) |
| <**c**in-co> | (*five*) |
| <**z**a-pa-to> | (*shoe*) |

The phoneme /**t**/ in Spanish is represented by the letter <t> and it is pronounced like an English <t>.

## Example

| | |
|---|---|
| <**t**an-go> | (*tango*) |

## B. Semiconsonant Sounds

The phoneme /**y**/ in Latin American Spanish is represented by the letter <y>, by the letter <i> when the latter is followed by <a, e, o, u>, and by the letter <ll> when the latter is followed by <a, e, i, o, u>. It is pronounced like the English <y> in "**y**ou."

## Example

| | |
|---|---|
| <**y**a> | (*already*) |
| <ha-**ci**a> | (*towards*) |
| <**hie**-lo> | (*ice*) |
| <**vio**> | (*saw*) |
| <**viu**-da> | (*widow*) |
| <ca-**lle**> | (*street*) |

The phoneme /**w**/ in Spanish is represented by the letter <u> when it is followed by <a, e, o, i>. It is pronounced like the English <w> in "**w**ell."

## Example

| | |
|---|---|
| <c**u**an-do> | (*when*) |
| <h**ue**-vo> | (*egg*) |
| <c**uo**-ta> | (*quota*) |
| <c**ui**-dar> | (*to take care of*) |

**Exercise 1.** Read the following words aloud and divide them into syllables.

| | | | | | |
|---|---|---|---|---|---|
| 1. | furia | _____ | muerto | _____ | rabia | _____ |
| 2. | huevo | _____ | Diana | _____ | cuidado | _____ |
| 3. | tiempo | _____ | verde | _____ | Juan | _____ |
| 4. | juego | _____ | agua | _____ | río | _____ |
| 5. | viaja | _____ | carroña | _____ | guarida | _____ |
| 6. | ciudad | _____ | tregua | _____ | lengua | _____ |
| 7. | puente | _____ | recuerdo | _____ | abuelo | _____ |
| 8. | nieve | _____ | tiempo | _____ | reumatismo | _____ |
| 9. | viuda | _____ | Luisa | _____ | viruela | _____ |
| 10. | pañuelo | _____ | azalea | _____ | Europa | _____ |
| 11. | antiguo | _____ | cuanto | _____ | cuadro | _____ |

**Exercise 2.** Pronounce and memorize the following tongue twisters.

1. Erre con erre cigarro,
   erre con erre barril,
   rápido corren los carros,
   cargados de azúcar al ferrocarril.

   Translation:
   *R with an R, cigar.*
   *R with an R, barrel.*
   *Rapid travel the cars (of the train)*
   *carrying the railroad's sugar.*

2. Tres tristes tigres comían trigo,
   en tres tristes trastos repletos de trigo.

   Translation:
   *Three sad tigers ate wheat.*
   *From three sad pots full of wheat.*

3. Compadre, cómprame un coco.
   Compadre, coco no compro,
   que el que poco coco come,
   poco coco compra.

   Translation:
   *"Friend, buy me a coconut."*
   *"Friend, I don't buy coconuts,*
   *because he who eats few coconuts,*
   *few coconuts buys."*

4. Pablito clavó un clavito,
   ¿qué clavito clavó Pablito?

   Translation:
   *Pablito nailed a nail.*
   *Which nail nailed Pablito?*

5. El amor es una locura
   que sólo el cura lo cura,
   pero el cura que lo cura
   comete una gran locura.

   Translation:
   *Love is a crazy thing*
   *that only a priest can cure,*
   *but the priest who cures it*
   *commits a crazy act.*

# III. Intonation

> **TIP BOX**
>
> Words are built by a process of combining consonants and vowels in characteristic patterns that are unique for each language that uses the alphabetic system. Once you understand the sound system in Spanish, the next step is to understand the rules for intonation.

Intonation means the stress you put on a specific syllable in a word as well as the pitch you apply on syllables when you pronounce a whole sentence. In Spanish, words are built by stressed (tonal) and non-stressed (atonal) syllables. In contrast with English, words in Spanish have only one stressed syllable.

> **TIP BOX**
>
> In Spanish, stress placement may have a grammatical function, that is, changing the stress to another syllable can change the part of speech and the meaning of the word.
>
> **Example**
>
> | | |
> |---|---|
> | *pa-pá (father)* | *pa-pa (potato)* |
> | *lás-ti-ma (pity)* | *las-ti-ma (hurt)* |

In Spanish, sentences are pronounced with some intonation at the beginning that is maintained before ending abruptly.

## Example

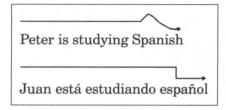

**Exercise 3.** Read the following verses to practice intonation in Spanish.

Nuestras vidas son los ríos
que van a dar en la mar,
que es el morir.
Jorge Manrique (1440–1479)

Translation:
*Our lives are rivers*
*that flow into the sea,*
*which is death.*

Verde que te quiero verde.
Verde viento. Verdes ramas.
El barco sobre la mar
y el caballo en la montaña.
Federico García Lorca (1898–1936)

Translation:
*Green, how I want you green.*
*Green wind. Green branches.*
*The ship out on the sea*
*and the horse on the mountain.*

¡Juventud, divino tesoro,
ya te vas para no volver!
Cuando quiero llorar, no lloro
y a veces lloro sin querer...
Rubén Darío (1867–1916)

Translation:
*Youth, divine treasure,*
*you leave never to return!*
*When I want to cry, I cannot*
*and sometimes I cry without wanting to...*

La más bella niña
de nuestro lugar,
hoy viuda y sola,
y ayer por casar,
viendo que sus ojos
a la guerra van,
a su madre dice,
que escucha su mal:
"Dejadme llorar
a orillas del mar".
Luis de Góngora (1521–1627)

Translation:
*The loveliest girl in all our countryside,*
*today forsaken, yesterday a bride,*
*Seeing her love ride forth to join the wars,*
*to her mother says, "Let me cry at the seashore."*

# IV. The Spanish Accentuation System

## A. Words Ending in *Vowel* or Consonant *n* or *s*

The accentuation system in Spanish is very simple. When words end in a **vowel** or the consonant **n** or **s**, the next to last syllable is stressed.

### Example

**ca**-lle (*street*), es-tu-**dian**-te (*student*), **be**-llo (*beautiful*), es-tu-**dian**-tes (*students*), **can**-tan (*they sing*)

## B. Words Ending in *Consonants* Other than *n* or *s*

For words ending in a consonant other than **n** or **s**, the stress falls on the last syllable.

### Example

co-**lor**     (*color*)
a-**rroz**     (*rice*)
fe-**liz**     (*happy*)

Exceptions for the rules above are words marked with an accent showing which syllable is stressed.

### Example

*lá*-piz     (*pencil*)
a-*vión*     (*airplane*)

## C. Diphthongs

When two vowels are side by side (example: viuda: *widow*), it is important to distinguish if both vowels are part of the same syllable or are divided into different syllables. To understand how this is done, remember that the combination of a strong vowel (a, e, o) with a weak vowel (i, u) or the combination of two weak vowels (i, u) together form **one** unique sound.

In these cases, however, when the stress is on the syllable that contains the combination of the two vowels, the stress is placed on the strong vowel (a, e, o) or on the second vowel when two weak vowels are combined.

In the following examples, the stressed syllable is marked in bold; the combination of two vowels together is underlined; and the strong vowel or the second vowel when the combination is formed by two weak vowels is marked in italics.

### Example

| Strong + Weak Vowel | Weak + Strong Vowel | Weak + Weak Vowel |
| --- | --- | --- |
| **a*i***-re (*air*) | **Di*a***-na (*Diana*) | ci*u*-**dad** (*city*) |
| **a*u***-llar (*howl*) | re-na-**cu*a***-jo (*toad*) | **ru*i***-do (*noise*) |
| **re*i***-na (*queen*) | **vi*e*n**-to (*wind*) | |
| *e*u-ca-**lip**-to (*eucalyptus*) | **tru*e***-no (*thunder*) | |
| *o*i-**dor** (*hearer*) | a-**vi*ó*n** (*airplane*) | |
| **S*o*u-sa** (*Souza*) | in-di-**vi**-d*u*o (*individual*) | |
| re*u*-**nir** (*to gather*) | **du*e***-lo (*sorrow*) | |

All other words that **do not** follow the preceding rules have a marked accent on the weak vowel (i, u), or on the second weak vowel when the combination is formed by two weak vowels. The accent mark indicates that the stress must be applied there.

### Example

| Strong + Weak Vowel | Weak + Strong Vowel | Weak + Weak Vowel |
| --- | --- | --- |
| ra-**íz** (*root*) | **dí**-a (*day*) | í-u (*there are no words*) |
| ma-**ú**-llo (*meow*) | **grú**-a (*tow truck*) | ú-i (*there are no words*) |
| pro-te-**í**-na (*protein*) | son-**rí**-e (*smile*) | |
| re-**í** (*I laughed*) | a-cen-**tú**-e (*stress*) | |
| o-**í**-do (*ear*) | **rí**-o (*river*) | |
| no-**ú**-me-no (*neumenon*) | **dú**-o (*duet*) | |
| re-**ú**-na (*gather*) | | |

Two strong vowels, however, are always divided in two different syllables.

## Example

| Strong + Strong Vowel |
|---|
| tr**a-er** (*to bring*) |
| ba-ca-l**a-o** (*codfish*) |
| al-d**e-a** (*village*) |
| **a-é**-re-o (*by air*) |
| an-ch**o-a** (*anchovy*) |
| r**o-e**-dor (*rodent*) |

---

**TIP BOX**

Adverbs ending in "-mente" have an accent mark only if the adjectives from which they derive have an accent mark.

**Example**

 fácil → fácilmente (*easy → easily*)
 cortés → cortésmente (*courteous → courteously*)

---

## D. Accents Distinguish a Word With Different Meanings

In Spanish, some words with the same spelling may or may not have an accent depending on their meaning or grammatical function.

 **a.** Demonstrative adjectives and demonstrative pronouns (este/a/os/as, ese/a/os/as, aquel, aquella/as/os) are written similarly, but they are distinguished by the context. However, in cases of ambiguity (the cases of actual ambiguity are rare), demonstrative pronouns take an accent mark.

## Example

Esta habla del pueblo.
*This talk (as a dialect) of the town.*

Ésta habla del pueblo.
*This (woman) talks about the town.*

**b.** The following possessive adjectives and personal pronouns are distinguished by an accent mark.

| **Possessive Adjectives** | **Personal Pronouns** |
|---|---|
| mi (*my*) | mí (*me*) |
| tu (*your*) | tú (*you*) |

## Example

Julia me regaló el libro a <u>mí</u> y no a ti.
*Julia gave the book to me, not to you.*

<u>Mi</u> perro Tobías ladra muy fuerte.
*My dog, Tobías, barks very loud.*

**c.** All interrogative words have a written accent that distinguishes them from other pronouns; these interrogatives are accented when used to introduce an interrogative sentence.

| ¿Cómo? | *How?* |
|---|---|
| ¿Cuál(es)? | *Which (which ones)?* |
| ¿Cuándo? | *When?* |
| ¿Cuánto(o), (a)? | *How much?* |
| ¿Cuánto(os), (as)? | *How many?* |
| ¿Dónde? | *Where?* |
| ¿Qué? | *What?* |
| ¿Quién(es)? | *Who, whom?* |

## Example

<u>¿Cuándo</u> vamos a cine?
*"When are we going to go to the movies?"*

<u>Cuando</u> tenga tiempo.
*"When I have time."*

**d.** Other words.

- **aún** (*still, yet*)    **aun** (*even*)

## Example

Que pasará con María que <u>aún</u> no llega.
*What happened to María that she's not here yet.*

<u>Aun</u> después de comer Jorge seguía con hambre.
*Even after eating Jorge continued to be hungry.*

- **cómo** (*how*) **como** (*as, like*)

## Example

¿<u>Cómo</u> te llamas?
*What's your name?*

María es tan alta <u>como</u> José.
*María is as tall as José.*

- **más** (*more*) **mas** (*but*)

## Example

Quiero <u>más</u> helado, por favor.
*I want more ice cream, please.*

Te busqué <u>mas</u> no te encontré.
*I looked for but I did not find you.*

- **sí** (*yes*) **si** (*if*)

## Example

María vendrá <u>si</u> quiere.
*María will come if she wants to.*

—¿Estás contento?
*"Are you happy?"*

—<u>Sí</u>, estoy muy contento.
*"Yes, I am very happy."*

- **sólo** (*only*) **solo** (*alone*)

## Example

José vive <u>solo</u>.
*José lives alone.*

Iremos <u>sólo</u> si nos invitas.
*We will go, [but] only if you invite us.*

- **té** (*tea*) **te** (*you*)

## Example

Los ingleses beben <u>té</u> todos los días a las cinco.
*The English drink tea every day at five o'clock.*

<u>Te</u> recomiendo que veas la última película de Almodóvar.
*I recommend that you see Almodóvar's last film.*

- **él** (*he*)        **el** (*the*)

## Example

Él está cansado.
*He is tired.*

El niño está aburrido.
*The child is bored.*

**Exercise 4.** Divide the following words into syllables and underline the stressed syllable.

| | | | | | | |
|---|---|---|---|---|---|---|
| 1. ahora | idea | deshacer | toalla | cuerda | maestro | ciudad |
| 2. adiós | ciencia | inspirar | durazno | abstracto | completo | destruir |
| 3. reconstruir | cuidado | temprano | septiembre | peligro | resplandor | lápiz |
| 4. emperatriz | aire | Eugenia | baúl | frío | alcohol | lección |
| 5. azul | calle | Islam | desplazar | influir | león | cereal |
| 6. baile | héroe | mercader | feliz | película | título | gramática |

**Exercise 5.** The following words have the stressed syllable in bold. Put an accent on the words that require it.

| | | | | | | |
|---|---|---|---|---|---|---|
| 1. **jo**ven | re**loj** | **la**piz | **an**gel | **de**bil | ho**tel** | se**gun** |
| 2. a**mor** | **ce**lebre | ol**vi**do | pe**li**cula | musul**man** | **jo**venes | **an**geles |
| 3. direc**tor** | **or**denes | **ti**tulo | **cre**dito | **ter**mino | ter**mi**no | **vic**tima |
| 4. in**fe**liz | **fe**liz | ani**mal** | **u**nico | mu**jer** | se**ñor** | sim**pa**tico |
| 5. **vir**genes | inte**res** | **es**ta | **es**ta | gra**ma**tica | pe**li**gro | ameri**ca**nos |
| 6. chi**me**nea | **sa**la | e**xa**men | e**xa**menes | ra**zon** | ra**zo**nes | **ar**bol |
| 7. a**za**lea | ta**re**a | mu**jer** | hipo**po**tamo | **pa**pa | an**ti**guo | **pa**pa |

**Exercise 6.** The following sentences are missing accent marks or have unnecessary accent marks. Put an accent on the words that require it or remove the accent mark.

1. Julio está sólo con su mascota.
2. Él te es una bebida.
3. Te invito a cine.
4. Lola y Josefa quieren más te.
5. ¿Cuanto cuesta aquél sombrero?
6. Cómo no he cumplido 21 años, aun no puedo ir a la discoteca contigo.
7. Todos creímos que el sabía que estabas casada.
8. Solo iremos sí nos invitas.
9. Tu no querrás ir, pero yo si.
10. Queremos ir, más no tenemos tiempo.

# Chapter 2

# THE NOUN AND THE ARTICLES

hat is a noun?

**Yo soy un sustantivo.**
*(I am a noun.)*

In Spanish (as in English) a **noun** refers to a person (*José*), an animal (*el gato*—the cat), a place (*el barrio*—the neighborhood), a thing (*el libro*—the book), an event (*la fiesta*—the party) or an abstract concept (*la justicia*—justice). However, nouns in Spanish are characterized by gender with a corresponding article. The definite article **el** accompanies a masculine noun and the definite article **la** accompanies a feminine noun. Nouns are usually classified as either common or proper.

**TIP BOX**

Common nouns name concrete things that are tangible and nonspecific including persons, animals, places, things, and events. Examples are *persona* (person), *animal* (animal), *perro* (dog), *gato* (cat), *casa* (house), *manzana* (apple), *agua* (water), *hada* (fairy), *árbol* (tree), *mesa* (table), and *dragón* (dragon). Common nouns also name abstract concepts such as *la justicia* (justice), *la inteligencia* (intelligence), *la pobreza* (poverty), or *la vida* (life).

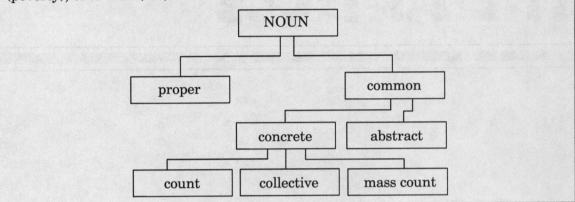

# I. The Gender of Nouns

## A. Nouns that Refer to Human Beings

Nouns that refer to human beings (the man, the woman) or animals (the horse, the mare), show their gender by their inherent meaning.

In order to deduce the masculine or feminine form of a noun, the following rules apply.

## Gender Rules

**a.** Nouns that end in **-o** (masculine), change to feminine by replacing the final **-o** with an **a**.

| Masculine | Feminine | English Translation |
|---|---|---|
| el abuel**o** | l**a** abuel**a** | *grandfather/grandmother* |
| el amig**o** | l**a** amig**a** | *male friend/ female friend* |
| el compañer**o** | l**a** compañer**a** | *male classmate/female classmate* |
| el cuñad**o** | l**a** cuñad**a** | *brother-in-law/sister-in-law* |
| el herman**o** | l**a** herman**a** | *brother/sister* |
| el muchach**o** | l**a** muchach**a** | *boy/girl* |
| el prim**o** | l**a** prim**a** | *male cousin/female cousin* |
| el sobrin**o** | l**a** sobrin**a** | *nephew/niece* |
| el suegr**o** | l**a** suegr**a** | *father-in-law/mother-in-law* |
| el tí**o** | l**a** tí**a** | *uncle/aunt* |
| el vecin**o** | l**a** vecin**a** | *male neighbor/female neighbor* |

**Exercise 1.** Complete the following sentences using the genealogical tree above.

1. Liliana es ___ _____ preferida de ___ _____ Rosario.
2. ___ _____ de María Sol es Andrés.
3. Felipe es ___ _____ de Gabriela.
4. María es ___ _____ de Julián.
5. Margarita es ___ _____ de Andrés.
6. Tobías es ___ _____ de la familia.
7. Rosario es ___ _____ de Gabriela.
8. Julián es ___ _____ de María Sol.
9. Laura es ___ _____ de Alfonso y Gabriela.
10. Gabriela es ___ _____ de Margarita.

**Exercise 2.** Change the underlined nouns either to masculine or feminine.

### Example

El amigo de tu hermana tiene sueño.
***La amiga** de tu hermana tiene sueño.*

1. El hermano de José tiene hambre.
   _____ de José tiene hambre.

2. <u>El vecino</u> de mi tía tiene treinta años.

_____ de mi tía tiene treinta años.

3. <u>La amiga</u> de mi prima baila bien.

_____ de mi prima baila bien.

4. <u>El sobrino</u> de María estudia en Boston.

_____ de María estudia en Boston.

5. <u>La abuela</u> cumple ochenta años.

_____ cumple ochenta años.

6. <u>El sicólogo</u> trabaja en el consultorio.

_____ trabaja en el consultorio.

7. <u>El gato</u> toma leche.

_____ toma leche.

8. <u>La perra</u> juega con los niños.

_____ juega con los niños.

9. <u>La tía</u> llega del trabajo temprano.

_____ llega del trabajo temprano.

10. <u>El primo</u> de Cecilia tiene doce años.

_____ de Cecilia tiene doce años.

**b.** Nouns that end in the consonants **-n, -r, -l** (masculine) change to the feminine by adding an **-a**.

| Masculine | Feminine | English Translation |
|-----------|----------|---------------------|
| el leó**n** | la leon**a** | *lion* |
| el peató**n** | la peaton**a** | *pedestrian* |
| el auto**r** | la autor**a** | *author* |
| el docto**r** | la doctor**a** | *doctor* |
| el escrito**r** | la escritor**a** | *writer* |
| el profeso**r** | la profesor**a** | *professor* |

**Exercise 3.** Complete the following sentences using the appropriate definite article **el** or **la**.

1. __ doctor trabaja en el hospital.
2. __ escritor escribe una novela.
3. __ leona cuida sus crías.
4. __ peatón cruza la calle.
5. __ profesora escribe en el tablero.
6. María, __ española, es de Madrid.
7. __ profesor de español es simpático.
8. __ escritora Gabriela Mistral ganó el premio Nobel de literatura.
9. __ león atrapó una cebra.
10. __ doctora examina al paciente.

**Exercise 4.** Change the underlined nouns and articles either to masculine or feminine.

## Example

El fundador del instituto cumplió cien años de muerto.

*La **fundadora** del instituto cumplió cien años de muer**ta**.*

1. La patrona paga muy bien a sus empleados.
   _____ paga muy bien a sus empleados.
2. El señor Mendoza trabaja mucho.
   _____ Mendoza trabaja mucho.
3. La doctora examina al paciente.
   _____ examina al paciente.
4. El rector del colegio renunció.
   _____ del colegio renunció.
5. La directora anunció un aumento de salarios.
   _____ anunció un aumento de salarios.
6. El embajador renunció a su cargo.
   _____ renunció a su cargo.
7. La vendedora promociona su nuevo producto.
   _____ promociona su nuevo producto.
8. El conductor de la escuela conduce despacio.
   _____ de la escuela conduce despacio.
9. El explorador llegó al Polo Norte.
   _____ llegó al Polo Norte.
10. El administrador de la compañía llegó tarde esta mañana.
    _____ de la compañía llegó tarde esta mañana.

**c.** Some nouns are identical in both masculine and feminine forms, and the only way to determine their gender is by the adjacent word (an article or an adjective) or by the word's context.

| Masculine | Feminine | English Translation |
| --- | --- | --- |
| **el** adolescente | **la** adolescente | adolescent |
| **el** agente | **la** agente | agent |
| **el** artista | **la** artista | artist |
| **el** astronauta | **la** astronauta | astronaut |
| **el** atleta | **la** atleta | athlete |
| **el** camarada | **la** camarada | comrade |
| **el** cantante | **la** cantante | singer |
| **el** cliente | **la** cliente | client |
| **el** espía | **la** espía | spy |
| **el** estudiante | **la** estudiante | student |
| **el** joven | **la** joven | youth |
| **el** testigo | **la** testigo | witness |
| **el** visitante | **la** visitante | visitor |

**Exercise 5.** According to the context, complete the following sentences using the appropriate definite article *el* or *la*.

1. María, ____ estudiante, está content**a**.
   José, ____ estudiante, está content**o**.
2. Juan es ____ testigo del crimen.
   Marta es ____ testigo del crimen.
3. El señor Rodríguez es ____ visitante más importante.
   La señora Rodríguez es ____ visitante más importante.
4. ____ cliente es amig**a** de mi padre.
   ____ cliente es amig**o** de mi padre.
5. ____ guía es amig**o** de mi madre.
   ____ guía es amig**a** de mi madre.
6. ____ novelista es muy famos**a**.
   ____ novelista es muy famos**o**.
7. ____ astronauta Julia se prepara para viajar a Marte.
   ____ astronauta Carlos se prepara para viajar a Marte.
8. Teresa, ____ adolescente, juega para el equipo de fútbol de su escuela.
   Jorge, ____ adolescente, juega para el equipo de fútbol de su escuela.
9. ____ cantante Isabel recibió muchos aplausos anoche en el concierto.
   ____ cantante Romeo recibió muchos aplausos anoche en el concierto.

**Exercise 6.** According to the context, complete the following sentences using the appropriate definite article *la, el, las,* or *los*.

1. ___ joven Sofía estudia biología en la Universidad Autónoma de México.
2. ___ mejor atleta de la universidad está enferma.
3. Juliana, ___ astronauta, hace experimentos en el transbordador espacial.
4. ___ agentes secretos descubrieron el crimen.
5. ___ cantantes del grupo de música Las Bandidas llegaron a Nueva York.
6. Todos ___ estudiantes de la universidad protestaron en contra de la guerra.
7. Aquellas mujeres son ___ clientes del salón de belleza de tu madre.
8. Ella es ___ artista de que te hablé el otro día.
9. ___ espías fueron sorprendidos por el Servicio Secreto.

**d.** Some nouns have special masculine and feminine forms.

| Masculine | Feminine | English Translation |
|-----------|----------|---------------------|
| **el** actor | **la** actriz | *actor/actress* |
| **el** barón | **la** baronesa | *baron/baroness* |
| **el** hombre | **la** mujer | *man/woman* |
| **el** rey | **la** reina | *king/queen* |

| **el** príncipe | **la** princesa | *prince/princess* |
| **el** yerno | **la** nuera | *son-in-law/daughter-in-law* |
| **el** caballo | **la** yegua | *horse/mare* |
| **el** caballero | **la** dama | *gentleman/lady* |
| **el** padre | **la** madre | *father/mother* |

**Exercise 7.** Complete the following crossword puzzle using the opposite or inverse masculine or feminine corresponding noun.

**Across:**
1 yerno
4 dama
6 príncipe
8 actor
10 barón
11 nuera
12 padre
13 hombre

**Down:**
2 rey
3 princesa
4 yegua
5 reina
7 caballero
9 madre
11 caballo

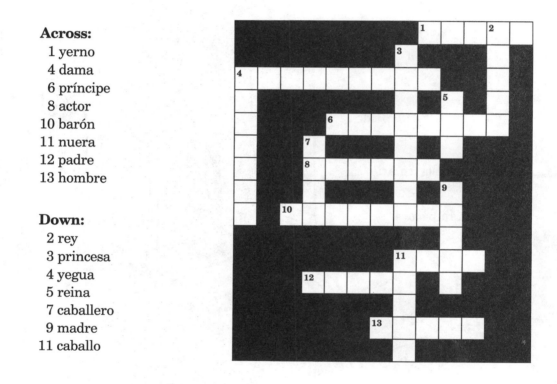

# B. Gender of Nouns With an Arbitrary Referent

To determine the gender of a noun that has an arbitrary referent, the following rules apply:

**a.** Nouns are feminine if they end in **-a, -d, -is, -sión, -ción,** and **-z.**

la vid**a** (*life*)
la realida**d** (*reality*)
la sínte**sis** (*synthesis*)
la deci**sión** (*decision*)
la can**ción** (*song*)
la lu**z** (*light*)

**b.** All others nouns are masculine if they end in **-o, -e, <u>an accented vowel</u>**, consonants that are neither **-d** or **-z**, and nouns ending in **-is**, **-sión**, and **-ción**.

el per**ro** (*dog*)
el perfum**e** (*perfume*)
el coli<u>brí</u> (*hummingbird*)
el árbo**l** (*tree*)
el coj<u>ín</u> (*cushion*)
el mot<u>or</u> (*engine*)

**Vocabulary**

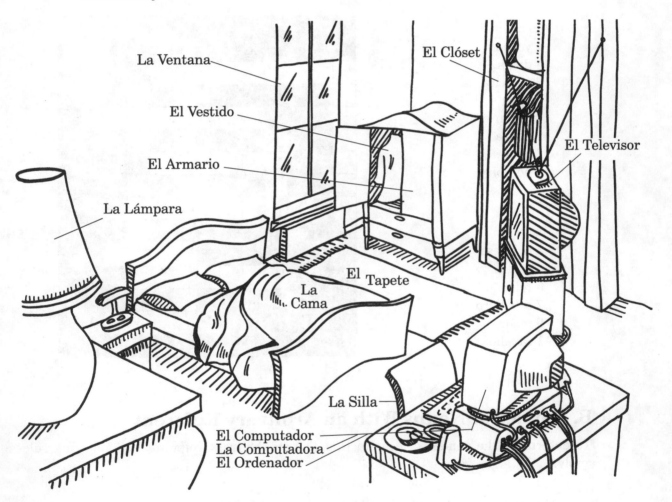

**Exercise 8.** Complete the following sentences using the appropriate definite article *el* or *la*.

1. ___ señora olvidó hacer ___ cama está mañana.
2. En ___ habitación está ___ computador, ___ silla, ___televisor, ___ cama y ___ lámpara.

3. ___ ventana está cerrada y ___ clóset está abierto.
4. María compró ___ vestido en ___ almacén.
5. ___ tapete de la sala está sucio.
6. Mi abrigo negro está en ___ armario.

**Vocabulary**

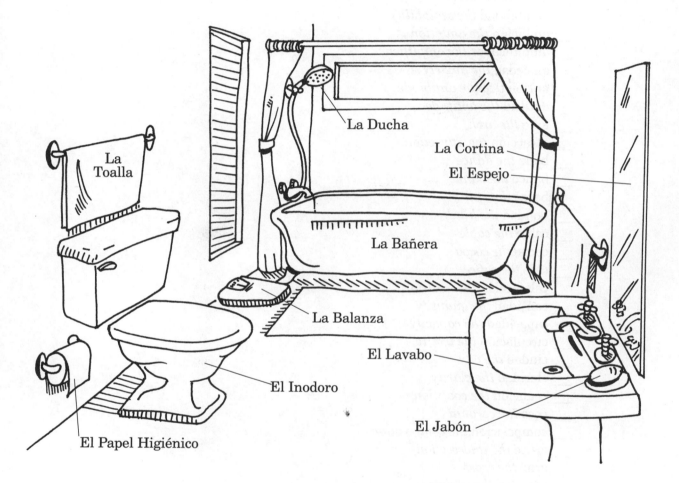

La Ducha

La Cortina

El Espejo

La Toalla

La Bañera

La Balanza

El Lavabo

El Inodoro

El Jabón

El Papel Higiénico

**Exercise 9**. Complete the following sentences using the appropriate definite article *el* or *la*.

1. El señor se resbaló en ___ bañera de su casa.
2. Las manos se lavan en ___ lavabo.
3. Laura se pesa en ___ balanza.
4. Rosario se lava las manos con ___ jabón y se seca con ___ toalla.
5. Gabriela se peina mirándose en ___ espejo.
6. Margarita olvida siempre cerrar ___ cortina de baño cuando está en ___ ducha.

**Exercise 10.** Put the appropriate definite article *el* or *la* for the following nouns.

___ acné *the acne*
___ actividad *the activity*
___ admiración *the admiration*
___ afiche *the poster*
___ agresividad *the aggressiveness*
___ aljibe *the cistern*
___ amabilidad *the amiability*
___ ambición *the ambition*
___ amplificador *the amplifier*
___ ansiedad *the anxiety*
___ antibiótico *the antibiotic*
___ aptitud *the aptitude*
___ arco *the arch*
___ atracción *the attraction*
___ baile *the dance*
___ banco *the bank*
___ barco *the ship*
___ bondad *the kindness*
___ cable *the cable*
___ cacao *the cocoa*
___ café *the coffee*
___ calefacción *the heating*
___ cantidad *the quantity*
___ capacidad *the capacity*
___ circulación *the traffic*
___ ciudad *the city*
___ claridad *the clarity*
___ coalición *the coalition*
___ coco *the coconut*
___ composición *the composition*
___ cruce *the intersection*
___ cruz *the cross*
___ decisión *the decision*
___ declaración *the declaration*
___ depresión *the depression*
___ destornillador *the screwdriver*
___ dirección *the direction*
___ domingo *the Sunday*
___ dulce *the sweet*
___ educación *the education*
___ electrodoméstico *the appliance*
___ embarcación *the vessel*

___ equipaje *the baggage*
___ escasez *the shortage*
___ estupidez *the stupidity*
___ evaluación *the evaluation*
___ habilidad *the skill*
___ humidificador *the humidifier*
___ infección *the infection*
___ liberación *the liberation*
___ libertad *the freedom*
___ luz *the light*
___ madurez *the maturity*
___ meteoro *the meteor*
___ monitor *the monitor*
___ nación *the nation*
___ nariz *the nose*
___ niñez *the childhood*
___ operación *the operation*
___ pared *the wall*
___ pasión *the passion*
___ piedad *the piety*
___ prisión *the prison*
___ profesión *the profession*
___ propiedad *the property*
___ publicidad *the advertising*
___ reflector *the reflector*
___ retrovisor *the rearview mirror*
___ revolución *the revolution*
___ salud *the health*
___ sed *the thirst*
___ selección *the selection*
___ sencillez *the simplicity*
___ superstición *the superstition*
___ tabaco *the tobacco*
___ televisión *the television*
___ televisor *the television*
___ tempestad *the tempest*
___ tensión *the tension*
___ timidez *the shyness*
___ tóxico *the toxic*
___ tronco *the trunk*
___ vapor *the steam*
___ vegetación *the vegetation*
___ versión *the version*
___ virtud *the virtue*
___ voz *the voice*

**c.** Feminine exceptions.

- Nouns that are Greek in origin generally end in **-ma** and are masculine.

## Example

| | |
|---|---|
| **el** problema (*the problem*) | **el** sistema (*the system*) |
| **el** clima (*the weather*) | **el** dilema (*the dilemma*) |
| **el** tema (*the theme*) | **el** drama (*the drama*) |
| **el** teorema (*the theorem*) | **el** enigma (*the enigma*) |
| **el** esquema (*the outline*) | **el** idioma (*the language*) |

- The following nouns that end in **-a**, **-d**, **-is,** and **-z** are **NOT** feminine.

| -a | -d | -is | -z |
|---|---|---|---|
| **el** día (*day*) | **el** césped (*lawn*) | **el** análisis (*analysis*) | **el** aprendiz (*apprentice*) |
| **el** mapa (*map*) | **el** huésped (*host*) | | **el** avestruz (*ostrich*) |
| **el** planeta (*the planet*) | **el** ataúd (*coffin*) | | **el** cáliz (*goblet*) |
| **el** tranvía (*street car*) | | | **el** arroz (*rice*) |
| | | | **el** pez (*fish*) |
| | | | **el** lápiz (*pencil*) |
| | | | **el** ajedrez (*chess*) |
| | | | **el** antifaz (*mask*) |
| | | | **el** altavoz (*speaker*) |
| | | | **el** maíz (*maize*) |

**Exercise 11.** Complete the following paragraph, using the following words and their corresponding articles: **el problema, el esquema, el teorema, el clima, el dilema, el idioma, el tema**

María Sol utilizó ___ _____ de Pitágoras para resolver ___ _____ de matemáticas. Ahora tiene que terminar la tarea de español. ___ _____ español es muy fácil. La tarea de ciencias es más difícil. María Sol debe escribir un ensayo. _____ del ensayo es sobre ___ _____ tropical. ___ _____ de María es escribir directamente el ensayo o hacer primero ___ _____.

**Exercise 12.** Give the appropriate noun for each picture and remember to give it its corresponding article.

1. _____

2. _____

3. _____

4. _____

5. _____

6. _____

7. _____

8. _____

9. _____

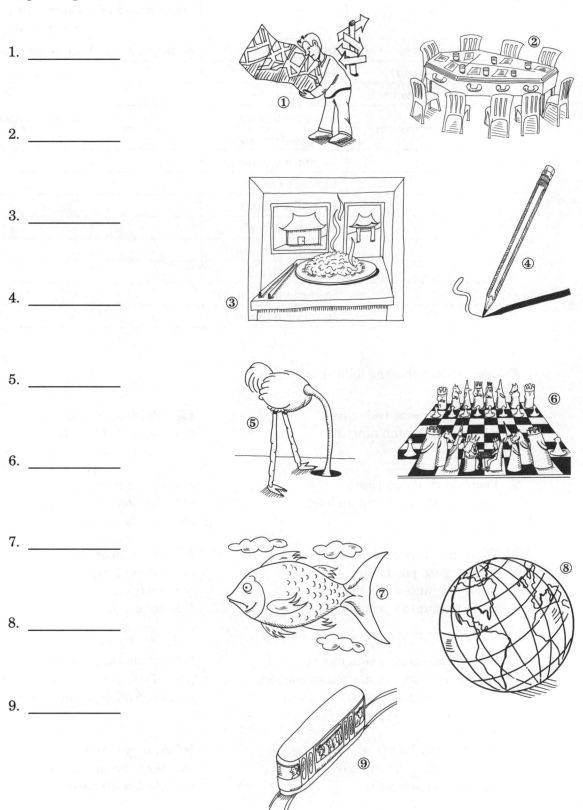

**d.** Masculine exceptions.

| -o | -e | -stress vowel | Consonants that Are Neither -d nor z |
|---|---|---|---|
| **la** foto (*photo*) | **la** llave (*key*) | **la** fe (*faith*) | **la** miel (*honey*) |
| **la** mano (*hand*) | **la** calle (*street*) | | **la** sal (*salt*) |
| **la** moto (*motorcycle*) | **la** fiebre (*fever*) | | **la** hiel (*bile*) |
| | **la** carne (*meat*) | | **la** piel (*skin*) |
| | **la** frase (*sentence*) | | |
| | **la** gente (*people*) | | |
| | **la** nieve (*snow*) | | |
| | **la** noche (*night*) | | |
| | **la** nube (*cloud*) | | |
| | **la** sangre (*blood*) | | |
| | **la** suerte (*luck*) | | |
| | **la** tarde (*afternoon*) | | |
| | **la** muerte (*death*) | | |

**Exercise 13.** Solve the following riddles.

1. Cinco hijos tiene cada una
   y dan golpes como ninguna.

   _____

2. Pequeña como un ratón
   y guarda la casa como un león.

   _____

3. Todos pasan por mí
   y yo no paso por nadie;
   todos preguntan por mí,
   yo no pregunto por nadie.

   _____

4. Cuando no estoy cocida roja soy,
   cuando me cocinan me pongo marrón,
   y soy alimento del león.

   _____

5. Blanca, muy blanca eres;
   pero cuando calienta el sol,
   rápido desapareces.

   _____

*Five children has each one
and they give blows as no one.*

*Small as a mouse,
but as a lion
she guards the house.*

*Everybody steps on me,
and I do not step on anybody;
everybody asks for me,
I do not ask for anybody.*

*When I am raw, red I am;
when I am cooked, brown I get,
and the food of the lion I am.*

*White, very white you are,
but when the sun heats,
quickly you disappear.*

6. Soy enemiga del sol y en mí
   brillan los soles
   y a pesar de tantas luces
   me iluminan con faroles.

   _____

*I am an enemy of the sun, in me*
*the suns shine, and*
*in spite of so many lights*
*with lanterns they illuminate me.*

7. Una señora
   que se deshace
   llora que llora.
   ¿Quién es?

   _____

*A lady that dissolves*
*while crying and crying.*
*Who is she?*

8. Rojo ha sido siempre mi vivir,
   pero algunos de azul
   me quieren vestir.

   _____

*All my life I have been red,*
*but some in blue*
*want me to dress.*

9. Blanca soy,
   nací en el mar;
   y en tu bautizo
   tuve que estar.

   _____

*White I am,*
*I was born in the sea;*
*and in your baptism*
*I had to be.*

**Exercise 14.** Give each picture the appropriate noun and corresponding definite article.

1. _____

2. _____

3. _____

4. _____

5. _____

## C. Nouns With Different Meanings

The meanings of some nouns depend on how the article is used.

| Spanish | | English Translation | |
|---|---|---|---|
| **Masculine** | **Feminine** | **Masculine** | **Feminine** |
| el capital | la capital | *capital (money)* | *capital (city)* |
| el corte | la corte | *cut* | *court* |
| el cura | la cura | *priest* | *healing* |
| el guía | la guía | *guide (person)* | *guidebook* |
| el modelo | la modelo | *model (example)* | *fashion model* |
| el orden | la orden | *order (arrangement)* | *order (command)* |
| el papa | la papa | *pope* | *potato* |
| el policía | la policía | *policeman* | *police* |

**Exercise 15.** Using the list above, choose the appropriate noun and its corresponding article.

1. ___ _____ de ojos negros ganó el concurso de moda.
2. ___ _____ en el salón de clase era perfecto.
3. ___ _____ vive en el Vaticano.
4. ___ _____ del museo del Prado es excelente.
5. ___ _____ para tu enfermedad es el reposo.
6. ___ _____ de España es Madrid.
7. ___ _____ determinó que la ley era inconstitucional.
8. ___ _____ de coche que compraste me gusta mucho.
9. ___ _____ recibió ____ _____ de captura.
10. ___ _____ de tu vestido es hermoso.
11. ___ _____ es una raíz comestible.
12. ___ _____ nos mostró todos los lugares turísticos.

# II. The Plural Forms of Nouns

In Spanish, plural nouns are formed in three ways:

**a.** When the noun ends in an unstressed vowel, an **-s** is added.

### Example

| el <u>li</u>bro | los <u>li</u>bro**s** | *book/books* |
|---|---|---|
| la <u>ca</u>sa | las <u>ca</u>sa**s** | *house/houses* |
| la <u>ma</u>dre | las <u>ma</u>dre**s** | *mother/mothers* |

**Exercise 16.** Rewrite the following sentences in the plural.

### Example

El libro está en la estantería.
*Los libros están en la estantería.*

1. El chocolate está sobre la mesa.
   _____

2. La cama está sin tender.
   _____

3. La casa está al norte de la ciudad.
   _____

4. El tigre está en la jaula.
   _____

5. El problema está en los gobernantes.
   _____

6. La tienda está en el barrio.
   _____

**Exercise 17.** Use the correct definite articles *el, la, el, los* with the following nouns.

1. _____ casas _____ perros _____ gatas
2. _____ dormitorios _____ problemas _____ manos
3. _____ teorema _____ días _____ motos
4. _____ noches _____ luna _____ Tierra
5. _____ sistemas _____ viaje _____ planetas
6. _____ mapas _____ poemas _____ programas

## Vocabulary

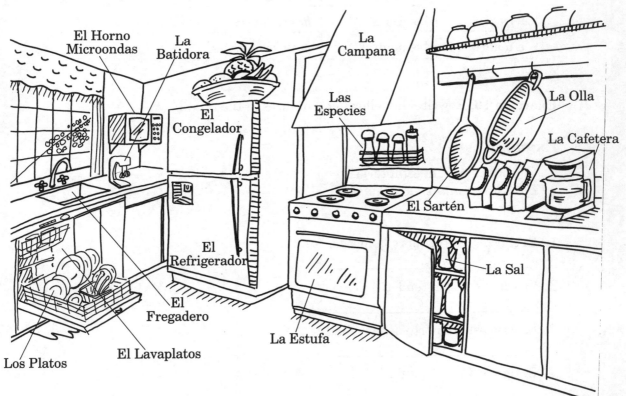

El Horno Microondas
La Batidora
La Campana
Las Especies
La Olla
El Congelador
La Cafetera
El Sartén
El Refrigerador
La Sal
El Fregadero
La Estufa
El Lavaplatos
Los Platos

**Exercise 18.** Rewrite the following sentences in the plural.

## Example

La ventana es transparente.
*Las ventanas son transparentes.*

1. El horno microondas es negro.

   _____

2. La batidora es verde.

   _____

3.  El fregadero es metálico.

    _____

4.  La olla es grande.

    _____

5.  La cafetera es eléctrica.

    _____

6.  La estufa es blanca.

    _____

**b.** When the noun ends in a consonant, a <u>stressed vowel</u>, or a *-y*, **-es** is added.

| el árbol | los árbol**es** | *tree/trees* |
| el actor | los actor**es** | *actor/actors* |
| el maniquí | los maniquí**es** | *mannequin/mannequins* |
| la ley | las ley**es** | *law/laws* |
| el tren | los tren**es** | *train/trains* |
| el pan | los pan**es** | *loaf/loaves* |

## TIP BOX

Note that if the noun ends in **-z**, the singular form becomes a **-c-** before the **-es** in the plural.

| el pez | los pe**ces** | *fish/fishes* |
| el lápiz | los lápi**ces** | *pencil/pencils* |
| la nuez | las nue**ces** | *nut/nuts* |

## TIP BOX

Exceptions to this rule are:

| el café | los café**s** | *coffee/coffees* |
| el esquí | los esquí**s** | *ski/skies* |
| el menú | los menú**s** | *menu/menus* |
| el papá | los papá**s** | *daddy/daddies* |
| el pie | los pie**s** | *foot/feet* |

**Exercise 19.** Rewrite the following sentences in the plural.

## Example

El señor es alt**o**.
***Los** señore**s** **son** altos*.

1. El refrigerador del hotel es blanco.
   _____

2. El congelador de mi casa es eficiente.
   _____

3. El tren es lento.
   _____

4. La ley es obsoleta.
   _____

5. El ataúd es de madera.
   _____

6. El sartén es de hierro.
   _____

**Exercise 20.** Rewrite the following sentences in their singular form.

## Example

Los señores están animados.
*El señor está animado*.

1. Los empleados están cansados.
   _____

2. Los motores están encendidos.
   _____

3. Los reyes están presos.
   _____

4. Los actores están desesperados.
   _____

5. Los maniquíes están vestidos elegantemente.
   _____

6. Los panes están crujientes.
   _____

**Vocabulary**

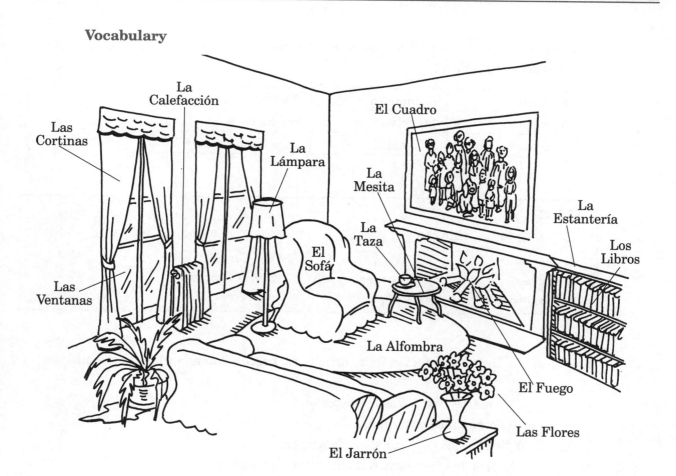

**Exercise 21.** Use the preceding vocabulary to write the appropriate definite article and corresponding noun, in plural or singular form.

Todos los días la abuela Rosario entra a _____ y mira _____ pintado por su hijo. Luego toma uno de _____ que están en _____ al lado de la mesita y se sienta en _____ próximo al sofá. Cuando hace frío, enciende _____ o prende _____ en _____. En _____ coloca _____ de té. A la abuela Rosario le encantan _____ frescas.

**Exercise 22.** Rewrite the following words in the plural.

1. la nuez

   _____

2. el lápiz

   _____

3. el pez

   _____

4. el pie

   _____

5. el café

   _____

6. el papá

   _____

c. Nouns ending in **-s** in the singular remain the same in the plural unless the last syllable is <u>stressed</u>.

| el martes | los martes | *Tuesday/Tuesdays* |
|-----------|------------|--------------------|
| la crisis | las crisis | *crisis/crises* |
| el análisis | los análisis | *analysis/analyses* |

**TIP BOX**

Exceptions to this rule are:

| el bus | los bus**es** | *bus/buses* |
|--------|---------------|-------------|
| el ciprés | los cipres**es** | *cypress/cypresses* |
| el burgués | los burgues**es** | *bourgeois* |

**Exercise 23.** Use the correct definite articles **el, la, los, las** according to the meaning.

1. Todos _____ martes voy a clase de español.
2. _____ crisis económica es mundial.
3. El doctor tiene todos _____ análisis de sangre.
4. _____ miércoles de la próxima semana iremos a bailar.
5. _____ diabetes es una enfermedad.
6. _____ tesis sobre el calentamiento global son muchas.

**Exercise 24.** Underline the stressed syllable, then rewrite the words in the plural.
Model: finland<u>és</u>—*finlandeses*

1. el microbús _____
2. el compás _____
3. el gas _____
4. el mes _____
5. el cortés _____
6. el burgués _____

## TIP BOX

Note that some nouns are only used in their plural form.

| | |
|---|---|
| las esposas | *handcuffs* |
| las gafas | *glasses* |
| las tijeras | *scissors* |
| los calzoncillos | *underwear* |
| los celos | *jealousy* |
| los prismáticos | *binoculars* |
| las vacaciones | *vacation* |

### Variation in the Plural

Note also that plural variation usually causes changes in the syllables of the word. Since the stressed syllable vowel is maintained in the singular, an accent may be dropped or added.

### Example

el jo-ven/los jó-ve-nes (*the young one/the young ones*)
el in-te-rés/los in-te-re-ses (*interest/interests*)

# III. Articles

An article is a word placed before a noun or an adjective. As in English, in Spanish there are two types of articles, **definite** and **indefinite**.

| | Spanish | | | | English | | | |
|---|---|---|---|---|---|---|---|---|
| | Masculine | | Feminine | | Masculine | | Feminine | |
| | Singular | Plural | Singular | Plural | Singular | Plural | Singular | Plural |
| **Indefinite** | un | unos | una | unas | a/an | some | a/an | some |
| **Definite** | el | los | la | las | the | the | the | the |

## A. Definite Agreement Patterns

Definite articles agree with nouns according to the following pattern.

**a.** The singular article *el* agrees with singular masculine words.

**Example**

**el** hij**o**, **el** gat**o**, **el** libr**o**, **el** Añ**o** Nuev**o** (*son, cat, book, New Year*)

**b.** The plural article *los* agrees with plural masculine words.

**Example**

**los** hij**os**, **los** gat**os**, **los** libr**os**, **los** añ**os** nuev**os** (*sons, cats, books, New Years*)

**c.** The singular article *la* agrees with singular feminine words.

**Example**

**la** hij**a**, **la** gat**a**, **la** cam**a**, **la** Navida**d** (*daughter, cat, bed, Christmas*)

**d.** The plural article *las* agrees with plural feminine words.

**Example**

**las** hij**as**, **las** gat**as**, **las** cam**as**, **las** navida**des** (*daughters, cats, beds, Christmas*)

---

**TIP BOX**

**1.** When the article *el* is preceded by the preposition *a* or *de*, a contraction occurs as follows:

a) **a + el = al**

**Example**

Todos los días, voy *al* (**a + el**) restaurante.
*Every day I go to the restaurant.*

b) **de + el = del**

**Example**

Mis amigos *del* (**de + el**) colegio me invitaron a cenar.
*My friends from school invited me to dinner.*

This rule does NOT apply to formal nouns, such as the names of countries.

**Example**

Acabo de llegar de El Salvador.
*I just arrived from El Salvador.*

**2.** When the noun that qualifies the definite article is singular and feminine and begins with a stressed **a-** or **ha-**, the article **el** (not **la**) is used.

**Example**

| el **a**gua negra | las aguas negras | *wastewater* |
|---|---|---|
| el **á**guila blanca | las águilas blancas | *the white eagle, the white eagles* |
| el **ha**cha afilada | las hachas afiladas | *the sharp ax, the sharp axes* |
| el **a**lma perdida | las almas perdidas | *the lost soul, the lost souls* |

**Exercise 25.** Underline the stressed syllable of the words in boldface, then write the definite articles that correspond to the following nouns.

**Example**

*el* **á̲nima** bendita. *las* **á̲nimas** benditas.
*la* **alco̲ba** grande. *las* **alco̲bas** grandes.

1. _____ **abeja** africana
   _____ **abejas** africanas
2. _____ **agua** mineral
   _____ **aguas** minerales
3. _____ **águila** calva
   _____ **águilas** calvas
4. _____ **ala** del avión
   _____ **alas** del avión
5. _____ **alcaparra** en vinagre
   _____ **alcaparras** en vinagre
6. _____ **alma** muerta
   _____**almas** muertas
7. _____ **almendra** tostada
   _____ **almendras** tostadas
8. _____ **almohada** de plumas
   _____ **almohadas** de plumas
9. _____ **arma** de fuego
   _____ **armas** de fuego

10. _____ **azalea** es una flor
    _____ **azaleas** son unas flores
11. _____ **hacha** de piedra
    _____ **hachas** de piedra
12. _____ **hambruna**
    _____ **hambrunas**

**Exercise 26.** Complete the following sentences; use contractions when necessary.

1.  La familia va de vacaciones a_____ playa.
2.  Federico escribe una carta a_____ presidente.
3.  Gabriela es hermana de_____ señor Alfonso Naranjo.
4.  Margarita y Federico van todos los días a jugar a_____ parque.
5.  Laura llega de_____ trabajo a_____ seis de la tarde.
6.  Tobías le ladra a_____ cartero.
7.  Mario va a_____ fiesta esta noche.
8.  Salimos de_____ casa temprano.

## B. Indefinite Agreement Patterns

Indefinite articles agree with nouns in the following pattern:

a. The article **un** agrees with singular masculine words.

### Example

**un** hij**o**, **un** gat**o**, **un** libr**o**, **un** Añ**o** Nuev**o** (*a son, a cat, a book, a New Year*)

b. The article **unos** agrees with plural masculine words.

### Example

**unos** hij**os**, **unos** gat**os**, **unos** libr**os**, **unos** añ**os** nuev**os** (*some sons, some cats, some books, some New Years*)

c. The article **una** agrees with singular feminine words.

### Example

**una** hij**a**, **una** gat**a**, **una** cam**a**, **una** Navida**d** (*a daughter, a cat, a bed, a Christmas*)

d. The article **unas** agrees with plural feminine words.

### Example

**unas** hij**as**, **unas** gat**as**, **unas** cam**as**, **unas** Navida**des** (*some daughters, some cats, some beds, some Christmases*)

**Exercise 27.** Rewrite the following nouns with an indefinite article.

**Example**

    **el** libro — *un libro*

1. los problemas _____
2. la balanza _____
3. la decisión _____
4. el perfume _____
5. el hombre _____
6. el escritor _____

7. el idioma _____
8. la toalla _____
9. las canciones _____
10. el príncipe _____
11. las yeguas _____
12. los leones _____

**Exercise 28.** Complete the following sentences using the correct indefinite article *un, una, uno, unas, unos.*

1. Hay _____ museo de historia natural en la ciudad.
2. Todos los años, Gabriela visita a _____ amiga de la familia en Madrid.
3. Rosario prepara _____ delicioso plato con mariscos.
4. Federico enseña en _____ universidad del estado.
5. Los niños juegan en _____ parque al norte de la ciudad.
6. El arqueólogo estudia _____ huesos de mamut.

# C. Uses of the Definite and Indefinite Articles

**a.** If the noun refers to an entity that is considered a generic whole or an abstract concept, a definite article is used.

**Example**

El vino es bueno para la salud.
*Wine is healthy.*

*El vino* (wine) in this sentence is considered a generic whole; therefore a definite article is used.

**Exercise 29.** Complete the following sentences using the correct definite article *la, el, las, los.*

1. _____ vino es bueno para _____ salud.
2. _____ leche es un buen alimento.
3. _____ azúcar tiene muchas calorías.
4. _____ justicia y _____ paz son inseparables.
5. _____ tiempo es un concepto abstracto.
6. _____ matemáticas y _____ física son ciencias exactas.

**b.** If the noun refers to an entity that is specific or is considered unique among others, a definite article is used.

## Example

El vino de California es excelente.
*The wine from California is excellent.*

In this sentence *vino* (wine) is considered a specific entity.

**Exercise 30.** Complete the following sentences using the correct singular plural definite articles *la, el, las, los.*

1. _____ vino de Francia es delicioso.
2. _____ leche de vaca es un buen alimento.
3. _____ azúcar de caña sabe igual que _____ azúcar de remolacha.
4. _____ justicia no existe en algunos países.
5. _____ tiempo para mañana es nublado con posibilidad de lluvia.
6. _____ matemáticas y _____ física en tu universidad son fáciles de aprender.

**c.** If the noun is located after the verb and refers to an entity that is singular and non-countable, no article is used.

## Example

Quiero beber vino.
*I want to drink wine.*

**Exercise 31.** Determine which of the following sentences needs an article. Then decide if it needs a definite or indefinite article.

1. Quiero beber _____ vino de California.
2. Hay _____ leche en el supermercado.
3. Rosario compra _____ azúcar de caña.
4. No hay _____ justicia en algunos países.
5. Sin tiempo, no podré terminar _____ ensayo de español.
6. Estudia _____ matemáticas y _____ física en la universidad.
7. Nosotros hablamos _____ inglés.

**d.** If the noun refers to an entity that is a part of a whole or, in other words, that is countable (one in some), an indefinite article is used.

## Example

Quiero beber una copa de vino.
*I want to drink a glass of wine.*

**Exercise 32.** Complete the following sentences using the correct indefinite article.

1. _____ **copa** de vino va muy bien con la comida.
2. _____ **vaso** de leche de vaca es un buen alimento.
3. _____ **cucharadita** de azúcar de caña sabe igual que _____ **cucharadita** de azúcar de remolacha.
4. En algunos países hace falta _____ **poco** de justicia.
5. Quiero dejar de fumar por _____ tiempo.
6. _____ **poco** de matemáticas y _____ **poco** de física son indispensables.

**Exercise 33.** Complete the following sentences using the correct definite or indefinite article.

1. ___ domingo pasado vimos ___ globos en ___ parque del barrio.
2. ___ niño encontró ___ guante en ___ puerta del teatro.
3. Necesitamos ___ libra de azúcar y ___ par de huevos para preparar ___ postre preferido de papá.
4. Juan tuvo que esperar ___ minutos antes de entrar a ___ oficina de su jefe.
5. En ___ zoológico de la ciudad vimos ___ jirafa, ___ león, ___ elefante, ___ tigre y ___ tortugas.
6. ___ animal preferido de todos fue ___ gorila.

**Exercise 34.** Complete the following paragraph using the correct definite or indefinite article.

___ joven Javier, todos ___ días se levanta a ___ seis de ___ mañana. Se baña, se viste y bebe ___ taza de café con ___ galleta. Luego, se cepilla ___ dientes y toma ___ bus para ir a ___ universidad. ___ martes a ___ ocho de ___ mañana tiene clase de estadística. Javier es ___ mejor estudiante de la clase. ___ vez a la semana juega fútbol con ___ amigos que conoció en la universidad.

## Review

**Exercise 35.** Complete according to the model.
Un amigo ecuatoriano y *una amiga ecuatoriana.*

1. Un señor triste y _____.
2. Un hombre fiel y _____.
3. Un marido celoso y _____.
4. Un oficial intrépido y _____.
5. Un policía valiente y _____.
6. Un gato negro y _____.
7. Un rey déspota y _____.
8. Un gobernador popular y _____.

**Exercise 36.** Complete the following sentences according to the model.

### Example

Gabriel es un muchacho adorado. Liliana *es una muchacha adorada.*

1. El señor Gutiérrez es un artista famoso. La señora Gómez _____.
2. Julio es un actor famoso. Lucía _____.
3. Pedro es un campeón de tenis. Martina _____.
4. Roberto es un cantante excepcional. María _____.

**Exercise 37.** Rewrite the following text to the feminine.

1. Tengo un perro valiente, _____,
2. un caballo inteligente, _____,
3. un gato divertido, _____,
4. un ratón entrometido, _____,
5. y un marido desesperante. _____.

**Exercise 38.** Put the following sentences in the plural according to the model.

### Example

Gabriela Mistral es una poeta conocida.
Gabriela Mistral *y César Vallejo son unos poetas conocidos.*

1. John Glenn es un astronauta intrépido.
   John Glenn y Neil Armstrong _____.
2. Nicole Kidman es una actriz famosa.
   Nicole Kidman y Tom Cruise _____.
3. Lance Armstrong es un ciclista veloz.
   Lance Armstrong y Robbie McEwen _____.
4. Batistuta es un futbolista estupendo.
   Batistuta y Romario _____.

**Exercise 39.** Complete the following sentences using the correct (plural or singular) definite or indefinite article.

1. ____ casa de Julia está en ____ centro de ____ ciudad.
2. ____ hermanos de José viven en ____ apartamento pequeño.
3. ____ filosofía es ____ ciencia olvidada.
4. ____ verano es ____ estación maravillosa.
5. ____ vacas y ____ caballos son mamíferos.
6. ____ actriz Morella y ____ papa viven en Roma.

# Chapter 3

# ADJECTIVES

n adjective is a word that qualifies a noun or a pronoun. Depending on how the adjective qualifies the noun or the pronoun, an adjective is classified as **descriptive, possessive, interrogative** or **demonstrative.**

## A. Descriptive Adjectives

As its name indicates, a descriptive adjective describes the noun or pronoun it qualifies.

**Example**
El coche **rojo**
*The red car*

### a. The Gender of the Adjective

In terms of gender, **two** types of adjectives exist: those with four possible endings and those with two possible endings.

## Tip box
Adjectives agree in number and gender with the noun or pronoun they modify:

Four possible endings

| la casa amarilla | (*the yellow house*) |
| el coche amarillo | (*the yellow car*) |
| las casas amarillas | (*the yellow houses*) |
| los coches amarillos | (*the yellow cars*) |

Two possible endings

| la mujer elegante | (*the elegant woman*) |
| las mujeres elegantes | (*the elegant women*) |
| el hombre elegante | (*the elegant man*) |
| los hombres elegantes | (*the elegant men*) |

## TIP BOX
### The Number of the Adjective
The plural for adjectives is formed by adding -es if the adjective ends in a stress vowel or consonant. In other cases, only an -s is added. (In general, the same number rules that apply to nouns, apply to adjectives.)

| Singular | Plural | English |
| --- | --- | --- |
| grande | grandes | *big* |
| rico | ricos | *rich* |
| blanco | blancos | *white* |
| iraní | iraníes | *Iranian* |
| atroz | atroces | *awful* |
| azul | azules | *blue* |

1. Adjectives that are characterized as having four endings always end with an unstressed **-o**, or with a **consonant** when referring to nationalities.

|  | Masculine | Feminine | English |
| --- | --- | --- | --- |
| **Singular** | alto | alta | *tall* |
| **Plural** | altos | altas | *tall* |
| **Singular** | alemán | alemana | *German* |
| **Plural** | alemanes | alemanas | *Germans* |

- Adjectives that end in **-o:**

Other adjectives of this type include amarillo *(yellow)*, blanco *(white)*, negro *(black)*, rojo *(red)*.

**Exercise 1.** Choose the appropriate adjective from the list below and fill in the blanks. Use the pictures as clues.

    alto/a/os/as
    delgado/a/os/as
    hermoso/a/os/as
    sucio/a/os/as
    caro/a/os/as
    largo/a/os/as

1. Jaime es un muchacho _____ ; no come mucho.

2. La camisa de Carlos está _____ ; acaba de jugar un partido de fútbol.

3. La familia Sandoval vive en una casa _____ ; costó mucho dinero.

4. El avestruz tiene piernas _____ ; es muy veloz.

5. Los plátanos de la tienda son muy  ; no puedo creer cómo han subido los precios.

6. La torre de la iglesia es muy _____ ; allí viven muchas palomas.

**Exercise 2.** Draw a line from the noun on the left to the appropriate adjective on the right.

1. hombres     a. sucios
2. salud     b. gordo
3. plumas     c. asquerosas
4. platos     d. simpáticos
5. dedo     e. negras
6. basuras     f. buena

- Adjectives ending in a consonant that refer to nationalities:

| Masculine | Feminine | English |
|-----------|----------|---------|
| alemán | alemana | *(German)* |
| danés | danesa | *(Danish)* |
| dominicano | dominicana | *(Dominican)* |
| español | española | *(Spaniard)* |
| finlandés | finlandesa | *(Finnish)* |
| francés | francesa | *(French)* |
| irlandés | irlandesa | *(Irish)* |
| japonés | japonesa | *(Japanese)* |
| libanés | libanesa | *(Lebanese)* |
| tailandés | tailandesa | *(Thai)* |

**Example**

| Un estudiante danés | Una estudiante dane**sa** | *(A Danish student)* |
|---------------------|---------------------------|----------------------|
| Unos estudiantes dane**ses** | Unas estudiantes dane**sas** | *(Some Danish students)* |

> **TIP BOX**
> Note that nationalities are not capitalized in Spanish.

**Exercise 3.** Complete the following sentences with the appropriate form of the adjective (remember that number and gender must agree).

1. Federico es _____ (español)
2. María es _____ (ecuatoriano)
3. El coche de tu padre es _____ (americano)
4. Los aviones del ejército son _____ (sueco)
5. Los camiones de la empresa son _____ (japonés)
6. Las compañeras de Gabriela son _____ (suizo)
7. La compañía donde trabaja tu padre es _____ (inglés)
8. Los quesos que compraste son _____ (francés)
9. La madre de Federico es _____ (portugués)
10. La suegra de Pedro _____ (boliviano)
11. Los marineros que están en el puerto son _____ (alemán)
12. Las señoritas Delgado son _____ (panameño)
13. Tu amiga es _____ (salvadoreño)
14. Ximena y Carmen son _____ (argentino)

**2.** Adjectives that are characterized as having two possible endings always end in **-e** or a **consonant**.

- Two-form adjectives ending in **-e**:

| La niña está triste. (*The girl is sad.*) | Las niñas están tristes. (*The girls are sad.*) |
| --- | --- |
| El niño está triste. (*The boy is sad.*) | Los niños están tristes. (*The boys are sad.*) |

agradable (*pleasant*)
alegre (*happy*)
brillante (*brilliant*)
desconcertante (*disconcerting*)
excelente (*excellent*)
firme (*firm*)
fuerte (*strong*)
grande (*big*)
importante (*important*)
insignificante (*insignificant*)
inteligente (*intelligent*)
interesante (*interesting*)
miserable (*miserable*)
rebelde (*rebellious*)
reconfortante (*comforting*)
torpe (*clumsy*)
triste (*sad*)
verde (*green*)

**Exercise 4.** Fill in the blank with the adjective that best completes each sentence.

interesante
importante
grande
rebelde
alegre
verde

1. El ejercicio es_____ para la salud; dicen que prolonga la vida.
2. Vimos una película _____ y nos reímos mucho.
3. La casa _____ de la esquina es de mis tíos.
4. Este es un libro _____de ciencia ficción; es muy entretenido.
5. Julián es un niño desobediente y _____; su mamá lo castiga mucho.
6. Gloria perdió su bolso _____; lo olvidó en el parque.

**Exercise 5.** Choose the adjective in parentheses that best completes each sentence.

1. No pudo contener sus impulsos _____ (hipócritas, homicidas) y mató a su rival.
2. ¿Escuchas ese sonido _____ en el sótano? (chocante, fuerte) ¿Será la tubería?
3. Revisé mis ejercicios y sólo encontré errores _____. (insignificantes, miserables)
4. Admiro a las personas _____. (desconcertantes, inteligentes)
5. El café te quedó _____; (excelente, firme) va muy bien con el postre de manzana.
6. José le dio a su amigo un abrazo _____ (excelente, reconfortante) después de la pérdida de su abuelo.

## TIP BOX

These two adjectives have **only** two forms, singular and plural.

| Singular | Plural |
| --- | --- |
| La mujer hipócrita<br>*(The hypocritical woman)* | Las mujeres hipócritas<br>*(The hypocritical women)* |
| El hombre hipócrita<br>*(The hypocritical man)* | Los hombres hipócritas<br>*(The hypocritical men)* |
| El hombre homicida<br>*(The homicidal man)* | Los hombres homicidas<br>*(The homicidal men)* |
| La mujer homicida<br>*(The homicidal woman)* | Las mujeres homicidas<br>*(The homicidal women)* |

The **-a** ending remains the same regardless of the noun gender.

• Adjectives taking only two endings that end in a consonant:

| La casa **azul** (*The blue house*) | Las casas **azules** (*The blue houses*) |
| El coche **azul** (*The blue car*) | Los coches **azules** (*The blue cars*) |

atroz (*atrocious*)
azul (*blue*)
cortés (*polite*)
cruel (*cruel*)
difícil (*difficult*)
especial (*special*)
fácil (*easy*)
feliz (*happy*)
gris (*grey*)
joven (*young*)
mejor (*best*)
peor (*worst*)
pertinaz (*persistent*)
sutil (*subtle*)
útil (*useful*)
virgen (*virgin*)

## TIP BOX

Adjectives ending in *-án, -ón, -or,* and *-in,* have **four** endings when referring to a person.

| holgazán | holgazana | *(lazy)* |
| charlatán | charlatana | *(charlatan)* |
| trabajador | trabajadora | *(worker)* |
| creador | creadora | *(creative)* |

**Exercise 6.** Claudia talks with her sister Ana while she gets ready to go to a party. Use adjectives from the box below to fill in the blanks.

| cortés | fácil | atroz |
| especial | joven | cruel |
| peor | gris | feliz |

1. Ana:—Te ves _____ con ese vestido; te hace ver gorda.
2. Claudia:—No seas tan _____. Es el mejor que tengo.
3. Ana:—Puedes ponerte mi vestido _____, es perfecto para un baile.
4. Claudia:—¿Estás loca? Ese vestido es _____.
5. Ana:—No es verdad. Eres _____ y todo te luce bien.
6. Claudia:—Gracias, Ana. Si eso te hace _____, me pondré tu vestido.

**Exercise 7.** Match the noun on the left with one of the adjectives on the right.

1. selva (*jungle*)          a. sutil
2. caballero (*knight*)      b. difícil
3. ejercicio (*exercise*)    c. virgen
4. asunto (*issue*)          d. fácil
5. lluvia (*rain*)           e. pertinaz
6. maquillaje (*makeup*)     f. cortés

---

## TIP BOX

An adjective that refers to two or more nouns takes the plural form. If the nouns are masculine, the adjectives also will be in the masculine form. Adjectives accompanying feminine nouns will be in the feminine form.

### Example

El coche y el vestido de José son roj**os**.
*José's car and suit are red.*

Tanto la planta como la flor son blanc**as**.
*This plant and flower are both white.*

When the nouns are from both genders, the masculine adjective form is used.

### Example

María, Liliana, Josefina y José son tímid**os**.
*María, Liliana, Josefina, and José are timid.*

---

## b. Short-Form Adjectives

Some adjectives have a shortened form; they lose their last vowel or syllable when they precede a masculine singular noun. An exception occurs when the adjective is preceded by the adverb **más** (*more*) or **menos** (*less*).

Adjectives that drop their last syllable are **bueno, malo,** and **grande** (*good, bad,* and *big*).

### Example

Un **buen** hombre
*A good man*

Una **buena** mujer
*A good woman*

Un **mal** comienzo
*A bad beginning*

Una **mala** persona
*A bad person*

**TIP BOX**

Note that the adjective **grande** loses its last syllable when it precedes either a masculine or feminine singular noun.

Un **gran** hombre
*A great man*

Una **gran** mujer
*A great woman*

**TIP BOX**

Note that Catholic saints in Spanish drop the last syllable of the word **santo** when it precedes a masculine proper noun in the case of *San Juan, San Andrés, San Francisco, San Ignacio.*

Exceptions: *Santo Tomás* and *Santo Domingo*.

**Exercise 8.** Complete the following sentences with the appropriate form of the adjective.

1. La isla de _____ Juan de Puerto Rico está en el mar Caribe. (San *or* Santo)
2. Federico es un _____ amigo. (grande *or* gran)
3. Liliana es la más _____ de todas nuestras amigas. (grande *or* gran)
4. _____ Teresa de Jesús es famosa por sus poemas. (San *or* Santa)
5. Todos tenemos a veces un _____ día. (malo *or* mal)
6. No es bueno estar rodeado de _____ compañías. (mal *or* malas)

**TIP BOX**

Descriptive adjectives exist in two categories, depending how they are connected to the noun or pronoun they modify.

**Predicative adjectives** are connected by a linking verb such as *estar* (to be), *ser* (to be), *sentirse* (to feel), *resultar* (to result), *parecer* (to seem), *semejar* (to like), *continuar* (to continue), *seguir* (to follow) to the noun or pronoun they modify.

**Example**

La señora está aburrida.
*The woman is bored.*

El señor es mexicano.
*The man is Mexican.*

El señor parece argentino.
*The man seems to be Argentinean.*

Attributive adjectives follow or precede the noun or pronoun they qualify. In Spanish, however, attributive adjectives commonly **follow** the noun they modify and, in doing so, make the noun more specific.

### Example

Las chicas chilenas están en la biblioteca.
*The Chilean girls are in the library.*

El coche rojo de Juan es nuevo.
*Juan's red car is new.*

When the adjective **precedes** the noun, it is because the noun is not specific and the adjective is describing a noun that reflects a totality or something general.

### Example

Los dorados cabellos de María.
*Maria's golden hair.*

Las hermosas playas del Caribe.
*The beautiful Caribbean beaches.*

## TIP BOX

Many adjectives have different meanings depending on if they precede or follow the noun or pronoun they qualify.

### Example

Pobre hombre (pobre = miserable, desgraciado)
*Poor man!, He is lonely.*

Hombre pobre (pobre = sin dinero)
*That man is poor; he has no money.*

Mi casa nueva (nueva = reciente, construida hace poco)
*My house was recently built.*

Mi nueva casa (vivía en otra hace poco)
*My new house is near to the old address I had.*

## c. Adjectives as Nouns

An adjective may have the function of a noun.

### Example

Los pobres no tienen que comer.
*The poor do not have anything to eat.*

El rojo es mi color preferido.
*Red is my favorite color.*

**Exercise 9.** Change the following sentences by transforming the adjectives into nouns.

**Example**

La mujer rubia está trabajando.
*La rubia está trabajando.*

1. El pobre hombre está sin trabajo. _____.
2. La señorita joven ganó el concurso de belleza. _____.
3. Los empleados trabajadores pidieron un aumento de salario. _____.
4. El chico alemán viajó por Sudamérica. _____.
5. Las mujeres argentinas son muy simpáticas. _____.
6. El coche negro es mi preferido. _____.

# B. Demonstrative Adjectives

A demonstrative adjective is a word used to signal or emphasize a noun.

**Example**

**Este** oso está mirando.
***This** bear is looking.*

**Ese** león está dormido.
***That** lion is sleeping.*

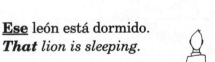

**Aquellos** monos están jugando.
*Those other monkeys are playing.*

## Forms of the demonstrative adjectives

| Masculine | | Feminine | |
|---|---|---|---|
| **Singular** | **Plural** | **Singular** | **Plural** |
| este *this* | estos *these* | esta *this* | estas *these* |
| ese *that* | esos *those* | esa *that* | esas *those* |
| aquel *that over there* | aquellos *those over there* | aquella *that over there* | aquellas *those over there* |

**Exercise 10.** Write the correct form of the adjective on the line provided.

1. Me gustan _____ flores. (este)
2. _____ restaurante es el mejor de la ciudad. (aquel)
3. Te traje _____ pasteles para la cena. (este)
4. Ten cuidado con _____ copas. Son muy delicadas. (ese)
5. _____ periódico dice que hará frío hoy. (este)
6. ¿Por qué tienes _____ libros en el suelo? (este)

**Exercise 11.** Gabriela and her mother are at the supermarket. Fill in the blanks with the demonstrative adjective that corresponds to the one in parenthesis.

—Mamá, compremos _____ jabón. *(this)*

—Vamos a comprar _____ jabón rosado, Gabriela. Es mi marca favorita. *(that, over there)*

—Pero no me gusta el perfume de _____ marca de jabón, mamá. *(that)*

—¿Qué te parece _____ jabón cremoso? *(this)*

—Me gusta mucho más. ¿Ves _____ flores? *(these)*

—¡Qué lindas! Quedan perfectas en _____ jarrón que te regaló papá. *(that, over there)*

# C. Possessive Adjectives

Spanish has two forms of possessive adjectives, a short form that is used before nouns, and a long form that is used after nouns.

## a. Short-Form Possessive Adjectives

| Singular | Plural | Translation |
|---|---|---|
| mi | mis | *my* |
| tu | tus | *your (informal)* |
| su | sus | *your (formal), its, his, her, their* |
| nuestro(a) | nuestros(as) | *our* |
| vuestro(a) | vuestros(as) | *your* |

Short-form possessive adjectives precede the noun they modify and agree with that noun in number and, in the case of **nuestro** and **vuestro**, also in gender.

### Example

¿Dónde están **mis** llaves?
*Where are my keys?*

**Nuestra** casa es blanca.
*Our house is white.*

---

### TIP BOX

Possessive adjectives are not used when possession is evident. For example:

Me puse la camisa.
*I put my shirt on.*

Me lavo la cara.
*I wash my face.*

**Vuestro** is only used in Spain, as it refers to the **vosotros** pronoun.

**Exercise 12.** Fill in the blanks in the paragraph with the correct adjective from the box.

| | |
|---|---|
| mis | su |
| mi | tu |
| nuestra | mis |

Estoy buscando _____ mochila. Me voy de viaje con _____ primos Arturo y Gonzalo. _____ tía Carmen y _____ esposo tienen una casa en el campo y vamos a visitarlos. Préstame _____ auto y devuélveme _____ maletas. Las voy a necesitar.

**Exercise 13.** Somebody switched the adjectives in this exercise. Write the correct adjective in the parenthesis at the end of each sentence.

1. Así son, <u>tu</u> amigos. Esa es la pura verdad. (_____)
2. Dame <u>vuestras</u> teléfono. Te llamo mañana. (_____)
3. Lucía y Marta dejaron <u>tus</u> maletas en el hotel. (_____)
4. El panadero comienza <u>su</u> trabajo muy temprano. (_____)
5. Mi hermana y yo donamos <u>sus</u> ropa vieja a los pobres. (_____)
6. Pensad en la felicidad de <u>nuestra</u> familias. (_____)

## b. Long-Form Possessive Adjectives

Long-form possessive adjectives follow the noun they modify and agree with that noun in number and in gender.

| Singular | | Plural | | Translation |
|---|---|---|---|---|
| **Masculine** | **Feminine** | **Masculine** | **Feminine** | |
| mío | mía | míos | mías | *my, of mine* |
| tuyo | tuya | tuyos | tuyas | *your (singular informal)* |
| suyo | suya | suyos | suyas | *your (singular or plural formal), its, his, her, their, of yours, of theirs* |
| nuestro | nuestra | nuestros | nuestras | *our, of ours* |
| vuestro | vuestra | vuestros | vuestras | *your (plural informal), of yours* |

### Example

¿Dónde están las llaves **mías**?
*Where are <u>my</u> keys?*

La casa **nuestra** es blanca.
*<u>Our</u> house is white.*

---

## TIP BOX

In Spanish, short-term possessive adjectives are more commonly used than long-term possessive adjectives. Both forms are interchangeable. However, when using the long-term possessive adjective, a definite or an indefinite article is usually used to determine the noun.

### Example

Miré los muros de <u>mi</u> patria.
Miré los muros de <u>la</u> patria <u>mía</u>.
(Francisco de Quevedo, 1580–1645)
*I looked upon my native country's walls.*

Also note that long-term possessive adjectives are identical to possessive pronouns.*

\* See Chapter 8, Pronouns.

---

**Exercise 14.** Replace in the following sentences the short-form possessive adjectives with the corresponding long-form possessive adjectives.

### Example

**Tu** camisa está sucia.
**La** camisa **tuya** está sucia.

1. Francisco me invitó a **su** finca el fin de semana.

   _____

2. Pero, yo prefiero quedarme en **mi** casa.

   _____

3. Felipe, **mi** novio, llega de Chile mañana.

   _____

4. Iremos a un bar el viernes en la noche con **nuestras** amigas de la universidad.

   _____

5. El sábado en la tarde iremos con **tus** hijos a la playa.

   _____

6. Santiago perdió **tus** libros.

   _____

7. Lola no puede abrir **su** coche porque perdió **sus** llaves.

   _____

8. El futuro de **vuestro** país no es muy prometedor.

   _____

# D. Cardinal and Ordinal Numbers

Cardinal numbers are used to refer to nouns that are of a specific quantity, and ordinal numbers refer to the order or position of a noun.

## a. Cardinal Numbers

> **TIP BOX**
>
> **ciento** *(one hundred)*
> Drop the last syllable when it precedes any noun.
>
> **Example**
>
>   cien hombres
>   *one hundred men*
>
>   cien mujeres
>   *one hundred women*

Cardinal numbers are formed by combining a series of basic numbers to form all possible numbers. Those basic numbers are:

| | |
|---|---|
| cero | 0 |
| uno (un)/ una | 1 |
| dos | 2 |
| tres | 3 |
| cuatro | 4 |
| cinco | 5 |
| seis | 6 |
| siete | 7 |
| ocho | 8 |
| nueve | 9 |
| diez | 10 |
| once | 11 |
| doce | 12 |
| trece | 13 |
| catorce | 14 |
| quince | 15 |
| (diez y seis or dieciséis, diez y siete or diecisiete, etc.) | 16–19 |

| | |
|---|---|
| veinte | 20 |
| (veintiuno, veintidós, etc.) | 21–29 |
| treinta | 30 |
| (treinta y uno, treinta y dos, etc., except numbers that are multiples of 10) | 31–100 |
| cuarenta | 40 |
| cincuenta | 50 |
| sesenta | 60 |
| setenta | 70 |
| ochenta | 80 |
| noventa | 90 |
| cien | 100 |
| (ciento uno/a, ciento dos, etc.) | 101–199 |
| doscientos/as* (hay doscientas mujeres, hay doscientos hombres, same pattern from 200 to 900) | 200 |
| quinientos/as | 500 |
| novecientos/as | 900 |
| mil | 1000 |
| un millón | 1,000,000 |

* Any number that has in one of its parts the ending **-tos**, if qualifying a feminine noun, changes to **-tas**.

## TIP BOX

**Notation of Cardinal Numbers**

In Spanish, notation numbering is as follows:

For currency, a decimal is used instead of a comma.

### Example

$ 1.000.000,00: un millón de dólares (*one million dollars*)

For weight, a comma is used instead of a decimal.

### Example

56,3 kg: cincuenta y seis kilos y trescientos gramos (*fifty-six kilograms point three hundred grams*)*

* 1 kilogram = 1000 grams

Exercise 15. Write out the following numbers.

| | | |
|---|---|---|
| 1. 245 | _____ | coches |
| 2. 45 | _____ | televisores |
| 3. 1282 | _____ | manzanas |
| 4. 145.765 | _____ | personas |
| 5. 554.898 | _____ | trabajadores |
| 6. 1.289.908 | _____ | naranjas |
| 7. 209 | _____ | muchachos |
| 8. 229.000 | _____ | mujeres |
| 9. 101 | _____ | niñas |
| 10. 590 | _____ | naranjas |
| 11. 21 | _____ | balones |
| 12. 33 | _____ | almacenes |

Exercise 16. Rewrite the following sentences using numbers.

1. Aquel pescado pesa siete kilos y medio. _____.
2. Tengo tres mil quinientos dólares en el banco. _____.
3. El préstamo es de un millón trescientas mil euros. _____.
4. El bebé pesó seis kilos y treinta gramos. _____.
5. La deuda externa de Argentina es de ciento cuarenta mil millones de dólares. _____.

# b. Ordinal Numbers

Ordinal numbers are adjectives that agree in gender and number with the noun they qualify. They refer to the order or position of a noun in a series.

Ordinal numbers *primero* (first) and *tercero* (third) drop the vowel **-o** when qualifying a masculine singular noun. For example:

El **primer** hombre *(the first man).*
El **tercer** piso *(the third floor).*

**Ordinal Numbers**

| 1° *primero / primer* | first |
|---|---|
| 2° *segundo* | second |
| 3° *tercero / tercer* | third |
| 4° *cuarto* | fourth |
| 5° *quinto* | fifth |

| | |
|---|---|
| 6° *sexto* | sixth |
| 7° *séptimo* | seventh |
| 8° *octavo* | eighth |
| 9° *noveno* | ninth |
| 10° *décimo* | tenth |
| 11° *undécimo* | eleventh |
| 12° *duodécimo* | twelfth |
| 13° *decimotercero /decimotercer* | thirteenth |
| 14° *decimocuarto* | fourteenth |
| 15° *decimoquinto* | fifteenth |
| 16° *decimosexto* | sixteenth |
| 17° *decimoséptimo* | seventeenth |
| 18° *decimoctavo* | eighteenth |
| 19° *decimonoveno* | nineteenth |
| 20° *vigésimo* | twentieth |

## TIP BOX

Ordinal numbers are also used to designate kings, queens, and popes.

**Example**

Siglo **XVI** (siglo **dieciséis**)
*XVI century* or *Sixteenth century*

Alfonso **VI** (Alfonso **sexto**)
*Alfonso the sixth*

Cardinal numbers are used for dates. The sole exception is the first of the month.

**Example**

Hoy es **primero** de julio.
*Today is the first of July.*

Mañana es **dos** de julio.
*Tomorrow is July second.*

**Exercise 17.** Complete the following sentences with the corresponding ordinal number.

1. Neil Armstrong fue el _____ (1°) hombre en pisar la Luna.

2. La _____ (3°) semana de marzo iremos a Madrid.

3. Juan fue el _____ (1°) en llegar, pero Alberto fue el _____ (1°) niño en cruzar la meta.

4. El apartamento de Rosario está en el _____ (3°) piso y el de Gabriela en el _____ (4°) piso.

5. María y José fueron los _____ (1°) invitados que llegaron a la fiesta.

6. En la competencia de ciclismo, Federico fue el _____ (13°) ciclista en cruzar la meta.

**Exercise 18.** According to the picture, answer the following sentences.

1. El hombre soltero baila solo en el _____ piso.

2. Los viejitos del _____ piso están comiendo.

3. La pastelería está en el _____ piso.

4. Los jóvenes se divierten en el _____ piso.

5. La señorita está usando la aspiradora en el _____ piso.

6. La madre del _____ piso está dándole de comer a su hijo.

# Review

**Exercise 19.** Put the adjective in the feminine according to the model.

## Example

José es boliviano. Lucía *es boliviana.*

1. Julio es colombiano.
   Marta _____.
2. Mi tío es español.
   Mi tía es _____.
3. Mi hermano es guapo.
   Mi hermana _____.
4. Mi amigo está contento.
   Mi amiga_____.
5. Pablo es inteligente.
   Liliana es _____.

**Exercise 20.** Put the adjective in the feminine according to the model.

## Example

Un coche amarillo y una casa *amarilla.*

1. Un helicóptero eficiente y un avión _____.
2. Un jugo refrescante y una fruta _____.
3. Un amigo fiel y una compañera _____.
4. Un actor famoso y una actriz _____.
5. Un empleado perezoso y una empleada _____.
6. Un profesor exigente y una profesora _____.

**Exercise 21.** Rewrite the following sentences by spelling the numbers.

1. Hay 200.000 soldados en Irak. _____.
2. Tenemos 3.673 francos suizos. _____.
3. José ganó 578.000.000 de pesos. _____.
4. Ese toro pesa 787 Kg. _____.
5. El premio mayor de la lotería es 231.537.000 dólares. _____.

**Exercise 22.** Complete the following sentences with the appropriate demonstrative adjective.

1. ¿Cuánto cuesta (that) _____ coche?
2. Me gusta (this) _____ casa.
3. (These) _____ niños me tienen desesperado.
4. (That) _____ lavadora de platos no sirve para nada.
5. Javier, ¿sabes quién es (that) _____ muchacha?

**Exercise 23.** Complete the following sentences with the appropriate possessive or demonstrative adjective.

1. (These)___ pantalones son ____ (de mí) pantalones. ____ (de ti) pantalones están sobre la cama.
2. (Those over there) ____ muchachos están compitiendo con ____ (de ellos) bicicletas.
3. (That) ____ señora tiene ____ (de ti) libros de español.
4. ¿(That over there) ____ muchacho tiene ____ (de ellos) perro?
5. (This) ____ es ____ (de nosotros) amigo Marco.
6. (This) ____ es ____ (de vosotros) casa, ¿verdad?

**Exercise 24.** Complete the following sentences with the corresponding ordinal number.

1. Fernando y Gabriel fueron los _____ (1º) en llegar a casa.
2. José, es la _____ (3º) vez que te lo digo. ¡Vete de aquí!
3. Jorge fue el _____ (1º) novio de Teresa.
4. ¡Este es el _____ (5º) día que paso sin comer!

# Chapter 4

# VERBS: SIMPLE TENSES OF THE INDICATIVE

mira
habla
trabaja
busca
compra
viaja

# I. The Present Indicative

There are three different verb classes in Spanish—those ending in **-ar, -er,** and **-ir**. Some verbs are **regular** whereas others are **irregular**.

## A. Regular Verbs

The **regular conjugation** in the present indicative is formed by adding the following endings to the stem of the verbs.

| Subject Pronoun | Verb Endings in the Present Indicative | | |
|---|---|---|---|
| | **-ar** | **-er** | **-ir** |
| yo | -o | -o | -o |
| tú | -as | -es | -es |
| él, ella, usted | -a | -e | -e |
| nosotros/as | -amos | -emos | -emos |
| vosotros/as | -áis | -éis | -ís |
| ellos, ellas, ustedes | -an | -en | -en |

## TIP BOX

### Example

To conjugate the verb *hablar* (to speak) in the present indicative, add to the stem **habl-** the corresponding verb ending for the verbs that end in -**ar**: -**o**, -**as**, -**a**, -**amos**, -**ais**, -**an**.

yo habl**o** (*I speak*)
tú habl**as** (*you speak*)
él, ella, usted habl**a** (*he, she speaks, you (sing.) speak*)
nosotros/as habl**amos** (*we speak*)
vosotros/as habl**áis** (*you (pl.) speak*)
ellos, ellas, ustedes habl**an** (*they speak*)

The following common verbs are regular in the present indicative.

| *-ar* class verbs | *-er* class verbs | *-ir* class verbs |
| --- | --- | --- |
| alistar *(to make ready)* | leer *(to read)* | insistir *(to insist)* |
| amar *(to love)* | aprender *(to learn)* | abrir *(to open)* |
| bailar *(to dance)* | correr *(to run)* | asistir *(to assist)* |
| buscar *(to look for)* | socorrer *(to help)* | decidir *(to decide)* |
| caminar *(to walk)* | emprender *(to start)* | escribir *(to write)* |
| comprar *(to buy)* | comer *(to eat)* | permitir *(to allow)* |
| ducharse* *(to take a shower)* | beber *(to drink)* | recibir *(to receive)* |
| enviar *(to send)* | comprender *(to understand)* | subir *(to go up)* |
| hablar *(to speak)* | creer *(to believe)* | vivir *(to live)* |
| llegar *(to arrive)* | responder *(to answer)* | reunirse* *(to meet)* |
| mirar *(to look)* | temer *(to fear)* | |
| necesitar *(to need)* | vender *(to sell)* | |
| retirar *(to withdraw)* | | |
| trabajar *(to work)* | | |
| viajar *(to travel)* | | |
| dibujar *(to draw)* | | |
| saltar *(to jump)* | | |
| casarse* *(to get married)* | | |
| graduarse* *(to graduate)* | | |
| ganar *(to win)* | | |

*See Chapter 7, Pronominal Verbs.

Exercise 1. Complete the following sentences using the present tense.

1. Yo _____ (llegar) siempre tarde.
2. Nosotros _____ (temer) que tu te extravíes si vas solo.
3. Ellos_____ (creer) ciegamente en sus dirigentes.
4. Mis padres _____ (vivir) en Cartagena.
5. Creo que tú nunca me _____ (responder) lo que te pregunto.
6. Ustedes _____ (mirar) de una manera extraña.
7. Marcelo _____ (insistir) en comprarme mi vaca.
8. Mi madre no me _____ (comprender).
9. León y Lucía _____ (necesitar) un lápiz, ¿les puedes prestar el tuyo?
10. Los perros no _____ (hablar).

# B. Verbs With Spelling Changes

This group of verbs are regular as they do not change in form. They only change their spelling to reflect their pronunciation. Such verbs are all those ending in **-cer, -cir; -ger, -gir; -guir; -uir; and -iar, -uar**.

**a.** Verbs that end in **-cer** and **-cir** change ONLY in the first person singular (*yo*) of the present indicative in two ways:

## Spelling Rules

| When the stem of the verb ends in consonant (**n** or **r**) the -c- from the ending **-cer** or **-cir** changes to **z** | | When the stem of the verb ends in vowel a **z** is added before the **c** | |
|---|---|---|---|
| conve**n**<u>**cer**</u> (*to convince*) | espa**r**<u>**cir**</u> (*to scatter*) | con<u>o</u>**cer** (*to know*) | cond<u>u</u>**cir** (*to drive*) |
| yo conven**zo** | yo espar**zo** | yo cono**zco** | yo condu**zco** |

Other verbs ending in **-cer** and **-cir** preceded by a consonant are:

ejer<u>**cer**</u> (*to exert*)
espar<u>**cir**</u> (*to disperse*)
frun<u>**cir**</u> (*to frown*)
ven<u>**cer**</u> (*to vanquish*)
zur<u>**cir**</u> (*to darn*)

Other verbs ending in **-cer, cir** preceded by a vowel are:

aborr<u>e</u>**cer** (*to detest*)
agrad<u>e</u>**cer** (*to thank*)
apet<u>e</u>**cer** (*to feel an urge for*)

dedu**cir** (*to deduce*)
desapar**ecer** (*to disappear*)
indu**cir** (*to induce*)
introdu**cir** (*to introduce*)
na**cer** (*to be born*)
recon**ocer** (*to recognize*)
redu**cir** (*to reduce*)

**Exercise 2.** Complete the following sentences using the present tense.

1. Él no_____(reconocer) pero yo sí _____(reconocer) que todo ha cambiado.
2. (yo) _____(vencer) a mis rivales si cometen errores.
3. (yo) _____ (esparcir) el grano de trigo sobre la tierra húmeda.
4. En cuanto veo a mis deudores, (yo) _____ (desaparecer).
5. Si (yo) me_____ (introducir) en la caverna paso desapercibido.
6. Todas las mañanas (yo) _____ (agradecer) al Señor por el nuevo día.
7. (yo) _____ (aborrecer) las tardes lluviosas.
8. Cada día me (yo) _____ (convencer) más de que estás loco.
9. (yo) _____ (conducir) siempre que Juan se emborracha.

**b.** Verbs that end in **-ger, -gir** change ONLY in the first person singular (*yo*) of the present indicative.

## Spelling Rules

| Verbs ending in **-ger, gir** change from **g** to **j** in the first person singular (*yo*) | |
|---|---|
| prote**ger** (*to protect*) | exi**gir** (*to demand*) |
| yo prote**jo** | yo exi**jo** |

Other verbs ending in **-ger, gir** that change **g** to **j** in the first person singular (*yo*) are:

aco**ger** (*to greet*)
afli**gir** (*to afflict*)
co**ger** (*to grab*)
corre**gir** (*to correct*)
diri**gir** (*to direct*)
ele**gir** (*to elect*)
emer**ger** (*to emerge*)
enco**ger** (*to shrink*)
esco**ger** (*to choose*)
exi**gir** (*to demand*)
fin**gir** (*to simulate*)

infrin**gir** (*to infringe*)
prote**ger** (*to protect*)
reco**ger** (*to pick up*)
restrin**gir** (*to restrain*)
resur**gir** (*to re-emerge*)
ru**gir** (*to roar*)
sumer**gir** (*to submerge, to drown*)
sur**gir** (*to emerge*)
ur**gir** (*to urge*)

**Exercise 3.** Complete the following paragraphs using the present tense.

1. Si quieres yo_____(recoger) el desorden de la fiesta. Pero a cambio te_____ (exigir) que no traigas más amigos. Así, además te _____(proteger) el bolsillo. Porque si yo _____ (acoger) bien esa gente es porque siempre me _____ (restringir) de decir lo que pienso y _____ (fingir) ser un cálido huésped.
2. Porque como bien lo sabes, yo no _____ (escoger) a quien traer y más bien siempre me_____ (dirigir) a mi habitación y me _____ (sumergir) en mis divagaciones. Pues con ellos no tengo nada de que hablar.

**c.** Verbs that end in **-guir** change ONLY in the first person singular (*yo*) in the present indicative.

## Spelling Rules

| Verbs ending in **-*guir*** change ***gu*** to ***g*** in the first person singular (yo) |
| --- |
| distin**guir** (*to distinguish*) |
| yo distin**g**o |

Other verbs ending in **-guir** that change **gu** to **g** in the first person singular (*yo*) are:

conse**guir*** (*to come by; to get*)
prose**guir*** (*to proceed*)
extin**guir** (*to extinguish*)
se**guir*** (*to follow*)
perse**guir*** (*to go after*)
er**guir*** (*to build*)

Note: *The stem of these verbs also changes from **e** to **i** (consigo, prosigo, etc.). Because the verb **erguir** starts with the vowel **e,** the beginning of the stem (**ie**) changes to **y** (yo yergo, tú yergues, él yergue...).

**Exercise 4.** Complete the following sentences using the present tense.

1. (yo) No _____ (distinguir) un sapo de una rana.
2. Al llegar al cerro siempre tomo un pequeño descanso y _____ (proseguir) mi camino.
3. Ve adelante que yo te _____ (seguir).
4. Este es el último incendio que (yo) _____ (extinguir). ¡En un mes me pensiono de bombero y voy a ser carpintero!
5. Él construye imperios financieros, yo en cambio sólo_____ (erguir) castillos de arena.
6. Nunca _____ (conseguir) terminar a tiempo mis deberes.
7. Cuando _____ (perseguir) la liebre durante una jornada de caza vuelvo animado a la casa.

**d.** Verbs that end in **-uir** change from **i** to **y** before **o** and **e** in all persons except in the first (*nosotros)* and second plural (*vosotros)* persons.

## Spelling Rules

| Verbs ending in **-uir** change **i** to **y** before **o** and **e** |
| --- |
| *conclu**uir*** (to conclude) |
| yo conclu<u>yo</u><br>tú conclu<u>ye</u>s<br>él, ella, usted conclu<u>ye</u><br>nosotros/as concluimos<br>vosotros/as concluís<br>ellos, ellas, ustedes conclu<u>ye</u>n |

Other verbs ending in **-uir** that change **i** to **y** before **o** and **e** are:

arg**üir** (*to argue*)
distrib**uir** (*to distribute*)
atrib**uir** (*to attribute to, to confer*)
h**uir** (*to run away*)
constit**uir** (*to constitute*)
incl**uir** (*to include*)
constr**uir** (*to construct*)
infl**uir** (*to influence*)
contrib**uir** (*to contribute*)
int**uir** (*to intuit*)
destit**uir** (*to dismiss*)
obstr**uir** (*to obstruct*)
destr**uir** (*to destroy*)
recl**uir** (*to confine*)
dil**uir** (*to dilute*)
reconstr**uir** (*to reconstruct*)
dismin**uir** (*to diminish*)
sustit**uir** (*to substitute*)

**Exercise 5.** Complete the following sentences using the present tense.

1. Como Robin Hood, todo lo que robas (tú) lo _____ (distribuir).
2. Te dejo este ejercicio y así (tú) lo _____ (concluir).
3. Dicen que ellos _____ (diluir) la gasolina para ganar más dinero.
4. Mis tíos _____ (destruir) toda la herencia en baratijas.
5. Me pagarán más si (nosotros) _____ (reconstruir) la casa.
6. El río _____ (obstruir) el paso.
7. Vosotros _____ (disminuir) la gravedad de los hechos.
8. La policía _____ (recluir) al ladrón en la cárcel.
9. ¿Quién _____ (sustituir) a un buen padre?
10. Los monopolios _____ (contribuir) al deterioro en la calidad de los productos y servicios.

**e.** Some verbs that end in **-iar** and **-uar** stress the **i** and **u** (in all persons except *nosotros* and *vosotros*) in the stem by splitting the semiconsonant group **-io-** and **-ia-** into two syllables : **í-o** and **í-a**. The semi-consonant group **-ua-** is also split in two: **ú-a**.*

## Spelling Rules

| Some verbs ending in **-iar** and **-uar** change **i** to **í** and **u** to **ú** in all forms except *nosotros* and *vosotros* | |
| --- | --- |
| en**viar** (to send) | act**uar** (to act) |
| yo en-**ví**-o | yo ac-t**ú**-o |
| tú en-**ví**-as | tú ac-t**ú**-as |
| él, ella, usted en-**ví**-a | él, ella, usted ac-t**ú**-a |
| nosotros/as en-via-mos | nosotros/as ac-tua-mos |
| vosotros/as en-viá-is | vosotros/as ac-tuá-is |
| ellos, ellas, ustedes en-**ví**-an | ellos, ellas, ustedes ac-t**ú**-an |

Other verbs ending in **-iar** and **-uar** that change the **i** to **í** and the **u** to **ú** are:

acent**uar** (*to accent, to emphasize*)
amp**liar** (*to enlarge*)
ans**iar** (*to wish*)
conf**iar** (*to trust*)
contin**uar** (*to continue*)
deval**uar** (*to devalue*)
efect**uar** (*to carry out*)
enfr**iar** (*to cool, to chill*)
evac**uar** (*to evacuate, to vacate*)

* See Chapter 1, Diphthongs.

evaluar (*to evaluate*)
graduarse (*to graduate)*
guiar (*to guide*)
insinuar (*to insinuate*)
perpetuar (*to perpetuate*)
situar (*to locate, to situate*)

**Exercise 6.** Complete the following sentences using the present tense.

1. Ellos _____(evaluar) sus propios ejercicios.
2. Si (vosotros) _____ (ampliar) vuestro apartamento, tendréis más espacio.
3. Él _____ (enfriar) su café antes de tomarlo.
4. ¡Tú siempre te _____ (situar) en el lugar más inoportuno!
5. El Señor _____ (guiar) mis pasos.
6. ¡Ese trabajo _____ (perpetuar) sus penas!
7. ¿Vosotros _____ (insinuar) que yo miento?
8. En tu país todos los días _____ (devaluar) la moneda.
9. Ellos _____ (efectuar) cambios que son fundamentales para nuestra compañía.
10. Ella _____ (continuar) trabajando en su proyecto de grado.

# C. Verbs With Stem Changes

Some verbs from any of the three conjugations (**-ar, -er, -ir**) have some systematic changes in the vowel (**e, i, o, u**) of their stem in all persons EXCEPT the first and second formal persons plural (*nosotros, vosotros*). These changes occur in the vowel of the stem in six different ways (**e** to **ie, e** to **i, i** to **ie, o** to **ue, o** to **hue, u** to **ue**).

**a.** Stem vowel change from **e** to **ie**.

| cerrar (*to close*) |
| --- |
| yo c**ie**rro |
| tú c**ie**rras |
| él, ella, usted c**ie**rra |
| nosotros/as cerramos |
| vosotros/as cerráis |
| ellos, ellas, ustedes c**ie**rran |

Other verbs with stems changing from **e** to **ie** are:

atender (*to attend to*)
atravesar (*to cross, to pierce*)
calentar (*to warm*)
comenzar (*to begin*)
confesar (*to confess*)

consentir (*to consent, to agree*)
defender (*to defend*)
descender (*to descend*)
despertar (*to wake up*)
divertir (*to have fun, to enjoy*)
empezar (*to begin*)
encender (*to switch on, to ignite, to light*)
encerrar (*to confine, to enclose*)
entender (*to understand*)
gobernar (*to govern*)
mentir (*to lie*)
negar (*to deny*)
pensar (*to think*)
perder (*to lose*)
preferir (*to prefer*)
querer (*to want*)
recomendar (*to recommend*)
sentar (*to sit*)
sentir (*to feel*)
sugerir (*to suggest*)

**Exercise 7.** Complete the following dialogue using the present tense:

**Visita al psiquiatra**

—Doctor, siempre temo cuando él _____(atravesar) la calle y (yo) _____ (pensar) que algo le va a pasar.

—¿Qué es lo que (tú) _____ (sentir)?

—No sé Dr. Algo _____ (gobernar) mis sentidos y (yo) _____ (preferir) alzarlo en mis brazos. Mis amigos me _____ (recomendar) comprar un cargador para bebés y (ellos) se _____ (divertir) burlándose de mí. Y me preguntan con quién me _____ (despertar) en las mañanas... Pero yo soy normal y sólo temo cuando (nosotros) _____(atravesar) la calle...

—Por favor empieza de nuevo, es que (yo) _____ (perder) el hilo con mucha facilidad. ¿Qué raza es tu perro?

**b.** Stem vowel change from **e** to **i**.

| **pedir (*to ask*)** |
|---|
| yo **pi**do |
| tú **pi**des |
| él, ella, usted **pi**de |
| nosotros/as pedimos |
| vosotros/as pedís |
| ellos, ellas, ustedes **pi**den |

Other verbs with stems changing from **e** to **i** are:

con**se**guir (*to get*)
cor**re**gir (*to correct*)
desp**e**dir (*to fire*)
el**e**gir (*to elect*)
imp**e**dir (*to impede*)
m**e**dir (*to measure*)
per**se**guir (*to follow*)
rep**e**tir (*to repeat*)
s**e**guir (*to follow*)
v**e**stirse* (*to get dressed*)

**Exercise 8.** Complete the following sentences using the present tense.

1. Ella sólo _____(vestir) diseños exclusivos.
2. Pilar _____ (repetir) las canciones y no _____ (conseguir) aprenderlas.
3. Mi profesor _____ (corregir) el libro de ejercicios todas las mañanas.
4. Él _____ (medir) más de un metro con ochenta centímetros, pero no es tan guapo.
5. Si tú no _____ (elegir) a alguien ahora te vas a quedar soltera.
6. ¡Vosotros os _____ (despedir) pero no os vais!
7. Nosotros _____ (impedir) que robaran la otra sucursal del banco.
8. Si (tú) _____ (seguir) estudiando vas a aprender español pronto.
9. La policía _____ (perseguir) al sospechoso.

**c.** Stem vowel change from **i** to **ie**. Only two common verbs are affected: **adquirir** (*to acquire*) and **inquirir** (*to inquire*).

| **adquirir (*to acquire*)** |
| --- |
| yo adqu**ie**ro |
| tú adqu**ie**res |
| él, ella, usted adqu**ie**re |
| nosotros/as adquirimos |
| vosotros/as adquirís |
| ellos, ellas, ustedes adqu**ie**ren |

**Exercise 9.** Complete the following sentences using the present tense.

1. Ellos _____(adquirir) prestigio con tu compañía.
2. Lucía _____ (adquirir) una mansión con el dinero de su herencia.
3. El juez _____ (inquirir) sobre lo ocurrido la noche del crimen.
4. Vosotros _____ (adquirir) conocimientos útiles.

*See Chapter 7, Pronominal Verbs.

**d.** Stem vowel change from **o** to **ue**.

| **recordar (*to remember*)** |
| --- |
| yo rec**ue**rdo |
| tú rec**ue**rdas |
| él, ella, usted rec**ue**rda |
| nosotros/as recordamos |
| vosotros/as recordáis |
| ellos, ellas, ustedes rec**ue**rdan |

Other verbs with stems changing from **o** to **ue** are:

abs**o**lver (*to absolve*)
alm**o**rzar (*to eat lunch*)
c**o**cer (*to boil, to bake*)
c**o**ntar (*to count*)
c**o**star (*to cost*)
dem**o**ler (*to demolish*)
dev**o**lver (*to return*)
dis**o**lver (*to dissolve*)
d**o**rmir (*to sleep*)
enc**o**ntrar (*to find*)
env**o**lver (*to wrap*)
ll**o**ver (*to rain*)
m**o**ler (*to grind*)
m**o**rir (*to die*)
m**o**strar (*to show*)
m**o**ver (*to move*)
**o**ler* (*to smell*)
p**o**der (*to be able to*)
pr**o**bar (*to taste, to prove*)
prom**o**ver (*to promote*)
rec**o**rdar (*to remember*)
rem**o**ver (*to remove*)
res**o**lver (*to resolve*)
ret**o**rcer (*to twist*)
rev**o**lver (*to mix*)
s**o**nar (*to sound*)
s**o**ñar (*to dream*)
t**o**rcer (*to twist*)

*Note: The verb **oler** changes the stem vowel from an **o** to **hue** (yo huelo, tú hueles, él huele...).

**Exercise 10.** Complete the following sentences using the present tense.

1. Si (tú) _____(volver) a preguntarle, él seguro que te lo va a decir.
2. ¡Él_____ (morir) por ti!
3. La guerra no _____ (resolver) nada, más bien complica todo.
4. Lo bueno de esa sinfonía es que todos los instrumentos _____ (sonar) de manera caótica.
5. Tomás y yo _____ (almorzar) todos los días donde mi mamá.
6. Vosotros _____ (dormir) como osos en invierno.
7. Ella _____ (poder) decir lo que quiera. Igual no le voy a hacer caso.
8. Como los perros, yo _____ (oler) todo antes de probar.
9. Ellos _____ (recordar) muy bien lo que el gobierno hizo con sus propiedades.
10. Nunca vamos a ver el final pues (tú) siempre _____ (devolver) la película en el mismo punto.

**e.** Stem vowel change from **u** to **ue**. Only one verb is affected: **jugar** (*to play*).

| jugar (*to play*) |
|---|
| yo **jue**go |
| tú **jue**gas |
| él, ella, usted **jue**ga |
| nosotros/as jugamos |
| vosotros/as jugáis |
| ellos, ellas, ustedes **jue**gan |

**Exercise 11.** Complete the following sentences using the present tense.

1. ¡Tú _____(jugar) con lo más sagrado!
2. La verdad, yo a eso no _____ (jugar).
3. Yo no entiendo. Gabriel y su amigos siempre practican mucho y _____ (jugar) muy mal.
4. Todos los niños _____ (jugar) con todo menos con sus juguetes.
5. A mí me parece que Lola _____ (jugar) muy bien tenis.

# D. Verbs With Irregular Forms

Verbs with irregular forms are mostly irregular in the present indicative, but only in the first person. A few others are irregular in all persons.

**a.** The following are irregular verbs in the present indicative in the first person.

| | **caber** *(to fit)* | **dar** *(to give)* | **saber** *(to know)* | **ver** *(to see)* |
|---|---|---|---|---|
| yo | **quep**o | doy | sé | veo |
| tú | cabes | das | sabes | ves |
| él, ella, usted | cabe | da | sabe | ve |
| nosotros/as | cabemos | damos | sabemos | vemos |
| vosotros/as | cabéis | dais | sabéis | veis |
| ellos, ellas, ustedes | caben | dan | saben | ven |

| | **decir** *(to say)* + **e** to **i** | **hacer** *(to do)* | **oír** *(to hear)* + **i** to **y** | **poner** *(to put)* | **salir** *(to go out)* | **tener** *(to have)* + **e** to **ie** | **traer** *(to bring)* | **venir** *(to come)* + **e** to **ie** | **valer** *(to value, to cost)* |
|---|---|---|---|---|---|---|---|---|---|
| yo | **di**go | hago | oigo | pongo | salgo | tengo | traigo | vengo | valgo |
| tú | dices | haces | oyes | pones | sales | tienes | traes | vienes | vales |
| él, ella, usted | dice | hace | oye | pone | sale | tiene | trae | viene | vale |
| nosotros/as | decimos | hacemos | oímos | ponemos | salimos | tenemos | traemos | venimos | valemos |
| vosotros/as | decís | hacéis | oís | ponéis | salís | tenéis | traéis | venís | valéis |
| ellos, ellas, ustedes | dicen | hacen | oyen | ponen | salen | tienen | traen | vienen | valen |

**Exercise 12.** Complete the following sentences using the present tense.

1. La casa se llena de vida cuando él _____(traer) los niños, yo en cambio no _____(traer) los míos nunca.

2. Vosotros _____ (dar) más de lo que tenéis, yo en cambio no _____ (dar) nada.

3. No sé qué pasa, siempre (tú)_____ (decir) una cosa y _____ (hacer) otra! Yo en cambio _____ (decir) y _____ (hacer) al mismo tiempo.

4. Selma _____ (venir) de estudiar, yo en cambio _____ (venir) de hacer ejercicio.

5. Ese sofá no _____ (caber) en la sala, y yo tampoco _____ (caber) en él; mejor lo tiro a la basura.

6. Vosotros siempre _____ (poner) orden en vuestra casa, yo en cambio nunca _____ (poner) orden.

7. Sólo una vez al año Lola _____ (venir) a visitarme, en cambio yo voy y _____ (venir) tres veces al año.

8. Casandra es la única que no_____ (ver) lo que yo _____ (ver) y todos los demás _____ (ver).

9. Todo lo que yo _____ (tener) es esta casa, en cambio tú _____ (tener) muchas propiedades.

10. Los esquimales _____ (saber) cazar focas, yo en cambio no _____ (saber).

11. Tulia y Francisco _____ (decir) que tú no _____ (saber) nada, yo en cambio _____ (decir) que eres un genio.

12. (Yo) _____ (oír) un ruido extraño. ¿Lo _____ (oír) tú?

13. En este juego (yo) siempre _____ (salir) perdiendo y tú _____ (salir) ganando.

14. Tú _____ (valer) mucho, yo en cambio no _____ (valer) nada.

**b.** The following are irregular verbs in the present indicative in all persons.

|  | estar *(to be)* | ser *(to be)* | haber *(to have)* | ir *(to go)* |
|---|---|---|---|---|
| yo | estoy | soy | he | voy |
| tú | estás | eres | has | vas |
| él, ella, usted | está | es | ha | va |
| nosotros/as | estamos | somos | hemos | vamos |
| vosotros/as | estáis | sois | habéis | vais |
| ellos, ellas, ustedes | están | son | han | van |

**Exercise 13.** Complete the following paragraph using the present tense.

Me gustan los libros de caballerías porque _____(ser) entretenidos. Por el contrario, los libros de gramática que (yo) _____ (haber) estudiado me aburren. Un libro de aventuras _____ (ser) siempre más divertido, y aún más, cuando _____ (estar) escrito con humor. Porque si vosotros _____ (estar) leyendo algo aburrido, _____ (ir) directo a dormir. De todas maneras, recuerda que con voluntad y entusiasmo _____ (ser) más fácil aprender cualquier idioma.

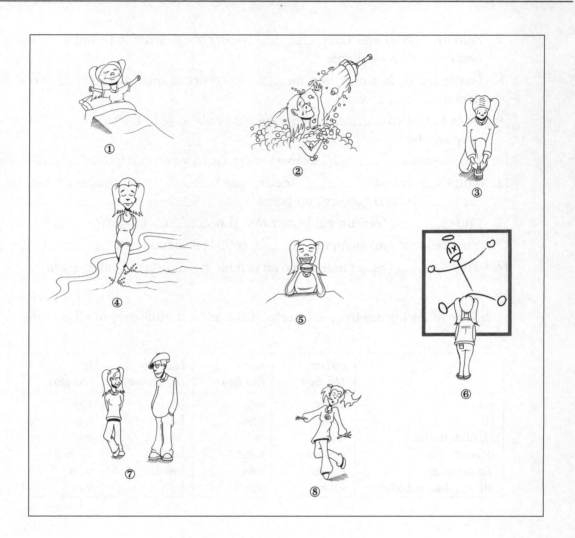

**Exercise 14.** Look at the pictures above and, using the present tense, write about one day in Sonia's vacation.

1. _____

2. _____

3. _____

4. _____

5. _____

6. _____

7. _____

8. _____

# E. Uses of the Present Tense

The present indicative refers to events which, in terms of order, are simultaneous with the event of speaking. The present indicative may represent one single event or express an habitual action. This distinction is always characterized by context. English, however, uses the simple present to express a single event and the present progressive for an habitual action.

| **Habitual action (Spanish)** | **Habitual action (English)** |
|---|---|
| (Simple Present) | (Simple Present) |
| —¿Qué **estudias**? | *"What do you study?"* |
| —**Estudio** economía. | *"I study economics."* |
| | |
| **Single event (Spanish)** | **Single event (English)** |
| (Simple Present) | (Present Progressive) |
| —¿Qué **estudias**? | *"What are you studying?"* |
| —**Estudio** para el examen de economía. | *"I am studying for the economics exam."* |

Others uses of the Spanish present indicative are similar to English. The present indicative describes **timeless** events and is also commonly used to express **future** events.

| **Timeless event (Spanish)** | **Timeless event (English)** |
|---|---|
| (Simple Present) | (Simple Present) |
| Todos los hombres **son** mortales. | *All men **are** mortal.* |
| | |
| **Future event (Spanish)** | **Future event (English)** |
| (Simple Present **ir** + **a** + infinitive) | (Present Progressive) |
| Mañana **vamos a ir** a la playa. | *Tomorrow we **are going to** the beach.* |

---

**TIP BOX**

In Spanish, the present progressive is used more frequently to emphasize a single event.

—¿Qué estás estudiando?                         *"What are you studying?"*
—**Estoy estudiando** para el examen de economía.      *"I am studying for the economics exam."*

**Exercise 15.** Complete the following text in the present tense using the following verbs: **llamarse, hacer, trabajar, estudiar, ir, querer, verse**

Paco:   —Hola, ¿Cómo te _____?

Pilar:  —Me _____ Pilar.

Paco:   —Yo me _____ Paco. ¿Qué _____? ¿ _____ o _____?

Pilar:  —_____ en una librería. ¿Y tú, qué _____?

Paco:   —_____ administración de empresas. ¿Quieres una cerveza?

Pilar:  —¡Vale!

Paco:   —Esta noche _____ a ir con unos amigos a un concierto de música de Senegal. ¿ _____ venir?

Pilar:  —¡Estupendo!

Paco:   —Entonces, nos _____ en el Teatro Real a las ocho en punto.

Pilar:  —De acuerdo. Hasta entonces.

Paco:   —Chao.

# Review

**Exercise 16.** Complete the following paragraph using the present tense.

Marta y Carlos _____ (ser) novios. Ambos _____ (asistir) a la Universidad Nacional y _____ (estudiar) Biología. En un mes _____ (ir) a graduarse, y por eso Marta _____ (buscar) un trabajo urgentemente. _____ (vivir) juntos porque no _____ (poder) estar separados un minuto. Los viernes _____ (jugar) tenis por la tarde y por la noche _____ (bailar) salsa. Los sábados, Marta _____ (dormir) hasta las ocho de la mañana, se _____ (vestir) y _____ (correr) siete kilómetros. Cuando Carlos _____ (decidir) ir con ella, siempre le dice: "Marta, esta vez sí te _____ (vencer)", pero la verdad es que nunca la _____ (vencer). Cuando ella lo _____ (socorrer), Carlos le _____ (contestar): "Mi amor te lo _____ (agradecer)". Yo les _____ (confesar) algo: "Carlos _____ (ser) un flojo" y Marta siempre lo _____ (proteger). Yo lo _____ (conocer) desde hace dos años. A Marta le _____ (reconocer) su ternura. Pero, también le _____ (exigir) prudencia. Ese hombre _____ (ser) un vividor. _____ (perseguir) a las muchachas dulces y las _____ (hacer) sentir diosas. Pero luego, cuando _____ (adquirir) confianza, se _____ (mudarse) a su apartamento. Allí, _____ (almorzar), _____ (comer) y _____ (dormir) y no _____ (traer) nada, sólo _____ (distribuir) sonrisas y palabras bonitas, y una las _____ (oír) como venidas del cielo. Luego que una se _____ (haber) ilusionado, _____ (tener) la desfachatez de decir que algo extraño le _____ (suceder) y dice: "Mi pasión se _____ (enfriarse), lo _____ (sentir) corazón pero me _____" (irse). Cuando _____ (decir) aquello, no _____ (caber) la menor duda que _____ (ser) porque _____ (haber) visto otra mujer. Lo _____ (decir) yo, que lo _____ (haber) vivido en carne propia.

# II. The Preterit

In Spanish two simple tenses are used to talk about the past: the **preterit** and the **imperfect.** The preterit is used **to narrate** in the past, and the imperfect is used **to describe** something in the past.

## A. Regular Verbs

The **regular conjugation** in the preterit is formed by adding the following endings to the stem of the verbs:

| | Verb Endings in the Preterit | |
|---|---|---|
| | **-ar** | **-er, -ir** |
| yo | -é | -í |
| tú | -aste | -iste |
| él, ella, usted | -ó | -ió |
| nosotros/as* | -amos | -imos |
| vosotros/as | -asteis | -isteis |
| ellos, ellas, ustedes | -aron | -ieron |

### TIP BOX

*Note that in the **first person of the plural** there is no difference between the present and the preterit. Therefore, the distinction is made by the context of the sentence.

### Example

**Ayer trabajamos toda la noche.**
*Yesterday we worked all night.*

**Nosotros trabajamos generalmente en las tardes.**
*We usually work every afternoon.*

**Exercise 17.** Complete the following sentences using the appropriate form of the preterit tense.

1. Dicen que el Libertador Simón Bolívar _____ (amar) a Manuelita Sáenz.
2. Yo _____ (aprender) un poco de español en la escuela.
3. Fernando _____ (abrir) la puerta y _____ (encontrar) algo terrible.
4. Amalia y Joaquín _____ (bailar) toda la noche.
5. No la pude alcanzar a pesar que _____ (correr) a gran velocidad.

6. ¿Cómo se llama la obra de teatro a la que (tú) _____ (asistir) anoche?
7. Yo _____ (socorrer) a mi gato cuando se cayó en la alberca.
8. Lo siento, (vosotros) _____ (decidir) muy tarde. La casa está vendida.
9. ¿Cuántas horas (usted) _____ (caminar) para atravesar la montaña?
10. Bolívar _____ (emprender) la campaña libertadora siendo muy joven.
11. ¿Quiénes _____ (escribir) la Biblia?
12. Te estoy diciendo que la linterna está en la maleta, porque (yo) _____ (alistar) todo antes de empacar.
13. Ella_____ (insistir) en comprar zapatos rojos.
14. Se quemó la tienda donde (tú) _____ (comprar) la mesa.
15. Ximena _____ (comer) grillos cuando estuvo en la China.
16. Anoche por fin (yo) _____ (hablar) con mis padres acerca de mi matrimonio.

**Exercise 18.** Rewrite the following sentences putting the underlined verb in the preterit tense.

1. La verdad es que nosotros no <u>comprendemos</u> nada.

   _____.

2. Miguel Induraín <u>sube</u> los Pirineos en el Tour de Francia en primer lugar.

   _____.

3. Otra vez Andrew <u>llega</u> tarde a clase.

   _____.

4. Martín Lutero <u>vive</u> entre 1483 y 1546.

   _____.

5. ¡La última semana de clase mi profesor <u>mira</u> los ejercicios de todo el curso!

   _____.

6. Andrea le <u>responde</u> muy mal al jefe.

   _____.

7. Yo siempre le estoy agradecido, porque cuando <u>necesito</u> dinero, ella me lo <u>presta</u>.

   _____.

8. Todos <u>tememos</u> el terremoto.

   _____.

9. Exactamente un año después del exilio en Elba, Napoleón <u>retorna</u> a Francia en febrero de 1815.

   _____.

10. Ellos <u>venden</u> todo antes de partir.

    _____.

11. Darwin y Wallace <u>trabajan</u> independiente y simultáneamente para elaborar la teoría de la evolución.

    _____.

12. Pedro y su esposa <u>viajan</u> en avión a Bruselas.

    _____.

13. Los padres de mis primos les <u>permiten</u> muchas cosas a sus hijos.

    _____.

14. Lucho <u>envía</u> sus cartas por correo rápido.

    _____.

15. Sócrates <u>bebe</u> una infusión de cicuta antes de morir.

    _____.

16. Los estudiantes <u>reciben</u> sus calificaciones el lunes.

    _____.

# B. Verbs With Spelling Changes

This group of verbs changes their spelling to reflect their pronunciation.

**a.** Verbs ending in **-car, -gar, -guar, -zar** are affected only in the first conjugation of the singular (*yo*).

## Spelling Rules

|  | **-car** | **-gar** | **-guar** | **-zar** |
|---|---|---|---|---|
|  | **c** to **qu** | **g** to **gu** | **u** to **ü** | **z** to **c** |
|  | **colocar** (*to place*) | cargar (*to carry*) | averiguar (*to find out*) | alcanzar (*to reach*) |
| yo | colo**qu**é | car**gu**é | averi**gü**é | alcan**c**é |
| tú | colocaste | cargaste | averiguaste | alcanzaste |
| él, ella, usted | colocó | cargó | averiguó | alcanzó |
| nosotros/as | colocamos | cargamos | averiguamos | alcanzamos |
| vosotros/as | colocasteis | cargasteis | averiguasteis | alcanzasteis |
| ellos, ellas, ustedes | colocaron | cargaron | averiguaron | alcanzaron |

Other verbs ending in **-car, -gar, -guar,** and **-zar** are:

| *-car* | *-gar* | *-guar* | *-zar* |
|---|---|---|---|
| acercar *(to bring closer)* | abrigar *(to shelter)* | apaciguar *(to appease)* | abrazar *(to embrace)* |
| ahorcar *(to hang)* | agregar *(to add)* | atestiguar *(to testify)* | adelgazar *(to make thin)* |
| aparcar *(to park)* | ahogar *(to drown)* | averiguar *(to find out)* | alcanzar *(to reach)* |
| arrancar *(to start [a* | alargar *(to extend)* | desaguar *(to drain)* | almorzar *(to have lunch)* |
|   *machine, a car], to pull out)* | albergar *(to harbor)* | fraguar *(to forge)* | alzar *(to raise)* |
| atacar *(to attack)* | apagar *(to turn off)* | | analizar *(to analyze)* |
| buscar *(to look for)* | arriesgar *(to risk)* | | aplazar *(to postpone)* |
| calificar *(to grade)* | cabalgar *(to ride)* | | aterrizar *(to land)* |
| cercar *(to surround, to fence)* | cargar *(to charge)* | | aterrorizar *(to terrify)* |
| clasificar *(to classify)* | castigar *(to punish)* | | autorizar *(to authorize)* |
| colocar *(to put)* | colgar *(to hang)* | | avanzar *(to advance)* |
| comunicar *(to communicate)* | conjugar *(to conjugate)* | | bautizar *(to baptize)* |
| criticar *(to criticize)* | descargar *(to discharge)* | | bostezar *(to yawn)* |
| dedicar *(to consagrate)* | descolgar *(to take down)* | | cazar *(to hunt)* |
| desempacar *(to unpack)* | despegar *(to separate)* | | comenzar *(to begin)* |
| destacar *(to emphasize)* | devengar *(to yield)* | | comercializar *(to market)* |
| diagnosticar *(to diagnose)* | dialogar *(to talk)* | | cruzar *(to cross)* |
| duplicar *(to duplicate)* | divulgar *(to divulge)* | | deslizar *(to slide)* |
| edificar *(to build)* | embriagar *(to intoxicate)* | | danzar *(to dance)* |
| educar *(to educate)* | encargar *(to entrust)* | | desplazar *(to displace)* |
| embarcar *(to embark)* | enjuagar *(to rinse)* | | destrozar *(to destroy)* |
| empacar *(to pack)* | entregar *(to deliver)* | | disfrazar *(to disguise)* |
| enfocar *(to focus)* | interrogar *(to interrogate)* | | economizar *(to save)* |
| enmarcar *(to frame)* | investigar *(to investigate)* | | empezar *(to begin)* |
| equivocar *(to mistake)* | jugar *(to play)* | | estabilizar *(to stabilize)* |
| especificar *(to specify)* | llegar *(to arrive)* | | esterilizar *(to sterilize)* |
| explicar *(to explain)* | madrugar *(to rise early)* | | generalizar *(to generalize)* |
| fabricar *(to manufacture)* | navegar *(to sail)* | | gozar *(to enjoy)* |
| falsificar *(to falsify)* | negar *(to deny)* | | idealizar *(to idealize)* |
| identificar *(to identify)* | obligar *(to force)* | | indemnizar *(to compensate)* |
| indicar *(to indicate)* | otorgar *(to offer)* | | inmortalizar *(to immortalize)* |
| justificar *(to justify)* | pagar *(to pay)* | | lanzar *(to launch)* |
| marcar *(to mark)* | pegar *(to hit)* | | localizar *(to locate)* |
| modificar *(to modify)* | prolongar *(to prolong)* | | memorizar *(to memorize)* |
| pecar *(to sin)* | rogar *(to beg)* | | modernizar *(to modernize)* |
| pescar *(to fish)* | | | organizar *(to organize)* |
| practicar *(to practice)* | | | privatizar *(to privatize)* |
| provocar *(to cause)* | | | rechazar *(to reject)* |
| publicar *(to publish)* | | | reemplazar *(to replace)* |
| roncar *(to snore)* | | | responsabilizar *(to blame)* |
| sacar *(to remove)* | | | rezar *(to pray)* |
| secar *(to dry)* | | | tranquilizar *(to calm down)* |
| simplificar *(to simplify)* | | | tropezar *(to trip)* |
| suplicar *(to entreat)* | | | visualizar *(to visualize)* |
| tocar *(to touch)* | | | |
| ubicar *(to locate)* | | | |

**Exercise 19.** Complete the following sentences with the appropriate form of the preterit tense.

1. Ellos _____ (ubicar) sus campamentos lejos de la ciudad.
2. Con ese poema creo que (yo) _____ (tocar) tu corazón.
3. A pesar de que yo _____ (suplicar) clemencia. El jurado lo condenó.
4. Los pinos _____ (secar) la tierra a su alrededor.
5. En la última película me dormí cuando Clint Eastwood _____ (sacar) el revólver.
6. *El País* de España _____ (publicar) un reportaje sobre toreras hace dos semanas.
7. En la última temporada yo _____ (pescar) con esa misma clase de anzuelos.
8. Vosotros _____ (fabricar) ese engaño para quedaros con mi herencia.
9. La profesora _____ (explicar) el ejercicio dos veces; sin embargo, sigo sin entender.
10. Adelaida dijo que ellos _____ (empacar) todo lo necesario.
11. El invierno _____ (duplicar) la energía que consumo regularmente.
12. Sus problemas radican en que yo les _____ (dedicar) demasiado tiempo.
13. Lo que yo _____ (buscar) no fue la fama ni el oro. Ellos llegaron por añadidura.
14. Yo la _____ (atacar) por estar en contra de mí.
15. Todos _____ (calificar) de excelente la última película de Almodóvar.
16. (Yo) _____ (colocar) la mesa en medio del patio. ¿Estás de acuerdo?

**Exercise 20**. Complete the following sentences with the appropriate form of the preterit tense.

1. Sólo me pude dormir cuando el conductor _____ (apagar) el radio.
2. Vosotros siempre _____ (arriesgar) sus intereses.
3. Cuando llegó la mañana (yo) _____ (cargar) mi carro y desaparecí.
4. (yo) _____ (colgar) mi ropa en el patio.
5. ¡Buenos días señor! Me da por favor los víveres que mi mamá le _____ (encargar) hace un momento por teléfono.
6. No sé cómo siguen creciendo estas matas si (yo) _____ (fumigar) todo el terreno dos veces.
7. Nosotros _____ (jugar) como nunca y perdimos como siempre.
8. La razón por la cual no conseguimos boletos es porque tú _____ (llegar) tarde.
9. Afortunadamente el jefe _____ (pagar) toda la cuenta anoche.
10. A pesar del intenso verano, el jardín está muy lindo gracias a que (yo) lo _____ (regar) dos veces por semana.

**Exercise 21**. Complete the following sentences with the appropriate form of the preterit tense.

1. En cuanto vio a su madre el niño _____ (apaciguar) su llanto.
2. Ellos lo asesinaron; supongo que (él) _____ (atestiguar) contra la mafia.
3. No sé cómo, pero (yo) _____ (averiguar) su escondite.
4. Vino el plomero y _____ (desaguar) la bañera.
5. Todos saben que (yo) _____ (fraguar) el complot con astucia.
6. Juan Pablo II _____ (santiguar) a la multitud al final de la ceremonia.

**Exercise 22.** Complete the following sentences with the appropriate form of the preterit tense.

1. Él _____ (abrazar) a su hija y sin decir nada partió.
2. Creo que Lucila y Juan _____ (adelgazar) porque tomaron esta nueva droga.
3. (yo) _____ (alcanzar) todo lo que quería.
4. No gracias. Nosotros _____ (almorzar) hace un ratito.
5. Nosotros _____ (alzar) los niños y pararon de llorar.
6. Yo _____ (analizar) toda la situación y creo que lo mejor es construir un nuevo parqueadero.
7. Los cazadores _____ (cazar) tantos elefantes, que los exterminaron.
8. Los hombres que poblaron América _____ (cruzar) el estrecho de Bering.
9. ¡Tú y tu pelota _____ (destrozar) mi jarrón de cristal!
10. Si confías en mí, continúo la obra que (tú) _____ (empezar).
11. Antonio _____ (encabezar) la marcha por la paz.
12. En cuanto recibí el balón (yo) _____ (lanzar) a la canasta y anoté dos puntos en contra de mi propio equipo.
13. Debes hacerte cargo de la fiesta que tu _____ (organizar).
14. El presidente Bush _____ (reemplazar) al presidente Clinton.
15. Ellos _____ (memorizar) todas las formas de los verbos en español.
16. Cuando vosotros _____ (localizar) el avión ya era demasiado tarde.
17. Sólo cuando Julia _____ (tranquilizar) a mi gato, pude ver que estaba herido.
18. El gato _____ (tropezar) cuando saltaba el balcón y se lastimó.

**b.** Verbs ending in **-caer, -eer, -oer, -oír,** and **-uir** are affected in the third conjugation of the singular *(él, ella, usted)* and in the third conjugation of the plural *(él, ellos, ellas, ustedes).*

| caer<br>*(to fall)* | leer<br>*(to read)* | roer<br>*(to gnaw)* | oír<br>*(to listen)* | huir<br>*(to escape)* |
|---|---|---|---|---|
| yo caí | leí | roí | oí | huí |
| tu caíste | leíste | roíste | oíste | huiste |
| el, ella, usted cayó | leyó | royó | oyó | huyó |
| nosotros/as caímos | leímos | roímos | oímos | huimos |
| vosotros/as caísteis | leísteis | roísteis | oísteis | huisteis |
| ellos, ellas, ustedes cayeron | leyeron | royeron | oyeron | huyeron |

Other verbs ending in **-caer, -eer, -oer, -óir,** and **-uir** are:

| -caer | -eer | -oer | -óir | -uir |
|---|---|---|---|---|
| decaer *(to decay)* <br> recaer *(to fall again)* | creer *(to believe)* <br> poseer *(to possess)* <br> proveer *(to provide)* <br> releer *(to reread)* | corroer *(to corrode)* | entreoír *(to half-hear)* | atribuir *(to attribute)* <br> concluir *(to conclude)* <br> constituir *(to constitute)* <br> construir *(to build)* <br> contribuir *(to contribute)* <br> destituir *(to dismiss)* <br> destruir *(to destroy)* <br> diluir *(to dilute)* <br> disminuir *(to diminish)* <br> distribuir *(to distribute)* <br> incluir *(to include)* <br> influir *(to influence)* <br> intuir *(to sense)* <br> obstruir *(to block)* <br> recluir *(to imprison)* <br> sustituir *(to substitute)* |

**Exercise 23.** Complete the following sentences with the appropriate form of the preterit tense.

1. El ácido del acumulador _____ (corroer) parte de las latas de mi coche.
2. Durante la segunda guerra mundial, ¿exactamente en qué año_____ (caer) Kiev en manos de los alemanes?
3. El _____ (poseer) tierras y ganados y hoy todo lo ha perdido.
4. Los ratones _____ (roer) el queso de la alacena.
5. A la muerte de su madre las responsabilidades de la casa _____ (recaer) sobre sus hombros.
6. Yo no _____ (creer) lo que dijiste. Lo siento mucho.
7. Ese mismo manantial_____ (proveer) de agua a toda la región por muchos años.

**Exercise 24.** Complete the following sentences with the appropriate form of the preterit tense.

1. Traté de advertírselo pero Laura no_____ (oír).
2. La policía _____ (atribuir) el crimen al novio de la víctima.
3. El juez _____ (concluir) que la policía estaba equivocada.
4. Todos ellos _____ (reconstruir) los hechos con evidencia falsa.
5. Así fue como los abogados _____ (destruir) los argumentos del fiscal durante el juicio.
6. El nivel del agua _____ (disminuir) 1,3% en todos los lagos de la cordillera de los Andes.
7. Ese almacén no_____ (distribuir) buena mercancía; sólo baratijas.
8. Quiero saber, ¿por qué (tú) no me _____ (incluir) en la lista de tus invitados?
9. Vosotros _____ (influir) en la decisión que él tomó.
10. Angelita _____ (sustituir) a Ana en la vicepresidencia de las Hermanas de la Caridad.

# C. Stem-Changing *–ir* Verbs Only

**a.** Stem-changing *–ir* verbs (**e** to **ie**, **e** to **i**, **o** to **u**) in the present tense* change their corresponding vowel of the stem in the preterit in the third conjugation singular (*él, ella, usted*) and plural (*ellos, ellas, ustedes*) in two different ways: **e** to **i** and **o** to **u**.

## Stem-Changing Rules

| e to **ie** | e to **i** | o to **u** |
| --- | --- | --- |
| **sentir** *(to feel)* | **pedir** *(to ask)* | **morir** *(to die)* |
| yo sentí | pedí | morí |
| tú sentiste | pediste | moriste |
| él, ella, usted s**i**ntió | p**i**dió | m**u**rió |
| nosotros/as sentimos | pedimos | morimos |
| vosotros/as sentisteis | pedisteis | moristeis |
| ellos, ellas, ustedes s**i**ntieron | p**i**dieron | m**u**rieron |

Other such stem-changing verbs are:

| e to **ie** | e to **i** | o to **u** |
| --- | --- | --- |
| cons**e**ntir *(to agree)* | cons**e**guir *(to get)* | d**o**rmir *(to sleep )* |
| div**e**rtir *(to amuse)* | corr**e**gir *(to correct)* | m**o**rir *(to die)* |
| m**e**ntir *(to lie)* | desp**e**dir *(to fire)* | |
| pref**e**rir *(to prefer)* | el**e**gir *(to elect)* | |
| recom**e**ndar *(to recommend)* | imp**e**dir *(to impede)* | |
| s**e**ntir *(to feel)* | m**e**dir *(to measure)* | |
| sug**e**rir *(to suggest)* | pers**e**guir *(to follow)* | |
| | r**e**ír *(to laugh)* | |
| | rep**e**tir *(to repeat)* | |
| | s**e**guir *(to follow)* | |
| | sonr**e**ír *(to smile)* | |
| | v**e**stir(se) *(to get dressed)* | |

**Exercise 25.** Complete the following sentences with the appropriate form of the preterit tense.

1. Los padres de mi abuela _____ (consentir) en su matrimonio.
2. Él _____ (divertir) al público con su humor exquisito.

*For a list of stem-changing *–ir* verbs (**e** to **ie**, **e** to **i**, **o** to **u**) see the present tense section in this chapter.

3. Cuando llegaron mis padres nosotros _____ (mentir) para evitar un terrible castigo.
4. Carlos _____ (preferir) vivir en París y no en Honolulu.
5. He mejorado desde que hice lo que el Dr. me _____ (recomendar).
6. Andrés y Daniel _____ (sentir) mucha alegría al saber sus notas de geografía.
7. Recuerdo que (nosotros) _____ (sugerir) ir a Honolulu.

**Exercise 26.** Complete the following sentences with the appropriate form of the preterit tense.

1. La familia Rojas _____ (conseguir) casa nueva.
2. El profesor no _____ (corregir) los ejercicios.
3. Andrés _____ (despedir) a todos los empleados y ahora tiene problemas.
4. Sara _____ (elegir) este vestido rojo para su boda.
5. La lluvia _____ (impedir) zarpar la noche acordada.
6. Esto sucedió porque el piloto no _____ (medir) las consecuencias de salir tan tarde.
7. Pero la policía británica nunca _____ (perseguir) a Jack el destripador.
8. Todos _____ (reír) de todo lo que el presidente dijo por la televisión esta mañana.
9. Ana y Mary _____ (repetir) todos los ejercicios hasta comprender el pretérito.
10. Él _____ (seguir) el mismo camino que su padre.
11. Vosotros _____ (sonreír) cuando hice mi presentación.
12. El año pasado nosotros _____ (vestir) a la virgen para la procesión.

**Exercise 27.** Complete the following sentences with the appropriate form of the preterit tense.

1. En su primera noche en casa, el bebé _____ (dormir) sin interrupciones.
2. El presidente McKinley y el Presidente Kennedy _____ (morir) en actos públicos.
3. En su viaje al Amazonas mis padres _____ (dormir) en un bohío indígena.
4. No recuerdo bien a mis abuelos pues yo era muy niño cuando ellos _____ (morir).

# D. Verbs With Irregular Forms

**a.** The verbs **ir** (to go) and **ser** (to be) are both irregular, but note that they also share the same conjugation form.

| ir/ser |
| --- |
| yo **fui** |
| tú **fuiste** |
| él, ella, usted **fue** |
| nosotros/as **fuimos** |
| vosotros/as **fuisteis** |
| ellos, ellas, ustedes **fueron** |

**b.** The verb **dar** (to give) is conjugated with the endings of the **-er** and **-ir** verbs.

| dar |
| --- |
| yo d**i** |
| tú d**iste** |
| él, ella, usted d**io** |
| nosotros/as d**imos** |
| vosotros/as d**isteis** |
| ellos, ellas, ustedes d**ieron** |

**Exercise 28.** Rewrite the following sentences in the preterit.

1. Carlos le da las gracias al taxista.

   _____.

2. María y José le dan un regalo de cumpleaños a su hijo.

   _____.

3. Tú contribuyes con dinero para proteger el medio ambiente.

   _____.

4. Nosotros le damos la bienvenida al astronauta.

   _____.

5. Yo doy lo mejor de mí.

   _____.

**c.** The following verbs are irregular. Memorize the first conjugation form and then add to the irregular stem the corresponding preterit endings.

| -ar | -er | -ir |
| --- | --- | --- |
| andar<br>yo **anduve** | tener<br>yo **tuve** | venir<br>yo **vine** |
| estar<br>yo **estuve** | caber<br>yo **cupe** | decir<br>yo **dije** |
| | haber<br>yo **hube** | producir<br>(plus verbs ending in **-cir**)<br>yo **produje** |
| | poder<br>yo **pude** | traer<br>(plus verbs ending in **-traer**)<br>yo **traje** |
| | poner<br>yo **puse** | |
| | saber<br>yo **supe** | |
| | hacer*<br>yo **hice** | |
| | querer<br>yo **quise** | |

* The verb **hacer** changes the **c** to **z** in the third conjugation of the singular *(él, ella, usted hizo).*

## TIP BOX

The following rule may be used for these irregular verbs.

 For example, to conjugate the verb **andar** (to go, to walk):

1. Memorize its first-person conjugation (**Yo anduve**)
2. Take the irregular stem (**anduv**)
3. Add the corresponding ending (**-e, iste, -o, -imos, -isteis, -ieron**)

| andar |
| --- |
| yo anduv**e** |
| tú anduv**iste** |
| él, ella, usted anduv**o** |
| nosotros/as anduv**imos** |
| vosotros/as anduv**isteis** |
| ellos, ellas, ustedes anduv**ieron** |

**Exercise 29.** Complete the following sentences with the appropriate form of the preterit tense.

1. Ayer, nosotros _____ (andar) por el parque.
2. La liebre _____ (estar) en su guarida toda la mañana.
3. Javier y sus amigos_____ (tener) unas veladas muy amenas.
4. Todo era gris hasta que (tú)_____ (venir) a mi vida.
5. La verdad es que tú nunca _____ (caber) en esta familia.
6. Los periódicos_____ (decir) esta mañana que el agua escasea en la Tierra.
7. _____ (haber) una tormenta terrible anoche y ahora no hay energía.
8. Los hindúes fueron los primeros que _____ (producir) arroz, y sólo en el medioevo se expandió su consumo al sur de Europa.
9. Las labores de asistencia social _____ (reducir) la cifra de muerte de niños recién nacidos en un 30%.
10. Los romanos _____ (poder) conquistar un vasto territorio.
11. Yo _____ (traer) mis pinturas para mostrártelas.
12. Él se _____ (retraer) mucho después de la muerte de su esposa.
13. Los niños _____ (poner) la mesa.
14. Nosotros _____ (saber) sólo después que era prohibido traer el perro a la iglesia.
15. La torta de queso está deliciosa, la (yo) _____ (hacer) anoche.
16. He oído que _____ (querer) más a tu primer esposo que a mí. ¿Es verdad?

# E. Uses of the Preterit

As previously mentioned, the preterit is used to narrate in the past; in other words, it expresses an action accomplished and completed in the past and not connected with the present.

### Example

Ayer estuve en la biblioteca hasta las once de la noche.
*Yesterday, I was in the library until eleven p.m.*

José me acompañó luego a casa.
*Afterwards, José accompanied me home.*

**Exercise 30.** Complete the following sentences with the appropriate form of the preterit tense.

1. Brasil no _____ (incluir) a Romario en la lista de su seleccionado nacional para las próximas eliminatorias al mundial.
2. Nos quedamos sólo un par de horas tomándonos unos vinos después que te _____ (retirar) a tu cuarto.
3. Yo _____ (repetir) estos ejercicios hasta que me quedaron bien.
4. Cuando llegamos a esta ciudad nosotros _____ (pagar) por adelantado el alquiler de la casa.
5. La cultura romana_____ (influir) grandemente sobre todo el mundo occidental.
6. Ellos te _____ (explicar) que es importante usar protector solar para no contraer cáncer.
7. Yo _____ (destrozar) todas tus cartas, para no recordarte.
8. En el viaje nosotros_____ (caminar) dos días antes de encontrar un ser humano.
9. Yo _____ (temer) no verte nunca más.
10. El niño se _____ (reír) cuando su padre se resbaló.
11. Aboné 100.000 dólares a la deuda y de esta manera (yo) _____ (reducir) las cuotas mensuales a sólo 500 dólares.
12. Todo era tranquilo en este pueblo hasta que ellos _____ (llegar) con sus dos mil jaulas de pericos.
13. Todavía seguimos utilizando el mismo vidrio que los fenicios_____ (fabricar).
14. Nosotros _____ (decidir) aprender español porque nos gusta la música latina.
15. ¿Ustedes _____ (cruzar) la cordillera por el lado menos inclinado?

**Exercise 31.** Complete the following sentences with the appropriate form of the preterit tense.

1.  Todo salió bien cuando hice lo que mi madre me _____ (sugerir).
2.  Los bandidos _____ (socorrer) a los periodistas perdidos en la noche.
3.  Jorge era un necio hasta que Dios le _____ (proveer) sabiduría.
4.  Fue en las costas de Jamaica donde nosotros _____ (pescar) un mero por primera vez.
5.  Ella lo _____ (perseguir) hasta que logró casarse con él.
6.  Mi amiga siempre estuvo ahí cuando yo la _____ (necesitar).
7.  Nosotros _____ (jugar) bien pero nuestros contrincantes lo hicieron mejor.
8.  _____ (haber) aguaceros torrenciales en Europa el mes pasado.
9.  Los misioneros _____ (distribuir) los alimentos entre los damnificados del terremoto.
10. Mira este conejito que Lucas _____ (cazar) para la cena de esta noche.
11. Todos nosotros_____ (sentir) mucho la muerte de tu padre.
12. Esta mañana Lola _____ (responder) toda su correspondencia acumulada de una semana.
13. La primera novela que Faulkner _____ (publicar) fue *La paga de los soldados*.
14. La torta quedó dura porque Berta no _____ (medir) bien la harina.
15. Ayer (yo) _____ (fumigar) esta casa y todavía hay hormigas por todas partes.
16. Los computadores _____ (disminuir) el mercado de máquinas de escribir pero no de calculadoras.

**Exercise 32.** Complete the following sentences with the appropriate form of the preterit tense.

1.  La madre chimpancé _____ (abrazar) a su hijo y lo protegió de la mirada de los curiosos.
2.  Finalmente los argentinos _____ (poder) estabilizar el valor de su divisa.
3.  Te felicito por la ambiciosa carrera que (tú) _____ (emprender).
4.  Tu abuelita _____ (empezar) a sufrir de sonambulismo desde que perdió su osito de felpa.
5.  La linterna debe estar en alguna de las cajas pues recuerdo bien que nosotros la _____ (empacar).
6.  Después de que yo _____ (andar) por la ciudad de Granada me salieron callos.
7.  Perdiste la partida porque desde el principio _____ (ubicar) mal a tu dama.
8.  Es extraño, pero ellos aseguran que _____ (oír) lobos anoche.
9.  Susana y Mario_____ (dormir) en una cabaña en lo alto de la montaña.
10. Por su buena actuación Charlotte _____ (conseguir) un óscar como mejor actriz de reparto.
11. Mi problema fue que mis padres nunca me _____ (comprender).
12. El incendio se _____ (apagar) dejando un gran sector del bosque destruido.
13. No es cierto cuando dicen que Beethoven _____ (amar) muchas mujeres.

May 21, 1920          June 5, 1941          March 7, 1942          July 23, 1945

May 3, 1950          August 3, 1955          May 5, 1969          April 3, 1970

**Exercise 33.** Based on the pictures above, tell some souvenirs about the life of abuelo Marco. Use the following verbs: **tener un hijo, casarse, arrestar a su hijo, graduarse, accidentarse, ganar un concurso, ir a un matrimonio**.

1. *El abuelo Marco nació el 21 de mayo de 1920.*

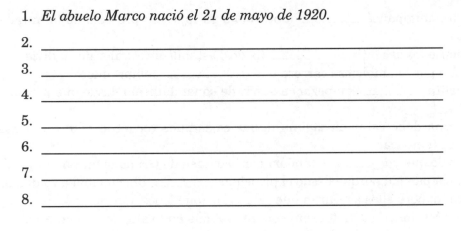

2. _____

3. _____

4. _____

5. _____

6. _____

7. _____

8. _____

# III. The Imperfect

The **imperfect,** as stated before, is mostly used **to describe** something in the past.

## A. Regular Verbs

The **regular conjugation** in the imperfect indicative is formed by adding the following endings to the stem of the verbs.

|  | Verb Endings of the Imperfect | |
| --- | --- | --- |
|  | **-ar** | **-er /-ir** |
| yo | -aba | -ía |
| tú | -abas | -ías |
| él, ella, usted | -aba | -ía |
| nosotros/as | -ábamos | -íamos |
| vosotros/as | -abais | -íais |
| ellos, ellas, ustedes | -aban | -ían |

---

**TIP BOX**

There are no stem-changing verbs in the imperfect.

---

**Exercise 34.** Complete the following sentences using the appropriate form of the imperfect tense.

1. Cuando niño, todos los días, _____ (recoger) piedritas.
2. Cuando Arnoldo era joven_____ (hacer) cien abdominales diarias.
3. Era mejor cuando tú _____ (almorzar) fuera de la casa.
4. Los árboles que derrumbaron _____ (proteger) los nacimientos de agua.
5. Nosotros fuimos a casa a hacer una fiesta, mientras vosotros _____ (insistir) en ir a la fiesta del club.
6. Dicen que Antonio _____ (escribir) su último libro cuando sufrió el infarto.
7. Él advirtió que nosotros perderíamos el dinero si_____ (decidir) no tomar el apartamento.
8. Mis padres_____ (asistir) todos los años a la celebración de año nuevo en casa de la familia Torres, mientras ellos estuvieron vivos.
9. Cuando era estudiante Tonino _____ (vender) emparedados en la universidad.
10. Todos los inversionistas _____ (temer) una nueva caída de los precios en la bolsa de Nueva York.

11. Liliana, cuando era adolescente, _____ (responder) mal con sus deberes escolares.
12. Los fenicios _____ (creer) en un solo dios.
13. Cuando era joven no _____ (comprender) a los adultos y ahora tampoco.
14. Mientras Sara _____ (buscar) un sitio de reposo, sus hijos gritaban sin parar.
15. A esta misma hora hace dos años, Teresa _____ (bailar) con Joaquín Sabina en un bar de Madrid.
16. En el año 1988 mis primos_____ (tener) la misma novia y no sabían.
17. Cuando Susana era joven, _____ (dormir) profundamente; ahora sufre de insomnio.

# B. Verbs With Irregular Forms

Only three verbs are irregular in the imperfect: **ir, ser,** and **ver.**

|            | ir     | ser    | ver     |
|------------|--------|--------|---------|
| yo         | iba    | era    | veía    |
| tú         | ibas   | eras   | veías   |
| él, ella, usted | iba | era  | veía    |
| nosotros/as | íbamos | éramos | veíamos |
| vosotros/as | ibais  | erais  | veíais  |
| ellos, ellas, ustedes | iban | eran | veían |

**Exercise 35.** Complete the following sentences using the appropriate form of the imperfect tense.

1. A los seis años Diego pensaba que _____ (ir) a ser bombero.
2. Cuando mi abuela vivía, nosotras _____ (ir) en la tardes a caminar por el campo.
3. Vosotros _____ (ser) más divertidos antes de tener tanto dinero.
4. Orlando _____ (ser) mas feliz cuando vivía en Bolivia.
5. Mis amigos y yo _____ (ver) cine mudo todos los viernes en la tarde cuando salíamos de la escuela.
6. La familia López _____ (ser) sus mejores amigos antes de su divorcio.
7. ¿Adónde _____ (ir) ustedes de vacaciones cuando vivían con sus padres?
8. ¡Sí, ya recuerdo ese grupo! Pero mis amigos _____ (ser) Javier y Tomás, a los otros chicos realmente no los conocí bien.
9. ¿Por qué David no _____ (ir) a la escuela con los otros niños del barrio cuando vivía en Lima?
10. Cuando llegaba del colegio todas las tardes, Germán _____ (ver) Plaza Sésamo en la tele.
11. Antes, Jaime _____ (ser) más amable con las visitas.
12. ¿Cómo se llamaba esa muchacha que (tú) _____ (ver) con frecuencia mientras vivimos en Buenos Aires?
13. La vida cotidiana_____ (ser) muy distinta antes de la popularización de los computadores.

# C. Uses of the Imperfect Tense

The imperfect is used to describe the past in the following ways.

**a.** To describe a routine or an habitual action that used to occurr in the past.

## Example

Cuando era niño, todos los días jugaba con mi vecino.
*When I was a child, I used to play with my neighbor every day.*

Los domingos íbamos a comer en un restaurante.
*Every Sunday, we would go to a restaurant for dinner.*

Durante las vacaciones viajábamos a la costa Atlántica para disfrutar de la playa.
*During our vacations, we would travel to the Atlantic Coast to enjoy the beach.*

**Exercise 36.** Complete the following text using the appropriate form of the imperfect tense of the following verbs.

**beber, caminar, comer, divertirse, esconderse, estar, enviar, ir, jugar, organizar, venir**

Ahora, recuerdo que cuando _____ en la escuela secundaria, para poder ir de paseo _____ rifas. En los paseos muchos de mis compañeros _____ aguardiente a escondidas y les _____ serenatas a sus prometidas sin el consentimiento de sus padres. En casa, nuestros padres eran muy estrictos. Todos los días _____ en una mesa diferente a la de los adultos. Allí, en esa mesa exclusiva para nosotros los niños, nos _____ monstruosamente, especialmente con mis primos que todos los años _____ en las vacaciones a visitarnos. Después de comer, durante el verano todas las tardes _____ a la playa y _____ voleibol. A veces, _____ por la montaña y nos _____ de mi hermano menor.

**b.** To describe a situation that occurred in the past.

## Example

En aquel tiempo, vivíamos en el campo.
*In those days, we lived in the countryside.*

Yo tenía ocho años y ayudaba a mi padre ordeñando las vacas.
*I was eight years old and I used to help my father milk the cows.*

**Exercise 37.** Complete the following exercise as shown in the example below.

## Example

Actualmente, mi hermana es la mejor estudiante, *pero antes era la peor.*

1. Ricardo tiene dos novias, _____. (sólo una)
2. Adriana canta rock, _____. (tango)
3. Alberto y Daniel escriben para el diario más importante del país, _____. (para el diario local)
4. Mi madre sonríe sólo de vez en cuando, _____. (todo el tiempo)
5. Lucrecia no duerme mucho, _____. (muchas horas)
6. Ahora nunca miento, _____. (todo el tiempo)
7. Rosa corre tres kilómetros, _____. (diez kilómetros)
8. Mi padre no tiene mucho dinero, _____. (mucho)
9. Hoy, mi madre no posee nada, _____. (una fortuna)

c. To describe a person in the past either physically or morally.

## Example

Mi profesora tenía los ojos negros y era muy amable.
*My teacher had dark eyes and she was very charming.*

**Exercise 38.** Following the example below, put the following sentences in the past, using the imperfect tense.

## Example

Mi abuelo tiene los ojos azules. *Mi abuelo tenía los ojos azules.*

1. Mi perra es grande y blanca y es muy juguetona.

   _____

2. Mi profesora tiene el cabello negro y es muy estricta.

   _____

3. Los niños son muy inquietos y tienen mucha energía.

   _____

4. María y Josefa son altas y bondadosas, y además tienen mucha paciencia.

   _____

5. Rosa es muy simpática y se viste muy elegante.

   _____

6. Fernando es guapo, tiene los ojos negros y el cabello oscuro. Además es inteligente.

   _____

**d.** To describe either a condition affecting the psyche or a mood in the past.

### Example

Se sentía triste y abandonada.
*She felt sad and abandoned.*

Estaba enferma y tenía fiebre.
*She was sick and had a fever.*

**Exercise 39.** Complete the following text using the appropriate form of the imperfect tense of the following verbs.

**aburrir, creer, decir, entrar, estar, gustar, ir, llorar, mirar, pensar, reprender, sentir, sentirse, tener**

Julia _____agobiada cuando nuestra madre la _____. A ninguno nos _____estudiar. La escuela nos _____ y (nosotros) _____ desconsoladamente todos los lunes cuando _____ camino a la escuela. (nosotros) _____ a los pescadores y al mar con nostalgia. (nosotros) _____ que la libertad era lanzar piedras desde el acantilado. Julia además siempre _____ miedo cuando _____a la clase de latín. Muchas veces para no ir a la escuela _____ que _____ enferma y que _____ náuseas. Pero mamá nunca le _____.

**e.** To describe attitudes and convictions in the past.

### Example

Todos creían que el chamán tenía el poder de la curación.
*All of them believed the shaman had healing power.*

Pensábamos que iba a morir.
*We thought he would die.*

**Exercise 40.** Following the example below, put the following sentences in the past using the imperfect tense.

### Example

Todos estamos convencidos de tu inocencia. *Todos estábamos convencidos de tu inocencia.*

1.  Mis padres piensan que soy un perezoso.

    _____

2.  Yo creo que tengo una enfermedad grave.

    _____

3.  Mi hermana está segura de mi lealtad.

    _____

4. Raúl nos asegura que tiene un secreto.

   _____

5. Andrea piensa que yo nunca tengo la razón, y es cierto.

   _____

6. Yo no reconozco que me equivoco.

   _____

7. Clemente insinúa que yo pierdo todo.

   _____

8. Yo insisto en ser astronauta.

   _____

9. Ellas siempre averiguan dónde es la fiesta.

   _____


**f.** To describe an action in process in a specific moment of the past.

### Example

   —¿Qué hacías cuando oíste la explosión?
   —Compraba el periódico en el kiosco.

   *"What were you doing when you heard the explosion?"*
   *"I was buying a newspaper in the kiosk."*

**Exercise 41.** Complete the following sentences using the appropriate form of the imperfect tense.

1. Él _____ (hacer) sus maletas cuando se inundó la casa.
2. Lola y María _____ (mirar) al cielo cuando cayó una estrella fugaz.
3. Nosotros _____ (vivir) en Santiago cuando ocurrió el golpe de estado.
4. Yo_____ (trabajar) en el segundo piso cuando escuché unos pasos en el corredor.
5. Mi abuelo_____ (recoger) los tomates en la huerta cuando sufrió el infarto.
6. Ellos_____ (encender) las luces de Navidad en el momento que todo Chicago sufrió el apagón.
7. Yo _____ (aparcar) dando marcha atrás y no vi el poste que estaba a mi izquierda. Por eso lo choqué.
8. ¿Exactamente qué oración _____ (rezar) cuando dices que la imagen apareció?
9. Yo _____ (leer) a Byron cuando decidí ser escritor.
10. Ellos _____ (vender) las joyas de su familia cuando su madre entró y los descubrió.

**g.** To describe the setting of a story that happened in the past.

## Example

Era una mañana de junio; alegre, tibia y sonrosada.
*It was a joyful, warm, and reddish June morning.*

El sol anunciaba sus rayos en los colores vivos de las nubes de Oriente.
*The sun announced its lively colored rays on the eastern clouds.*

---

## TIP BOX

Most of the time, the Spanish imperfect corresponds to the English expression *used to* + *infinitive* or to the progressive past form *was/were* + *present participle (-ing).*

---

**Exercise 42.** Complete the following text using the imperfect tense.

1. Todo _____ (ser) armonía en la casa de mis padres.
2. El riachuelo _____ (hacer) un ruido tenue sobre el silencio de la montaña.
3. _____ (llover) torrencialmente y no había lugar dónde guarecerse.
4. La música _____ (seguir) sonando en el salón mientras afuera _____ (nevar).
5. _____ (hacer) un claro día de invierno.
6. La mar_____ (estar) en calma, no _____ (hacer) viento.
7. _____ (ser) un terreno pantanoso y difícil de transitar.
8. El sol _____ (haber) caído y se acercaba una tormenta.
9. La tarde _____ (correr) lentamente en el sopor del trópico.

**Exercise 43.** Describe what Mom saw when she came back from the party. Use the following verbs: **dibujar, beber, mirar, destruir**

1. _____
2. _____
3. _____
4. _____

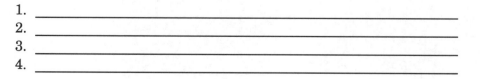

# D. The Imperfect Vs. the Preterit

**a.** As previously stated, the imperfect is used to evoke memories or remembrances.

## Example
Cuando era niño, tenía un labrador.
*When I was a child, I had a golden retriever.*

**b.** The preterit is used to narrate or recount events.

## Example
Un día perdí mi labrador.
*One day, I lost my golden retriever.*

In a past narrative, both past tenses are used: the preterit to recount events and the imperfect for descriptions and situations.

## Example
Aquel día en que perdí mi labrador, estaba en el parque. Jugaba con mis amigos. En aquella época tenía doce años y lloré inconsolablemente la pérdida de mi perro.

*The day I lost my golden retriever, I was in the park. I was playing with my friends. I was twelve years old at that time and I cried inconsolably for the loss of my dog.*

A good metaphor for the imperfect is a photograph that describes the setting of a situation, whereas for the preterit it is the plot of a film that shows a sucession of events.

Hacía sol, todos disfrutábamos del hermoso día. De repente, escuchamos una fuerte explosión. Corrimos al lugar y encontramos un cráter de por lo menos 10 metros de diámetro. Un meteorito había caído a tan sólo un kilómetro de donde estábamos.

*It was sunny and we were enjoying the beautiful day. Suddenly, we heard a strong explosion. We ran to the place and we found a crater which was at least 10 meters in diameter. A meteorite had fallen only one kilometer from where we had been.*

**c.** The preterite is used when we talk about periods of time that are well defined (with a beginning and a precise end). The imperfect, on the contrary, is used when talking about indefinite periods of time.

| Definite period of time |
|---|
| Entre 1989 y 1999, toqué el harpa. <br> *Between 1989 and 1999, I played the harp.* <br><br> Durante 10 años, toqué el harpa. <br> *For 10 years, I played the harp.* <br><br> Desde que tenía ocho años hasta cumplir 18 años, toqué el harpa. <br> *Between the ages of eight and 18, I played the harp.* |

| Indefinite period of time |
|---|
| Antes, tocaba el harpa con frecuencia. <br> *Before, I played the harp regularly.* <br><br> Cuando era joven, tocaba el harpa con frecuencia. <br> *When I was young, I played the harp regularly.* <br><br> En aquella época, tocaba el harpa con frecuencia. <br> *During that time, I played the harp regularly.* |

**d.** The preterit indicates a change in relation to a common habit or a change in relation to a given situation.

| Imperfect <br> (common habit) |
|---|
| Antes pasábamos las vacaciones en la finca de mi abuelo. <br> *We used to spend our vacation on my grandfather's farm.* |

| Preterit <br> (change in relation to a common habit) |
|---|
| Pero un día mi abuelo murió y no volvimos nunca más. <br> *But, one day my grandfather died and we never returned.* |

| Imperfect <br> (given situation) |
|---|
| Ayer hacía un día hermoso. <br> *Yesterday, it was a beautiful day.* |

| Preterit <br> (change in the given situation) |
|---|
| De repente se nubló y cayó un agacuero torrencial. <br> *Suddenly, it became cloudy and a strong rain fell.* |

**Exercise 44.** Divide the following text into one column with the phrases in the imperfect doing the same for the other column in the preterit.

Era alrededor de las ocho de la mañana cuando oímos gritos en la calle. Marta y yo nos levantamos y nos asomamos a la ventana. Afuera había miles de personas gritando. Era un día de verano y el cielo estaba completamente azul. Todos en la calle iban vestidos con disfraces de variados colores y cantaban y bailaban como locos.

—Ya comenzó el Carnaval—, le dije a Marta. Nos vestimos rápidamente, tomamos la cámara y salimos a la calle. Todos nos miraban de manera extraña. No había duda que éramos un par de idiotas turistas.

| **Imperfect** | **Preterit** |
|---|---|
| *Era alrededor de las ocho de la mañana* | *oímos gritos en la calle.* |
| _____ | _____ |
| _____ | _____ |
| _____ | _____ |
| _____ | _____ |
| _____ | _____ |

**Exercise 45.** Put the following text in the past, using either the imperfect or the preterit.

### El Bogotazo

El señor Torres es un hombre maduro, casado con una mujer que trabaja en la oficina de correos. El 9 de abril de 1948, se encuentra bebiendo una cerveza en el Café Royal, sobre la calle Séptima. De repente, escucha una multitud de hombres armados que vienen enfurecidos de todas partes, con palos y machetes. Como no tiene tiempo suficiente para levantarse y salir corriendo, decide refugiarse en el bar. Desde la ventana ve cómo hombres enfurecidos destruyen y saquean todo lo que está a su alrededor. Todo el centro de la ciudad de Bogotá está en llamas. El señor Torres pasa la noche en el bar y sólo al día siguiente logra salir. Se dirige a su casa, preocupado por su mujer. No sabe si está viva. Aunque hay muertos por todas partes, el señor Torres encuentra a su mujer sana y salva.

**Exercise 46.** Answer the following questions, using the preterit or the imperfect.

1. ¿Por qué apagaste la calefacción?

   _____

2. ¿Por qué vendiste tu auto?

   _____

3. ¿Por qué no me invitaste a la fiesta?

   _____

4. ¿Por qué te quedaste en casa ayer?

_____

5. ¿Por qué no fuiste a trabajar?

_____

# IV. Progressive Tenses

## A. Forms of the Progressive Tenses

The progressive tenses are formed with the auxiliary verb **estar** (in any tense) plus the gerund (or present participle).*

| | Progressive Tenses | | |
|---|---|---|---|
| | **Present** | **Preterit** | **Imperfect** |
| | cantar | correr | abrir |
| yo | estoy cantando | estuve corriendo | estaba corriendo |
| tú | estás cantando | estuviste corriendo | estabas corriendo |
| él, ella, usted | está cantando | estuvo corriendo | estaba corriendo |
| nosotros/as | estamos cantando | estuvimos corriendo | estábamos corriendo |
| vosotros/as | estáis cantando | estuvisteis corriendo | estabais corriendo |
| ellos, ellas, ustedes | están cantando | estuvieron corriendo | estaban corriendo |

## B. Uses of the Progressive Tenses

Progressive tenses are used to emphasize an action or to express that which is specific or exceptional.

### Example

¡Silencio! Estoy estudiando.
_Silence! I am studying!_

Ayer estuve corriendo toda la tarde.
_Yesterday, I ran all afternoon._

Ayer estaba paseando y me encontré un anillo de oro.
_Yesterday, I was walking and I found a gold ring._

* See Chapter 5, II. The Gerund.

**Exercise 47.** Describe what people at the airport are doing. Use the following verbs: **tocar, leer, dormir, retirar**

1. _____

2. _____

3. _____

4. _____

**Exercise 48.** Complete the following sentences using the appropriate form of the present progressive tense.

1. Debes esperar porque apenas _____ _____ (encender) el horno.
2. No llores, si aún no nos _____ _____(despedirse).
3. En esta región de Colombia siempre _____ _____ (llover).
4. ¡Tan pronto (tú) _____ _____ (alistar) tus maletas para el viaje!
5. No lo saques del revelador todavía, que la imagen apenas _____ _____(aparecer).
6. No me gusta este libro que (tú) _____ _____(escribir).
7. (yo) _____ _____(leer) la vida espiritual de sor Juana Inés.
8. El padre _____ _____(asistir) a una ceremonia en otra población. Ahora no va a poder atenderte.
9. (yo) _____ _____ (comprar) una nueva casa y por eso no debo excederme en gastos.
10. Te he dicho que no hables mientras (tú) _____ _____ (comer).

**Exercise 49.** Form sentences using the appropriate form of the preterit progressive tense.

1. Durante el otoño las hojas / caer / sobre el jardín.
2. El año pasado / Tomás /escribir/ sus memorias.
3. Anoche / Nicolás / alistar / todo su equipaje.
4. Ayer / nosotros / mirar / su última obra de teatro pero no nos gustó.
5. Ayer en la tarde / el profesor /corregir / las partes mal escritas de las composiciones.
6. ¿Por qué ayer (ustedes) / recoger / las uvas si aún no estaban maduras?
7. ¡Durante toda la comida (tú) / sonreír / con el esposo de tu amiga!
8. Nos duelen las piernas porque / caminar / ayer toda la tarde.
9. ¿Cómo se llamaba esa muchacha con la que (tú) / vivir / en Bruselas?
10. Los niños están cansados/ toda la tarde / subir / los muros de los vecinos.

**Exercise 50.** Complete the following sentences using the appropriate form of the imperfect progressive tense.

1. Cuando la madre de Joselito entró en la casa, su hermano y sus amigos _____ (beber) el whisky de su papá.
2. Lo detuvo la policía porque al parecer lo encontraron cuando _____ (vender) narcóticos.
3. Mi perro cayó al hueco porque _____ (buscar) huesos.
4. La señora se enojó porque cuando llegó, su esposo y la secretaria _____ (bailar) encima del escritorio.
5. Mis padres _____ (viajar) cuando mi abuela murió.
6. Yo _____ (oír) a mi madre cuando él entró.
7. Tú _____ (leer) una revista de autos la tarde en que te vi por primera vez.
8. Nosotros _____ (asistir) al matrimonio de mis primos cuando nuestro perro se enfermó.
9. Ellos _____ (construir) el ferrocarril cuando descubrieron las minas de oro.

# V. The Future Tense

## A. Regular Verbs

The **regular conjugation** in the future indicative is formed by adding the following endings to the infinitive of the verb.

|  | Verb Endings of the Future Indicative | amar (to love) |
|---|---|---|
| yo | -é | amar**é** |
| tú | -ás | amar**ás** |
| él, ella, usted | -á | amar**á** |
| nosotros/as | -emos | amar**emos** |
| vosotros/as | -éis | amar**éis** |
| ellos, ellas, ustedes | -án | amar**án** |

**TIP BOX**

Note that the endings correspond to the endings of the irregular verb **haber** in the present indicative.

|  | haber (to have) |
|---|---|
| yo | he |
| tú | has |
| él, ella, usted | ha |
| nosotros/as | hemos |
| vosotros/as | habéis |
| ellos, ellas, ustedes | han |

**Exercise 51.** Complete the following sentences using the appropriate form of the future tense.

1. Michael Jackson _____ (escribir) sus memorias.
2. Hoy estoy cansada. Mañana (yo) _____ (alistar) lo del viaje.
3. Nosotros _____ (leer) su libro.
4. No sé que decir porque de todas manera él _____ (insistir) en que tengo que ir.

5. El próximo invierno Rosalba _____ (comprar) una piel de jabalí.

6. El sábado la familia Aznar_____ (comer) con vosotros.

7. Mis primos me_____ (permitir) usar su computador esta noche.

8. Él _____ (enviar) el dinero mañana en la tarde.

9. Mañana no estaré, ¿te _____ (beber) el remedio antes de dormir?

10. Hoy estamos muy ocupados pero mañana (tú) _____ (recibir) una sorpresa.

# B. Irregular Verbs

The irregular verbs in the future either drop the vowel of their infinitive ending or they replace it with the consonant **d.**

a. The **-er** verbs **caber, haber, saber, poder, querer** drop the vowel **e.**

|  | **Future** (irregular verbs that drop the **e**) | | | | |
|---|---|---|---|---|---|
|  | **caber** | **haber** | **saber** | **poder** | **querer** |
| yo | cabré | habré | sabré | podré | querré |
| tú | cabrás | habrás | sabrás | podrás | querrás |
| él, ella, usted | cabrá | habrá | sabrá | podrá | querrá |
| nosotros/as | cabremos | habremos | sabremos | podremos | querremos |
| vosotros/as | cabréis | habréis | sabréis | podréis | querréis |
| ellos, ellas, ustedes | cabrán | habrán | sabrán | podrán | querrán |

**Exercise 52.** Complete the following sentences using the appropriate form of the future tense.

1. No te preocupes el coche es grande y _____(caber) tus maletas y las mías.

2. Para cuando llegues yo ya me _____ (haber) ido.

3. Si insistes en molestarme_____ (saber) de lo que soy capaz.

4. Este paquete es muy chico, seguro que _____ (caber) en tu maleta de mano.

5. Con esfuerzo, nosotros_____ (poder) ir a conocer la biblioteca de Alejandría el próximo verano.

6. Mariela está hoy muy triste pero mañana ya lo _____ (haber) olvidado todo.

7. Los extraterrestres no _____ (querer) irse de nuestro planeta después de que conozcan Acapulco.

8. No pensemos que es difícil y mañana ya lo _____ (haber) hecho.

9. Los científicos creen que en unos años _____ (saber) cómo funciona el cerebro humano.

**b.** The verbs **poner, salir, tener, valer, venir** replace the ending vowel by **d.**

|  | **Future** (irregular verbs that replace the ending vowel by **d**)* | | | | |
|---|---|---|---|---|---|
|  | **poner** | **salir** | **tener** | **valer** | **venir** |
| yo | pondré | saldré | tendré | valdré | vendré |
| tú | pondrás | saldrás | tendrás | valdrás | vendrás |
| él, ella, usted | pondrá | saldrá | tendrá | valdrá | vendrá |
| nosotros/as | pondremos | saldremos | tendremos | valdremos | vendremos |
| vosotros/as | pondréis | saldréis | tendréis | valdréis | vendréis |
| ellos, ellas, ustedes | pondrán | saldrán | tendrán | valdrán | vendrán |

**Exercise 53.** Complete the following sentences using the appropriate form of the future tense.

1. Dejaré la televisión en tus manos y para mañana sé que tú la _____ (componer).
2. Si trabajamos más duro, en un año _____ (tener) ahorrado suficiente para comprar una granja.
3. Cuando deje de llover las ardillas _____ (salir) de sus madrigueras.
4. Él_____ (poner) el capital y nosotros la fuerza de trabajo.
5. Para el año 2020 un galón de agua _____ (valer) lo mismo que uno de petróleo.
6. Vosotros_____ (sobresalir) en la competencia porque sois los mejores.
7. Tú, sal por la puerta de atrás que nosotros lo _____ (entretener).
8. Rocío _____ (venir) más temprano para ir al cine en la tarde.
9. Un yen en los próximos diez años _____ (equivaler) a lo mismo que dos hoy.
10. Mis padres _____ (intervenir) en las decisiones de mis hermanos, pero en las mías no.

* Related verbs that follow the same pattern are **componer** (to compose), **deponer** (to depose), **descomponer** (to break down), **disponer** (to arrange), **imponer** (to impose), **oponer** (to oppose), **presuponer** (to assume), **proponer** (to propose) **suponer** (to suppose), **sobresalir** (to excel), **abstener** (to abstain), **contener** (to contain), **detener** (to stop), **entretener** (to entertain), **mantener** (to maintain), **obtener** (to obtain), **retener** (to retain, to maintain), **sostener** (to equal), **equivaler**, **contravenir** (to contravene), **convenir** (to agree), **intervenir** (to intervene), **prevenir** (to prevent), **sobrevenir** (to happen unexpectedly).

**d.** The verbs **decir** and **hacer** and related verbs* are also irregular, because they drop the **-ec-** or the **-ce-**.

| | **Future** (irregular verbs that drop **-ec-** or **-ce-**) | |
|---|---|---|
| | **decir** (*to say*) | **hacer** (*to do*) |
| yo | diré | haré |
| tú | dirás | harás |
| él, ella, usted | dirá | hará |
| nosotros/as | diremos | haremos |
| vosotros/as | diréis | haréis |
| ellos, ellas, ustedes | dirán | harán |

**Exercise 54.** Complete the following sentences using the appropriate form of the future tense.

1. Mis hijos _____(decir) mañana que yo los eduqué con disciplina.
2. Tú _____ (hacer) lo que yo diga.
3. Si le cuentas a todos (yo) _____ (contradecir) tus palabras y nada podrás probar.
4. Tú_____ (decir) y yo obedeceré.
5. Algunos de nuestros descendientes_____ (deshacer) lo que hemos construido.
6. Nosotros _____ (decir) exactamente lo que pasó.
7. Con esfuerzo (ellos) _____ (rehacer) la casa destruida.
8. Francisca esta cansada, (ella) _____ (hacer) sus deberes mañana.
9. Él _____ (satisfacer) todos sus caprichos.
10. Julián _____ (rehacer) el documento.

*Related verbs that follow the same pattern are **contradecir** (to contradict), **deshacer** (to untie, to undo), **rehacer** (to do again, to redo), **satisfacer** (to satisfy).

**Exercise 55.** Write about what the kids will do after school. Use the following verbs: **hacer, jugar, comer, ver**.

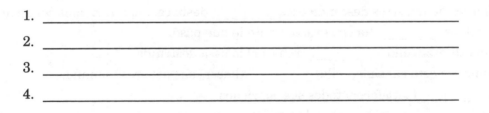

1. _____

2. _____

3. _____

4. _____

# C. Uses of the Future Tense

**a.** The future tense refers to future actions by imagining the future or by planning future projects.

### Example

Mañana compraremos el coche.
*Tomorrow we will buy the car.*

Iremos de vacaciones a España el próximo año.
*Next year we will go on vacation to Spain.*

En cinco años, tendremos nuestro primer hijo.
*In five years, we will have our first child.*

**Exercise 56.** Following the example below, put the following sentences in the future tense.

### Example

Ahora vivo en Boston, *pero el próximo año viviré en Madrid.*

1. Ahora no tengo bastante dinero, _____.
2. Ahora no hablo muy bien español, _____.
3. Ahora trabajo en Estados Unidos, _____.
4. Ahora no hago mucho ejercicio, _____.
5. Ahora te obedezco en todo, _____.
6. Ahora soy muy responsable, _____.

**Exercise 57.** Complete the following mini-dialogues using the appropriate form of the future tense.

—Todos las Nochebuenas vamos a la Misa de Gallo. ¿ _____(ir, tú) este año?
—No lo sé porque el párroco está enfermo y no sabemos si la _____ (celebrar).

—He oído que ganaste la lotería. ¿Qué _____ (hacer) con todo ese dinero?
—Me voy a Ibiza, _____ (comprar) un carro nuevo y el resto se lo _____(regalar) a los pobres.

—¿Cuándo_____(ir) al odontólogo?
—La semana entrante y también _____(visitar) a mi psicólogo.

—Son la cinco de la tarde y el bus no pasa. ¿Crees que_____ (pasar) pronto?
—No lo sé, pero de seguro que _____ (dejar) la estación a las 5:30 así que _____ (estar) acá a las 5:35 a más tardar.

—Vete ahora, que en un momento_____ (llegar) mi padre y nos _____(sorprender).
—Espero que pronto me _____ (presentar) a tu familia como tu novio oficial.

—Nosotros _____ (organizar) la venta de las boletas y tú _____ (prestar) tu casa para la rifa. ¿Qué dices?
—Esta bien, ¿pero yo cuánto _____ (ganar)?

**Exercise 58.** Complete the following sentences using the appropriate form of the future tense.

—¿Quién crees que _____ (ganar) las elecciones para el cargo de alcalde?
—No sé, pero dicen que Guerra de seguro _____ (tratar) de hacer trampa.

—En el futuro cercano todo lo que haces y dices lo _____ (saber) el gobierno.
—¿Dijiste lo _____ (saber)? Hace tiempo ya lo saben.

—Ayer un virus atacó el internet a nivel mundial. ¿Cómo sabremos que esto no se _____ (producir) de nuevo?
—Creo que eso nadie lo _____ (garantizar).

**b.** The future tense expresses probability and conjecture in the present.

### Example

—¿Qué pasa con Javier que aún no llega?
*"What happened to Javier that he's not here yet?"*

—Estará retrasado su avión.
*"His airplane is probably late."*

—Estará durmiendo.
*"He's probably sleeping."*

—Estará discutiendo con su novia.
*"He's probably arguing with his girfriend."*

**Exercise 59.** We do not know why Jorge is not in class at this time. We will try to guess what he is most probably doing at this very instant.

Rewrite the following sentences using the future as shown.

### Example

Probablemente Jorge está durmiendo. *Estará durmiendo.*

1. Probablemente Jorge está enfermo. _____
2. Probablemente Jorge y Juan están jugando fútbol. _____
3. Probablemente Jorge y yo estamos viendo televisión. _____
4. Probablemente yo estoy en la corte. _____
5. Probablemente tú estás en un embotellamiento de tráfico. _____
6. Probablemente Jorge está hablando con sus amigos. _____
7. Probablemente vosotros estáis escuchando música. _____

---

## TIP BOX

The future tense can be expressed by using the verb **ir** in the present indicative + the preposition **a + an infinitive.**

### Example

Mañana <u>**voy a bailar**</u> en una discoteca.
*Tomorrow I <u>am going to dance</u> in a discotheque.*

---

**Exercise 60.** Change the following sentences in the future tense to the present tense form that expresses future action.

### Example

Pasado mañana iremos al cine.
*Pasado mañana vamos a ir al cine.*

1. Las golondrinas saldrán con el sol.

   _____

2. El precio de la carne aumentará.

   _____

3. Las computadoras serán más baratas en unos años.

   _____

4. Tendré una entrevista para un nuevo empleo el próximo mes.

   _____

5. Tú emprenderás un largo viaje.

   _____

6. Tus planes serán exitosos.

   _____

7. Esta historia tomará un rumbo impredecible.

   _____

8. Dos grandes editoriales españolas se fusionarán en el transcurso de este año.

   _____

9. Si todo sale bien compraremos un yate en abril.

   _____

# VI. The Conditional Tense

## A. Regular Verbs

The **regular conjugation** of the conditional is formed by adding the following endings to the infinitive of the verb.

|  | Verb Endings in the Conditional Tense | amar (*to love*) |
|---|---|---|
| yo | -ía | amar**ía** |
| tú | -ías | amar**ías** |
| él, ella, usted | -ía | amar**ía** |
| nosotros/as | -íamos | amar**íamos** |
| vosotros/as | -íais | amar**íais** |
| ellos, ellas, ustedes | -ían | amar**ían** |

**TIP BOX**

Note that the conditional is formed by adding the imperfect endings from the **-er, -ir** verbs to the infinitive form of the verb.

# B. Irregular Verbs

The conditional tense follows the same rules as the future tense.

| | Conditional (irregular verbs) | | | | |
|---|---|---|---|---|---|
| | **caber** (to fit) | **poner** (to put/ to place) | **salir** (to leave/ to go out) | **decir** (to say) | **hacer** (to do) |
| yo | cabría | pondría | saldría | diría | haría |
| tú | cabrías | pondrías | saldrías | dirías | harías |
| él, ella, usted | cabría | pondría | saldría | diría | haría |
| nosotros/as | cabríamos | pondríamos | saldríamos | diríamos | haríamos |
| vosotros/as | cabríais | pondríais | saldríais | diríais | haríais |
| ellos, ellas, ustedes | cabrían | pondrían | saldrían | dirían | harían |

# C. Uses of the Conditional Tense

The conditional expresses either a future or possible action. It is used to express advice, desire, or wishes as well as politeness. It is also used to express a future event in relation to another event that is in the past, and to express probability or conjecture in the past.

**a.** To express advice, desire, and/or politeness.

- Advice

### Example

En tu lugar, no gastaría tanto dinero en ese coche.
*If I were in your shoes, I would not spend so much money on that car.*

Antes de irte deberías terminar tus deberes.
*Before leaving you should finish your homework.*

**Exercise 61.** Following the example, write correct sentences.

### Example
presentar el examen/Francisca/estudiar más
***Antes de presentar** el examen, Francisca **debería** estudiar más.*

1. gritar/Julio/razonar _____
2. salir a jugar/(ellos)/comer _____
3. comenzar un nuevo proyecto/(nosotros)/terminar este _____

4. precipitarte/(tú)/calmarte _____

5. lanzar al país a una guerra/el presidente/reflexionar un poco más _____

6. subir la montaña/(vosotros)/preparar el equipo _____

7. comprar una casa/(usted)/comprar un coche _____

8. comer/(tú)/lavarte las manos _____

**Exercise 62.** Following the example, answer the questions with an expression of advice.

### Example

—¿Compramos la casa?

—*Yo que ustedes, no la compraría.* (or) —*Yo que vosotros, no la compraría.*

1. —¿Voy a Colombia?

—_____.

2. —¿Invertimos en la bolsa?

—_____.

3. —¿Me retiro de la universidad?

—_____.

4. —¿Me salgo del equipo de fútbol?

—_____.

5. —¿Nos ponemos estos disfraces?

—_____.

6. —¿Salgo con Jorge?

—_____.

• Desire or wishes

### Example

Me gustaría* verte otra vez.

*I would like to see you again.*

**Exercise 63.** Following the example below, make sentences that express desire or wishfulness.

### Example

hablar español (a mí)

*Me gustaría hablar español.*

1. tener más tiempo libre (a nosotros) _____

2. conocer más gente (a él) _____

*See Chapter 15, Special Constructions With Indirect Objects.

3. vivir en Granada (a mí) _____

4. salir más a menudo por la noche (a ellos) _____

5. ir con más frecuencia a cine (a vosotros) _____

6. tener más libertad (a nosotros) _____

- Politeness

## Example

¿Me podría traer un vaso de agua?
*Could you bring me a glass of water?*

**Exercise 64.** Following the example below, create sentences using the form that expresses politeness or courtesy.

## Example

el menú
*¿Me podría usted traer el menu, por favor?*

1. pan

    _____.

2. un vaso de agua

    _____.

3. una garrafa de vino

    _____.

4. una paella

    _____.

5. flan de postre

    _____.

6. la cuenta, por favor

    _____.

**Restaurante *El Vasco***
**Menú**

**Entradas**
Plato de jamón y lomo ibérico
Ensalada natural
Pimientos rellenos de bacalao en su propia salsa

**Carnes**
Solomillo al oporto con setas
Delicias de solomillo rellenas de *foie* con salsa *roquefort*

**Pescados**
Merluza en salsa verde con almejas y gambas
Chipirones rellenos en su tinta con flan de arroz

**Postres**
Cuajada de leche de oveja con miel
Queso con membrillo y nueces
Helados variados

**Bebidas**
Botella de vino
Caña de cerveza

**Exercise 65.** Using the menu above, write about what the customer is ordering.

1. _____ -
2. _____ -
3. _____ -
4. _____ -
5. _____ -

**Exercise 66.** Following the example, answer the questions expressing politeness.

## Example

—¿El señor quiere una taza de chocolate o una taza de café?
—*Quisiera una taza de café.*

1. —¿Quiere azúcar o miel?
   —_____

2. —¿Quiere una tostada o un panecillo?
   —_____

3. —¿Quieren agua o jugo de naranja?
   —_____

4. —¿Quiere huevos fritos o huevos revueltos?
   —_____

5. —¿Quieren fruta o helado?
   —_____

6. —¿Quieren pagar en efectivo o con tarjeta de crédito?
   —_____

**b.** In subordinated clauses, the conditional expresses a future event in relation to another event that is in the past.

## Example

El profesor nos dijo que tendríamos el examen la próxima semana.
*The teacher told us that we would have the exam next week.*

**Exercise 67.** Following the example, answer the questions expressing desire.

## Example

María

—¿Qué dijo María? (enviar las cartas en una hora)
—*Dijo que enviaría las cartas en una hora.*

1. —¿Qué dijeron Julia y Luis? (recoger el niño en la guardería) _____
2. —¿Qué dijo el abogado? (retirar la demanda) _____
3. —¿Qué dijeron los senadores? (aprobar la ley) _____
4. —¿Qué dijo el presidente? (ir a la guerra) _____
5. —¿Qué dijeron los manifestantes? (protestar hasta el final) _____
6. —¿Qué dijo la policía? (meter a la cárcel) _____

**c.** To express probability or conjecture in the past.

## Example

—¿Qué pasó con Lucía que no vino?
—*What happened to Lucía that she did not come?*

—Perdería su avión.
—*Probably she missed her flight.*

—No se despertaría a tiempo.
—*She probably did not wake up on time.*

—Preferiría no venir.
—*She probably preferred not to come.*

**Exercise 68.** We do not know why María was not at work yesterday. We will try to guess what she was probably doing yesterday. Rewrite the following sentences using the conditional as shown in the example below.

## Example

Probablemente María estaba durmiendo. *Estaría durmiendo.*

1. Probablemente María estaba enferma.
   _____

2. Probablemente María estaba discutiendo de política.
   _____

3. Probablemente María estaba escuchando un concierto.
   _____

4. Probablemente María estaba hablando por teléfono.
   _____

5. Probablemente María estaba en una reunión muy importante.
   _____

6. Probablemente María estaba redactando la composición.
   _____

7. Probablemente María estaba visitando su médico.
   _____

# Chapter 5

# VERBS: THE INFINITIVE AND PARTICIPLE FORMS

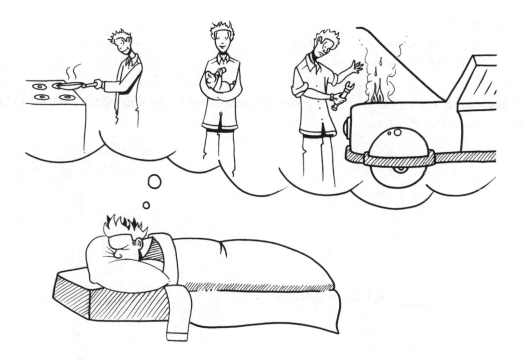

## I. The Infinitive

As stated previously, Spanish verbs are grouped in three categories according to the ending of the infinitive form: **-ar, -er, -ir.** The infinitive is the verb form that Spanish uses as a noun.

# A. Forms of the Infinitive

The infinitive has two forms: The simple infinitive and the perfect infinitive.

|  | Verb Endings | | |
|---|---|---|---|
|  | **-ar** | **-er** | **-ir** |
| Simple Infinitive | cant**ar** *(to sing)* | com**er** *(to eat)* | viv**ir** *(to live)* |
| Perfect Infinitive | hab**er** cant**ado** | hab**er** com**ido** | hab**er** viv**ido** |

# B. Uses of the Infinitive

In Spanish, the infinitive is the noun form of the verb. Like all nouns, the infinitive may function as a subject, an object of the verb, or an object of the preposition.

**a.** The infinitive as a subject.

**Example**

<u>**Aprender**</u> español es divertido.
*Learning Spanish is fun.*

**Exercise 1.** Complete the following sentences with the appropriate verb in the infinitive shown in the picture.

1. _____ es interesante.

2. _____ fila es aburrido.

3. _____ es divertido.

4. Me gusta _____ cerveza.

5.

Me gusta _____ al cine.

6.

_____ es buen ejercicio.

7.

_____ sano es muy importante.

8.

_____ distraído es peligroso.

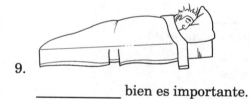

9.

_____ bien es importante.

10.

_____ rápido es peligroso.

**b.** The infinitive as an object of the verb.

### Example

Quiero **viajar** a España este año.
*I want to travel to Spain this year.*

Necesito **comprar** el boleto de avión pronto.
*I need to buy the airplane ticket soon.*

Escuché **llorar** a tu bebé.
*I heard your baby crying.*

**Exercise 2.** Change the following sentences using the infinitive as shown in the example.

**Example**

Como langosta en la playa.
*Quiero comer langosta en la playa.*

1. Paseo en el parque.
   _____.

2. Nado con frecuencia para sentirme bien.
   _____.

3. Corto el césped del jardín durante el fin de semana.
   _____.

4. Voy al cine porque estrenan una película interesante.
   _____.

5. Leo una novela antes de dormirme.
   _____.

6. Voy a un concierto de jazz con mis amigos.
   _____.

**Exercise 3.** Transform the following sentences using the infinitive as shown.

**Example**

Ayer vimos cómo volaban los gansos.
*Ayer vimos volar los gansos.*

1. Observaré cómo preparas esta receta.
   _____.

2. Escuché cómo la orquesta ensayaba para el concierto.
   _____.

3. Oí a un chico que pedía auxilio en la calle.
   _____.

4. ¿Ves cómo sale el sol desde tu habitación?
   _____.

5. Miramos cómo los niños patinaban sobre el hielo.
   _____.

6. ¿Escuchaste cómo el guitarrista daba un concierto?
   _____.

7. Sentiste que tu hermano cerraba la puerta.*
   _____.

8. Contemplaremos cómo Óscar hace una escultura.*
   _____.

9. Vi cómo Patricia entraba en correos.*
   _____.

10. Oyes cómo suena el teléfono.
    _____.

* Note that the personal **a** is needed in these sentences.

**c.** The infinitive as an object of the preposition.
In Spanish the infinitive is always used after a preposition in the following ways.

- Use as a prepositional phrase.

### Example

Al **llegar** a casa, me acosté en la hamaca.
*Upon arriving home, I lay down in the hammock.*

---

### TIP BOX

In Spanish the contraction **al** (a + el) followed by the infinitive is equivalent in English to *upon, when,* or *as.*

---

- Use as a modifier of an adjective.

### Example

Estoy ansioso de **verte.**
*I am anxious to see you.*

- Use as a modifier of a noun.

### Example

La torta para **regalar** está lista.
*The cake that we are bringing is ready.*

- Use as a modifier of an adverb.

### Example

Yo lo abracé antes de **partir**.
*I hugged him before leaving.*

**Exercise 4.** Change the following sentences using the infinitive as shown in the example.

### Example

Mientras subía las escaleras, me caí.
*Al subir las escaleras, me caí.*

1. Cuando me gradué, viajé a Chile.
   _____.

2. Mientras abría la puerta, escuché a alguien hablar dentro de la casa.
   _____.

3. Cuando leí el libro, aprendí mucho sobre la cultura azteca.
   _____.

4. Cuando vimos las noticias, nos enteramos de que nevaría mañana.
   _____.

5. Cuando hablé con Laura por teléfono, me dijo que no estabas.
   _____.

6. Mientras salíamos del museo, nos encontramos a Pepe.
   _____.

7. Mientras hacías la compra, descubriste que habías olvidado el dinero.
   _____.

8. Cuando abrí el mapa, supe dónde estaba.
   _____.

9. Mientras tomaba un café, mi hermano entró en la cocina.
   _____.

10. Mientras manejaba al trabajo, escuchaba las noticias por la radio.
    _____.

# II. The Gerund (or Present Participle)

## A. Forms of the Gerund

The gerund is formed in regular verbs by adding the ending **-ando** to the stem of the **-ar** verbs and **-iendo** to the stem of **-er** and **-ir** verbs.

| -ar | -er | -ir |
|-----|-----|-----|
| cant**ar** | ten**er** | decid**ir** |
| cant**ando** | ten**iendo** | decid**iendo** |

---

**TIP BOX**

Stem-change verbs ending in **-ir\*** have an irregular stem in the gerund. They change as follows:

- The **e** of the stem changes to **i**.

  **Example**
  > h**e**rir (ie) changes to h**i**riendo.

- The **o** of the stem changes to **u**.

  **Example**
  > d**o**rmir (ue) changes to d**u**rmiendo.

When the stem of the verbs **-er** and **-ir** ends in a vowel, as in verbs such as **caer, creer, leer, construir, ir, oír**, the gerund is **–yendo**.

**Example**
> La nieve está **cayendo**. *(The snow is falling.)*
> María está **leyendo**. *(Maria is reading.)*

\* See Chapter 4 for a list of stem-change **-ir** verbs.

---

# B. Uses of the Gerund

**a.** The gerund (or present participle) is used with the progressive tenses. Progressive tenses are formed with the verb **estar** and the gerund.

### Example

No entres que me estoy **bañando.**
*Do not enter; I am taking a bath.*

**Exercise 5.** Complete the following sentences using the gerund of the verb shown.

### Example

Camilo se está _____ (bañar) en el lago.
*Camilo se está bañando en el lago.*

1. Isabel está _____ (plantar) un árbol en su jardín.
2. Eva está _____ (comer) un helado.
3. Pedro y Andrés están _____ (dar) un paseo en bicicleta.
4. En nuestra ciudad están _____ (construir) más edificios porque ahora hay más habi-tantes.
5. Miguel todavía está _____ (dormir) porque anoche trabajó hasta muy tarde.
6. Estoy _____ (leer) mi correo electrónico.

**b.** The gerund is used with an adverbial function that may indicate manner, cause, reason, time, or condition.

### Example

María salió de la casa **gritando.**
*María left the house screaming.*

Ayer, **bailando** en la discoteca, vi a tu novia.
*Yesterday, dancing in a discotheque, I saw your girlfriend.*

**Exercise 6.** Transform the following sentences using the present participle, as shown.

### Example

Mientras escribía me acordé de ti.
*Escribiendo me acordé de ti.*

1. Mientras vivía en Madrid conocí a Pepe.

   _____

2. Si haces ejercicio, te sentirás mejor.

   _____

3. Cuando viajé a Guatemala aprendí a cocinar tamales.

   _____

4. Mientras veía el partido de tenis, llamaron a la puerta.

   _____

5. Si lees el periódico, estarás informado.

   _____

6. Mientras entraba a la oficina, me dijeron que había una reunión importante.

   _____

---

**TIP BOX**

The gerund (-ando, -iendo) is the equivalent of the English gerund (-ing). The Spanish gerund or present participle, however, cannot be used as a noun as it is used in English. In Spanish the infinitive is used instead.

**Example**

> Correr es buen ejercicio.
> *Running is good exercise.*

Another important difference is that the Spanish gerund cannot be used as an adjective to directly modify a noun, as can the English -ing form. In Spanish, a relative clause is used instead.

**Example**

> El niño que llora es mi hijo.
> *The crying baby is my son.*

---

# III. The Past Participle

## A. Forms of the Past Participle

a. The past participle is formed in regular verbs by adding the ending **-ado** to the stem of the **-ar** verbs and **-ido** to the stem of the **-er** and **-ir** verbs.

| -ar | -er | -ir |
|---|---|---|
| **cantar** *(to sing)* | **tener** *(to have)* | **venir** *(to come)* |
| cant**ado** | ten**ido** | ven**ido** |

**b.** There are, however, exceptions in which the past participle is irregular.

| Infinitive | Irregular Past Participle |
|---|---|
| abrir (*to open*) | abierto (*opened*) |
| absolver (*to absolve*) | absuelto (*absolved*) |
| cubrir (*to cover*) | cubierto (*covered*) |
| decir (*to say*) | dicho (*said*) |
| descubrir (*to discover*) | descubierto (*discovered*) |
| encubrir (*to cover up*) | encubierto (*covered up*) |
| escribir (*to write*) | escrito (*written*) |
| hacer (*to do*) | hecho (*done*) |
| morir (*to die*) | muerto (*died*) |
| poner (*to put*) | puesto (*put*) |
| podrir (*to rot*) | podrido (*rotten*) |
| romper (*to break*) | roto (*broken*) |
| satisfacer (*to satisfy*) | satisfecho (*satisfied*) |
| volver (*to come back*) | vuelto (*come back*) |

# B. Uses of the Past Participle

**a.** The past participle, used together with the verb **haber** (to have), forms the perfect tense.* Note that in this case there is NO concordance between the past participle and the subject of the sentence. The past participle does not vary.

**Example**

La joven **ha encontrado** la felicidad.
*The young girl has found happiness.*

Los muchachos **han nadado** en el río.
*The boys have swum in the river.*

*Refer to Chapters 6 and 7 about the perfect tenses.

**b.** The past participle, used with a linking verb (**estar**—*to be*, **ser**—*to be*, **parecer**—*to seem*), has the aspect of a predicative adjective. In this case it agrees with the subject of the verb.

### Example

La novela *El Quijote* **fue escrita** por Miguel de Cervantes Saavedra.
*The novel* El Quijote *was written by Miguel de Cervantes Saavedra.*

Los niños **están encerrados** en el cuarto.
*The kids are locked in the room.*

María **parece cansada.**
*María seems tired.*

**c.** The past participle, when it has the aspect of an adjective, agrees with the noun it modifies.

### Example

Cuando llegamos a la casa encontramos la puerta **abierta.**
*When we arrived home we found the door opened.*

Los arqueólogos encontraron las momias bien **preservadas.**
*Archeologists found the mummies well preserved.*

**Exercise 7.** Complete the following sentences using the appropriate past participle (Perfect Tenses).

1. Ya habíamos _____ (salir) cuando nos llamó.
2. Eduardo se ha _____ (entrenar) mucho durante este año.
3. Siempre habías _____ (llevar) una vida sana hasta hace un año.
4. ¿No fuiste al espectáculo? Te habrías _____ (divertir).
5. He _____ (trabajar) cuarenta horas durante esta semana.
6. Para cuando te llame, ¿habrás _____ (decidir) qué quieres hacer?
7. Paula ha _____ (abrir) la ventana porque hacía calor.
8. Jaime habría _____ (preferir) descansar, pero Amalia quería salir a pasear.
9. Víctor ha _____ (decir) la verdad.
10. Para el lunes habré _____ (mandar) la solicitud.

**Exercise 8.** Complete the following sentences using the appropriate past participle.

1. En el metro hay letreros _____ (escribir) en español.
2. El cheque ya está _____ (firmar).
3. Tenemos la mesa _____ (poner) y la cena _____ (preparar).
4. Tras una larga investigación, las joyas fueron _____ (encontrar).
5. Esta casa fue _____ (construir) hace más de un siglo.
6. El presidente fue _____ (elegir) la semana pasada.
7. Encontré la puerta _____ (cerrar).
8. Los marineros fueron _____ (rescatar) del naufragio.

9. Esta foto fue _____ (tomar) desde el balcón de mi casa.
10. No te preocupes, ese problema ya está _____ (resolver).

**Exercise 9.** Complete the following sentences using the appropriate past participle.

1. No puedo escuchar su mensaje porque lo he _____ (borrar) accidentalmente.
2. El cuadro *Guernica* fue _____ (pintar) por Pablo Picasso.
3. Los libros _____ (usar) son más baratos.
4. Durante este año hemos _____ (tener) éxito en nuestro trabajo.
5. Cuando fui a su casa, él ya se había _____ (ir).
6. ¿No estás _____ (preocupar) por el medio ambiente?
7. Maite se ha _____ (hacer) socia de un gimnasio que hay cerca de su casa.
8. Javier Bardem es un actor muy _____ (conocer).
9. Machu Pichu fue _____ (construir) por los incas.
10. Antes del 2002 no había _____ (correr) en un maratón.

**Exercise 10.** Give the past participle and gerund form of the following verbs as shown below.

**Example**

| **cantar** | *cantado* | *cantando* |

1. abrir _____ _____
2. absolver _____ _____
3. amar _____ _____
4. beber _____ _____
5. comer _____ _____
6. cubrir _____ _____
7. decir _____ _____
8. descubrir _____ _____
9. encubrir _____ _____
10. escribir _____ _____
11. estar _____ _____
12. hablar _____ _____
13. hacer _____ _____
14. jugar _____ _____
15. leer _____ _____
16. morir _____ _____
17. pedir _____ _____
18. podrir _____ _____
19. poner _____ _____
20. reunir _____ _____
21. romper _____ _____
22. satisfacer _____ _____
23. servir _____ _____
24. venir _____ _____
25. volver _____ _____

**Exercise 11.** Complete the following text with the appropriate infinitive, past participle or gerund.

Claudia está _____ (comer) con Rebeca. Ambas están _____ (discutir) sobre la situación política mundial. El profesor de Historia ha _____ (convencer) a Claudia que estamos _____ (vivir) un momento muy importante en la historia. Rebeca está _____ (sorprender), para ella todo sigue igual. Trabaja mucho y está _____ (cansar). Lo único que quiere es _____ (descansar) y _____ (ver) televisión. Claudia por el contrario está _____ (preocupar) y _____ (enojar) con la indiferencia de Rebeca. Claudia ha _____ (escribir) varios correos electrónicos a sus amigos que están _____ (vivir) fuera del país para_____ (saber) qué piensan.

# Chapter 6

# THE PERFECT TENSES OF THE INDICATIVE

## I. Forms of the Perfect Tenses

The perfect tenses of the indicative are formed with the verb *haber* in the corresponding tense (present, imperfect, or future) + the past participle.*

**Yo he recibido un pescado.**
*(I have received a fish.)*

| | Perfect Tenses | | | |
|---|---|---|---|---|
| | amar (*to love*) | | | |
| | **Present Perfect** | **Past Perfect** | **Future Perfect** | **Conditional Perfect** |
| yo | **he** amado | **había** amado | **habré** amado | **habría** amado |
| tú | **has** amado | **habías** amado | **habrás** amado | **habrías** amado |
| él, ella, usted | **ha** amado | **había** amado | **habrá** amado | **habría** amado |
| nosotros/as | **hemos** amado | **habíamos** amado | **habremos** amado | **habríamos** amado |
| vosotros/as | **habéis** amado | **habíais** amado | **habréis** amado | **habríais** amado |
| ellos, ellas, ustedes | **han** amado | **habían** amado | **habrán** amado | **habrían** amado |

*See Chapter 5 to learn more about the past participle.

**TIP BOX**

Remember, the past participle in the perfect tenses does NOT agree with the subject.

**Example**

José y Julián <u>han viajado</u> a Bolivia tres veces.
*José and Julián have traveled three times to Bolivia.*

María <u>ha viajado</u> a Bolivia tres veces.
*María has traveled three times to Bolivia.*

Note also that no word falls between the verb *haber* and the participle.

**Example**

Marta <u>no</u> ha viajado a Bolivia.
*Marta has <u>not</u> traveled to Bolivia.*

Marta <u>ya</u> **ha regresado** de Bolivia.
*Marta has <u>already</u> returned from Bolivia.*

# II. Uses of the Perfect Tenses

Perfect Tenses in Spanish (as in English) are used when the speaker wants to emphasize the fact that the action performed by the verb (in past participle) has begun or has ended before a particular point of reference. The use of perfect tenses is very similar in both the English and Spanish languages.

## A. Present Perfect

|  | cantar<br>(*to sing*) | oler<br>(*to smell*) | partir<br>(*to leave*) |
|---|---|---|---|
| yo | he cantado | he olido | he partido |
| tú | has cantado | has olido | has partido |
| él, ella, usted | ha cantado | ha olido | ha partido |
| nosotros/as | hemos cantado | hemos olido | hemos partido |
| vosotros/as | habéis cantado | habéis olido | habéis partido |
| ellos, ellas, ustedes | han cantado | han olido | han partido |

In the present perfect the action referred to by the verb is located prior to the point of reference.

**Example**

Lina ya **ha llegado;** ya podemos servir la comida.
*Lina has arrived; we may now serve the meal.*

In the previous example, the fact of arriving occurs before the reference point, which in this case is in the present tense.

When there is no obvious point of reference, the reference point is usually the moment of the act of speaking.

Los niños **han comido** muy bien.
*The children have eaten very well.*

---

## TIP BOX

The present tense is usually used with the adverbs *ya* and *todavía*.

### Example

—¿**Ya** han llegado los niños?
—*Have the children already arrived?*

—No, **todavía** no han llegado.
—*No, they have not arrived yet.*

---

**Exercise 1.** Complete the following sentences using the appropriate form of the present perfect tense.

1. (yo) _____ _____ (caminar) diez kilómetros y no veo un alma.
2. Él _____ _____ (escribir) muchos libros sin publicar ni uno.
3. Ella _____ _____ (leer) todo lo que escribió Agatha Christie.
4. Nosotros _____ _____ (comprar) esta casa en muy mal estado.
5. Los invitados se _____ _____ (comer) todo lo que había.
6. No _____ _____ (permitir, nosotros) invitarlos a casa.
7. (vosotros) _____ _____ (beber) todo el vino de su cava.
8. (yo) _____ _____ (insistir) en verte para decirte algo muy importante.
9. A pesar de tus intrigas no (tú) _____ _____ (conseguir) separarnos.
10. El gobierno me _____ _____ (enviar) a cumplir una misión fuera del país.

**Exercise 2.** Complete the following sentences using the appropriate form of the present perfect tense.

1. Yo_____ _____ (escribir) mil versos.
2. Tú no_____ _____ (decir) nada esta noche.
3. Yo_____ _____ (volver) sólo para verte.
4. Nosotros no _____ _____ (morir) por una suerte loca.
5. Las cocineras no _____ _____ (freír) el pescado.
6. Sus amigos_____ _____ (leer) todos sus libros por pura cortesía.
7. Tú no _____ _____ (ver) nada. Eres demasiado joven.
8. Los chinos _____ _____ (descubrir) un dinosaurio volador con cuatro alas entre otras muchas cosas maravillosas.
9. Los arqueólogos_____ _____ (abrir) las tumbas sin establecer aún la fecha exacta del entierro.
10. Mis hermanos me _____ _____ (cubrir) el rostro con crema de afeitar.

**Exercise 3.** Answer the following sentences using the present perfect or the preterit tense.

**Example**

—¿Ya llevaste los niños al colegio?
—*No, todavía no los he llevado.* (or) —*Sí, ya los llevé.*

1. —¿Ya fuiste al banco?
   —No, _____

2. —¿Ya limpiaste la loza de la comida?
   —Si, _____

3. —¿Ya comiste?
   —Sí, _____

4. —¿Ya conoces el nuevo teatro?
   —No, _____

5. —¿Ya hiciste tus ejercicios de español?
   —No, _____

6. —¿Ya terminaste de leer el libro?
   —No, _____

7. —¿Ya grabaste tus archivos en otro disco?
   —Sí, _____

8. —¿Sabes si Andrés ya hizo sus deberes?
   —Sí, _____

9. —¿Anita y Milena ya terminaron el bordado?
   —No, _____

10. —¿La compañía de teatro ya se fue del pueblo?
    —No, _____

# B. Past Perfect

|  | cantar | oler | partir |
|---|---|---|---|
| yo | había cantado | había olido | había partido |
| tú | habías cantado | habías olido | habías partido |
| él, ella, usted | había cantado | había olido | había partido |
| nosotros/as | habíamos cantado | habíamos olido | habíamos partido |
| vosotros/as | habíais cantado | habíais olido | habíais partido |
| ellos, ellas, ustedes | habían cantado | habían olido | habían partido |

In the past perfect, the action referred to by the verb is also located before the point of reference.

### Example

Lina ya **había llegado** cuando servimos la comida.
*Lina had already arrived when we served the meal.*

The fact of arriving occurs before the reference point (serving the meal), but in this case, the reference point is located in the past. Therefore, the past perfect is used in Spanish as it is used in English: to express a past action completed prior to another past action.

**Exercise 4.** Complete the following sentences using the appropriate form of the present perfect tense.

1. Yo no _____ _____(abrir) la puerta cuando el ladrón me atacó.
2. Tú ya _____ _____(bailar) con ella cuando decidiste hacerlo conmigo.
3. Antes de estudiar medicina el _____ _____(estudiar) biología
4. No le creí cuando dijo que nunca antes _____ _____ (venir) a Málaga.
5. No era su primera experiencia en Europa, antes ellos_____ _____ (vivir) en Austria.
6. Mi mamá fue la última en enterarse que nosotros _____ _____ (romper) el jarrón.
7. Dijeron que ya _____ _____ (comer).
8. No, nunca antes Jorge _____ _____ (visitar) Estocolmo.
9. A pesar de que Mónica no _____ _____ (llegar) decidimos iniciar la reunión.
10. Mis padres ya _____ _____ (morir) cuando decidimos destruir la antigua casa.

**Exercise 5.** Complete the following dialogue using the past perfect or the simple preterit.

1. —¿Ya (tú) _____(ver) la última película de Penélope?
   —¿Cuál? ¿Una en que _____ (hacer) el papel de monja?
   —¡No! Esa ya la _____ (hacer) antes de venir a Hollywood.

2. —Cuando Martín _____ (entrar) a la casa, ya Andrea____ ____(hacer) sus maletas y se disponía a partir.
   —¿Y él qué _____ (hacer)?
   —Le pidió la llave del buzón del correo, pero ella le dijo que ya la _____ (dejar) encima de la nevera con una carta para él.

3. —¡La última vez que te vi aún no _____ (dejar) los pantalones cortos! ¡Y mira ya hasta te _____ (salir) bigote!
   —Sí es verdad, la última vez que te _____ (ver), fue cuando _____ (venir) a visitar a mi padre. Ud. recientemente _____(publicar) su primer libro, ¿verdad?

# C. Future Perfect

|  | **cantar** | **oler** | **partir** |
|---|---|---|---|
| yo | habré cantado | habré olido | habré partido |
| tú | habrás cantado | habrás olido | habrás partido |
| él, ella, usted | habrá cantado | habrá olido | habrá partido |
| nosotros/as | habremos cantado | habremos olido | habremos partido |
| vosotros/as | habréis cantado | habréis olido | habréis partido |
| ellos, ellas, ustedes | habrán cantado | habrán olido | habrán partido |

**a.** The future perfect is used to express a future action located further in the future and related to a particular point of reference.

### Example

Para la próxima semana ya se **habrá reanudado** la producción de petróleo en Venezuela.
*By next week, Venezuela's oil production will have resumed.*

Lina ya **habrá llegado** cuando sirvamos\* la comida.
*Lina will have already arrived when we serve dinner.*

**Exercise 6.** Complete the following sentences using the appropriate form of the future perfect.

1. Para mañana, ya _____ _____(terminar/yo) de leer el libro.
2. En diez años ya _____ _____(casarse/tú) y _____ _____ (tener) dos hijos.
3. Mañana_____ _____(estudiar/él) su lección y podremos salir a un bar.
4. Espero que al final del año _____ _____ (realizar) ustedes todos sus proyectos.
5. En un año ya _____ _____ (hacer/nosotros) nuestra casa de campo.
6. Sé que es duro el divorcio, pero antes de que me dé cuenta ya _____ _____ (comenzar/yo) de nuevo mi vida.
7. Para cuando yo me pensione tú ya _____ _____(ir) a la universidad y serás independiente.
8. Antes de que regreses ya_____ _____(oír) muy buenas noticias de nuestro proyecto.
9. No te preocupes, para entonces yo ya_____ _____(llegar).
10. Cuando llegue el aburrido de Juan, nosotros ya _____ _____(partir).

---

\*For an explanation regarding the use of the subjunctive in this sentence, see The Present Subjunctive in Adverbial Clauses, Chapter 10.

**b.** The future perfect is also used to express probability in the past, when the action is seen as finished. (This is very similar to the use of the conditional when expressing probability.)

**Example**

—¿Por qué no vino?
*"Why did he not come?"*

—Se **habrá ido** a otra parte.
*"He probably went to another place."*

—¿Dónde está Liliana? Aún no llega.
*"Where is Liliana? She has not arrived yet."*

—**Habrá perdido** el avión.
*"Maybe she missed her plane."*

**Exercise 7.** Rewrite the following sentences using the future perfect as shown.

**Example**

El detenido probablemente ha hablado y los detectives descubrirán el asesinato.
*El detenido habrá hablado y los detectives descubrirán el asesinato.*

1. Los asesinos probablemente se han llevado el cadáver.

   _____

2. La policía probablemente perdió la pista de los delincuentes.

   _____

3. Un testigo probablemente estuvo en el lugar del crimen.

   _____

4. El testigo probablemente lo vio todo.

   _____

5. La policía ha entrevistado al testigo.

   _____

6. El testigo probablemente es uno de los asesinos.

   _____

**Exercise 8.** Make conjectures about what a lonely dog could do. Follow the example and key words.

**Example**

dormir/calle
Probablemente el perro habrá dormido en la calle.

1. comer/basura

   _____

2. recorrer/ la ciudad con otros perros

   _____

3. entrar/ a un restarante a comer

   _____

4. morder/ un policía

   _____

5. jugar/ con niños en el parque

   _____

6. bañarse/ en el lago

   _____

# D. Conditional Perfect

|  | **cantar** | **oler** | **partir** |
|---|---|---|---|
| yo | habría cantado | habría olido | habría partido |
| tú | habrías cantado | habrías olido | habrías partido |
| él, ella, usted | habría cantado | habría olido | habría partido |
| nosotros/as | habríamos cantado | habríamos olido | habríamos partido |
| vosotros/as | habríais cantado | habríais olido | habríais partido |
| ellos, ellas, ustedes | habrían cantado | habrían olido | habrían partido |

## Uses of the Conditional Perfect

**a.** The conditional perfect is used to indicate a future action related to a moment in the past, but previous to another moment existent in the sentence.

### Example
Te dije que cuando llegaran,* ya **habrían comido**.
_I told you that by the time they arrived, they would have already eaten._

**Exercise 9.** Rewrite the following sentences using the conditional perfect as shown.
Aquella tarde/(yo)/salir/contigo/no tener dinero.
_Aquella tarde habría salido contigo pero no tenía dinero._

1. Aquel día/nosotros/comer/no tener hambre

   _____

2. Esa noche/(yo)/acostarse/no tener sueño

   _____

*For an explanation regarding the use of the subjunctive in this sentence, see The Present Subjunctive in Adverbial Clauses, Chapter 10.

3. Aquella mañana/(yo)/besarte/no conocerte lo suficiente

   _____

4. Esa tarde/(yo)/jugar/contigo al fútbol/no tener el balón

   _____

5. Aquel año/(yo)/estudiar/no tener dinero para pagar la matrícula

   _____

6. Aquella noche/(yo) decirte/ la verdad/no tener la valentía de decírtelo

   _____

7. Ese día/(yo)/quedarse contigo en casa/no tener tiempo

   _____

8. Jorge y Tomás/ ir/a la fiesta/tener que estudiar para un examen

   _____

9. Ellos/construir/la casa/no tener los medios

   _____

10. Lucía/saludarme/seguro no verme

    _____

**b.** The second use of the conditional perfect is to express probability of an action that has already been completed.

### Example

—¿Por qué no vino?
*"Why did he not come?"*

—Se **habría ido** a otra parte.
*"He probably went to another place."*

---

### TIP BOX
Other uses are related with conditional clauses.*

### Example

De tener tiempo te <u>habríamos visitado</u>.
*If we had had time, we would have visited you.*

Si hubiéramos tenido tiempo, te <u>habríamos visitado</u>.
*If we had had time, we would have visited you.*

*See Chapter 11, Conditional Clauses.

---

**Exercise 10.** Rewrite the following sentences using the conditional perfect as shown.

**Example**

La cantante probablemente ya había terminado de cantar cuando llegamos al teatro.
*La cantante ya habría terminado de cantar cuando llegamos al teatro.*

1. Marcela probablemente ya había probado las albóndigas en casa de su abuela.
   _____.

2. El señor Rodríguez probablemente ya había muerto cuando llegó al hospital.
   _____.

3. Mi madre probablemente ya había llamado cuando yo llegué a casa.
   _____.

4. Roberto probablemente ya había salido del trabajo cuando yo lo llamé.
   _____.

5. Filomena y su hija probablemente ya habían hecho las maletas cuando llegó el taxi.
   _____.

6. El presidente probablemente ya había tomado la decisión de ir a la guerra cuando asumió la presidencia.
   _____.

7. Lucía probablemente ya había pensado abandonar a su esposo cuando se marchó.
   _____.

# Chapter 7

# PRONOMINAL VERBS

## I. Reflexive Verbs

A reflexive verb requires a reflexive pronoun when it refers to an action affecting the subject of the sentence.

| | Reflexive Pronouns |
|---|---|
| me | *myself* |
| te | *yourself (informal)* |
| se | *himself, herself, itself, yourself (formal)* |
| nos | *ourselves* |
| os | *yourselves (informal)* |
| se | *themselves, yourselves (formal)* |

**Yo <u>me</u> cepillo el pelo.**
*(I comb my hair.)*

Reflexive pronouns are used to indicate that the direct or indirect object in a sentence is the same as its subject. In this case, the subject performs and receives the action.

### Example

Laura <u>**se**</u> lava las manos.
*Laura washes her hands.*

The reflexive pronoun varies according to the personal pronoun.

| | | |
|---|---|---|
| yo | **me** | levant**o** |
| tú | **te** | levant**as** |
| el | | |
| ella | **se** | levant**a** |
| usted | | |
| | | temprano |
| nosotros | **nos** | levant**amos** |
| vosotros | **os** | levant**áis** |
| ellos | | |
| ellas | **se** | levant**an** |
| ustedes | | |

## TIP BOX

Reflexive pronouns are similar to direct and indirect object pronouns in terms of positioning.* They usually precede a conjugated verb, but in the presence of an **infinitive verb**, a **present participle**, or an **affirmative direct command**, they are usually attached. A reflexive pronoun precedes an object pronoun when they occur in the same sentence.

### Example

—Esta mañana **me** levanté temprano y **me** bañé.
*"This morning, I woke up early and I took a shower."*

—Y, ¿**te** lavaste el cabello?
*"And, did you wash your hair?"*

—Sí, **me** lo lavé.
*"Yes, I did."*

—Yo hace un mes no **me** lo lavo.
*"I haven't washed mine in a month."*

—**Lávatelo**, no seas sucio.
*"Wash it, don't be gross."*

—Mi peluquero **me** dijo que **lavarse** el cabello a menudo no es bueno.
*"My stylist told me that washing one's hair too often is not good."*

*See Chapter 8, Object Pronouns.

**Exercise 1.** Write a reflexive sentence based on the given words. You may choose the verb tense.

### Example

yo/lavarse/cabello
*Me lavo el cabello.*

1. Lucía/cepillarse/cabello _____
2. Los niños/tomarse/leche _____
3. Tú/cortarse/cuando cocinas _____
4. El bebé/levantarse/temprano _____
5. Yo/levantarse/tarde _____
6. Fernando/arreglarse/para salir _____
7. Nosotros/ducharse/con agua caliente _____
8. Ustedes/mirarse/en el espejo _____

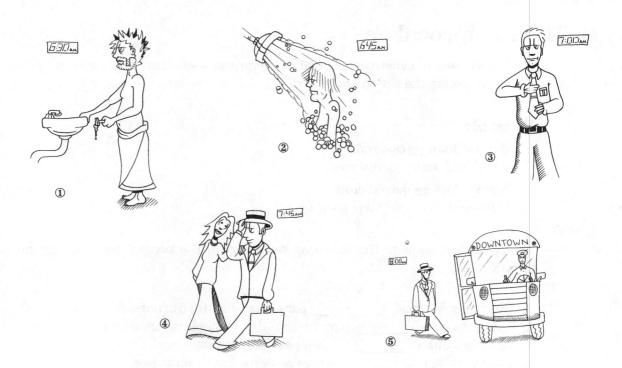

**Exercise 2.** Write five reflexive sentences describing one day in Jorge's life. Follow the suggestions of the drawings above.

### Example

*Jorge se levanta a las seis de la mañana.*

1. (afeitarse) _____ .
2. (bañarse) _____ .
3. (vestirse) _____ .
4. (ponerse, despedirse) _____ .
5. (subirse) _____ .

## TIP BOX

Some reflexive verbs use pronouns that do not obviously reflect back to the subject. Among these verbs are *atreverse a* (to dare), *burlarse de* (to make fun of), *fijarse en* (to notice), *acordarse de* (to remember), *quejarse de* (to complain about), *arrepentirse de* (to repent), *jactarse de* (to boast), *rebelarse contra* (to revolt against), *suicidarse* (to commit suicide). Notice that these verbs have the pronoun *se* attached to the infinitive form.

### Example

Toda la clase <u>se</u> burla de José menos yo.
*The whole class makes fun of José but me.*

Los estudiantes <u>se</u> rebelaron contra el profesor.
*The students rebelled against the teacher.*

# II. The Reciprocal *Se*

**Se** is also used in constructions (called reciprocal sentences) that have two or more subjects performing the action of the verb.

### Example

María y Juan **se** casaron.
*María and Juan got married.*

Pedro y José **se** despidieron.
*Pedro and José said their good-byes.*

**Exercise 3.** Complete the following sentences in the present tense using the verbs in parentheses.

1. Gonzalo y Marcos _____ para lavar el auto. (turnarse)
2. Los amigos _____ para jugar fútbol el domingo. (reunirse)
3. Rosario y Juan _____ con pasión. (besarse)
4. Julia y su hija _____ antes de despedirse. (abrazarse)
5. Los novios _____ a los ojos con dulzura. (mirarse)
6. Las olas _____ contra el acantilado. (estrellarse)

# III. The Passive *Se*

The **se** pronoun is used also in passive sentences; in this case, the object to which the verb refers is also the subject of the verb.

### Example

**Se** compran coches usados.
*Used cars are bought.*

**Se** necesita ingeniero con cinco años de experiencia.
*An engineer with five years of experience is needed.*

**Exercise 4.** Complete the following sentences in the present tense using the verbs in parentheses.

1. Se (buscar) _____ secretarios bilingües.
2. Se (necesitar) _____ vendedores con experiencia.
3. Se (vender) _____ coches europeos.
4. Se (alquilar) _____ apartamento en el barrio Miraflores.
5. Se (reparar) _____ relojes electrónicos.
6. Se (cocinar) _____ los tomates antes de licuarlos.
7. Se (preparar) _____ tamales para Navidad.

**Exercise 5.** Put the following instructions in the correct order by writing a number at the end of each sentence, and conjugate the verb in the present indicative.

**Receta de tortilla española**

1. Se _____ (servir) la tortilla en un plato y se come. _____
2. A fuego alto en una sartén, con una gota de aceite, se _____ (colocar) las patatas y los huevos. _____
3. Se _____ (cortar) las patatas y la cebolla en rodajas. **1**
4. Se les _____ (añadir) un poco de sal a las patatas. _____
5. Se _____ (sofreír) en aceite a fuego lento. _____
6. Una vez cocinadas, se _____ (sacar) las patatas del aceite. _____
7. Aparte en un recipiente, se _____ (batir) los huevos. _____
8. Se _____ (añadir) las patatas a los huevos. _____
9. Se le _____ (dar) la vuelta a la tortilla y se _____ (cocinar) a fuego bajo por cuatro minutos. _____

# IV. Impersonal Constructions With *Se*

Impersonal constructions with **se** are sentences in which the subject is unknown. The verb is always conjugated in the third person (*él, ella*).

---

### TIP BOX

Note that impersonal sentences with **se** are usually followed by a sentence preceded by a preposition, or by the relative pronoun **que**.

---

### Example

**Se** espera **a** los atletas del Perú.
*We expect the athletes from Peru.*

**Se** come muy bien **en** este restaurante.
*One eats well in this restaurant.*

**Se** necesita **que** los países protejan los recursos naturales de la Tierra.
*It is necessary that countries protect the earth's natural resources.*

**Exercise 6.** Complete the following sentences in the present tense using the verbs in parentheses.

1. Se (esperar) _____ a los delegados.
2. Se (encerrar) _____ a los presos.
3. Se (preocupar) _____ de sus hijos.
4. Se (ocupar) _____ de la ciudad.
5. Se (hablar) _____ de las elecciones presidenciales por todo el país.
6. Se (decir)_____ que va a llover toda la semana.
7. Se (saber)_____ que consumir muchas grasas es malo para la salud.
8. Se (preferir)_____ los libros nuevos a los usados.
9. Hoy en día, se (construir)_____ con materiales más resistentes.
10. No se (permitir)_____ el uso de cámaras fotográficas en el museo.

# Chapter 8

# PRONOUNS

## I. Personal Pronouns

### A. Subject Pronouns

Subject pronouns are words that replace a subject noun. They can be classified according to number, person, gender (male or female), and formality (formal or informal).

**Tú y yo jugamos.**
*(You and I play.)*

| | Spanish | | English | |
|---|---|---|---|---|
| | **Singular** | **Plural** | **Singular** | **Plural** |
| First person | yo | nosotros | *I* | *we* |
| Second person | tú *(informal)* usted *(formal)* | vosotros *(informal)* ustedes *(formal)* | *you* | *you* |
| Third person | él, ella | ellos, ellas | *he, she, it* | *they* |

The main difference between English and Spanish is that, in Spanish, subject pronouns may be omitted once the speaker knows who the subject is.

---

**TIP BOX**

The pronouns **nosotros**, **vosotros**, and **ellos** have feminine forms: **nosotras**, **vosotras**, and **ellas**. When referring to a mixed male and female group of people the **-os** form is used.

---

**TIP BOX**

**Vosotros**, the plural form for **tú**, is mainly used in Spain. In other Spanish-speaking countries the form **ustedes** is used.

There is also another second person singular form, **vos**, which is used in some Latin American countries, especially in the Southern Cone (Argentina, Chile, Paraguay, and Uruguay), and it is sometimes used in Costa Rica and Nicaragua.

**Exercise 1.** Change the noun in bold with a subject pronoun.

1. **Juan** (____) está cansado porque trabaja mucho en la oficina.
2. **Marta y Consuelo** (____) viven en un apartamento muy bonito.
3. **Julio y yo** (____) queremos ir al concierto de Shakira.
4. ¡**Arturo,** (____) estás loco! *(you informal)*
5. **Los niños** (____) juegan en el parque a ladrones y policías.

**Exercise 2.** Match the sentence with the corresponding personal pronoun.

| | |
|---|---|
| 1. Ayer, **Gabriel, María y yo** fuimos a la playa. | yo |
| 2. —¡**Jorge!** ¡Tienes la camisa sucia! *(you informal)* | él |
| 3. Quiero conocer a tus vecinos. *(I)* | nosotros |
| 4. **Lucía y Rosa** llegaron muy cansadas después del partido. | ellos |
| 5. **Lucero, María y yo** salimos de viaje esta noche. | ella |
| 6. **Marta** siempre está dedicada a su trabajo. | tú |
| 7. **Lola y Juan** están dispuestos a ayudarnos. | vosotros |
| 8. —¡**Marta y José!** ¿Salisteis por la puerta principal? *(you informal)* | ellas |

**Exercise 3.** Fill in the blank with the appropriate subject pronoun.

1. Helena tiene más hambre que ____. *(you formal)*
2. Cuando ____ llegó a la estación, el tren ya había salido. *(Susana)*
3. A ____ no les gusta ayudar en las labores de jardinería. *(the boys)*
4. El portero dijo que ____ viniste anoche. *(you informal)*
5. ____ no sé qué hora es. *(I)*
6. Cuando ____ oímos la noticia, nos preocupamos mucho. *(Simón and I)*
7. Catalina quiere que ____ compre los boletos para el concierto. *(Julio)*
8. Quiero que ____ vengan a la fiesta del sábado. *(Clara and Irene)*

## B. Object Pronouns

**a.** Forms of direct object pronouns. **Direct object pronouns** are used to avoid repetition. They may replace **a person** or **a thing**.

| Direct Object Pronouns: Singular | | Direct Object Pronouns: Plural | |
|---|---|---|---|
| me | *me* | nos | *us* |
| te | *you (informal)* | os | *you (informal)* |
| lo | *you (formal masculine), him, it* | los | *you (formal, masculine), them (masculine)* |
| la | *you (formal feminine), her, it* | las | *you (formal, feminine), them (feminine)* |

## TIP BOX

In some regions of Spain and Latin America, **le** and **les** are used as direct object pronouns instead of **lo** and **los** when referring to people. This practice is called "**leísmo**."

Direct object pronouns vary according to the person or thing they substitute.

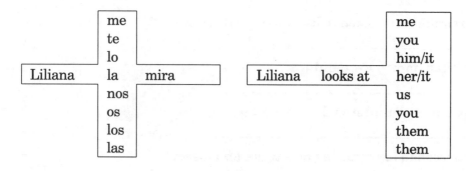

## TIP BOX

A direct object pronoun exists only in the presence of a transitive verb. A transitive verb is a verb that requires a direct object to complete its meaning.

### Example

| | |
|---|---|
| —¿Compraste las bebidas para la fiesta? | *"Did you buy the drinks for the party?"* |
| —No, no **las** compré. | *"No, I did not buy them."* |
| —Entonces, ¡**cómpralas**! | *"So, buy them!"* |
| —Y no te olvides de **ponerlas** en la nevera. | *"And don't forget to put them in the refrigerator."* |

## TIP BOX

A direct object pronoun usually precedes a conjugated verb; however, in the presence of an **infinitive verb**, a **gerund** or an **affirmative direct command**, a direct object pronoun usually is attached.

**Exercise 4.** Complete the following sentences with the appropriate direct object pronoun.

1. Victoria abraza a **Nicolás** todos los días. Victoria ___ abraza todos los días.
2. Recibimos a **la entrenadora** con un aplauso. ___ recibimos con un aplauso.
3. Compré estas **flores** en la calle. ___ compré en la calle.
4. El jugador lanzó **la pelota** con desgano. ___ lanzó con desgano.
5. Tengo que comprar **amortiguadores** para el auto. Tengo que comprar___.
6. Jorge y Mario vieron **la película** anoche. Jorge y Mario ___ vieron anoche.
7. Toma las llaves y abre **la puerta**. Ábre___.

**Exercise 5.** Rewrite the following sentence substituting the direct object (in bold) with the corresponding pronoun.

### Example

Marta envió **el paquete** ayer.
*Marta **lo** envió ayer.*

1. En la reunión el presidente discutió **el problema.**
   _____.

2. La multitud aprobó **los cambios**.
   _____.

3. Leí **las obras completas de Cervantes**.
   _____.

4. Estoy buscando **los apuntes que tomé en clase**.
   _____.

5. No conozco a **la nueva profesora de español**.
   _____.

6. Los científicos encontraron **la solución del experimento**.
   _____.

7. Gabriela vende **flores** en la feria.
   _____.

**b.** Forms of indirect object pronouns. **Indirect object pronouns** are used to avoid repetition. They replace **personal nouns.**

| Indirect Object Pronouns: Singular | | Indirect Object Pronouns: Plural | |
|---|---|---|---|
| me | *me* | nos | *us* |
| te | *you (informal)* | os | *you (informal)* |
| le, se | *you (formal), him, her* | les, se | *you (formal), them* |

Indirect object pronouns vary according to the person they substitute.

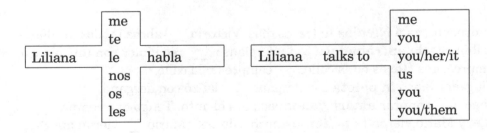

**TIP BOX**

What is an indirect object noun?

An indirect object noun is the recipient of the direct object noun.

**Example**

Laura <u>le</u> envía <u>una carta</u> a <u>su madre</u>.
                    DO          IO
*Laura sent <u>a letter</u> to <u>her mother</u>.*

Note that the indirect objects are frequently expressed twice in the same sentence. Notice that indirect and direct object pronouns are the same except for *le* and *les*. Since *le* and *les* may replace *él* or *ella* or *ellos* or *ellas*, a prepositional phrase is added to avoid ambiguity.

**Example**

Ayer <u>les</u> compré unos juguetes a <u>tus hijos</u>.
*Yesterday I bought some toys to <u>your kids</u>.*

Indirect object pronouns follow the same pattern as do direct object pronouns. They usually precede a conjugated verb; however, in the presence of an **infinitive verb**, a **gerund,** or an **affirmative direct command**, indirect object pronouns are usually attached.

**Example**

—Estamos aburridos. **Cuéntanos** algo divertido.
—Vale, voy a **contarles** un chiste.

*—We are bored. Tell <u>us</u> an amusing story.*
*—OK, I am going to tell <u>you</u> a joke.*

**TIP BOX**

Indirect object pronouns precede the direct object pronoun when the two are used together.

**Example**

—¿Pero, quién te contó esa mentira?
—<u>Me la</u> contó Liliana.

*"But, who told you that lie?"*
*"Liliana told it to me."*

**Exercise 6.** Complete the following sentences using the appropriate indirect object pronoun.

1. Marta ___ compra zapatos **a su hija**.
2. ¿Por qué no ___ diste un golpe **a la puerta**?
3. ___ dicen que vayamos primero a la oficina del director. *(a nosotros)*
4. Esta es la persona que ___ regaló tus botas nuevas. *(a ti)*
5. ¡___ advertí que no llegarais tarde! *(a vosotros)*
6. **Las ruedas** no suenan cuando ___ pongo aceite.
7. ¡Eres muy dulce! Siempre ___ traes las cosas que prefiero. *(a mí)*

**Exercise 7.** Match the indirect object to each indirect object pronoun.

1. El cartero **me** entregó las cartas.                         a él
2. **Te** trajimos una bicicleta nueva.                          a nosotros
3. Arturo se emocionó cuando **le** dimos el regalo.             a ustedes
4. Si **les** contara lo que me pasó, no me creerían.            a mí
5. Antes de salir, píde**les** a tus padres las llaves.          a ella
6. **Nos** dieron otra semana de plazo para presentar el examen.  a ellos
7. No creo que a Juana **le** parezca buena la idea.             a ti

**c.** Double object pronouns. The indirect object pronoun **se** is used instead of **le** and **les** before the direct object pronouns **lo, la, los,** and **las**.

## Example

Margarita:—¡Federico! ¿**Le** devolviste el libro a Liliana?
*Margarita: "Federico! Did you return the book to Liliana?"*

Federico:—Sí, **se lo** devolví ayer.
*Federico: "Yes, I returned it to her yesterday."*

**Exercise 8.** In a new, short sentence replace the words in bold with the appropriate object pronoun.

## Example

Mi padre me envió **un regalo**.
*Mi padre me **lo** envió.*

1. Quiero que le entregues a Sonia **esta carta.**

   _____.

2. Llamamos **a mamá** esta mañana.

   _____.

3. Los obreros cerraron **el túnel** durante el fin de semana.

   _____.

4. No esperes más **a tu tía Consuelo**.

   _____.

5. Es una lástima que hayamos perdido **el tren.**

   _____.

6. Los González invitaron a **Victoria y a Cristina** a cenar.

   _____.

7. Busca **la dirección** en esta libreta.

   _____.

**Exercise 9.** Complete the following dialogue with an appropriate direct or indirect object pronoun.

—¡Qué desorden hay en este cuarto! ¿Has visto mis **zapatos**?
—No ____ he visto. ¿Dónde los dejaste?
—Dentro de **una caja blanca**. ¿____ viste por aquí?
—Sí. ____ dejé sobre el escritorio.
—No veo **el escritorio**. ¿Dónde ____ pusiste?
—____ saqué a la calle para que alguien se lo lleve.
—¡No puede ser! ¿Desocupaste **los cajones**?
—Ni ____ miré. ¿Tenías algo dentro?
—Mi colección de **postales**. ¿Cómo voy a recuperar ____?
—Estaba bromeando. Aquí están tus **postales**. ____ guardé en este sobre.
—Casi ____ matas del susto (a mí). Me alegro de que no ____ hayas perdido.

# II. Possessive Pronouns

A possessive pronoun replaces a noun that is qualified by a possessive adjective.*

**Example**

possessive adjective        possessive pronoun
_____              _____
       ↓                          ↓
**Me gusta <u>mi</u> casa.**      **Me gusta la <u>mía</u>.**
*I like my house.*            *I like mine.*

*See Chapter 3, Adjectives.

Possessive pronouns have four forms and they agree in number and gender **with the noun they replace**.

| Singular | | Plural | | Translation |
|---|---|---|---|---|
| **Masculine** | **Feminine** | **Masculine** | **Feminine** | |
| mío | mía | míos | mías | *mine* |
| tuyo | tuya | tuyos | tuyas | *yours (informal)* |
| suyo | suya | suyos | suyas | *his/hers/its* |
| nuestro | nuestra | nuestros | nuestras | *ours* |
| vuestro | vuestra | vuestros | vuestras | *yours (informal)* |

**Exercise 10.** Answer the following questions using a possessive pronoun.

**Example**

¿Es tuya aquella chaqueta?                    ¿Son tuyas aquellas flores?
*Sí, es mía* or *No, no es mía.*              *Sí, son mías* or *No, no son mías.*

1. ¿Es de tu hermano aquel coche negro?
   _____.

2. ¿Son de vosotros las chaquetas que están sobre la silla?
   _____.

3. ¿Son de ellos los perros que ladraban anoche?
   _____.

4. ¿Es tuya esta botella de agua?
   _____.

5. ¿Son vuestros aquellos autos?
   _____.

6. ¿Es de ella esa libreta marrón?
   _____.

7. ¿Es de ellas esa mesa de madera?
   _____.

8. ¿Me pertenece el paraguas negro?
   _____.

**Exercise 11.** Complete the mini-dialogues using the appropriate possessive pronoun.

1. —Este es mi libro.
   —No, es el ___. *(mine)*

2. —¿Cómo está tu familia?
   —Muy bien, gracias. ¿Y la ____? *(yours)*

3. —El equipo visitante ganó el campeonato de tenis.
   —¿De veras? Pensé que el ___ había ganado. *(ours)*

4. —Me parece que Ricardo tiene la chaqueta de Manuel.
   —¿Sí? Entonces, Ricardo olvidó la ___ en el restaurante. *(his)*

5. ¿Recordáis la cámara que os presté?
   —¿Era ___? No lo sabíamos. *(yours informal)*

6. —Quisiera tener el cabello tan negro como el ___. *(yours)*
   —¡Qué gracioso! Yo quisiera que el ___ fuera rubio. *(mine)*

7. —Esta es la mejor computadora que tenemos.
   —¡Es la que necesitamos! La ___ no tiene suficiente memoria. *(ours)*

8. —¿De quién son estos zapatos?
   —Son de José. Los ___ están en mi cuarto. *(mine)*

9. —Marcela compró sus flores en el supermercado.
   —¿Ah, sí? Juliana cultivó las ___. *(hers)*

10. —Aquí está el dinero de Aníbal.
    —Lo pondré en mi gaveta. Aníbal tiene la ___ completamente llena. *(his)*

**Exercise 12.** Write the appropriate possessive pronoun under each picture.

1.
   —Esta miel es _____.
   —No, esa miel es de las abejas.

2.
   —¿Esta casa es de sus padres?
   No, esta casa es _____.

3.
   —¿Ese computador es _____?
   —Sí, es _____.

4.
   ¿Esos caballos son _____?
   Sí, son _____.

5.
   ¡No puedo creerlo! ¿Doctor, ese coche es _____?
   —Sí, es _____. Las apariencias engañan.

# III. Demonstrative Pronouns

| Singular Demonstrative Pronouns | | |
|---|---|---|
| **Masculine** | **Feminine** | **Translation** |
| éste | ésta | *this one (here)* |
| ése | ésa | *that one (there)* |
| aquél | aquélla | *that one (over there)* |

| Plural Demonstrative Pronouns | | |
|---|---|---|
| **Masculine** | **Feminine** | **Translation** |
| éstos | éstas | *these (here)* |
| ésos | ésas | *those (there)* |
| aquéllos | aquéllas | *those (over there)* |

## TIP BOX

Although demonstrative adjectives and demonstrative pronouns look identical, they are distinguished by the context. However, in cases of ambiguity, the demonstrative pronouns take an accent mark.

| Neuter Demonstrative Pronouns | |
|---|---|
| esto | *this (here)* |
| eso | *that (there)* |
| aquello | *that (over there)* |

Neuter demonstrative pronouns never bear an accent mark because they are always pronouns and therefore no ambiguity is possible. They are used to refer to nonspecific things, ideas, or situations in a general way.

## Example

—¿Qué es **eso?**
*"What's that?"*

—¿**Esto?** ¿Mis gafas?
*"This? My glasses?"*

—No, ¡**aquello!**
*"No, that!"*

—¡Ah! un encendedor.
*"Ha! A lighter"*

**Exercise 13.** Complete the following sentences with the appropriate demonstrative pronoun.

1. Estas flores están más frescas que _____ que están allí. (those, over there)
2. _____ me parece imposible. (this)
3. Tráeme la copa. No, _____ que está sobre el piano. (that)
4. De todos mis amigos, _____ es el más simpático. (this)
5. Ya leí estos libros. Ahora voy a leer _____. (those)
6. ¿Qué vestido prefieres? ¿_____? (this)
7. Me gusta más _____ (that) que está sobre la silla.
8. ¿_____? (that, over there) Tienes muy buen gusto.
9. La historia es verídica. _____ pasó hace mucho tiempo. (that)
10. Esta es mi sobrina Olga y _____ es su hermanita Liliana. (that, over there)

# IV. Relative Pronouns

Relative pronouns **que, quien, quienes, el cual, el que, cuyo** are capable of transforming a sentence into a dependent adjective clause (relative clause). Both relative pronouns and the adjective clause refer back to an antecedent that is usually a noun or a pronoun.

---

**TIP BOX**
Within the clause, the relative pronoun can function as:

**a. A subject**

**Example**

Necesitamos un líder **que** respete los derechos humanos.
*We need a leader that respects human rights.*

**b. A direct object**

**Example**

Compré el coche **que** me aconsejaste.
*I bought the car you told me to.*

**c. An indirect object**

**Example**

No encuentro a la mujer a **quien** le pregunté por el precio del coche.
*I can't find the woman whom I asked the price of the car.*

**d. The object of a preposition**

**Example**

Este es mi amigo con **quien** fuimos a la fiesta el año pasado.
*This is my friend with whom I went to the party last year.*

---

## A. The Relative Pronoun *que*

The relative pronoun **que** (*that, which, who, whom*) refers to both animated and non-animated antecedents.

### Example

El vendedor **que** nos atendió es boliviano. (The antecedent of **que** is the animated noun **el vendedor**.)

El café **que** te compré es colombiano. (The antecedent of **que** is the inanimated noun **el café**.)

---

**TIP BOX**

The relative pronoun que may be also be preceded by a preposition (**a, de, en, con**); in such a case, the antecedent is always a thing.

**Example**

El libro <u>de que</u> te hablé es *Las mil y una noches*.
*The book which I told you about is* A Thousand Nights and a Night.

---

**Exercise 14.** In the following sentences identify the antecedent of the relative pronoun **que**.

1. El teléfono **que** te compré es negro. _____
2. Tengo un amigo **que** tiene siete perros. _____
3. La música **que** más me gusta es el tango. _____
4. Las personas **que** esperaban en la fila tiritaban de frío. _____
5. El regalo **que** te traje está sobre la mesa. _____
6. Siento una pena **que** me oprime la garganta. _____
7. Las situaciones **que** no se pueden resolver son muy graves.
8. No creas los rumores **que** escuchas por la calle.
9. El barco **que** se acerca trae muchos turistas.
10. Los estudiantes **que** participaron en la manifestación eran muy alegres.

**Exercise 15.** Combine the following sentences according to the example.

### Example

El parque está en el centro de la ciudad. El parque es hermoso.
*El parque que está en el centro de la ciudad es hermoso.*

1. Las flores están en el jarrón. Las flores son de muchos colores.

   _____.

2. Julián le regaló a Claudia un collar de perlas. El collar le costó mucho dinero.

   _____.

3. Presentamos el examen de química el lunes pasado. El examen fue muy fácil.

   _____.

4. La niña llevaba una muñeca en su carrito. La niña perdió la muñeca.

   _____.

5. Quiero que me devuelvas el dinero. Te lo presté la semana pasada.

   _____.

6. Vimos una película de horror. Se llama "La pesadilla".

   _____.

7. Enviamos las invitaciones por correo. Las invitaciones no llegaron a tiempo.

   _____.

8. Silvia tiene una casa en la playa. La casa es muy valiosa.

   _____.

9. Encontré unos libros en el parque. Los libros eran de Gustavo.

   _____.

10. El camino lleva a la laguna. El camino está lleno de baches.

    _____.

## B. The Relative Pronouns *quien, quienes*

The relative pronoun **quien** always has the function of a noun, even if it has or does not have an antecedent. It also agrees with its antecedent in number (singular **quien** or plural **quienes**).

---

### TIP BOX

**a. With an antecedent**

**Example**

Y así le gritaba Doña Bárbara, <u>quien</u> tenía modales terribles.
   (**Quien** is antecedent of Doña Bárbara.)
*Doña Bárbara, who had terrible manners, screamed at him.*

**b. Without an antecedent**

**Example**

<u>Quien</u> tiene dinero, hace lo que quiere.
*Whoever has money, does whatever he wants.*

---

## TIP BOX

**Quien** or **quienes** is also used after a preposition.

### Example

No conozco a la mujer <u>**con quien**</u> hablabas ayer.
*I don't know the woman with whom you were talking yesterday.*

No conozco a la mujer <u>**a quien**</u> hablabas ayer.
*I don't know the woman to whom you were talking yesterday.*

No conozco a la mujer <u>**de quien**</u> hablabas ayer.
*I don't know the woman of whom you were talking yesterday.*

Tu hijo <u>**por quien**</u> te preocupas tanto, está muy consentido.
*Your son for whom you worry so much is very spoiled.*

La mujer <u>**para quien**</u> trabajas es mi hermana.
*The woman for whom you work is my sister.*

## TIP BOX

As a noun, **quien** or **quienes** may have the role of a subject, a direct object, or an indirect object.

### a. As a subject

Laura, <u>**quien**</u> baila muy bien, ganó el concurso de baile.
*Laura, who dances very well, won the dance contest.*

### b. As a direct object

Tu amiga, <u>**a quien**</u> conocí la semana pasada, es famosa.
*Your friend, whom I met last week, is famous.*

In this case, the relative pronoun **quien** preceded by the preposition **a** can be replaced by the relative pronoun **que**.

Tu amiga <u>**que**</u> conocí la semana pasada, es famosa.
*Your friend I met last week is famous*

### c. As an indirect object

Admiro mucho al poeta León de Greiff <u>**a quien**</u> tuve el gusto de conocer.
*I admire the poet, León de Greiff, whom I had the pleasure of meeting.*

**Exercise 16.** Complete the following sentences with the relative pronouns **que, quien, quienes, a quien, a quienes**.

1.  Los amigos _____ invitamos a la fiesta, no pudieron venir.
2.  El dueño de la tienda, _____ le pedimos señas de cómo llegar, nos dio todos los datos.

3.  Manolo se acercó a su madre, _____ lo abrazó con gran ternura.
4.  Margarita y Ana, _____ fueron a la misma escuela, son muy buenas amigas.
5.  El médico, _____ acudimos de inmediato, nos examinó minuciosamente.
6.  Los niños _____ no se les han aplicado vacunas pueden contraer enfermedades contagiosas.
7.  La joven _____ ves allí es mi hermana.
8.  La portera del edificio, _____ no ve muy bien, no reconoció a los recién llegados.
9.  El ministro, _____ acababa de posesionarse, se encargó de la situación.
10. Mi familia, _____ vive en Panamá, es muy hospitalaria.

**Exercise 17.** Complete the following sentences with the appropriate preposition and relative pronouns.

### Example

Tu amiga, **con quien** fuimos ayer a la fiesta, está dormida.

1.  No conozco a la chica _____ bailabas.
2.  Tú eres es la persona _____ me siento más a gusto.
3.  José es el abogado _____ trabaja mi novia.
4.  Ximena es la persona _____ hago tantos sacrificios.
5.  Las muchachas _____ me hablaste acaban de llegar.
6.  Mi abuela es la persona _____ más admiro.

## C. The Relative Pronouns *el que* and *el cual*

The relative pronouns **el que** (*which, who, whom*) and **el cual** (*which, who, whom*) refer to both a person or a thing. They agree with the antecedent in gender and number.

| Masculine | | Feminine | |
|---|---|---|---|
| **Singular** | **Plural** | **Singular** | **Plural** |
| el cual (*who*) | los cuales (*which, who*) | la cual (*which, who*) | las cuales (*which, who*) |
| el que (*he who*) | los que (*those which*) | la que (*she who*) | las que (*those which*) |

### Example

**Referring to a person:**

Tu abuelo, **el cual (*el que*)** tiene ochenta y nueve años, se encuentra muy bien de salud.
*Your grandfather, who is eighty years old, is in perfect health.*

**Referring to a thing:**

El avión, **el cual (*el que*)** se accidentó ayer, tenía una falla mecánica.
*The airplane, which had an accident yesterday, had a mechanical failure.*

- When preceded by a preposition (**a, en, con, para,** and so on), either **el cual** or **el que** may be used.

## Example

**Referring to a person:**

Mi abuelo, <u>**con el cual**</u> (<u>**con el que**</u>) viví cuando tenía siete años, se encuentra muy bien de salud.
*My grandfather, with whom I lived when I was seven years old, is in perfect health.*

**Referring to a thing:**

El avión, <u>**en el que**</u> (<u>**en el cual**</u>) viajaste la semana pasada, se accidentó ayer.
*The airplane, in which you flew last week, had an accident yesterday.*

- The relative pronoun **el cual** or **la cual** is used to avoid ambiguity in sentences where there is more than one possible antecedent of different gender.

## Example

Juan y su hermana María, <u>**la cual**</u> llegó ayer de Paris, vendrán a la fiesta.
*Juan and his sister Maria, who arrived from Paris, will come to the party.*

---

## TIP BOX

Note that the relative pronoun **el cual** refers to either a person or a thing. **El cual** may be replaced by the relative pronoun **que** when used in a restrictive clause (without commas). It may also be replaced in nonrestrictive clauses (with commas) by the relative pronoun **quien** or **quienes** preceded by the preposition **a**, when the antecedent is a person.

### Example

**Persons**
**(Restricted clause)**

Tus amigos <u>**que**</u> invitaste a la fiesta no podrán venir.
*Your friends, whom you invited to the party, will not be able to come.*

**(Nonrestricted clause)**

Tus amigos, <u>**los cuales**</u> (<u>**a quienes**</u>) invitaste a la fiesta, no podrán venir.
*Your friends, whom you invited to the party, will not be able to come.*

**Things**
**(Restricted clause)**

La serpiente <u>**que**</u> es verde con blanco es de Sudamérica.
*The snake, which is green and white, is from South America.*

**(Nonrestricted clause)**

La serpiente, <u>**la cual**</u> es verde con blanco, es de Suramérica.
*The snake, which is green and white, is from South America.*

---

**TIP BOX**

The pronoun **el cual** is more formal than **que**; therefore, when there is no ambiguity in every day conversation, **que** is preferred.

---

**Exercise 18.** Complete the following sentences with **el cual** or **que**.

1. El barco, _____ había zarpado minutos antes, se esfumó entre la niebla.
2. Con este anillo, _____ es una prueba de nuestro pacto, sellemos el trato.
3. Los saltamontes, _____ se habían escondido entre la hierba, formaron una nube sobre la granja.
4. El hidrógeno y el oxígeno, _____ tiene un peso molecular de 16, son los dos componentes del agua.
5. Las gerentes, _____ se habían reunido para discutir la reunión, tomaron una decisión importante.
6. El cielo, _____ se veía desde mi ventana, se estaba tornando gris.

## D. The Relative Pronouns *lo que* and *lo cual*

The neuter relative pronouns **lo que** and **lo cual** are only used to refer to a concept or a preceding idea.

The pronoun **lo que** is mainly used in restrictive clauses.

### Example

**Lo que** quiero es que vuelvas.
*What I want is you to come back.*

No se hace todo **lo que** uno quiere sino **lo que** uno puede.
*We do not do all we can but what we are able.*

In a nonrestrictive clause, either **lo cual** or **lo que** is used, and may be preceded by a preposition.

### Example

Estaba enfermo, **lo cual** (**lo que**) me entristeció enormemente.
*He was sick, which makes me extremely sad.*

Tenía miedo a la guerra, **por lo cual** (**por lo que**) deduje que era un hombre sensible.
*He was scared of the war, by which I deduced that he was a sensible man.*

**Exercise 19.** Write a new sentence using **lo que**, according to the example.

## Example

> **Quiero** que me acompañes al centro.
> *Lo que quiero es que me acompañes al centro.*

1. Me preguntó si quería salir con él.
2. Nos sentíamos muy cansados de viajar a caballo.
3. Perdimos el tren por haber salido tarde.
4. Me asusté cuando el teléfono timbró.
5. Me sorprendió no haberte visto en la fiesta.
6. Le pedí que se casara conmigo.

**Exercise 20.** Complete the following paragraph using **lo que** or **lo cual**.

1. Se escuchaban pasos en la planta baja, _____ nos preocupó mucho.
2. Los estudiantes se portaron muy bien, _____ llenó de orgullo a los maestros.
3. El campeón renunció a la medalla, _____ sorprendió a sus admiradores.
4. Tienes los ojos inflamados, _____ me hace pensar que estuviste llorando.
5. Subieron la colina muy deprisa, _____ los dejó sin aliento.
6. Marcela no invitó a su familia a la boda, _____ los ofendió enormemente.

## E. The Relative Pronoun *cuyo*

The relative pronoun **cuyo** (*whose*) agrees **with the noun it modifies** in number and gender.

## Example

> La industria pesquera, **cuya explotación** es indiscriminada, plantea problemas ecológicos a corto plazo.
> *The fishing industry, whose exploitation is indiscriminate, poses short-term ecological problems.*
>
> La madre, **en cuyo rostro** se reflejaba una infinita alegría, dio a luz un varón.
> *The mother, whose face reflects an immense happiness, gave birth to a boy.*

**Exercise 21.** Complete the following sentences with the appropriate **cuyo** form.

1. Los dueños, _____ foto ves aquí, murieron el año pasado.
2. Esta es la familia _____ gatos cuido en el verano.
3. Aquel, en _____ manos se encuentra la solución, debe actuar pronto.
4. Gonzalo, en _____ auto salimos anoche, tiene mucho dinero.
5. Estos son los libros _____ páginas debemos fotocopiar.
6. Llamé a mi abuela, _____ consejos siempre me ayudan.

# V. Prepositional Pronouns

Prepositional pronouns are subject pronouns preceded by a preposition (**a, por, con, ante,** etc.) with the exception of the **yo** and **tú** forms.

| Prepositional Pronouns | |
| --- | --- |
| mí | me |
| ti | you |
| él, ella | him, her |
| nosotros, nosotras | we |
| vosotros, vosotras | you |
| ellos, ellas | them |

## Example

Me gusta estar **contigo**.
*I love to be with you.*

Pilar habló muy bien de **ti**.
*Pilar talked well about you.*

La casa fue construida por **nosotros**.
*The house was built by ourselves.*

El jefe está hablando de **mí**.
*The boss is talking about me.*

---

**TIP BOX**

Note that subject pronouns differ from prepositional pronouns only in the forms **yo** and **tú**, which use the forms **mí** and **ti**. Also, it is important to notice that these two prepositional pronouns, when they are preceded by the preposition **con**, change to **conmigo** and **contigo**.

---

**Exercise 22.** Answer the following questions using the appropriate prepositional pronoun. Follow the example.

## Example

—¿Hablaste con Alicia?
—*Sí, hablé con ella.*

1. —¿Te asombraste por los precios de los autos?

   _____

2. —¿Soñaste conmigo anoche?

   _____

3. —¿Hablaste con tu mamá sobre tu amiga Gloria?

   _____

4. Según Alfonso, ¿cuánto dinero se necesita para viajar a Europa?

   _____

5. ¿Están los papás de Mimí preocupados por su hija?

   _____

6. ¿Voy a tener que ir sin que me acompañes?

   _____

**Exercise 23.** Lilo and Lola are twins. They are having an argument about one of the objects they have in their room. Fill in the blanks with the appropriate prepositional pronoun.

—Esta es mi silla. Papá la compró para _____ (me) el año pasado.

—¿Para _____ (you)? Creo que te equivocas. Yo estaba con _____ (him) ese día.

—Si te sientas en ella no vuelvo a hablar con _____ (you) nunca más.

—Tú no puedes pasar ni un día sin hablar con _____ (me), hermanita.

—Tienes razón. Soy tan charlatana como tú.

## Review

**Exercise 24.** Fill in the blank with the appropriate personal, possessive, object, or relative pronoun.

Fernando:—Hola Clarita y Laura.

Clara y Laura:—Hola Fernando.

Fernando:—Quiero que vengan a la fiesta de inauguración de mi apartamento la próxima semana.

Laura:—¿_____ vas invitar a _____?

Fernando:—¡Sí, a _____!

Laura:—Muchas gracias. Y, ¿cómo está tu novia?

Fernando:—¡Uhm! No sé... ¿Y tu novio, Clarita?

Clara: ¿El _____? _____ no tengo novio.

Laura: ¿Cómo está tu familia?

Fernando—Muy bien, gracias. ¿Y la _____?

Laura:—La verdad, no muy bien. A mi padre _____ despidieron del trabajo ayer.

Clara: Y recién ha comprado un apartamento.

Laura:—Sí, _____ compró hace justo una semana.

Fernando:—Quisiera conocer_____.

Laura: ¡_____ invito la próxima semana!

Clara:—¿Vieron la última película con Penélope Cruz?

Fernando:—No, no _____ he visto. De todas maneras no me gusta _____ como actriz.

Clara: —¡Laura! Olvidé mi bolso en la cafetería. Hasta luego.

Fernando:—¡Espera!

Clara: ¡ _____ vemos otro día!

Laura:—¡_____ advertí que no _____ olvidara!

Fernando—¿Por qué no _____dijiste que esperara un momento?

Laura:—Mejor así, así podemos estar solos. Anoche soñé con_____.

Fernando:—¿_____?

Fernando:—¡Oh! ¡Qué suerte tengo!

Laura:—¿Por qué?

Fernando:—Allí hay un letrero _____ dice: "Se reparan relojes". Y debo llevar el _____ a que _____ reparen.

Laura:—Déja_____ ver_____, que _____ _____ acompaño.

Fernando:—No es necesario. Gracias. ¡Bueno...! _____ vemos otro día.

Laura:—¿Cuándo es la fiesta?

Fernando:—¿Cuál fiesta?

Laura:—¡_____ a _____ que _____ invitaste a Clara y _____! ¡Idiota!

Fernando:—¡Espera Laura, no _____ enojes!... "¡A las mujeres no _____ entiende nadie!"

# Chapter 9

# THE ADVERB

Yo leí este libro <u>lentamente</u>.

Pedro <u>casi</u> leyó un libro.

Lo siento <u>mucho</u>, pero no me gusta leer.

**A**n adverb is a word that is used to modify a **verb**, an **adjective**, or **another adverb**. Adverbs indicate time, place, manner or quantity; unlike adjectives, they are **invariable.**

### Example

Modifying a <u>verb</u>:
Margarita **acaricia** a su gato **suavemente.**
*Margarita caresses her cat softly.*

Modifying an <u>adjective</u>:
José es **muy simpático.**
*José is very nice.*

Modifying an <u>adverb</u>:
El avión vuela **muy rápido.**
*The airplane flies very fast.*

Adverbs derived from adjectives end in **-mente**, and are usually adverbs of manner. Adverbs without any particular ending are generally adverbs of manner, time, or place.

# I. Adverbs Derived from Adjectives

Adverbs ending in **-mente** tell how something is done. They are formed by adding the suffix **-mente** to the feminine or to the invariable form of the adjective.

>    *lenta* → lentamente          (slow → slowly)
>    *alegre* → alegremente        (joy → joyfully)

---

**TIP BOX**

Adverbs ending in **-mente** are usually equivalent to the English suffix *-ly*. They are usually adverbs of manner because they denote the way in which something is done.

   When two or more adverbs ending in **-mente** modify the same word, only the last adverb in the series retains the ending **-mente**, while the others remain in the feminine adjective form.

**Example**

> El estudiante hizo su tarea <u>rápida</u> y <u>correctamente</u>.
> *The student did his homework fast and correctly.*

---

**Exercise 1.** Rewrite the following sentences replacing the word in bold by an adverb ending in **-mente.**

**Example**

> Todos comimos en el restaurante **con gusto.**
> *Todos comimos en el restaurante **gustosamente.***

1. El profesor habla **con rapidez**. _____.
2. Los gallos pelean **con violencia**. _____.
3. El pianista toca **con suavidad**. _____.
4. El jefe habla con sus empleados **de manera cortés**. _____.
5. El niño respondió a su maestro **de manera inteligente**. _____.
6. El padre juega con su hijo **con cariño.** _____.

**Exercise 2.** Combine the following elements to form sentences.

**Example**

> coches/circular/lento: *Los coches circulan lentamente.*

1. cantante/cantar/estupendo: _____.
2. María/simple/desear/invitarte/fiesta: _____.
3. niños/jugar/alegre: _____.
4. obra de teatro/ser/absoluto/fantástico: _____.
5. estudiantes/protestar/enérgico: _____.
6. profesora/hablar/suave: _____.

**Exercise 3.** Transform the following adjectives to adverbs according to the model.

**Example**

    hermoso → hermosamente

    1. largo _____
    2. sincero _____
    3. alegre _____
    4. absoluto _____
    5. discreto _____
    6. secreto _____
    7. rápido _____
    8. frecuente _____
    9. enorme _____
  10. gentil _____
  11. loco _____

# II. Other Adverbs

Other adverbs, or those that do not have any particular ending, are varied in their function. Those adverbs may denote the **way** (adverb of manner), **the intensity or degree** (adverb of degree), the **time** (adverb of time), and the **place** (adverb of place) in which or where something is done.

---

**TIP BOX**

An adjective may act as an adverb when used with an intransitive verb or with a verb that expresses a state or condition. The adjective modifies both the subject and the verb simultaneously and agrees with the subject.

**Example**

    Juan y María llegaron muy <u>contentos</u>.
    *Juan and María arrived very happy.*

---

## A. Adverbs of Manner

Study the following examples.

    **así** (*so, like this, like that, like what, thus*)

    —¿Por qué te pones **así**?
    *"Why do you get worked up like that?"*

    —¿Cómo **así**?
    *"Like what?"*

—**Así**, de mal genio.
*"Like in a bad mood."*

—Lo siento, pero **así** soy yo.
*"I am sorry, but that's the way I am."*

**bien** *(well, good)*

—Hola, ¿cómo estás?
*"Hello, how are you?"*

—**Bien**, gracias.
*"Well, thanks."*

—¿Dónde aprendiste español?
*"Where did you learn Spanish?"*

—En Costa Rica.
*"In Costa Rica."*

—Hablas muy **bien**.
*"You speak [it] very well."*

**como** *(like, as...as, about, around)*

—Ese queso se ve delicioso.
*"That cheese looks delicious."*

—Sí, sabe **como** a queso Manchego, ¿no?
*"Yes, it tastes a bit like 'Manchego' cheese, doesn't it?"*

—Pero es blanco **como** el queso fresco.
*"But, it is white like farmer cheese."*

—¿Quién lo trajo?
*"Who brought it?"*

—Lo trajo Liliana esta mañana **como** a las ocho.
*"Liliana brought it this morning around eight."*

**despacio** *(slowly)*

—¿Puedes hablar más **despacio**?
*"Can you speak more slowly?"*

---

## TIP BOX
**Despacio** is equivalent to *lentamente*.

---

**mal** *(badly)*

Los niños se portaron **mal** anoche.
*The children behaved badly last night.*

**pronto** (*soon, quickly*)

—¡Ven **pronto** que me muero por verte!
*"Come soon. I am dying to see you!"*

—¡Iré lo más **pronto** que pueda!
*"I will come as soon as possible!"*

**Exercise 4.** Underline the adjectives once and the adverbs twice.

1.  Aquel hombre está como loco.
2.  No me siento bien.
3.  Quiero que vengas pronto.
4.  Los caracoles se desplazan despacio.
5.  Ese muchacho está pálido; anda muy mal de salud.
6.  No es fácil trabajar así.

**Exercise 5.** Replace the underlined words using the following adverbs of manner:
**pronto, mal, así, bien, como, despacio.**

## Example

Los invitados llegaron <u>rápidamente</u>.
*Los invitados llegaron pronto.*

1.  Tus amigos vendrán <u>en un momento</u>.
    _____

2.  A nosotros nos gusta caminar <u>lentamente</u>.
    _____

3.  Rosalba se siente <u>apenada</u> por lo que te dijo anoche.
    _____

4.  No me gusta que me hables <u>de esa manera</u>.
    _____

5.  No te preocupes, que estamos <u>sin problemas</u>.
    _____

6.  Lo hice <u>de la manera que</u> me indicaste.
    _____

# B. Adverbs of Degree

## algo

As an adverb, the word *algo* means **a little** or **somewhat**.

Rosalba no puede ir al paseo porque se encuentra **algo** indispuesta.
*Rosalba cannot go on the trip because she is somewhat indisposed.*

## apenas (*hardly, scarcely*)

Pobre hombre, **apenas** tiene para vivir.
*Poor man, he scarcely has enough to live.*

**bastante** *(enough, fairly, very, quit a bit)*

Anoche comimos **bastante**.
*Last night we ate quite a bit.*

La fiesta estuvo **bastante** divertida.
*It was a very nice party.*

**casi** *(almost, nearly)*

**Casi** todos los días voy al trabajo a pie.
*Almost every day I walk to work.*

Hoy, fui en coche y ¡**casi** me estrello!
*Today I went by car and I almost crashed!*

**cuánto** *(as, as much as)*

¡**Cuánto** sufrí al creer que te habías marchado!
*How much I suffered when I thought you had left!*

---

**TIP BOX**

The adverb **cuánto**, when followed by an adjective or an adverb, changes its form to **cuán**.

¡**Cuán** enorme fue mi sufrimiento cuando supe que te habías marchado!
*How great was my suffering when I realized you had left!*

¡**Cuán** lejos estás de creer que volveré a quererte!
*How far are you from believing that I will love you again!*

---

**demasiado** *(too, too much)*

—Vamos al restaurante *Gorditos*.
*"Let's go to* Gorditos *restaurant."*

—Ni loco, la comida allí es **demasiado** pesada, tiene mucha grasa.
*"Are you crazy? The food there is too rich. It has too much fat."*

—¿No será más bien, que tú comes **demasiado**?
*"Maybe the problem is that you eat too much."*

**más*** *(more, better, past)*

—Papá, ¿puedo comer postre?
*"Dad, may I eat dessert?"*

—Primero, come un poco **más** de carne.
*"First, eat a little more meat."*

—¡Papá! No me gusta la carne.
*"Dad, I don't like meat."*

—¿Te gusta **más** el pescado?
*"Do you like fish better?"*

---

*See Chapter 17, Comparatives and Superlatives.

—Sí.
*"Yes."*

—Apúrate, que son **más** de las ocho y tienes que acostarte.
*"Hurry up, it's past eight o'clock, and you must go to bed."*

**menos\*** (*less, least, fewer, fewest*)

Ahora que estoy más viejo, salgo **menos**.
*Now that I am older, I go out less.*

**mucho** (*a lot, much*) and **muy** (*very, much*)
The adverb **mucho** is used before a verb.

—Tengo **muchas** ganas de ir al concierto de jazz latino. ¿Vienes?
*"I wish a lot to see the Latin jazz concert. Do you want to come?"*

—Lo siento **mucho**, pero no me gusta **mucho** el jazz.
*"I'm very sorry, but I don't like jazz very much."*

The adverb **muy** is used before an adjective, before a participle acting as an adjective, and before an adverb.

## Example

El profesor de química es **muy famoso**.
*The chemistry professor is very famous.*

Es un hombre **muy respetado**.
*He is a very respected man.*

Pero dicta clase **muy despacio**.
*But he teaches class at a very slow pace.*

---

## TIP BOX

Note that the word **mucho** used as an adverb always follows the verb it qualifies. When modifying an adverb or an adjective, it is placed in front the adjectives *mejor, peor, mayor,* or *menor* and the adverbs *más, menos, antes,* or *después*. On the other hand, the adverb **muy** is NEVER followed by the adjectives *mejor, peor, mayor,* or *menor,* nor by the adverbs *más, menos, antes,* or *después*.

### Example

Es **mucho** mejor que jueguen en el parque.
*It is much better that they play in the park.*

Por las malas, es **mucho** peor para todos.
*By force, it is much worse for all of us.*

Su esposa es **mucho** mayor, ¿no te parece?
*His wife is much older, don't you think?*

Jorge sabe **mucho** más.
*Jorge knows much more.*

---

\*See Chapter 17, Comparatives and Superlatives.

Alicia **tiene** <u>**mucho**</u> menos dinero de lo que pensaba.
*Alicia has less money than I thought.*

Julio **llegó** <u>**mucho**</u> antes que nosotros.
*Julio arrived a long time before we did.*

Los invitados **llegaron** <u>**mucho**</u> después de lo previsto.
*The guests arrived long after it was predicted they would.*

**nada** *(not at all, by no means)*

Vivir en el país que no es el tuyo, no es <u>**nada**</u> fácil.
*To live in a country that is not yours is not at all easy.*

Lo que hiciste ayer, no me gusta <u>**nada**</u>.
*What you did yesterday, I didn't like at all.*

**poco** *(little)*

Ese coche cuesta <u>**poco**</u>.
*This car doesn't cost much.*

Es <u>**poco**</u> probable que te visite este fin de semana.
*Is unlikely that I will visit you this weekend.*

**sólo** *(only)*

Tengo <u>**sólo**</u> dieciocho años.
*I am only eighteen years old.*

**también** *(also)*

Yo <u>**también**</u> estoy cansado.
*I am also tired.*

**tanto\* (tan)** *(as much as, as)*

No deberías comer <u>**tanto**</u>.
*You shouldn't eat so much.*

**Exercise 6.** Underline the adjectives once and the adverbs twice.

1. Hay apenas cinco naranjas en la mesa.
2. Hay muy poca gente en el parque.
3. Tú comes muy poco, menos de 400 calorías diarias.
4. Tengo demasiados amigos en la universidad.
5. ¡Cuán contento me siento hoy!
6. A nosotros nos gustan más las verduras frescas que la carne.
7. Casi pierdo el examen de física; estaba bastante difícil.
8. Me siento algo enfermo y también un poco cansado.
9. No hay nada que me guste; sólo dormir.
10. Hay tanto por aprender que es mejor no dormir tanto.

*See Chapter 17, Comparatives and Superlatives.

## C. Adverbs of Time

**ahora** *(now, soon)*

**Ahora,** creo que tenías razón.
*Now, I think you were right.*

—¿Cuándo vienes?
*"When will you come?"*

—**Ahora** voy.
*"I'm coming soon."*

**anoche** *(last night)*

**Anoche** me encontré con tu amigo Carlos.
*Last night I bumped into your friend Carlos.*

**anteayer** *(the day before yesterday)*

**Anteayer** fuimos a la playa.
*The day before yesterday, we went to the beach.*

**antes** *(before)*

**Antes** del mediodía estaremos en casa.
*Before noon, we will be at home.*

**aún** *(still, yet)*

**Aún** sigo sin ganas de trabajar.
*I am still not in the mood to work.*

**ayer** *(yesterday)*

**Ayer** era el Día de los muertos y fuimos de paseo al cementerio.
*Yesterday it was the Day of the Dead, and so we took a trip to the cemetery.*

**cuando** *(when)*

**Cuando** tengas tiempo, ven y nos tomamos una cerveza.
*When you have a moment, let's have a beer together.*

**después** *(after)*

**Después** del cine fuimos a bailar.
*After the movie we went dancing.*

**entonces** *(then)*

En aquel **entonces**, vivíamos en el campo.
*At that time, we lived in the countryside.*

**hoy** *(today)*

**Hoy** vivimos todos en la ciudad, menos mi abuelo.
*Today we all live in the city, except my grandfather.*

**jamás** and **nunca** *(never)*

Mi abuelo **jamás** quiso dejar el campo.
*My grandfather never wanted to leave the countryside.*

**Nunca** se acostumbró a la ciudad.
*He never got used to living in the city.*

---

## TIP BOX

Note that **jamás** and **nunca** in negative sentences are equivalent to both *ever* and *never.*

No quiero visitarlos **jamás**.
*I don't want to visit you ever.*
*I never want to visit you.*

---

**luego** *(then)*

Llegamos a la casa y **luego** preparamos la cena.
*We came home and then we fixed dinner.*

**mañana** *(tomorrow)*

**Mañana** saldremos para Bolivia.
*Tomorrow we leave for Bolivia.*

**mientras** *(while)*

**Mientras** tengamos salud, lo demás no importa.
*While we have our health, everything else is unimportant.*

**siempre** *(always)*

**Siempre** me encuentro con tu tía en el cine.
*I always bump into your aunt at the movies.*

**tarde** *(late)*

Siempre llegamos **tarde** a clase.
*We always arrive late to class.*

**todavía** *(still, yet)* and **ya** *(already)*

—¿**Todavía** tienes tu colección de estampillas?
*"Do you still have your stamp collection?"*

—Sí, **todavía** la tengo.
*"Yes, I still have it."*

—¿**Ya** tienes la estampilla en honor al escritor Ernesto Sabato?
*"Do you already have the stamp in honor of the writer Ernesto Sabato?"*

—No, **todavía** no.
*"No, not yet."*

**Exercise 7.** Underline the adjectives once and the adverbs twice.

1. Anteayer estuvimos en la casa de mis tíos. Nunca antes había estado en la casa de ellos.
2. Antes, cuando niña, siempre jugaba en el parque. En aquel entonces tenía ocho años.
3. Anoche, aún después de visitarte seguía extrañándote.
4. Ayer amanecí contento; hoy no lo estoy.
5. Mañana iremos a la playa en la mañana y luego, tarde en la noche, iremos a bailar.
6. Hoy todavía me siento un poco enfermo; ahora no podré salir contigo.
7. Luego te invito a mi casa; ahora vamos a comer un helado.
8. No he ido jamás a aquel restaurante. ¿Vamos?
9. Todavía tengo un poco de dinero; yo te invito.
10. Mientras comíamos llegó Lucía con su estúpido novio.
11. Ya es hora de partir; es muy tarde.

## D. Adverbs of Place

**abajo** *(below)* and **arriba** *(above)*

**Abajo** el infierno, **arriba** el cielo.
*Hell is below. Heaven is above.*

**acá**, **aquí** *(here)* / **allí, ahí** *(there)* / **allá** *(over there)* / **donde** *(where)* / **cerca** *(near)* / **lejos** *(far)*

**Acá**, **donde** vivo, es muy verde.
*Here, where I live, is very green.*

**Cerca** del río están los guaduales, y **allá**, a lo **lejos**, la sierra nevada.
*Near the river are the bamboo forests, and over there, in the distance, are the snow-peaked mountains.*

**Ahí** en el valle está el pueblo, **allá** en el cerro, la finca de mi abuelo.
*There in the valley is the village; over there, on the hill, is my grandfather's farm.*

**alrededor** *(around)*

**Alrededor** del pueblo hay cultivos de café.
*Around the village there are coffee fields.*

**debajo** *(under)* / **encima** *(on top)* / **detrás** *(behind)* / **delante** *(in front of)*

—¡Lola! ¿Dónde pusiste mis libros?
*"Lola, where did you put my books?"*

—Los puse **encima** de la mesa.
*"I put them on the table."*

—No, no están.
*"They are not there."*

—Entonces, búscalos **debajo** de la mesa.
*"Then, look for them under the table."*

—No, tampoco están.
*"No, they are not there either."*

—¡Míralos! Están ahí bajo tus narices.
*"Look at them! They are there right under your nose."*

—¿Dónde?
*"Where?"*

—**Detrás** de ti.
*"Behind you."*

—No los veo.
*"I don't see them."*

—¿Estás ciego? Los tienes **delante** y no los ves.
*"Are you blind? You have them right in front of you and you don't see them!"*

**dentro** *(inside)* and **fuera** *(outside)*

¡Qué desespero! **Dentro** de la casa hace un calor infernal y **fuera** un frío glacial.
*How frustrating! Inside the house it's hellishly hot and outside it's as cold as ice!*

**Exercise 8.** Underline the adjectives once and the adverbs twice.

1.  Cerca de tu casa hay un edificio grande.
2.  Allá a lo lejos veo un pájaro enorme.
3.  Abajo está el sótano oscuro y frío y arriba el ático.
4.  Ven acá, a mi lado, donde pueda verte.
5.  La Tierra gira alrededor del Sol.
6.  Las manzanas rojas están encima de la mesa.
7.  Detrás de mi casa hay un parque muy lindo.
8.  ¡Eres muy desordenado! Busca tus medias debajo de la cama.
9.  Delante de nosotros hay un coche sospechoso.
10. ¡No dejes la leche fresca fuera de la nevera!
11. Cuando oigo las noticias de la guerra siento una tristeza inmensa dentro de mí.

## E. Adverbial Expressions

- **Adverbial Expressions of Manner**

| | |
|---|---|
| **a ciegas** | *blindly* |
| **a cuestas** | *at the expense of* |
| **a diestra y siniestra** | *disorderly* |
| **a escondidas** | *secretly* |
| **a oscuras** | *in the dark* |
| **a la moda** | *stylish, in vogue* |
| **al revés** | *upside down, just the opposite* |
| **de buena gana** | *of good will* |
| **de golpe** | *suddenly, fast* |
| **de memoria** | *by heart* |
| **de mala gana** | *unwillingly* |
| **de prisa** | *fast* |
| **de pronto** | *suddenly* |

| de repente | suddenly |
| en resumen | in conclusion, in general |
| en vano | in vain |
| por desgracia | unfortunately |
| sobre todo | above all, especially |

- **Adverbial Expressions of Time**

| de ahora en adelante | hereafter, from here on |
| al anochecer | tonight, at dusk |
| de antemano | beforehand, before |
| de día | during daytime |
| de la noche a la mañana | overnight |
| de la tarde | afternoon, P.M. |
| de mañana | since morning; morningtime |
| de noche | at night, nightime |
| de vez en cuando | sometimes, once in a while |
| al fin | at last, finally |
| pasado mañana | the day after tomorrow |
| por ahora | presently, for now |
| por último | at last, finally |

- **Adverbial Expressions of Place**

| a la derecha | to the right |
| a la izquierda | to the left |
| de arriba a bajo | from top to bottom |
| de dónde | where... from? |
| dentro de | within, inside, indoors |
| en alguna parte | somewhere |
| en casa | at home |
| en cualquier parte | anywhere |
| en el extranjero | abroad |
| en ninguna parte | nowhere |
| en otra parte | elsewhere |
| en todas partes | everywhere |
| por aquí | this way |
| en ninguna parte | nowhere |

**Exercise 9.** Answer the following questions using the appropriate adverbial expression.

1. Mi hijo se aprendió la poesía _____. *(by heart)*
2. María le respondió a su madre _____. *(unwillingly)*
3. Los presos fueron encarcelados _____. *(abroad)*
4. Todos corren _____ para llegar a tiempo. *(fast)*
5. _____, descubrió que ya no era un niño. *(finally)*
6. Todos los empleados hicieron su trabajo _____. *(in vain)*

# Chapter 10

# THE SUBJUNCTIVE

There are three **moods** in Spanish —the indicative, the subjunctive, and the imperative,* which is used for direct commands.

**Quisiera tener un pescado.**
*(I would like to have a fish.)*

### What Is the Subjunctive?

**The subjunctive** is used in hypothetical or subjective situations. The indicative, on the other hand, is always used to express a more objective or "real" action or situation.

The **subjunctive** is often used when we **desire** for something to occur, when we want to **influence** someone, when we **doubt** something, or when we express **emotions**.

### Examples

#### Subjunctive Mood

- Desire or Influence

  El jefe quiere que **trabajemos** más.
  *The boss wants us to work harder.*

- Hope

  Los estudiantes quieren que no **haya** clase el lunes.
  *The students hope that there is no class on Monday.*

- Emotion

  Es maravilloso que **sea** fiesta hoy.
  *It is wonderful that it is a holiday today.*

- Doubt

  Tal vez **llueva** mañana.
  *It may rain tomorrow.*

*See Chapter 12, Commands.

### Indicative Mood

El jefe dice que **tenemos** que trabajar más.
*The boss says that we have to work harder.*

Los estudiantes **están** contentos porque no **hay** clase el lunes.
*The students are happy because there is no class on Monday.*

Hoy **es** fiesta.
*Today is a holiday.*

Mañana **va** a llover.
*It will rain tomorrow.*

---

## TIP BOX
**Some grammar definitions**
A **mood** indicates the point of view of the speaker toward what he or she is saying.

The **tense of a verb** means the time when the action of the verb takes place (present, past, or future).

The **aspect** refers to the manner in which a verb's action is distributed through the time-space continuum. The aspect may be **perfect** or **imperfect**. Perfect indicates that the action is seen by the speaker as complete, as ended, or as a fact. Imperfect indicates that the action is seen by the speaker as incomplete.

---

# I. The Present Subjunctive

## A. Regular Formation of the Present Subjunctive

The present of the subjunctive is formed by using the root of the conjugation of the first person (**yo**) of a verb in the present tense of the indicative plus the corresponding verb endings for the subjunctive.

|  | Verb Endings of the Present Subjunctive | |
|---|---|---|
|  | **-ar** | **-er / -ir** |
| yo | -e | -a |
| tú | -es | -as |
| él, ella, usted | -e | -a |
| nosotros/as | -emos | -amos |
| vosotros/as | -éis | -áis |
| ellos, ellas, ustedes | -en | -an |

**TIP BOX**

To conjugate the verb **tener** *(to have)* in the present tense of the subjunctive, use the root of the first person of the present tense of the indicative: **Yo <u>teng</u>o**.

Add to the root **teng-** the corresponding verb ending for the verbs that end in **-er**: *-a,-as, -a, -amos, -áis, -an.*

| Regular Formation of the Present Subjunctive | | **bail-ar**<br>*(to dance)* | **com-er**<br>*(to eat)* | **viv-ir**<br>*(to live)* |
|---|---|---|---|---|
| **Present of the Indicative** | yo | bail-**o** | com-**o** | viv-**o** |
| **Present of the Subjunctive** | yo | bail-**e** | com-**a** | viv-**a** |
| | tú | bail-**es** | com-**as** | viv-**as** |
| | él, ella, usted | bail-**e** | com-**a** | viv-**a** |
| | nosotros(as) | bail-**emos** | com-**amos** | viv-**amos** |
| | vosotros(as) | bail-**éis** | com-**áis** | viv-**áis** |
| | ustedes, ellos, ellas | bail-**en** | com-**an** | viv-**an** |

**Exercise 1. Part A.** Complete the following sentences in the present of the indicative and underline the root of the verb.

**Example**

Yo (tener) <u>teng</u>o una amiga increíble.

1. María (bailar) _____ salsa todas las noches.
2. Carmen y Carlos (caminar) _____ por el parque.
3. Julián (cocinar) _____ para sus amigos.
4. Carmen (compartir) _____ las mismas aficiones de Julián.
5. Todos ellos (vivir) _____ en el mismo barrio.
6. Carmen (ver) _____ por las tardes la televisión en español.
7. Carlos (poner) _____ la música demasiado alta por las mañanas.
8. María (hacer) _____ deporte con Carmen.

**Part B.** Using the preceding underlined roots complete the following sentences in the present subjunctive.

### Example

Es maravilloso que (tener/tú ) <u>teng</u>as una amiga increíble.

1. María quiere que (bailar/tú) _____ con ella esta noche.
2. Carlos le dice a María que (caminar) _____ más rápidamente.
3. Es fantástico que Julián (cocinar) _____ para sus amigos.
4. Es bueno que Carmen (compartir) _____ las mismas aficiones de Julián.
5. Es una pena que no todos (vivir) _____ en el mismo barrio.
6. María no quiere que Carmen (ver) _____ tanta televisión.
7. Los vecinos le piden a Carlos que no (poner) _____ la música tan alta.
8. María no cree que Carmen (hacer) _____ suficiente deporte.

# B. Irregular Formation of the Present Subjunctive

Not all verbs have a regular formation. Verbs ending in **-gar, -guar, -car, -zar,** and the following verbs are irregular:

| dar<br>(*to give*) | estar<br>(*to be*) | haber<br>(*to have*) |
|---|---|---|
| ir<br>(*to go*) | saber<br>(*to know*) | ser<br>(*to be*) |

**a.** Verbs ending in **-gar, -guar, -car,** and **-zar** do not have the same root in the first person either of the present indicative or in the present subjunctive. These verbs need to adopt the phonetic rules as shown in the examples below.

Verbs that end in **-gar** take the letter **u** after **g**:
    yo juego  →   yo jue**gu**e

Verbs that end in **-guar** take a **ü**:
    yo desaguo  →   yo desa**gü**e

Verbs that end in **-car** change to **qu**:
    yo busco  →   yo bus**qu**e

Verbs that end in **-zar,** by an orthographic convention, change the **z** to a **c**:
    yo almuerzo  →   yo almuer**c**e

| Present Subjunctive of Verbs Ending in *-gar, -guar, -car, -zar* | | peg-ar *(to hit)* | averigu-ar *(to investigate)* | busc-ar *(to look for)* | rez-ar *(to pray)* |
|---|---|---|---|---|---|
| **Present of the Indicative** | yo | peg-**o** | averigu-**o** | busc-**o** | rez-**o** |
| **Present of the Subjunctive** | yo<br>tú<br>él, ella, usted<br>nosotros(as)<br>vosotros(as)<br>ellos, ellas, ustedes | peg**u**-e<br>peg**u**-es<br>peg**u**-e<br>peg**u**-emos<br>peg**u**-éis<br>peg**u**-en | averig**ü**-e<br>averig**ü**-es<br>averig**ü**-e<br>averig**ü**-emos<br>averig**ü**-éis<br>averig**ü**-en | bus**qu**-e<br>bus**qu**-es<br>bus**qu**-e<br>bus**qu**-emos<br>bus**qu**-éis<br>bus**qu**-en | rec-e<br>rec-es<br>rec-e<br>rec-emos<br>rec-éis<br>rec-en |

| Other Verbs Following the Same Pattern | | | |
|---|---|---|---|
| **-gar** | **-guar** | **-car** | **-zar** |
| agregar *(to add)*<br>entregar *(to deliver)*<br>jugar *(to play)*<br>llegar *(to arrive)*<br>negar *(to deny)*<br>refregar *(to scrub)*<br>regar *(to water)*<br>rogar *(to beg)* | apaciguar *(to appease)*<br>desaguar *(to drain)*<br>menguar *(to diminish)* | cerrar *(to close)*<br>machacar *(to pound)*<br>picar *(to sting)*<br>buscar *(to search)*<br>salpicar *(to sprinkle)*<br>tocar *(to touch)* | abrazar *(to embrace)*<br>alcanzar *(to reach)*<br>almorzar *(to have lunch)*<br>empezar *(to begin)*<br>enderezar *(to straighten)* |

**b.** Verbs **haber, ir, saber, ser, dar, estar** are extremely irregular and they must be memorized.

| Present Subjunctive of the Verbs *haber, ir, saber, ser, dar, estar* | haber *(to have)* | ir *(to go)* | saber *(to know)* | ser *(to be)* | dar *(to give)* | estar *(to be)* |
|---|---|---|---|---|---|---|
| yo | haya | vaya | sepa | sea | dé | esté |
| tú | hayas | vayas | sepas | seas | des | estés |
| él, ella, usted | haya | vaya | sepa | sea | dé | esté |
| nosotros(as) | hayamos | vayamos | sepamos | seamos | demos | estemos |
| vosotros(as) | hayáis | vayáis | sepáis | seáis | deis | estéis |
| ellos, ellas, ustedes | hayan | vayan | sepan | sean | den | estén |

**Exercise 2.** Complete the following sentences in the present subjunctive.

1.  Quiero que (dormir/tú) _____ más, para que mañana trabajes mejor.
2.  Me alegro de que (ir/vosotros) _____ a mi boda.
3.  Es necesario que (pagar/usted) _____ sus facturas.
4.  Les aconsejo que (ustedes empezar) _____ a estudiar pronto.
5.  Es importante que (cerrar/ella) _____ la puerta antes de salir.
6.  No creo que (saber/nosotros) _____ la verdad de la historia.
7.  Es mejor que (agregar/usted) _____ la propina a la cuenta.
8.  Es necesario que (desaguar/usted) _____ la piscina.
9.  Es importante que (refregar/vosotros) _____ los platos todos los días.
10. Que maravilla que (ir/tú) _____ a Madrid con tu esposa.
11. No creo que (buscar/ella) _____ un apartamento para vivir con su novio.
12. Ojalá que (almorzar/ellas) _____ con sus padres.
13. Es mejor que (dar/ella) _____ el dinero para la matrícula pronto.
14. Quiero que (rogar/tú) _____ por mí en la iglesia.
15. Le aconsejo al presidente que (apaciguar/él) _____ los manifestantes.
16. Me alegro de que (entregar/tú) _____ tus trabajos.

# C. Uses of the Subjunctive

## The Subjunctive in Subordinate Noun Clauses

The subjunctive is used in subordinate clauses when the main clause indicates **influence, desire,** or **doubt.**

---

**TIP BOX**

**What Is a Subordinate Clause?**

**Subordinate clauses** are dependent clauses. This means that the sentence cannot stand alone. In Spanish there are three different types depending on their grammatical function as a noun (noun clauses), as an adjective (adjective or relative clauses), or as an adverb (adverbial clauses).

---

**a.** The subjunctive in sentences that express **influence** or **desire.** When the subject in the main clause expresses a desire to influence the subject in the subordinate clause to perform an action, the use of the subjunctive is required in the subordinate clause.

**Yo no quiero que tú <u>andes</u> tan sucia.**
*(I don't want you to go around so dirty.)*

### Example

El profesor quiere que María **<u>estudie</u>** más español.
*The teacher wants María to study more Spanish.*

In this example, **el profesor** wants to influence the behavior of the subject in the subordinate clause, **María,** to perform the action (**que estudie más**).

Different verbs and expressions are used to express desire or influence. When those verbs or expressions are present in the main clause, the use of the subjunctive is required in the subordinate clause. The following verbs and expressions are used in this case.

---

## TIP BOX
Note that the verb in the **main clause** is always in the **indicative** mood.

---

| Verbs that Express Influence or Desire | | |
|---|---|---|
| **Verb** | **Example** | **Translation** |
| aconsejar (*to advise*) | Te aconsejo que vengas. | *I advise you to come.* |
| decir (*to say*) | Te digo que te apresures. | *I tell you to hurry.* |
| dejar (*to leave*) | Deja que se vaya. | *Let him go.* |
| desear (*to desire*) | Luis desea que Lucía venga. | *Luis wants Lucía to come.* |
| esperar (*to expect*) | Espero que cumplas tu promesa. | *I expect you to keep your promise.* |
| exigir (*to demand*) | Él exige que le des una explicación. | *He demands that you give him an explanation.* |
| mandar (*to order*) | El cura le manda que rece. | *The priest orders him to pray.* |
| ordenar (*to order*) | El capitán ordena que zarpemos. | *The captain orders us to set sail.* |
| pedir (*to request, to ask*) | Me pide que le disculpe. | *He asks me to forgive him.* |
| permitir (*to allow*) | No te permito que la insultes. | *I do not allow you to insult her.* |
| preferir (*to prefer*) | Prefiero que se queden. | *I prefer you to stay.* |
| prohibir (*to forbid*) | Te prohibo que salgas con Juan. | *I forbid you to go out with Juan.* |
| querer (*to want*) | Quiero que te cases conmigo. | *I want you to marry me.* |
| recomendar (*to recommend*) | Te recomiendo que te olvides de ella. | *I recommend you forget about her.* |
| rogar (*to beg*) | Les ruega que rectifiquen la ley. | *He begs them to amend the law.* |
| sugerir (*to suggest*) | Mi madre me sugiere que estudie más. | *My mother suggests that I study more.* |

| Expressions that Express Influence or Desire | | |
|---|---|---|
| **Expressions** | **Example** | **Translation** |
| Es esencial... | que sigas los consejos del médico. | **It is essential** *for you to follow the doctor's advice.* |
| Es importante... | que prestes atención. | **It is important** *for you to pay attention.* |
| Es mejor... | que nos demos prisa. | **It is better** *for us to hurry.* |
| Es necesario... | que se cumplan las normas. | **It is necessary** *to comply with the rules.* |
| Es preciso... | que me ayudes. | **It is essential** *that you to help me.* |
| Es urgente... | que pagues la cuenta del gas. | **It is urgent** *that you pay the gas bill.* |
| Es indispensable... | que llames al médico. | **It is essential** *that you call the doctor.* |
| Es aconsejable... | que recojas tu desorden. | **It is advisable** *that you pick up your mess.* |

**Exercise 3.** Complete the following sentences in the present subjunctive. Imagine you are a teacher and it is your first day of class. Explain to your students the class rules. Use verbs and expressions that express influence or desire.

## Example

preparar la tarea todos los días
*Es esencial que ustedes preparen la tarea todos los días.*

1. Llegar puntuales a clase

   _____

2. Corregir los ejercicios

   _____

3. Repasar con regularidad

   _____

4. Escribir los trabajos en procesador de texto

   _____

5. Leer con cuidado el programa

   _____

6. Participar en las actividades comunes

   _____

7. Estudiar con anticipación los temas que se van a ver en clase

   _____

8. Hacer preguntas para aclarar dudas

   _____

9. Participar en los trabajos en equipo

   _____

10. Practicar antes y después de clase

    _____

**Exercise 4.** You and your parents are packing yours bags to go on vacation and there still is much to do.

## Example

comprar aspirinas
*Quiero que compres aspirinas.*

1. Ir al banco

   _____

2. Preparar tu ropa

   _____

3. Despedirte de tu hermana

   _____

4. Recoger los billetes de avión

   _____

5. Hacer la reserva del hotel

   _____

6. Regar las plantas

   _____

7. Llevar el perro a casa de tu primo

   _____

8. Cancelar la entrega del periódico

   _____

9. Avisar en la oficina de correos que estaremos de vacaciones

   _____

10. Empacar las vitaminas y los medicamentos

    _____

**b.** The subjunctive in sentences that express **doubt.** When the subject in the main clause expresses **doubt,** the subordinate clause requires the use of the subjunctive.

**Yo dudo que la perrita <u>quiera</u> quedarse.**
_(I doubt that the nice doggie would want to stay.)_

### Example

El profesor duda que María **<u>venga</u>** mañana a clase.
_The teacher doubts that María will come to class tomorrow._

(Yo) No creo que los unicornios **<u>existan</u>**.
_I don't believe that unicorns exist._

In the first example, **el profesor** doubts if **María** is coming to class tomorrow. In the second example the subject, **Yo,** doubts the existence of unicorns. In both examples the main clause expresses _doubt_. This is why the verb in the subordinate clause is in the subjunctive.

---

## TIP BOX

When the main clause expresses **certainty** or a **belief**, the subordinate clause should be in the indicative.

El profesor **no duda** que María **viene** mañana.
_The teacher has no doubt that María is coming tomorrow._

**Creo** que los unicornios **existen**.
_I believe unicorns exist._

**Pienso** que **tienes** razón.
_I think you are right._

In Spanish, different verbs and expressions are used to express **doubt**. When those expressions or verbs are present in the main clause, the use of the subjunctive is required in the subordinate clause. Those verbs and expressions are shown in the table that follows.

| Verbs that Express *Doubt* (Subjunctive) | | |
|---|---|---|
| **Verbs** | **Example** | **Translation** |
| no creer *(not to believe)* | No creo que tenga tiempo para comer contigo. | *I don't believe I will have time to eat with you.* |
| dudar *(to doubt)* | Nosotros dudamos que haya oro en esa cueva. | *We doubt that there is gold in that cave.* |
| no estar seguro de *(not to be certain)* | Eva no está segura que su madre pueda venir. | *Eva is not certain that her mother can come.* |
| no pensar *(not to think)* | No pienso que sea buena idea invitarlo a la fiesta. | *I don't think it's a good idea to invite him to the party.* |
| no parecer* *(not to seem)* | No nos parece que tengas razón. | *It doesn't seem to us that you are right.* |
| * This verb is conjugated as *gustar.* See Chapter 15. | | |

| Expressions that Express *Doubt* (Subjunctive) | | |
|---|---|---|
| **Expressions** | **Example** | **Translation** |
| Es dudoso… | que llueva mañana. | *It is doubtful that it will rain tomorrow.* |
| Es improbable… | que haga sol hoy. | *It is unlikely that it will be sunny today.* |
| Es posible… | que todos los empleados sean despedidos. | *It is possible that all the employees will be fired.* |
| Es probable… | que te compre un regalo si te portas bien. | *If you behave, it is likely that I will buy you a gift.* |
| No es cierto… | que todos los políticos sean corruptos. | *It is not true that all the politicians are corrupt.* |
| No es claro… | que su marido sea muy inteligente. | *It is not clear that your husband is very intelligent.* |
| No es evidente… | que la economía se esté recuperando. | *It is not evident that the economy is recovering.* |
| No es obvio… | que los avances técnicos mejoren la calidad de vida. | *It is not obvious that the technological advances improve the quality of life.* |
| No es posible… | que volvamos juntos. Ya no te quiero. | *It's not possible for us to get back together. I don't love you anymore.* |
| No es seguro… | que apruebe el examen de matemáticas. | *It is not certain that I will approve the Math exam.* |
| No es verdad… | que me lo pase jugando todo el día en la computadora. | *It is not true that I spend all day long playing on the computer.* |
| Puede ser que… | vayamos de vacaciones a las Islas Canarias este verano. | *Maybe we will go to the Canary Islands for vacation this summer.* |

Note that most of the verbs and expressions that express **doubt** have their corresponding opposite forms that express **certainty** or **belief**. In these cases the use of the **indicative mood** is required.

| Verbs that Express *Certainty* and *Belief* (Indicative) | | |
|---|---|---|
| **Verbs** | **Example** | **Translation** |
| creer *(to believe)* | Creo que tengo tiempo para comer contigo. | *I believe I will have time to eat with you.* |
| no dudar *(not to doubt)* | Nosotros no dudamos que hay oro en esa cueva. | *We don't doubt that there is gold in that cave.* |
| estar seguro de *(to be certain)* | Eva está segura que su madre puede venir. | *Eva is certain that her mother can come.* |
| pensar *(to think)* | Pienso que es buena idea invitarlo a la fiesta. | *I think it's a good idea to invite him to the party.* |
| parecer* *(to seem)* | Nos parece que tienes razón. | *It seems to us that you are right.* |

\* This verb is conjugated as *gustar*. See Chapter 15.

| Expressions that Express *Certainty* and *Belief* (Indicative) | | |
|---|---|---|
| **Expressions** | **Example** | **Translation** |
| Es cierto... | que todos los políticos son corruptos. | *It is true that all the politicians are corrupt.* |
| Es claro... | que su marido es muy inteligente. | *It is clear that your husband is very intelligent.* |
| Es evidente... | que la economía se está recuperando. | *It is evident that the economy is recovering.* |
| Es obvio... | que los avances técnicos mejoran la calidad de vida. | *It is obvious that the technological advances improve the quality of life.* |
| Es seguro... | que aprobaré el examen de matemáticas. | *It is not certain I will approve the Math exam.* |
| Es verdad... | que me lo paso jugando todo el día en la computadora. | *It is true that I spend all day long playing on the computer.* |

## TIP BOX

**Special Attention: Interrogative Sentences!**

In interrogative sentences the speaker's intent, viewpoint, or attitude determines whether the subjunctive or the indicative is to be used in the dependent clause after expressions of certainty or belief. If the speaker **doubts**, the verb in the subordinate clause should be in the subjunctive. But if the speaker **knows** or **has an opinion** about what he or she is asking, the verb in the subordinate clause should be in the indicative.

**Example**

¿Estás seguro de que Javier **tiene** hambre?
*Are you sure Javier is hungry?*

In this sentence the speaker has an opinion about whether Javier is or is not hungry. For this reason the indicative is used.

¿Estás seguro de que Javier **tenga** hambre?
*Are you sure Javier might be hungry?*

In this sentence the speaker has no opinion about whether Javier is or is not hungry. This is why the subjunctive is used here.

**Exercise 5.** Juan has many debatable opinions. Rewrite his opinions using expressions of doubt.

**Example**

*Juan:*—En Estados Unidos los estudiantes beben demasiado.
—*No estoy seguro de que los estudiantes **beban** demasiado.*

1. —Los políticos dicen siempre la verdad.
   —_____

2. —El presidente no cobra suficiente dinero.
   —_____

3. —Los ciudadanos no pagamos muchos impuestos.
   —_____

4. —Los programas de televisión son muy educativos.
   —_____

5. —Soy el mejor trabajador de mi empresa.
   —_____

6. —Los vinos alemanes son los mejores.
   —_____

7. —El fútbol americano es el deporte más inofensivo.
   —_____

8. —El precio de la gasolina ha estado estable en los últimos diez años.
   —_____

9. —Sólo los niños deben usar protector solar.
   —_____

10. —La pizza es un alimento con bajo contenido de grasas.
    —_____

**Exercise 6.** Imagine that María wants to go to the beach with her friend Roberto. Roberto doesn't want to go and he is absolutely sure of it. Complete the following sentences using the subjunctive or the indicative.

## Example

Estoy seguro/ haber / mucha gente en la playa
*Estoy seguro de que hay mucha gente en la playa.*

1. No creo / ser / sano tomar el sol

   _____

2. Es posible / encontrarse / con tu ex-novio

   _____

3. No es posible / gustar / ir a un lugar con tanta gente

   _____

4. Es evidente / tener / ganas de ver a Federico, tu ex-novio

   _____

5. Es posible / preferir / quedarme solo en casa

   _____

6. Creo / estar / celoso de Federico

   _____

7. Creo / no tener / traje de baño

   _____

8. Me parece / ir a llover / esta tarde

   _____

9. Prefiero / quedarnos / en casa

   _____

10. Quizá / nosotros / poder ir / mañana

    _____

**c.** The subjunctive in sentences that express **emotion**.
When the subject in the main clause expresses **emotion,** the subordinate clause requires the use of the subjunctive.

## Example

Me alegro mucho de que María **venga** a clase.
*I am very glad that María is coming to class.*

Es terrible que **haya** guerra.
*It is terrible that there is war.*

**Es maravilloso que <u>pueda</u> andar limpia.**
*(It's wonderful that I can go around clean.)*

In Spanish, different verbs and expressions are used to express **emotion**. When those expressions or verbs are present in the main clause, the use of the subjunctive is required in the subordinate clause. Those verbs and expressions are shown in the table that follows.

| Verbs that Express *Emotion* | | |
|---|---|---|
| **Verbs** | **Example** | **Translation** |
| alegrarse *(to be happy)* | Me alegro que puedas venir. | *I am happy that you can come.* |
| enojar* *(to make angry)* | ¿Te enoja que haga ruido? | *Does it make you angry that I make noise?* |
| gustar* *(to like)* | Me gusta que sonrías. | *I like that you smile.* |
| lamentar *(to regret)* | Luis lamenta mucho que no vengas a la fiesta. | *Luis regrets a lot that you cannot come to the party.* |
| maravillar* *(to astonish)* | Nos maravilla que seas tan valiente. | *It astonishes us that you are so brave.* |
| molestar* *(to bother)* | ¿Os molesta que escuche música? | *Does it bother you if I listen to music?* |
| quejarse *(to complain)* | Inés se queja de que no la escuches. | *Inés complains that you don't listen to her.* |
| sentir *(to be sorry)* | Siento mucho que no te puedas quedar a comer. | *I am very sorry that you cannot stay for dinner.* |
| sorprender* *(to be surprised )* | Nos sorprende que seas tan indelicado. | *It surprises us that you are so inconsiderate.* |

\* These verbs are conjugated as *gustar*. See Chapter 15.

| Expressions that Express *Emotion* | | |
|---|---|---|
| **Expression** | **Example** | **Translation** |
| Es difícil... | que podamos sobrevivir con tan poco dinero. | *It's difficult for us to survive with so little money.* |
| Es sorprendente... | que tengas tanto éxito. | *It's surprising that you have so much success.* |
| Es mejor... | que te relajes un poco. | *It's better if you relax a little bit.* |
| Es terrible... | que sufras tanto. | *It's terrible that you suffer so much.* |
| Es extraño... | que Luis nos llame; seguro que quiere un favor. | *It's strange for Luis to call us; he must need a favor.* |
| Es deplorable... | que comas como un cerdo. | *It's unfortunate that you eat like a pig.* |
| Es raro... | que él nos pida disculpas si es tan orgulloso. | *It's unusual for him to apologize since he is so proud.* |
| Es fácil... | que un político se convierta en un dictador. | *It is easy for a politician to become a dictator.* |
| Es estupendo... | que cumplas con tus promesas. | *It is wonderful that you keep your promises* |
| Es maravilloso... | que existas. | *It is marvelous that you exist.* |

| | | |
|---|---|---|
| Es agradable... | que aún te acuerdes de mí con cariño | *It's nice that you still remember me with love.* |
| Es bueno... | que te laves las manos antes de comer. | *It's good that you wash your hands before eating.* |
| Es interesante... | que el asesino sea el bueno de la película. | *It's interesting that the assassin is the good character in the movie.* |
| ¡Es el colmo... | que me grites de esa manera! | *It's unbelievable that you scream at me like that.* |
| Es increíble... | que por fin tengas un novio buena persona. | *It is incredible that finally you got yourself a nice boyfriend.* |
| Es normal... | que te enfermes si no te cuidas. | *It's normal for you to get sick if you don't take care of yourself.* |
| Es una lástima... | que Ana sea tan creída. | *It is a shame that Ana is so conceited.* |
| Es una pena | que tengamos que estudiar tanto. | *It is a shame we have to study so much.* |
| Es una desgracia... | que nuestro equipo favorito pierda siempre. | *It is disgraceful that our favorite team loses always.* |
| Es peor... | que no me digas la verdad. | *It is worse if you don't tell me the truth.* |
| Es vergonzoso... | que estés saliendo con otra mujer. | *It is shameful that you are going out with another woman.* |
| ¿Es natural... | que tenga hambre a toda hora? | *Is it natural that I feel hungry all the time?* |
| Es lamentable... | que no goces tu tiempo libre. | *It's deplorable that you don't enjoy your free time.* |
| Es malo... | que trabajes tanto. | *It's bad that you work so much.* |
| Es una suerte... | que te tenga a ti. | *It is lucky that I have you.* |

**Exercise 7.** Imagine that you are having an argument with one of your friends. You want to stress the negative aspects of his personality, but you also want to mention some of his virtues. Write six sentences using verbs and/or expressions of emotion. You can use the ideas in parenthesis or your own.

### Example

*Es el colmo que no escuches. Es estupendo que seas tan leal.*

1. _____ (eres sincero)
2. _____ (eres honrado)
3. _____ (eres de mal genio)
4. _____ (eres desordenado)
5. _____ (eres olvidadizo)
6. _____ (eres imprudente)
7. _____ (eres comprensivo)
8. _____ (eres entrometido)
9. _____ (eres divertido)
10. _____ (eres muy inteligente)

**Exercise 8.** Inspire yourself with the drawings and write a sentence choosing the expression that corresponds to what is shown in each frame: *es una suerte, es el colmo, es una desgracia, es increíble.*

1. _____

2. _____

3. _____

4. _____

## The Subjunctive in Adjectival Clauses or Relative Clauses

The adjectival or relative subordinate clauses modify nouns. When the noun that is modified is hypothetical and exists only in the mind of the speaker, the verb in the subordinate clause takes the subjunctive.

### Example

Necesito un profesor que **sepa** español.
*I need a teacher who knows Spanish.*

Busco un apartamento que **tenga** tres dormitorios.
*I am looking for an apartment that has three bedrooms.*

In these examples, the nouns that are modified by the subordinate clauses **profesor** and **apartamento** are hypothetical. They do not yet exist in the real world, but only in the mind of the speaker. The verbs in the subordinate clauses should therefore be in the subjunctive.

**Exercise 9.** Imagine that you want to meet someone to share your leisure time. Write six sentences describing the person that you are looking for.

### Example

(saber cocinar)
*Busco un amigo(a) que sepa cocinar.*

1.  (ser sincero)
    _____

2.  (tener tiempo para mí)
    _____

3.  (gustarle hablar y reír)
    _____

4.  (trabajar poco)
    _____

5.  (gozar la vida)
    _____

6.  (saber bailar)
    _____

7.  (gustarle leer)
    _____

8.  (no ser celoso)
    _____

9.  (ser chistoso)
    _____

10. (ser muy inteligente)
    _____

**Exercise 10.** Write three sentences describing the man in the woman's dream. Indicate that she would like him to be funny, rich, and smart. Then write three sentences describing her real husband (bald, serious, and poor).

1. Ella busca un hombre que sea guapo.

2. _____.

3. _____.

4. _____.

5. Ella se casa con un hombre que no es guapo.

6. _____.

7. _____.

8. _____.

**Exercise 11.** Imagine that you are looking for an apartment to share with a friend. Write six sentences describing the apartment you are looking for.

## Example

(tener dos dormitorios)
*Necesitamos (queremos, buscamos) un apartamento que tenga dos dormitorios.*

1. (tener una sala grande)

   _____

2. (estar bien ubicado)

   _____

3. (tener una cocina moderna)

   _____

4. (tener vista al mar)

   _____

5. (tener una sala amplia)

   _____

6. (tener garaje)

   _____

7. (tener portero)

   _____

8. (no ser costoso)
   _____

9. (estar en un último piso)
   _____

10. (ser claro)
    _____

**Exercise 12.** Complete the following text using the present subjunctive or present indicative.

Sonia y Javier _____ (tener) un apartamento en Houston que _____ (costar) mucho dinero. Ambos _____ (querer) una vida más divertida y _____ (aspirar) vender el apartamento que _____ (tener) en Estados Unidos y comprar uno en España. Sonia _____ (querer) que el apartamento _____ (estar) ubicado en la ciudad de Granada. Javier está de acuerdo, pero además _____ (querer) que el apartamento _____ (quedar) en el Albaicín, el antiguo barrio moro. Sonia _____ (desear) que _____ (tener) vista a la Sierra Nevada y a la Alhambra. Javier, también _____ (querer) que el apartamento no _____ (ser) ruidoso y _____ (tener) garaje.

## The Subjunctive in Independent Clauses

- The subjunctive is used in independent clauses in exclamatory sentences.

**Example**

¡**Muera** el rey!
*Death to the king!*

- In sentences that express **desire** after the expression **ojalá** (*I hope*).

**Example**

**Ojalá llegue** la primavera pronto.
*I hope spring will come soon.*

- When you want to express **doubt** after the expressions **tal vez, quizá, a lo mejor, acaso, probablemente** (*maybe*).

**Example**

**Tal vez vaya** a tu casa mañana.
*Maybe I will go tomorrow to your home.*

**Probablemente llueva** mañana.
*It might rain tomorrow.*

**Exercise 13.** Write six sentences about your possible plans for this summer using the expressions **tal vez, quizá, a lo mejor, probablemente**.

## Example

(ir de vacaciones a Madrid este verano)
*Tal vez (quizá, a lo mejor, probablemente) vaya de vacaciones a Madrid este verano.*

1. (trabajar durante el verano)
   _____

2. (ir a México este verano)
   _____

3. (tener que estudiar para los exámenes de doctorado)
   _____

4. (visitar a mi familia en España)
   _____

5. (tener suerte y poder [tú] venir a visitarme)
   _____

6. (comprar una casa este verano)
   _____

7. (jugar la final de la copa de fútbol)
   _____

8. (conseguir un perro)
   _____

9. (conducir a Montreal)
   _____

10. (ir al festival de cine en agosto)
    _____

## The Present Subjunctive in Adverbial Clauses

An adverbial subordinate clause acts as an adverb. These adverbial clauses normally modify the verb of the main clause of a sentence and are introduced by a conjunction. Adverbial subordinate clauses inform us about time, place, manner, condition, cause, purpose, and concession. An adverbial subordinate clause may either be in the indicative or subjunctive, depending on what is being expressed.

- **Dependent Adverbial Clauses of <u>Time</u>**

The following conjunctions introduce adverbial dependent clauses of time:

| | |
|---|---|
| **cuando** | *when* |
| **en cuanto** | *as soon as* |
| **tan pronto como** | *as soon as* |
| **antes de que** | *before* |

| | |
|---|---|
| **después de que** | *after* |
| **hasta que** | *until* |
| **luego que** | *soon after* |
| **mientras** | *while, when, as long as* |

Note that if the dependent adverbial clause expresses an action that does happen, has happened, or is certain to happen, the **indicative** is used.

### Example

Viajo **cuando tengo** dinero.
*I travel when I have money.*

Viajé **en cuanto recibí** el dinero.
*I traveled as soon as I received the money.*

But if the dependent adverbial clause expresses an action that it is uncertain, doubtful, or has not already happened, the **subjunctive** is used.

### Example

María vendrá a visitarnos **cuando tenga** tiempo.
*María will visit us when she has time.*

María vendrá a visitarnos **en cuanto pueda**.
*María will visit us as soon as she can.*

---

## TIP BOX

The conjunction **antes de que** (*before*) always takes the subjunctive.

### Example

Llámala **antes de que sea** demasiado tarde.
*Call her before it's too late.*

---

**Exercise 14.** Answer the following questions with sentences in the indicative or the subjunctive. Use the conjunction in parentheses.

1. ¿Cuándo volveremos a París? (después de que/terminar/los estudios)

   _____

2. ¿Cuánto tiempo nos quedaremos en esta esquina? (hasta que/aparecer/Luis)

   _____

3. ¿Cuándo les escribirás a tus padres? (en cuanto/tener/tiempo)

   _____

4. ¿En qué momento supieron que habían perdido el partido? (después de que/Jorge/tener que retirarse del juego)

_____

5. ¿Cuándo regresaste a casa? (luego que/nosotros/despedirse)

_____

6. ¿Cuándo dejaremos salir a jugar a los perros? (cuando/haber/comido)

_____

7. ¿A qué hora abren las puertas del teatro? (tan pronto como/ser/las siete en punto)

_____

8. ¿Cuándo pueden entregarnos el equipo de sonido? (cuando/repararlo/el técnico)

_____

9. ¿En qué momento viste salir el avión? (mientras/estar/comiendo)

_____

10. ¿Cuándo se puede tocar esta pintura? (en cuanto/estar/seca)

_____

**Exercise 15.** Answer the following questions with sentences in the simple preterit (indicative) or the present subjunctive.

1. ¿Cuándo te mudarás de casa? (pintar la casa nueva)
   Cuando _____

2. ¿Cuándo supieron que habían ganado la lotería? (leer el periódico)
   Después de que _____

3. ¿Cuándo encontraremos el balón que se perdió? (derretirse la nieve)
   Cuando _____

4. ¿Cuándo piensa recogerte tu mamá? (oscurecer)
   Antes de que _____

5. ¿Cuándo siembras las semillas de tomate? (comenzar la primavera)
   Tan pronto como _____

6. ¿Cuándo comenzó a trabajar Tania en esa oficina? (tener una entrevista con el jefe)
   En cuanto _____

7. ¿Cuándo podré pasar al equipo profesional de ciclismo de montaña? (cumplir 21 años)
   Cuando _____

8. ¿Cuándo me llamó Gonzalo? (dormir)
   Mientras _____

9. ¿A qué hora saldremos hacia Nueva York? (encontrar las llaves del auto)
   En cuanto _____

10. ¿Hasta cuándo estarán juntos? (acabarse el mundo)
    Hasta que _____

- **Dependent Adverbial Clauses of <u>Location</u>**

Adverbial clauses of location are introduced by the following conjunctions:

| | |
|---|---|
| **donde** | *where, wherever* |
| **por donde** | *whereby, by which* |
| **en donde** | *where, wherever* |
| **adonde** | *where, wherever* |

When the location referred to is known, clauses of location take the **indicative**.

## Example

Te espero donde nos **<u>vimos</u>** la última vez.
*I will wait for you where we last saw each other.*

However, if the location referred to is unknown, the **subjunctive** is used instead.

## Example

Te buscaré en donde **<u>estés</u>**.
*I will look for you wherever you are.*

Te llevo adonde **<u>digas</u>**.
*I will take you wherever you say.*

**Exercise 16.** Fill in the blanks with the present indicative or the present subjunctive.

1. Espérame donde _____ (poder) estacionar el auto.
2. Quiero que me lleves adonde _____ (vender) esas chaquetas de cuero tan hermosas.
3. Por donde _____ (nosotros / caminar), veremos las huellas de los venados.
4. Caminaremos por donde no _____ (haber) lodo.
5. Vamos adonde _____ (nosotros / poder) hablar en privado.
6. Lo dejaron donde _____ (terminar) el camino.
7. Vamos a un lugar donde _____ (poder) ir al baño.
8. No se preocupen, que nosotros los llevamos a donde _____ (querer).
9. Irá detrás de ella, a cualquier parte donde ella _____ (ir).
10. Vamos al bar donde nos _____ (ver) la última vez.

- **Dependent Adverbial Clauses of <u>Manner</u>**

The indicative is used in clauses of manner that are introduced by the following conjunction:

| | |
|---|---|
| **como** | *as, in any way* |

## Example

Los niños hicieron la tarea **<u>como</u>** les **<u>indicaron</u>**.
*The children did the homework as it was explained to them.*

**Exercise 17.** Complete the following sentences with the appropriate tense and mood.

1. Terminaré el trabajo como me _____ (decir/ustedes).
2. Nicolás pintó el cuadro como se lo _____. (haber/imaginado)
3. Conecta el televisor así como (él) te _____. (indicar)
4. Aquí estamos, como te _____. (prometer/yo)
5. Ana le contó a José las cosas como _____. (suceder)
6. Haz las tareas como te _____ (explicar/yo)
7. No olvides que las cosas son como _____ (ser).
8. Fernando nos explicó la película tal como _____ (ocurrir).
9. Todo sucedió como _____ (pronosticar) aquel historiador famoso.
10. Las cosas no salieron como las _____ (haber/planeado/ellos).

- **Dependent Adverbial Clauses of <u>Limitation</u>**

The subjunctive is used in clauses of limitation that are introduced by the following conjunctions:

| | |
|---|---|
| **a menos que** | *unless* |
| **a no ser que** | *unless* |
| **sin que** | *without* |
| **con tal de que** | *provided that* |

### Example

¡No pelearemos **<u>a menos que estemos</u>** dispuestos a jugarnos la vida!
*We won't fight unless we are all ready to die!*

Nos vemos mañana **<u>a menos que</u>** no **<u>tenga</u>** tiempo.
*We'll see each other tomorrow unless I don't have the time [to see you].*

**Exercise 18.** Complete the following sentences with the appropriate form of the verb.

1. Iremos a México a no ser que _____ los planes. (cambiar/él)
2. Le daremos el dinero del taxi con tal de que nos _____ . (esperar)
3. Carmela se irá sin que nadie la _____. (ver)
4. Los niños se quedarán sin comer a no ser que _____ de jugar pronto. (dejar)
5. Me iré sin ti a menos que _____ a tiempo. (llegar)
6. Voy a perder la partida a no ser que _____ salvar la reina. (poder)
7. El vecino me deja usar su podadora de césped con tal de que le _____ el jardín. (arreglar)
8. Te enfermarás a menos que _____ mejor. (comer)
9. ¿Sabes cómo envejecer sin que se _____? (notar)
10. Te daré la fórmula con tal de que no se la _____ a nadie. (decir)

- **Dependent <u>Causal</u> Adverbial Clauses**

The indicative is always used in adverbial clauses introduced by a causal conjunction.

| | |
|---|---|
| **como** | *since* |
| **porque** | *because* |
| **puesto que** | *since, because* |
| **ya que** | *since, because* |

## Example

<u>**Como**</u> no hiciste las tareas, no **podrás** ver televisión.
*Since you didn't finish your homework, you cannot see television.*

No **podré** comprarte el juguete **porque** no tengo dinero.
*I will not be able to buy you that toy because I don't have any money.*

**Exercise 19.** Complete the following sentences with the appropriate form of the verb.

1. Como no _____ (llegar/nosotros) temprano al concierto, no pudimos entrar.
2. Estos enfermos necesitan toda nuestra atención puesto que _____ (estar) desamparados.
3. Te llamé anoche porque _____ (necesitar) tus consejos.
4. Ya que _____ (llegar/tú), ayúdame a preparar la cena.
5. Como bien _____ (saber/ustedes), este es el monumento más importante de la ciudad.
6. Los estudiantes escogieron esta clase porque _____ (ser) la más interesante.
7. Como no _____ (venir) a la fiesta, no te vuelvo a invitar.
8. Ya que _____ (tener) ganas de divertirte, te invitó a bailar.
9. Puesto que hacer ejercicio _____ (ser) bueno para la salud, hagamos ejercicio.
10. Los siento mucho pero no podré ir al paseo con vosotros porque no _____ (tener) dinero.

- **Dependent Adverbial Clauses of <u>Purpose</u>**

The subjunctive is always used in an adverbial clause introduced by a conjunction of purpose.

| | |
|---|---|
| **a fin de que** | *in order that* |
| **para que** | *in order that* |
| **de manera que** | *so that* |
| **de modo que** | *so that* |

## Example

Debemos luchar **para que haya** paz en el mundo.
*We should struggle in order to have peace in the world.*

---

> **TIP BOX**
> Note, however, that some of the precedent conjunctions may express either consequence or purpose. When expressing consequence, the indicative is used.
>
> **Example**
>
> Te lo dije varias veces, **de manera que** no te **puedes** quejar.
> *I told you that many times, so you cannot complain.*

**Exercise 20.** Complete the following sentences with the appropriate form of the verb.

1. Graciela llamó a todas sus amigas a fin de que se _____ (enterarse) de la noticia.
2. Déjale tu número telefónico a la bibliotecaria para que te _____ (avisar) cuando tenga el libro.
3. Salgamos temprano de manera que _____ (llegar/tú) a tiempo.
4. Es muy tarde, de modo que _____ (irse/usted) a casa.
5. Arreglemos las flores en el jarrón para que no se _____ (caerse).
6. Los campesinos prepararán las parcelas de modo que _____ (estar) listas para la siembra.
7. A fin de que todos _____ (poder) comprar casa, hemos reducido las tasas de interés.
8. Cómprale libros a tu hijo para que _____ (aprender) a leer.
9. Explícale como venir de manera que no se _____ (perderse).
10. ¡No puedo creerlo! ¡De modo que _____ (tener) dos novios!

**Exercise 21.** As shown in the example below, answer the following questions.

**Example**

Pepe, ¿llamo a Liliana? (venir a la fiesta)
*Por supuesto, para que venga a la fiesta.*

1. —¿Le dejo a José las llaves en la portería? (poder entrar)
   —_____.

2. —¿Invitamos a Pedro? (traer cerveza)
   —_____.

3. —¿Salgo ya? (llegar temprano)
   —_____.

4. —¿Compro sillas? (tener donde sentarnos)
   —_____.

5. —¿Comemos ahora? (no tener hambre después)
   —_____.

6. —¿Limpiamos el apartamento? (estar limpio para cuando /llegar/ los invitados)
   —_____.

- **Dependent Concessive Adverbial Clauses**

A dependent concessive adverbial clause is introduced by the following conjunctions:

**aunque**          *though, although, even though*
**bien sea que**    *although*
**pese a que**      *even though*

These clauses express difficulties or obstacles that do not prevent what is being said in the main clause to be carried out. If the obstacle or difficulty is considered hypothetical, the subjunctive is used.

### Example

Saldré **aunque llueva**.
*I will go out even though it is raining.*

**Aunque** me **pida** disculpas, no lo perdonaré.
*Even though he apologizes, I won't forgive him.*

But if the obstacle or difficulty is considered real, the indicative is used instead.

### Example

**Aunque** me **ha pedido** disculpas, no lo perdonaré.
*Even though he has apologized to me, I won't forgive him.*

**Exercise 22.** Complete the following sentences with the appropriate form of the verb.

1. Aunque _____ (tener/tú) noventa años, esta música te hace sentir romántico.
2. Bien sea que te _____ (inscribirse) o no, tendrás que pagar el curso.
3. Pese a que les _____ (advertir/nosotros), no nos hicieron caso.
4. Aunque _____ (querer/ellas) disimular, se les nota la curiosidad.
5. Aunque _____ (ver/nosotros) lo que pasó, no reconocimos al asaltante.
6. Mónica se levantó temprano, pese a que se _____ (acostarse) tarde.

# II. The Imperfect Subjunctive
## A. Regular Formation of the Imperfect Subjunctive

The imperfect of the subjunctive is formed by using the root of the conjugation of the third person plural **ellos, ellas, ustedes** in the simple preterit tense of the indicative, plus the corresponding verb endings for the imperfect subjunctive. The imperfect subjunctive has two sets of endings: **-ra, -ras, -ra, -ramos, -rais, -ran** (used more frequently in spoken language), and **-se, -ses, -se, -semos, -seis, -sen** (used more in written language).

| | Verb Endings of the Imperfect Subjunctive | amar<br>root:<br>ellos amar~~on~~ | comer<br>root:<br>ellos comier~~on~~ | vivir<br>root:<br>ellos vivier~~on~~ |
|---|---|---|---|---|
| | **(-ra) form** | | | |
| yo | -ra | amar**a** | comier**a** | vivier**a** |
| tú | -ras | amar**as** | comier**as** | vivier**as** |
| él, ella, usted | -ra | amar**a** | comier**a** | vivier**a** |
| nosotros/as | -ramos | am**á**r**amos** | comi**é**r**amos** | vivi**é**r**amos** |
| vosotros/as | -rais | amar**ais** | comier**ais** | vivier**ais** |
| ellos, ellas, ustedes | -ran | amar**an** | comier**an** | vivier**an** |
| | **(-se) form** | | | |
| yo | -se | am**ase** | comi**ese** | vivi**ese** |
| tú | -ses | am**ases** | comi**eses** | vivi**eses** |
| él, ella, usted | -se | am**ase** | comi**ese** | vivi**ese** |
| nosotros/as | -semos | am**á**s**emos** | comi**é**s**emos** | vivi**é**s**emos** |
| vosotros/as | -seis | am**aseis** | comi**eseis** | vivi**eseis** |
| ellos, ellas, ustedes | -sen | am**asen** | comi**esen** | vivi**esen** |

## TIP BOX

Note that since the formation of the imperfect subjunctive is formed using the root of the third person plural of the simple preterit, all verbs that are irregular in the third person of the plural of the simple preterit maintain the same irregularity in the imperfect of the subjunctive.

See Chapter 4 to review verbs that have irregularities in the simple preterit.

**Exercise 23.** Conjugate the following verbs using the preterit indicative and underline the root of the verb.

### Example

Ellos *leyer*on (leer)

1. Ellos _____ (incluir)
2. Ellos _____ (retirar)
3. Ellos _____ (repetir)
4. Ellos _____ (pagar)
5. Ellos _____ (influir)
6. Ellos _____ (explicar)
7. Ellos _____ (destrozar)

8.  Ellos _____ (caminar)
9.  Ellos _____ (temer)
10. Ellos _____ (reír)
11. Ellos _____ (reducir)
12. Ellos _____ (producir)
13. Ellos _____ (llegar)
14. Ellos _____ (fabricar)
15. Ellos _____ (decidir)
16. Ellos _____ (cruzar)

**Exercise 24.** Complete the following sentences using the imperfect subjunctive.

1.  Era importante que Lucía_____ (incluir) a Jorge en la lista de invitados.
2.  El director nos dijo que mejor nos_____ (retirar) del comité.
3.  No me entenderías aunque te _____ (repetir) mil veces lo mismo.
4.  Salomé dijo que compraría este vestido cuando le _____ (ellos pagar) su sueldo.
5.  No creo que su madre _____ (influir) en su decisión de casarse.
6.  Quisiera que me _____ (explicar/tú) este ejercicio.
7.  Aunque me _____ (destrozar) el corazón, te seguiría queriendo.
8.  Omar prometió que cuando _____ (caminar) de nuevo aprendería a esquiar.
9.  Era increíble que Juan, siendo tan valiente, _____ (temer) a un simple ratoncito.
10. Me dijo que no me _____ (reír) de su peinado.
11. Era normal que el banco _____ (reducir) las tasas de interés.
12. Fue un milagro que no se _____ (producirse) un accidente peor.
13. ¡Te dije que _____ (llegar) temprano!
14. Jorge nos pidió que _____ (fabricar) una máquina fotográfica como las antiguas.
15. Era necesario que Carmen _____ (decidir) con quién se iba a casar.
16. Los autos se detuvieron para que la anciana_____ (cruzar) la calle.

# B. Uses of the Imperfect Subjunctive

The imperfect subjunctive is used following the same rules used in the present subjunctive, but with the difference that the action referred to is in **the past.**

### a. Uses of the Imperfect Subjunctive in Subordinated Noun Clauses.

- In sentences that express **influence** or **desire.**

### Example

Necesitaba que **llegaras** pronto pero no apareciste.
*I needed you to come quickly but you didn't show up.*

**Exercise 25.** You are going camping with a couple of friends. On the day you are leaving, you find out that your friends did not do what they were supposed to. Express your disappointment using the imperfect subjunctive. Use verbs and expressions of influence or desire.

## Example

comprar los víveres
*Era importante que ustedes compraran los víveres.*

1. preparar la tienda de campaña

   _____

2. conseguir combustible para la estufa portátil

   _____

3. traer un botiquín

   _____

4. hacer un mapa del recorrido

   _____

5. averiguar cómo llegar al sitio del campamento

   _____

6. comprar repelente de insectos

   _____

**Exercise 26.** Put the following text in the subjunctive according to the example.

| | |
|---|---|
| Me parece que mi casa es un poco pequeña. | *Yo quisiera que fuera más grande...* |
| no tiene suficiente luz. | que _____. |
| Me parece que la cocina no es moderna, | Yo quisiera que _____. |
| y el color de las paredes es triste. | y_____. |
| Además, no tiene clósets para guardar la ropa. | Además yo quisiera que _____. |
| Tampoco hay restaurantes cerca. | y que _____. |

• In sentences that express **doubt.**

## Example

Juan no creía que María **llegara** temprano a casa.
*Juan did not believe that María would come home early.*

**Exercise 27.** Use the following words to make sentences in the imperfect subjunctive. Use verbs and expressions of doubt.

## Example

Pedro / dudar/ haber guerra
*Pedro dudaba que hubiera guerra.*

1. Nosotros / no pensar / tú / venir

   _____

2. Los ingenieros / no creer / el terreno / hundirse

   _____

3. La policía / dudar / producirse / un nuevo atentado

   _____

4. Mi madre/ no estar segura/ yo/ venir/ a ayudarla

   _____

5. El juez / no creer / el testigo / estar diciendo / la verdad

   _____

6. Quizás si nosotros / llevar / mucho dinero / poder / comprar anillo

   _____

- In sentences that express **emotion.**

## Example

Él tenía miedo de que lo **mordieran** los perros.
*He was afraid of being bitten by the dogs.*

**Exercise 28.** Use the following words to make sentences in the imperfect subjunctive. Use verbs and expressions of emotion.

## Example

ser terrible / haber / tanta contaminación.
*Era terrible que hubiera tanta contaminación.*

1. Marisela / temer / mojársele / el cabello

   _____

2. Yo / preocuparse / el dinero / perderse

   _____

3. ¡Qué miedo / haber / una avalancha!

   _____

4. Alegrarme / ir / juntos / a la fiesta

   _____

5. Me preocupar/ el gato/ no comer

   _____

6. La anciana / emocionarse / nosotros / venir / de visita

   _____

### b. The Imperfect Subjunctive in Adjectival Clauses or Relative Clauses.

### Example

En aquella época, necesitaba a alguien que me **comprendiera**.
*At that time, I needed someone who would understand me.*

Buscaba un apartamento que **tuviera** tres dormitorios.
*I was looking for an apartment that had three bedrooms.*

**Exercise 29.** Imagine that last year you were looking for a car to buy. Write six sentences describing the car you were looking for.

### Example

ser económico
*Necesitaba un coche que fuera económico.*

1. ser de color amarillo
   _____.

2. tener cuatro puertas
   _____.

3. marchar rápido
   _____.

4. frenar bien
   _____.

5. estar entre los diez mejores
   _____.

6. no ser muy costoso
   _____.

### c. The Imperfect Subjunctive in Adverbial Clauses

- Dependent Adverbial **Clauses of Time**

### Example

María dijo que vendría a visitarnos cuando **tuviera** tiempo.
*María told us she would visit us when she had time.*

Te lo advertí antes de que **fuera** demasiado tarde.
*I warned you before it was too late.*

Exercise 30. Complete the following sentences with the imperfect subjunctive.

1.  Le prometí a mi sobrino que vendría a verlo después de que _____ (regresar) de la oficina.
2.  Silvia dijo que esperaría hasta que Juan y José _____ (llegar).
3.  Los músicos prometieron comenzar la serenata en cuanto_____ (ser) las doce.
4.  Mientras no _____ (tú/sentir) dolor, todo estaría bien.
5.  Fernando dijo que luego que _____ (usted/escribir) la carta, la llevaría al correo.
6.  Los niños le pidieron que comprara chocolates cuando _____ (ella/ir) a la tienda.
7.  Le dije a María que me buscara tan pronto como me _____ (necesitar).
8.  Todos le dijimos que cuando tus amigas te _____ (ver), no te reconocerían.
9.  Cuando niño mi mamá me decía que mientras _____ (yo/vivir) en esta casa, debería respetar sus normas.
10. Todos estuvimos de acuerdo que en cuanto _____ (terminar) de llover volveríamos a salir.

- Dependent Adverbial **Clauses of Location**

## Example

Me dijo que te buscaría donde **estuvieras**.
*He told me he would look for you wherever you might be.*

Me contó que te llevaría adonde **dijeras**.
*He told me he would take you wherever you say.*

Exercise 31. Fill in the blanks with the imperfect subjunctive of the verb in parentheses.

1.  Le advertimos a Horacio que lo encontraríamos donde se _____. (esconderse)
2.  Quería llevarte adonde _____ (poder) comprar el vestido.
3.  Los vigilantes nos dejarían entrar por donde _____ (haber) menos gente.
4.  Era obvio que las gaviotas llegarían donde _____ (haber) más desperdicios.
5.  Los gitanos iban de pueblo en pueblo, acampando donde_____ (poder) pasar la noche.

- Dependent Adverbial **Clauses of Manner**

## Example

Quedó dicho que los niños harían la tarea como les **indicaran**.
*It was stated that the children would do the homework as it was indicated to them.*

Exercise 32. Complete the following sentences with the imperfect subjunctive.

1.  Los invitados vendrían a la fiesta vestidos como _____ (querer).
2.  Como si _____ (tener) todo el dinero del mundo, se dedicó a despilfarrarlo.
3.  Se acordó que la modista haría los trajes como le _____ (indicar) el diseñador.
4.  Beatriz amaba a Mimí como si _____ (ser) su propia hija.

- Dependent Adverbial **Clauses of Limitation**

## Example

Nunca discutían a menos que **tuvieran** un problema muy grave.
*They never fought unless they had a terrible problem.*

**Exercise 33.** Complete the following sentences with the appropriate form of the verb.

1. Pedro no contestaba las cartas, a no ser que_____ (ser) de su madre.
2. Los vendedores regalaban muestras del producto con tal que lo _____. (probar/nosotros)
3. No podíamos dar marcha atrás a menos que_____ (querer) reconocer nuestro error.
4. Era seguro que se descongelarían a no ser que _____ (andar/ellas) más deprisa.

- Dependent Adverbial **Clauses of Purpose**

## Example

Lucharon toda su vida para que **hubiera** paz en el mundo.
*They fought all their lives so there would be peace in the world.*

**Exercise 34.** Complete the following sentences with the appropriate form of the verb.

1. Pintamos el exterior de la casa a fin de que se _____ (conservarse) en buen estado.
2. La invitó a entrar para que no se_____ (mojarse) con la lluvia.
3. Organicé las tarjetas de manera que _____ (quedar) en orden alfabético.
4. La fotógrafa retrocedió unos pasos de modo que el sol no la _____. (deslumbrar)
5. El departamento de agricultura asesoró a los granjeros para que _____ (alternar) las cosechas.
6. Revisamos todos los documentos de modo que _____ (cumplir) todos los requisitos.

- Dependent **Concessive** Adverbial Clauses

## Example

Nos dijo que no se entregaría aunque lo **mataran**.
*He told us he would not surrender even though they would kill him.*

Aunque me **pidiera** disculpas, no lo perdonaría.
*Even if he apologized, I wouldn't forgive him.*

**Exercise 35.** Complete the following sentences with the appropriate form of the verb.

1. Aunque _____ (yo/querer), no podría realizar este experimento.
2. Aunque _____ (ella/saber) la verdad, jamás nos la diría.
3. Pese a que _____ (nosotros/pagar) las deudas, nuestra reputación quedaría arruinada.
4. Nadie la admiraba aunque se _____ (vestirse) de seda.
5. Aunque los impuestos _____ (bajar), los ciudadanos seguirían quejándose.

# III. The Perfect Tenses of the Subjunctive

## A. Formation of the Perfect Subjunctive Tenses

The perfect subjunctive tenses are formed with the present or imperfect subjunctive of the auxiliary verb **haber** and the past participle of the verb to be conjugated.

|  | **Present Perfect** | **Past Perfect (-ra form)** | **Past Perfect (-se form)** |
|---|---|---|---|
| yo | haya comido | hubiera comido | hubiese comido |
| tú | hayas comido | hubieras comido | hubieses comido |
| él, ella, usted | haya comido | hubiera comido | hubiese comido |
| nosotros/as | hayamos comido | hubiéramos comido | hubiésemos comido |
| vosotros/as | hayáis comido | hubierais comido | hubieseis comido |
| ellos, ellas, ustedes | hayan comido | hubieran comido | hubiesen comido |

## B. Uses of the Present Perfect Subjunctive

The present perfect subjunctive is used in a dependent clause that requires the subjunctive. When the verb in the main clause is in the present, present perfect, or future, the present perfect may be used in the subordinate clause when the action refers to a past action.

### Example

No creo que María **haya pasado** el examen.
*I don't believe María passed the exam.*

Me ha dolido mucho que usted no **haya sido** capaz de llamarme.
*It has hurt me very much that you have not called me.*

No te imaginarás que te **haya creído** esa historia extraordinaria.
*You could not have imagined that I would have believed that outrageous story.*

**Exercise 36.** Complete the following sentences using the present perfect subjunctive.

1. ¡No puedo creer que _____ (tú/perder) tanto dinero!
2. Me preocupa mucho que papá _____ (subir) tanto de peso.
3. Es imposible que no _____ (nosotros/encontrar) ninguna huella.
4. ¿Cree usted que el centro comercial _____ (cerrar) temprano?
5. No pienso que los espectadores _____ (ver) el truco.
6. Cuando Beto y Daniel _____ (demostrar) que son responsables, les enseñaremos a conducir.

**Exercise 37.** Rewrite the following sentences as shown in the example.

### Example

Es imposible que María llegue temprano.
*Es imposible que María haya llegado temprano.*

1. No creo que Luis te preste la motocicleta.
   _____.

2. ¡Es un milagro que Martín llegue sano y salvo!
   _____.

3. Es posible que la tía Magdalena venda su colección de sombreros.
   _____.

4. No se sabe si Nubia se vaya en el tren de las cuatro.
   _____.

5. ¡Qué bueno que consigamos todos los disfraces para la obra!
   _____.

6. No es cierto que me sienta solo.
   _____.

## C. Uses of the Past Perfect Subjunctive

The past perfect subjunctive is used in a dependent clause that requires the subjunctive. When the verb in the main clause is in the past tense (preterit, imperfect) or conditional and the verb of the subordinate clause refers to an action that was completed prior to that of the verb in the main clause, the past perfect subjunctive is used in the dependent clause.

### Example

**Era importante que todos <u>hubiéramos</u> ido a votar.**
*It was important that we all had gone to vote.*

**Todos te agradecieron que lo <u>hubieras ayudado</u>.**
*All of them thanked you for having helped him.*

**Todos habrían querido que no te <u>hubieras aparecido</u> a la reunión.**
*All of them wished that you had not showed up to the meeting.*

**Exercise 38.** Complete the following sentences using the past perfect subjunctive.

1. Aunque no _____ (tú / venir), te habríamos guardado torta.
2. Con tristeza, Laura dijo que sus compañeras _____ (poder) ayudarle.
3. Me sorprendió que no _____ (tú / escribir) el ensayo.
4. Ramón y Consuelo no se _____ (reconciliar) de no ser por tu ayuda.
5. Si _____ (nosotros / cantar) en el festival, seríamos famosos.
6. ¿Qué _____ (ser) de mí sin tu apoyo?

**Exercise 39.** Rewrite the following sentences using the past perfect subjunctive as shown in the example.

### Example

Era imposible que María llegara temprano.
*Era imposible que María hubiera llegado temprano.*

1. Ojalá tengamos suerte en el concurso.

   _____.

2. Era imposible que terminara de escribir el libro a tiempo.

   _____.

3. Ojalá ganemos el campeonato de fútbol.

   _____.

4. Ojalá vengas a mi graduación.

   _____.

5. Ojalá nos escriba a menudo.

   _____.

6. Sin la ayuda del viento, es posible que la casa no se quemara.

   _____.

# Chapter 11

# CONDITIONAL CLAUSES

## I. Factual Conditions

### A. Expression in the Present or in the Past

To express a factual or real condition in the present or in the past, we use the indicative tenses that express either the past or the present.

**¡Si tuviera dinero, iría a comer como Dios manda!**
*(If I had money, I would eat like a king!)*

**Example**

**Present**

Si no comes, te mueres.
*If you don't eat, you will die.*

**Past**

La invité a ver una película cómica para ver si se reía un poco.
*I invited her to see a funny movie to see if she would laugh a bit.*

**Exercise 1.** Connect the following sentences; make sure that they make sense.

| | |
|---|---|
| 1. Si come mucho, | a. siempre voy al trabajo caminando. |
| 2. Lo llamé para saber | b. no abro la boca. |
| 3. Si no tengo nada que decir, | c. se engorda. |
| 4. Si estoy haciendo fila, | d. me aburro. |
| 5. Si mis compañeros hacen mucho ruido, | e. no me puedo concentrar. |
| 6. Si puedo, | f. si quería ir a cine. |

## B. Expression in the Future

To express the possibility that a factual or real condition will happen in the future, the main **si** clause must express the idea of future (the verb may be either in the present indicative, future or present subjunctive, or expressed as a command), and the tense used in the **si** clause must be the present indicative.

### Example

**Present indicative**

Si te invito, ¿vienes?
*If I invite you, will you come?*

¿Qué te parece si me acompañas de compras mañana?
*How about coming shopping with me tomorrow?*

**Future**

Llegaré a las ocho si no hay tráfico.
*I will arrive at eight if there is no traffic.*

**Present subjunctive**

Mejor que no te aparezcas, si tienes demasiado trabajo.
*It's preferable that you don't show up, if you have too much work to do.*

**Command**

No vengas si no tienes tiempo.
*Don't come if you don't have the time.*

**Exercise 2.** Complete the following sentences using the appropriate form and tense of the verb.

1. Si podemos, _____ (ir/nosotros) con ustedes al zoológico mañana.
2. Tendré éxito en la vida si me _____(concentrarse/yo) un poco más.
3. Cuando era niña, lloraba si sus padres se _____(burlarse) de ella.
4. Iremos al cine si _____ (llegar/ustedes) temprano.
5. Te espero esta noche si _____ (salir/tú) del trabajo temprano.
6. Si me _____ (animarse/yo), participaré en el concurso.
7. Si ella me mira, me _____ (ponerse/yo) nervioso.
8. Si no vienen a trabajar les _____ (escribir/yo) un memorándum.
9. No me _____ (empujar/tú) si no quieres que me caiga.

**Exercise 3.** Make chain sentences, according to the example.
accidentarse - ir al hospital - no poder trabajar - no tener dinero para las vacaciones - no poder ir a Grecia - aburrirse

*Si conduces ebrio te accidentarás, si te accidentas ...*

_____

_____

_____

_____

**Exercise 4.** Make four hypotheses according to the drawing above regarding the thief's options.

1. *Si el ladrón pasa con los dos lingotes de oro, se caerá al vacío.*
2. _____.
3. _____.
4. _____.
5. _____.

# II. Nonfactual Conditions

## A. Conditions for Different but Possible Realities

The **si** clause is also used to express a condition that is contrary to the present reality, but still possible. In this case, the verb in the main clause uses either the conditional or perfect conditional and the **si** clause uses the imperfect subjunctive.

### Examples

Si fuera rico, no trabajaría.
*If I were rich, I would not work.*

Si no trabajaras, me enloquecerías.
*If you were not working, you would make me crazy.*

Si me amaras, no te habría abandonado.
*If you loved me, I would not have left you.*

**Exercise 5.** Complete the following sentences using the appropriate form and tense of the verb.

1.  Si pudiera, te _____ (comprar) el cielo.
2.  Si tuvieras tiempo, _____ (ir) a la fiesta.
3.  Le _____ (ayudar) si me lo pidiera.
4.  Llamaría a Julia si _____ (tener) su número de teléfono.
5.  Te esperaría en la estación si me _____ (decir) a qué horas llegas.
6.  Si las encontráramos, las _____ (saludar).
7.  Si le pagaran lo suficiente, él _____ (trabajar) más horas.
8.  Si lo _____ (intentar), lo _____ (lograr).
9.  Si te lo explicara, me _____ (entender).
10. Si supieras lo que debes hacer, no _____ (cometer) tantos errores.
11. ¡Qué objeto tenía correr, si cuando _____ (llegar), sería demasiado tarde!
12. La máquina no se detendría si _____ (fabricar/nosotros) una fuente constante de energía.
13. Si Victoria _____ (decidir) aprender varios idiomas, podría hacerlo.

**Exercise 6.** According to the example answer the following sentences.

### Example

Si vuelves a Nueva York, ¿dónde vivirás?
*Si volviera a Nueva York, viviría en Manhattan.*

1.  Si invitaras a Carmen a comer, ¿dónde la llevarías? (a un restaurante elegante)
    _____.

2.  Si tuvieras dinero, ¿a dónde viajarías? (a Grecia)
    _____.

3.  Si hicieras una fiesta, ¿a quién invitarías? (a Carmen)
    _____.

4.  Si cambiaras de carro, ¿qué carro comprarías? (un Alfa Romeo)
    _____.

5.  Si fuera viernes, ¿qué harías? (ir a cine)
    _____.

## B. Conditions for Different and Impossible Realities

**Si** clauses are also used to express conditions that are contrary to the present reality, but which are also **impossible** because they have already occurred. In this case, the verb in the main clause uses either the conditional or perfect conditional and the **si** clause takes the past perfect subjunctive.

### Example

Si hubieras bebido menos, no tendrías dolor de cabeza.
*If you had drunk less, you would not have a headache.*

Si hubieras terminado los deberes, habrías podido salir con tus amigos.
*If you had finished your homework, you would have been able to go out with your friends.*

**Exercise 7.** Complete the following sentences using the appropriate form and tense of the verb.

1. Si hubiéramos sabido que el museo estaba cerrado, no _____ (venir).
2. Si se _____ (detenerse) la tormenta, no se habrían inundado estos terrenos.
3. Si me hubiera casado más joven, _____ (tener) más hijos.
4. Si Carlos hubiera visto el semáforo en rojo, no _____ (tener) ese accidente.
5. Si mis padres no _____ (llegar) temprano, habríamos podido hacer una fiesta.
6. Si me hubieras escuchado, no te _____ (pasar) esa desgracia.
7. Si _____ (estar) menos oscuro, no me habría tropezado.
8. Si el pastelero hubiera usado la receta, el pastel _____ (quedar) más delicioso.
9. Si el gallo no hubiera cantado, no nos _____ (despertar).
10. Si tu papá no _____ (cargar) esa caja tan pesada, la espalda no se le habría maltratado.

**Exercise 8.** According to the example, answer the following sentences.

### Example

necesitar/tú/dinero (ir a un cajero)
—*Si hubieras necesitado dinero,¿qué habrías hecho?*
—*Habría ido a un cajero.*

1. tener/una semana de vacaciones (ir a España)

   _____.

2. tener/ la oportunidad de escoger un coche (un Peugeot)

   _____.

3. perder/el examen (retirarse de la universidad)

   _____.

4. Carmen/abandonar/ (a mi)/ (ponerse a llorar)

   _____.

5.  tener/un hija/ llamarla Gabriela

    _____.

6.  incendiar/tu casa (llamar a los bomberos)

    _____.

7.  tener que salir/del país (irse a Italia)

    _____.

8.  ir/a cine (ver la película sueca)

    _____.

9.  dar (a ti)/su teléfono (llamar [a ella])

    _____.

10.  invitar (a mi)/ (llevar un regalo [a ti])

    _____.

## C. *Como si* Clauses

**Como si** or "as if" clauses are followed by the imperfect or past perfect subjunctive.

### Example

Juanita le miró con complicidad, **como si le conociera** de toda la vida.
*Juanita observed him with complicity as if she had known him all her life.*

Fue **como si** Dios se **hubiera olvidado** de nosotros.
*It was as if God had forgotten us.*

---

**TIP BOX**

The order of the main and subordinate clause may be transposed in all **si** and **como si** clauses.

For example, it is correct to say:

**Si** tuviera dinero, viajaría por el mundo.
*If I had money, I would travel the world.*

or

Viajaría por el mundo, **si** tuviera dinero.
*I would travel the world, if I had money.*

**Exercise 9.** Complete the following sentences using the appropriate form and tense of the verb.

1. Me saludó con una sonrisa, como si _____ (haber/olvidar) nuestra pelea.
2. Caminó a pasos largos por el pasillo, como si _____ (tener) prisa.
3. Las velas se hincharon, como si el viento las _____ (estar/empujar).
4. Bailé toda la noche, como si aún _____ (tener) veinte años.
5. Llovía como si se _____ (haber/derretir) todas las nubes.
6. Los chiquillos nos miraban, como si _____ (ser/nosotros) monstruos.
7. El perro arrastraba una de las patas, como si _____ (estar) herido.
8. El acusado bajó la cabeza, como si _____ (saber) el veredicto.
9. Me acusas como si no me _____ (conocer).
10. Puse todo mi empeño, como si _____ (ser) mi última oportunidad.

**Exercise 10.** According to the example below, answer the following questions.

## Example

—¿Cómo reaccionó Lucía al verte? (nada/haber/pasado)
—*Como si nada hubiera pasado.*

1. —¿Cómo reaccionó Lucía al verte? (no/conocerme)
   _____.

2. —¿Cómo encontraste al abuelo? (tener/quince años)
   _____.

3. —¿Cómo anduvo el coche? (ser/cohete)
   _____.

4. —¿Cómo se portaron los niños? (ser/unos ángeles)
   _____.

5. —¿Cómo habló el presidente? (estar/muerto de risa)
   _____.

6. —¿Cómo funcionó tu bote de vela? (ser/nuevo)
   _____.

7. —¿Cómo cantó Julieta? (tener/una papa en la boca)
   _____.

8. —¿Cómo bailó Carmen? (tener/una pata de palo)
   _____.

9. —¿Cómo te atendió el jefe? (ser/un/perro)
   _____.

10. —¿Cómo comieron los niños? (ser/marranos)
   _____.

# Chapter 12

# COMMANDS

Commands (or the imperative form of the verb) are used to tell someone to do something in a very direct manner. In Spanish, two speech forms are used: the informal (**tú, vosotros**) and the formal (**usted, ustedes**). Both forms can be used in commands. When addressing friends, relatives, or children, informal commands are used. But when a certain distance is desired or required, formal commands are used to express this distance or respect.

**¡Come bien!**
*(Eat decently!)*

**¡Siéntate bien!**
*(Sit down correctly!)*

**¡No hables con la boca llena!**
*(Do not talk while eating!)*

**¡Cállate! ¡No grites!**
*(Be quiet! Do not yell!)*

**¡No te rías!**
*(Do not laugh!)*

**¡No llores!**
*(Do not cry!)*

# I. Formal Commands

## The Form of Formal Commands

Formal commands use the present subjunctive.*

| **caminar** (*to walk*) | **responder** (*to answer*) | **ir** (*to go*) |
|---|---|---|
| camine (usted) | responda (usted) | vaya (usted) |
| caminen (ustedes) | respondan (ustedes) | vayan (ustedes) |

---

### TIP BOX

Note that reflexive and object pronouns are affixed to the endings of all commands in **affirmative sentences** only.

### Example

No quiero verlo a usted más. ¡**Váyase** de aquí!
*I don't want to see you anymore. Leave!*

No quiero perder ese trabajador. Por favor, ¡no lo **deje** ir!
*I don't want to lose this worker. Please, don't let him go!*

¡**Dígaselo** al jefe!
*Tell it to the boss!*

¡No se lo **diga** al jefe!
*Don't tell that to the boss!*

---

**Exercise 1.** Answer the following questions according to the example.

### Example

¿Envío la carta?
*Sí, envíela.* (or) *No, no la envíe.*

1. ¿Quiere que le empaque esta camisa?

   _____.

2. ¿Desea que la llame mañana?

   _____.

3. ¿Subimos a este autobús?

   _____.

*See Chapter 10, Regular and Irregular Formations of the Present Subjunctive.

4. ¿Podo todos estos árboles?

    _____.

5. ¿Quiere que le corte el cabello?

    _____.

6. ¿Lleno el tanque de la gasolina?

    _____.

7. ¿Digo la verdad?

    _____.

8. ¿Quiere que le cuente un secreto?

    _____.

9. ¿Apagamos las luces del corredor?

    _____.

10. ¿Me siento en esta silla?

    _____.

**Exercise 2.** Help write the instructions for submitting a short story to a local Spanish magazine. Use formal commands.

## Example

(resumir el cuento) *Resuma el cuento.*

1. (escoger un título breve)

    _____.

2. (incluir el nombre del autor)

    _____.

3. (mencionar el tema del cuento)

    _____.

4. (hacer una lista de vocabulario nuevo)

    _____.

5. (enviar dibujos o fotografías que ilustren el cuento)

    _____.

6. (preparar tres originales en sobres diferentes)

    _____.

7. (poner los sobres al correo)

    _____.

8. (esperar con paciencia la respuesta del comité de publicación)

    _____.

# II. Informal Commands

## The Form of Informal Commands

Informal commands (**tú** and **vosotros**) are irregular in **affirmative** sentences. They do not take the subjunctive. In **negative** sentences, however, they use the present subjunctive.

### a. Affirmative Sentences

- **Tú** form

The form **tú** takes the third singular conjugation (**él, ella, usted**) of the present indicative; however, some verbs have an irregular form.

| caminar (to walk) | responder (to answer) | vivir (to live) |
|---|---|---|
| camina (tú) | responde (tú) | vive (tú) |

Irregular **tú** command verbs are:

| Verb | Irregular Form |
|---|---|
| venir (to come) | ven |
| dar (to give) | da |
| tener (to have) | ten |
| poner (to put) | pon |
| hacer (to do) | haz |
| decir (to say) | di |
| ir (to go) | ve |
| salir (to go out) | sal |
| ser (to be) | sé |

**Example**

¡__Canta__! (tú)
*Sing!*

¡__Ven__ aquí!
*Come here!*

- **Vosotros** form

The informal command **vosotros** uses a special form that consists of the infinitive form of the verb, where the letter **r** is replaced by the letter **d.**

### Example

**(cantar)**
¡**Cantad**! (vosotros)
*Sing!*

¡**Cantadle** una canción a Lucía! (vosotros)
*Sing a song to Lucía!*

**(entregar)**
¡**Entregad** aquello!
*Bring that!*

¡**Entregadle** la carta!
*Bring him the letter!*

#### b. Negative Sentences

- **Tú** form

In negative sentences, the informal command form **tú** uses the second person singular conjugation (**tú**) of the present subjunctive.

### Example

¡**No vengas**!
*Don't come!*

¡**No** le **entregues** las cartas!
*Don't give the letters to him!*

- **Vosotros** form

In negative sentences, the informal command form **vosotros** takes the second person plural conjugation (**vosotros**) of the present subjunctive.

### Example

¡**No vengáis**!
*Don't come!*

¡**No** le **entreguéis** las cartas!
*Don't give the letters to him!*

## TIP BOX

All commands in Spanish use the subjunctive form with the **exception** of informal commands (**tú** and **vosotros**) in **affirmative** sentences.

The form **tú** uses the third person singular conjugation (**él, ella, usted**) of the present indicative or an irregular form.*

### Example

¡<u>Canta</u>! (tú)
*Sing!*
¡<u>Ven</u> aquí!
*Come here!*

The informal command **vosotros** uses a special form that consists of the infinitive form of the verb in which the letter **r** is replaced by the letter **d**.

### Example

(for the verb **comer**) (*to eat*)
¡**Comed**! (vosotros)
*Eat!*

*For a list of irregular verbs see Affirmative Sentences in this chapter.

**Exercise 3.** Answer the following sentences using informal commands.

### Example

¿Cierro la puerta?
*Si, ciérrala.* (or) *No, no la cierres.*

1. ¿Te presto algo de dinero?
   _____.

2. ¿Mezclo la harina con el azúcar?
   _____.

3. ¿Llamo por teléfono a Laura?
   _____.

4. ¿Te busco a la salida del trabajo?
   _____.

5. ¿Escribo esta carta?
   _____.

6. ¿Te pago lo que te debo?
   _____.

7. ¿Llevo las fotos de los niños?
   _____.

8. ¿Anoto tu dirección?

   _____.

9. ¿Preparo la cena esta noche?

   _____.

10. ¿Intento cruzar el río?

   _____.

**Exercise 4.** Miguel's mother needs to remind him of all the things he needs to help with at home. Fill in the blanks with the appropriate form of the verb, using informal commands.

## Example

Miguel, _____ los platos del desayuno. (lavar)
*Miguel, lava los platos del desayuno.*

1. _____ a pasear al perro. (sacar)

2. _____ tu ropa del piso. (levantar)

3. _____ la cama antes de salir de casa. (tender)

4. _____ el periódico. (traer)

5. _____ la alfombra de la sala. (aspirar)

6. _____ a tu papá a cortar el césped. (ayudar)

7. _____ las compras del auto. (sacar)

8. _____ tus libros. (recoger)

9. _____ gasolina al auto. (poner)

10. _____ temprano esta noche. (llegar)

**Exercise 5.** Answer the following sentences as shown in the example below.

## Example

Rewrite the following sentences using informal commands, negative commands, formal commands, and informal commands with **vosotros,** as shown in the example.

## Example

Cuide las plantas del jardín.
*Cuida las plantas del jardín.*
*No cuides las plantas del jardín.*
*Cuidad las plantas del jardín.*
*No cuidéis las plantas del jardín.*

1.  Juegue hasta que oscurezca.

    _____.
    _____.
    _____.
    _____.

2.  Venga a almorzar con nosotros.

    _____.
    _____.
    _____.
    _____.

3.  Sueñe con el futuro.

    _____.
    _____.
    _____.
    _____.

4.  Perdone la interrupción.

    _____.
    _____.
    _____.
    _____.

5.  Olvide los disgustos que hemos tenido.

    _____.
    _____.
    _____.
    _____.

6.  Haga un diseño del mobiliario.

    _____.
    _____.
    _____.
    _____.

7. Diga sólo lo estrictamente necesario.

   _____.
   _____.
   _____.
   _____.

8. Coma todo lo que le sirvan.

   _____.
   _____.
   _____.
   _____.

9. Váyase de inmediato.

   _____.
   _____.
   _____.
   _____.

10. Entienda la gravedad de la situación.

   _____.
   _____.
   _____.
   _____.

**Exercise 6.** Use the words in parentheses to write negative commands.

## Example

   (arrancar las flores, tú)
   *No arranques las flores.*

1. (cortarse el cabello, tú)

   _____.

2. (salir tan tarde, vosotros)

   _____.

3. (empujar, tú)

   _____.

4. (ser ingenuo, usted)

   _____.

5. (tocar esos cuadros, ustedes)

   _____.

6. (pensar en cosas tristes, vosotros)

   _____.

7. (olvidar tus promesas, tú)

   _____.

8. (cerrar los ojos, usted)

   _____.

# III. The *Nosotros* Commands

When expressing a command in the first person plural, (**nosotros**), two forms are used: the verb **ir** or the subjunctive.

## A. The Verb *Ir* Form

**a.** In affirmative sentences the verb **ir** is used in the first person plural of the present indicative to express the **nosotros** commands.

### Example

¡**Vamos** a comer!
*Let's go eat!*

¡**Vamos** al restaurante Los Girasoles!
*Let's go to the restaurant Los Girasoles!*

¡Buena idea! ¡**Vámonos**!
*Good idea! Let's go!*

---

### TIP BOX

Note that reflexive and object pronouns are affixed to the endings of both affirmative forms only.

   Also note that when the verb **ir** is used in its pronominal form, the form **vámonos** is used instead of **vámosnos**, which is incorrect.

#### Example

¡**Vámonos** de aquí!
*Let's get out of here!*

---

**b.** In negative sentences the **ir** (**nosotros**) command form uses the first person plural of the present subjunctive of the verb **ir**.

¡**No vayamos** a comer!
*Let's not go eat!*

## B. The Subjunctive Form

**a.** The subjunctive form in affirmative sentences uses the first person plural of the present subjunctive.

### Example

¡**Llamémoslos**!
*Let's call them!*

**b.** The subjunctive form in negative sentences uses the first person plural of the present subjunctive of the verb **ir**.

¡**No** los **llamemos**!
*Let's not call them!*

**Exercise 7.** Use the words in parentheses to write commands.

## Example

(comprar leche, nosotros)
*¡Compremos leche!*

1. (comprar esa marca de jabón, nosotros)

   _____.

2. (ir a jugar al parque, nosotros)

   _____.

3. (no hablar de política, nosotros)

   _____.

4. (gritar, nosotros)

   _____.

5. (irse a la cafetería, nosotros)

   _____.

6. (mandar la carta a Julia, nosotros)

   _____.

7. (ir a bailar, nosotros)

   _____.

8. (no irse de aquí, nosotros)

   _____.

9. (no ir a cine, nosotros)

   _____.

10. (irse a la playa, nosotros)

    _____.

# Chapter 13

# AFFIRMATIVE, NEGATIVE, AND INTERROGATIVE SENTENCES

## I. Affirmative and Negative Sentences

To make a negative sentence, the word **no** is added to an affirmative sentence before the verbal expression.

### Example

Marcos come carne.
*Marcos eats meat.*

Marcos **no** come carne
*Marcos doesn't eat meat.*

**¿Me quiere?**
*(She loves me?)*

**No me quiere.**
*(She loves me not.)*

---

**TIP BOX**

Note that when answering a question negatively, the word **no** is used twice.

**Example**

—María, ¿Eres vegetariana?
*"María, are you vegetarian?"*

—**No, no** soy vegetariana.
*"No, I am not a vegetarian."*

The following are some common affirmative and negative words.

| Affirmative Words | | Negative Words | |
|---|---|---|---|
| alguien | *somebody* | nadie | *nobody* |
| algo | *something* | nada | *nothing* |
| algún (-o, -os, -a, -as) | *some, something* | ningún (-o, -os, -a, -as) | *no, no one, none, any* |
| alguna vez | *ever* | nunca, jamás | *never* |
| siempre | *always* | nunca, jamás | *never* |
| también | *also* | tampoco | *neither, not either* |
| todavía, aún | *still* | ya no | *no longer* |
| ya | *already* | todavía no | *not yet* |
| o | *or* | ni | *nor* |
| o...o | *either...or* | ni...ni | *neither...nor* |

## Example

—Alguna vez has preguntado: "¿Hay alguien ahí?" y te han respondido: "¡No, no hay nadie!"
—No, ¡nunca!
—¡Ah! A mi siempre me ocurre.
—A mí, ¡jamás!
—Tal vez, algún día te ocurra a ti también algo parecido.
—Espero que nunca. Nadie se atrevería a hacerme un chiste como ese.
—Yo tampoco creo que se deban hacer ese tipo de chistes, y nunca me imaginé que me ocurriera. De todas maneras no sé si fue una burla, o fue verdad.
—¡No, hay nada que hable! Empiezo a creer que estás loco.
—Todavía no estoy loco, ni quiero estarlo, pero... algunas cosas hablan. Y siempre responden que no hay nadie.
—No, ¡jamás!
—¡Sí! Cuando hay alguien ahí que no quiere hablar contigo. ¡Ja! ¡Ja!
—Me estás tomando del pelo, ¿no?

*"Have you ever asked, 'Is anybody there?'*
*and somebody answered,*
*'No, there isn't'?"*
*"No. Never!"*
*"Oh! It always happens to me."*
*"It NEVER happens to me!"*
*"Maybe some day, something like that will happen to you."*
*"I hope not. Nobody would ever dare to play such a prank on me."*
*"I don't think it is right to play such pranks, and I never imagined that something like that would ever happen to me. In any case, I do not know if it was a joke or a true event."*
*"Things don't talk. I am beginning to think you are crazy."*
*"I am not crazy yet, and I don't want to be, but... some things talk. And they always respond that there is nobody there."*
*"No. Never!"*
*"Of course! If that somebody doesn't want to talk to you!"*
*"You are kidding, aren't you?"*

**TIP BOX**

Note that object pronouns always precede the verb in negative sentences.

**Example**

No **le** devolviste el libro a Juan.
*You didn't bring the book back to Juan.*

**TIP BOX**

When **nada, nadie,** or **ninguno** precedes the verb, there is no double negation.

**Example**

**Nada** le gusta.
*He likes nothing.*

**Nadie** lo quiere.
*Nobody loves him.*

**Ningún** amigo lo visita.
*No friend visits him.*

However, when **nada, nadie,** or **ninguno** follows the verb, there is double negation.

**Example**

**No** le gusta **nada**.
*He doesn't like anything.*

**No** lo quiere **nadie**.
*Nobody loves him.*

**No** lo visita ningún **amigo**.
*No friend visits him.*

Exercise 1. Complete the following sentences using negative and affirmative words.

1. —¿Haces algo esta tarde?
   —No, no hago _____.
2. —¿Comprendiste todo?
   —No, no comprendí _____.
3. —¿Vieron ustedes a alguien?
   —No había _____.
4. —¿Tienes algún amigo latinoamericano?
   —Sí, tengo _____.
5. —¿Todas tus amigas van a ir la fiesta?
   —No, no va _____.
6. —¿Hay algún problema?
   —No, no hay _____ problema.

Exercise 2. Complete the following dialogue using negative and affirmatives words.

1. —¿Hay alguien en la oficina?
   —No, no hay _____.
2. —Hay algo horrible adentro.
   —Estás loco, si no hay _____.
3. —¿Siempre sientes miedo?
   —No, _____.
4. —¿Encontraste alguna pista en el lugar del crimen?
   —No, no encontré _____.
5. —¿Alguna vez has visto un extraterrestre?
   —No, _____.
6. —Sabes, voy a renunciar a mi cargo.
   —¿Sí?, yo _____.
7. —No me gusta mi jefe.
   —A mí _____, es un déspota.

## II. Interrogative Sentences

The following are the interrogative words used most frequently in Spanish:

| | |
|---|---|
| ¿Cómo? | *How?* |
| ¿Cuál(es)? | *Which (which ones)?* |
| ¿Cuándo? | *When?* |
| ¿Cuánto(o), (a)? | *How much?* |
| ¿Cuánto(os), (as)? | *How many?* |
| ¿Dónde? | *Where?* |
| ¿Qué? | *What?* |
| ¿Quién(es)? | *Who, whom?* |

All interrogative words take a written accent when used to introduce an interrogative sentence, so they can be distinguished from other pronouns. A preposition may precede the interrogative word when needed.

Note that in interrogative sentences, when a stated subject is present, the subject follows either the verb or the complement of the verb.

## Example

Notice that the underlined interrogatives all have accent marks.

**En una tienda de animales**

Cliente:—¿<u>Cómo</u> se llama ese perro y de dónde es?

Vendedor:—¿Cuál?

C:—El que tiene manchas.

V:—Pero si son todos casi idénticos. ¿<u>Cuántas</u> manchas tiene?

C:—El que tiene tres o cuatro manchas.

V:—Veamos, ¿<u>dónde</u> tiene las manchas?

C:—Una en la cola y las otras en las patas.

V:—¿En <u>qué</u> patas, las delanteras o las traseras?

C:—¿<u>Cómo</u> puedo saber si se mueven todo el tiempo?

V:—Entonces, explíqueme mejor. ¿<u>Con quién</u> está el perro? ¿Con ese de manchas chicas o grandes?

C:—Está con el de manchas grandes y orejas caídas.

V:—¿<u>Cuáles</u> manchas, las redondas o las cuadradas?

C:—Las ovaladas.

V:—Igual estos perros no vienen de ninguna parte, nacieron aquí y aún no tienen nombre. ¿<u>Cuál</u> quiere el señor?

C:—No, ninguno, sólo preguntaba... Ese tiene cara de llamarse Pedro como yo.

V:—¿<u>Cuál</u>?

C:—¡El que tiene manchas!

*In a pet store*

*Customer: What is that dog's name and where is it from?*

*Salesman: Which one?*

*C: The one with the spots.*

*S: But they are almost identical! How many spots does it have?*

*C: The one with three or four spots.*

*S: Let's see... Where are the spots?*

*C: It has one on the tail and the other ones on the legs.*

*S: On which legs, the front or the rear?*

*C: How can I know, if they are moving all the time?*

*S: Then you should explain yourself better. Which other dog is it with? With the one with small spots or with the one with big spots?*

*C: With the one with big spots and droopy ears.*

*S: Which spots? The round ones or the square ones?*

*C: The oval ones.*

*S: Anyway, these dogs are not from any particular place. They were all born here and do not have a name. Which one do you want?*

*C: None. I was just asking... That one looks like it could be a Pedro, just like me.*

*S: Which one?*

*C: The one with spots!*

---

**TIP BOX**

It is important to note that **qué** and **cuél** followed by the verb **ser** are equivalent to *what* in English. In Spanish, **cuál** is used almost always as *what* with the verb **ser**, except when the verb **ser** is used in sentences that ask to characterize something, in which case **qué** is used instead.

**Example**

> ¿**Cuál** es el problema?
> *What's the problem?*

> ¿**Qué** es la filosofía?
> *What is philosophy?*

> ¿**Qué** es lo que te pasa?
> *What is wrong with you?*

---

**Exercise 3.** Complete the following sentences using **qué** or **cuál(es)**.

1. ¿ _____ de estas dos camisas prefieres?
2. ¿ En _____ barrio de la ciudad vives?
3. ¿A _____ hora sales para el trabajo?
4. ¿De _____ es tu anillo? ¿De plata o platino?
5. David, ¿ _____ tienes en tu bolsillo?
6. Doctor, ¿ _____ es la solución a mi problema?
7. Doctor, ¿ _____ son los riesgos de beber alcohol?
8. José, ¿ _____ es la diferencia entre vivir en el campo o vivir en la ciudad?
9. Julia tengo hambre, ¿ _____ tienes en la nevera?
10. Laura, ¿ _____ ingredientes tiene una tortilla de patatas?
11. Liliana, ¿ _____ es tu hermana, la de ojos azules o la de ojos negros?
12. Profesor, ¿ _____ opina sobre la crisis económica de Argentina?
13. Lucho, ¿ _____ es el avión más rápido del mundo?
14. Lucía, ¿ _____ de tus amigos sabe bailar?
15. Marta, ¿ _____ es tu hermano, médico o abogado?
16. Patricia, ¿ _____ es la mejor manera de enamorar a una mujer?
17. Profesor, ¿ _____ es un dromedario?
18. Santiago, ¿ _____ es tu color preferido?
19. Señorita, ¿ _____ síntomas tiene usted?
20. Tina, ¿ _____ son los números telefónicos de tu oficina?

# Chapter 14

# SER AND ESTAR

T he verb *to be* in Spanish corresponds (in most cases) to the verbs **ser** and **estar**. These two forms create some difficuties for English speakers.

**¡Este hombre está loco!**
*(This man is being crazy!)*

## I. Uses of *Ser*

The verb **ser** is used to denote the essential quality of something. **Ser** is always used to denote possession, origin, or the material from which something is made. It is also used to express time and when events take place.

**¡Este hombre es loco!**
*(This man is crazy!)*

### Example

Ese disco compacto **es** de mi hermana.
*That compact disc belongs to my sister.*

Don Quijote **es** de La Mancha.
*Don Quixote comes from La Mancha.*

El barco **es** de madera.
*The ship is made of wood.*

El concierto **es** a las siete de la noche.
*The concert is at seven P.M.*

> **TIP BOX**
> The verb **ser** is always used with a noun, a pronoun, or an infinitive.
>
> **Example**
>    El esposo de Julia **es** arquitecto.
>    *Julia's husband is an architect.*
>
>    Ese coche azul **es** mío.
>    *That blue car is mine.*
>
>    Querer **es** poder
>    *Where there is a will there is a way.*

**Exercise 1.** Complete the following sentences using the appropriate form of the verb **ser**.

**Example**
   El periódico _____ de papel.
   *El periódico es de papel.*

1. Adela _____ periodista.
2. Estas _____ las llaves de mi hermano.
3. La bicicleta _____ de metal.
4. Hoy _____ martes.
5. Esa pluma no _____ tuya.
6. ¿ _____ ustedes de Puerto Rico?
7. La conferencia _____ a las 7 de la tarde.
8. Francisco _____ pintor.
9. Maite y Lucas _____ de México.
10. Estas películas _____ de la filmoteca de la universidad.
11. La silla _____ de plástico.
12. La casa azul _____ de Lorena.

# II. Uses of *Estar*

The basic function of **estar** is to denote position.

**Example**
   María **está** en el trabajo.
   *María is at work.*

   Argentina **está** en América del Sur.
   *Argentina is in South America.*

> **TIP BOX**
>
> Remember that the verb **estar** is also used to form the progressive tenses.
>
> No me interrumpas, que **estoy** leyendo.
> *Don't interrupt me, I am reading.*

**Exercise 2.** Complete the following sentences using the appropriate form of the verb **estar**.

**Example**

María _____ en la biblioteca.
*María está en la biblioteca.*

1. Tomás _____ en San Juan.
2. Carlos y yo _____ en la playa.
3. Ellos _____ viendo una obra de teatro.
4. ¿Qué _____ haciendo?
5. Julio _____ escribiendo unas postales.
6. Patricia no _____ en casa. Salió hace un rato.
7. Mario _____ escuchando música.
8. Luisa todavía _____ en la oficina.
9. Andrés y yo _____ buscando el museo.
10. La calculadora _____ en el cajón.
11. Margarita _____ esperando a que llegue el autobús.
12. ¿Sabes dónde _____ los libros que te presté?

# III. *Ser* and *Estar* + Adjective

Both **ser** and **estar** may be used with an adjective. When denoting inherent, permanent qualities, **ser** is used. To describe temporary and changeable conditions, **estar** is used.

**Example**

Tatiana **es** muy alegre, pero hoy **está** muy triste porque su gato murió.
*Tatiana is very happy, but today she is very sad because her cat died.*

María Clara no **es** una mujer alegre, pero hoy **está** muy contenta.
*María Clara is not generally a happy person, but today she is very happy.*

**Exercise 3.** Complete the following sentences using the appropriate form of the verb **ser** or **estar**.

### Example

La profesora _____ muy exigente con sus estudiantes.
*La profesora es muy exigente con sus estudiantes.*

1.  El documental sobre El Salvador _____ fabuloso.
2.  Carmen _____ alta.
3.  Podemos cruzar. Este puente _____ seguro.
4.  Martín y Maribel se casaron hace años y _____ muy felices juntos.
5.  Las uvas _____ verdes.
6.  Mi hermano _____ muy listo, por eso saca muy buenas notas.
7.  Nosotros _____ aburridos porque llevamos treinta minutos esperando.
8.  Las uvas _____ verdes, todavía no podemos comérnoslas.
9.  Los niños _____ guapísimos hoy porque van a una fiesta de cumpleaños.
10. Romeo y Julieta _____ enamorados.
11. Podemos salir, ya _____ lista.
12. El gato _____ vivo.
13. Miguel _____ cansado porque trabajó mucho ayer.

## Review

**Exercise 4.** According to the illustration use the appropriate form of the verb **ser** or **estar** to describe each member of the family.

| La madre | El padre | El adolescente | El bebé |
|---|---|---|---|
| 1. *La madre está de mal humor.* | 1. *El padre..* | 1. *El adolescente...* | 1. *El bebé...* |
| 2. _____ | 2. _____ | 2. _____ | 2. _____ |
| 3. _____ | 3. _____ | 3. _____ | 3. _____ |
| 4. _____ | 4. _____ | 4. _____ | 4. _____ |
| 5. _____ | 5. _____ | 5. _____ | 5. _____ |

**Exercise 5.** Complete the following dialogue using the appropriate form of the verb **ser** or **estar**.

Alberto:—¡Hola! ¿Cómo te llamas?

Lola:—Me llamo Lola.

Alberto:—¿De dónde _____?

Lola:—_____ de España. ¿Y tú, cómo te llamas?

Alberto:—Yo me llamo Alberto y _____ argentino.

Lola:—¿Qué haces?

Alberto:—_____ matemático.

Lola:—¡_____ matemático!

Alberto:—Sí, la verdad es que _____ una profesión inútil pero divertida.

Lola:—Sabes, hoy _____ un poco aburrida. Te invito a una cerveza.

Alberto:—¡Genial! Vamos al bar "La Casita de Piedra", _____ buenísimo.

Lola:—¿Cuál? ¿El bar que _____ en la calle Bolívar?

Alberto:—Sí, _____ un bar tranquilo y además podemos oír tangos.

Lola:—¿Te gustan los tangos? _____ un poco pasado de moda, ¿no te parece?

Alberto:—Quizá. Y dime una cosa, ¿tú que haces?

Lola:—Yo _____ estudiante de administración de empresas.

Alberto:—¿Dónde estudias?

Lola:—En el Instituto de Negocios y Finanzas.

Alberto:—¿Dónde _____ ese instituto?

Lola:—_____ en la avenida Las Américas.

Alberto:—¡Ah! ¡Ya sé cuál _____! ¡Qué tal si vamos al bar!

Lola:—¡Vale! Vamos que me _____ muriendo de sed.

# Chapter 15

# SPECIAL CONSTRUCTIONS WITH INDIRECT OBJECTS

In some Spanish and English verbs the action of the verb is received by an indirect object that is always a person or a personified object or a thing.

## I. Nonreflexive Verbs

### Example

Las serpientes me asustan.*
*Snakes scare me.*

Tu visita nos sorprendió.*
*Your visit surprised us.*

Le fastidia tu egoísmo.
*Your selfishness annoys him (or her).*

**Lo siento, pero se me perdió la billetera.**
*(I am sorry, but I lost my wallet.)*

---

*The verbs **asustarse** and **sorprenderse** are also used as reflexive verbs (when the subjects of the verb and the pronoun correspond to the same person) and without an indirect object.

**(Yo) <u>Me</u>** asusto al ver serpientes. **(me = yo)**
*I get scared when I see snakes.*

**(Nosotros) <u>Nos</u>** sorprendimos con tu visita. **(nos = nosotros)**
*We were surprised by your visit.*

**TIP BOX**

However, in many cases this kind of verb does not function in the same way in English. In such cases the subject in the sentence in English becomes an indirect object in the Spanish sentence.

**Example**

Me gusta tu vestido.
*I like your dress. (or) Your dress is pleasing to me.*

Study the following verbs.

**agradar** (*to please*)
Me agrada tu visita.
*I am pleased by your visit.*

**alegrar** (*to gladden*)
Me alegra que viniste.
*I am glad you came.*

**apasionar** (*to arouse passion, to love* )
A don Quijote le apasionaban los libros de caballería.
*Don Quijote loved stories about knights.*

**apetecer** (*to feel like*)
Me apetece una copa de vino con la comida.
*I feel like having a glass of wine with my meal.*

**atraer** (*to attract*)
Me atraen los coches deportivos.
*I am attracted to sports cars.*

**bastar** (*to be enough*)
Sólo me basta tu presencia para estar feliz.
*Your mere presence is enough to make me happy.*

**caber** (*to fit, to fill*)
Me cabrían más muebles en esta alcoba.
*I could fit more furniture in this room.*

**convenir** (*to be better for*)
Creo que me convendría mejor que vinieras en la tarde.
*I think it would be better for me if you arrived in the afternoon.*

**corresponder** (*to be responsibile for*)
A ti te corresponde lavar el baño esta semana.
*It is your responsibility [or turn] to clean the bathroom this week.*

**costar** (*to cost, to make an effort*)
Aquel abrigo me costó trescientos dólares.
*That coat cost me 300 dollars.*

**encantar** (*to please, to delight, to love*)
A Juanita le encantan los chocolates.
*Juanita loves chocolates.*

**extrañar** (*to be surprised*)
Me extraña mucho que no hayas venido a la fiesta.
*I'm surprised that you didn't come to the party.*

**hacer falta** (*to be lacking, to miss*)
A Andrea le hace falta mucho su hijo.
*Andrea misses her son very much.*

**fascinar** (*to like very much*)
Nos fascina ir a cine.
*We like very much going to the movies.*

**fastidiar** (*to annoy*)
A Rocío le fastidian los hombres.
*Rocío finds men annoying.*

**gustar** (*to be pleasing, to like*)
A nosotros nos gusta bailar salsa.
*We like to dance salsa.*

**importar** (*to matter*)
Me importa mucho que te alejes de mí.
*It matters to me that you are distancing yourself from me.*

**interesar** (*to interest*)
¿Os interesaría ir de compras?
*Are you interested in going shopping?*

**molestar** (*to be a nuisance, to bother*)
A Gabriel y Teresa les molesta el ruido.
*Gabriel and Teresa are bothered by noise.*

**quedar** (*to remain*)
A Julia le quedan un par de años para terminar sus estudios.
*Julia has two more years remaining before finishing her studies.*

**sobrar** (*to have left over, to be in excess*)
A Jacobo le sobra el dinero.
*Jacob has money left over.*

**tocar** (*to have to, to be responsible for*)
A muchas mujeres todavía les toca hacer la comida y los quehaceres de la casa.
*Many women still have to [have the responsibility to] make meals and clean the house.*

**Exercise 1.** Form sentences according to the example.

## Example

Lucía/ gustar/ los tomates
*A Lucía le gustan los tomates.*

1. Pedro y José/corresponder/lavar la ropa

   _____.

2. nosotros/convenir/no gastar tanto dinero

   _____.

3. Daniel/tener/tanta hambre que/caber/un pollo entero

   _____.

4. Jorge/extrañar/que María no haya vuelto

   _____.

5. vosotros/bastar/una comida al día

   _____.

6. ¿ti/apetecer/ una bebida?

   _____.

7. yo/alegrar/que vengas pronto

   _____.

8. ¿vosotros/atraer/ese hombre?

   _____.

9. nosotros/agradar/tu visita

   _____.

10. Pedro/apasionar/la literatura

    _____.

11. nosotros/ese perro/costar/un ojo de la cara

    _____.

**Exercise 2.** Complete the following sentences with the appropriate indirect object pronoun and form of the verb in the present tense.

1. A nosotros ___ _____ (encantar) tu cocina.
2. A Julia ___ _____ (hacer falta) un amigo simpático como yo.
3. A mi madre ___ _____ (fascinar) los pistachos.
4. Mañana a nosotros ___ _____ (tocar) limpiar la casa.
5. A Clara ___ _____ (sobrar) el dinero.
6. A Teresa y su marido ___ _____ (molestar) que tú los llames.
7. A vosotros ___ _____ (quedar) cinco minutos para terminar el examen.
8. A mí no ___ _____ (interesar) tu amistad.
9. A nosotros ___ _____ (importar) mucho el bienestar de todos.
10. A Santiago ___ _____ (gustar) ir a cine.
11. ¿A ti ___ _____ (fastidiar) estudiar gramática?

# II. Reflexive Verbs

A similar construction occurs in Spanish when an accidental action occurs, such as losing one's keys or dropping one's eyeglasses. The following reflexive verbs are the most commonly used.

**caerse** (*to drop*)
Se me cayeron las gafas.
*I dropped my eyeglasses.*

**olvidarse** (*to forget*)
Se me olvidaron los libros.
*I forgot my books.*

**perderse** (*to lose*)
A Juan, se le perdieron las llaves.
*Juan lost his keys.*

**romperse** (*to break*)
A Rebeca se le rompieron los huevos.
*Rebecca broke the eggs.*

**quemarse** (*to burn*)
¡Se me quemó el arroz!
*I burned the rice!*

① ② ③ ④

**Exercise 3.** Look at the illustrations and describe what is happening.

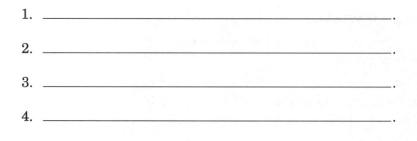

1. _____.

2. _____.

3. _____.

4. _____.

**Exercise 4.** Change the following according to the example.

## Example

Ximena y yo quemamos nuestra casa.
*A Ximena y a mí se nos quemó la casa.*

1. Julio perdió su perro.
   _____.

2. Pablo y Marcela perdieron su anillo de matrimonio.
   _____.

3. Andrea rompió los platos.
   _____.

4. Santiago dejó caer el armario.
   _____.

5. Vosotros perdisteis las llaves del carro.
   _____.

6. Clemente y yo olvidamos los pasaportes en la casa.
   _____.

7. Federico quemó las tostadas del desayuno.
   _____.

8. Teresa rompió el florero.
   _____.

9. Ellos perdieron la maleta en el aeropuerto.
   _____.

10. El niño dejó caer la pelota.
    _____.

**Exercise 5.** Answer the following questions according to the example.

## Example

¿Quién rompió la copa? (yo)
*A mí se me rompió.*

1. ¿Quién dejo caer el vaso? (Juan)
   _____.

2. ¿Quién quemó la carne? (tú)
   _____.

3. ¿Quién rompió los platos? (nosotros)
   _____.

4. ¿Quién perdió las llaves? (vosotros)
   _____.

5.  ¿Quién olvidó los libros? (ellos)

    _____.

6.  ¿Quién quemó la casa? (yo)

    _____.

7.  ¿Quién olvidó el dinero? (nosotros)

    _____.

8.  ¿Quién perdió la billetera? (Pedro)

    _____.

9.  ¿Quién olvidó pagar las cuentas? (ustedes)

    _____.

10. ¿Quién dejo caer el niño? (Lucía)

    _____.

# Chapter 16

# SPECIAL VERBS AND VERB EXPRESSIONS

The following verbs and verb expressions have peculiar uses in Spanish, which is why it is necessary to study them carefully.

> **TIP BOX**
> In Spanish, many expressions are formed by combining two verbs. When this occurs, the first verb is conjugated, while the second verb remains in the infinitive form.

## I. *Acabar*

The Spanish verb **acabar** usually means *to finish*; however, if the verb is followed by the preposition **de**, the meaning changes to *to have just*. Finally, if the verb is followed by the preposition **por**, the meaning changes to *to end up*.

- **Acabar** *(to finish)*

    Él **acabó** todo el helado.
    *He finished all of the ice cream.*

- **Acabar de + infinitive** *(to have just)*

    **Acabo de** llamar al teatro y me dicen que las entradas están agotadas.
    *I have just called the theater and they told me the tickets are sold out.*

- **Acabar por + infinitive** (*to end up*)

Finalmente el policía **acabó por** creer en mi inocencia.
*The police finally ended up believing in my innocence*

---

### TIP BOX
Remember that a verb after a preposition is always in the infinitive.

---

**Exercise 1.** Complete the following sentences with the appropriate form of the verb **acabar, acabar de,** or **acabar por.**

1. Manuel _____ comer y se fue a jugar.
2. ¡Mamá! Ya _____ los deberes. ¿Puedo ver televisión?
3. Aunque Roberto no es simpático _____ invitarlo a la fiesta.
4. ¡Qué mala suerte! Se nos _____ la gasolina.
5. Todos en la clase _____ el ejercicio al mismo tiempo.
6. Mis padres _____ comprar un apartamento.
7. Lucía _____ volver de España
8. Se nos _____ la leche.

## II. *Acordarse de*

The verb expression **acordarse de** is equivalent to the verb **recordar**, which means *to remember*.

### Example

Anoche me **acordé de** nuestro viaje a Tulúm.
*Last night I remembered our trip to Tulúm.*

Anoche te **recordé**.
*Last night I remembered you.*

**Exercise 2.** Transform the following sentences using the verb expression **acordarse de**.

### Example

Ayer te recordé.
*Ayer me acordé de ti.*

1. Siempre recordaré aquellos años dichosos.
   _____.

2. El abuelo no recuerda nada; ha perdido la memoria.
   _____.

3. Las tortugas recuerdan el lugar donde nacieron durante toda su vida.

   _____.

4. El niño no recordó que tenía que hacer los deberes.

   _____.

5. El otro día mientras comíamos te recordamos con alegría.

   _____.

## III. *Ahorrar, Salvar*

The verb **ahorrar** (*to save*) means to save things, such as money or time, whereas **salvar** is used for *saving a life* or *surviving*.

### Example

Tu padre **ahorra** mucho tiempo trabajando en casa.
*Your father saves a lot of time by working at home.*

El dodo no se **salvó** de la extinción.
*The dodo bird did not survive extinction.*

**Exercise 3.** Complete the following sentences with the appropriate form of the verb **ahorrar** or **salvar**.

1. Los ecologistas _____ energía.
2. ¡Gracias! Me _____ (tú) la vida.
3. El año pasado _____ (nosotros) tres mil dólares.
4. Como no ganamos mucho no _____ nada.
5. ¡Hay que _____ las ballenas! Están en vía de extinción.

## IV. *Andar, Ir, Irse*

The verb **andar** means *to walk* and *to go* when referring to walking or going without a specific destination. It also has the meaning of *running* when referring to nonanimated things (a car, a refrigerator). When talking about going to a specific destination, the verb **ir** is used instead. **Irse,** the pronominal form of the verb **ir,** means *to go away.*

### Example

Ayer **anduvimos** por el parque.
*Yesterday, we walked around the park.*

Este coche **anda** muy bien.
*This car runs well.*

Anoche **fuimos** al teatro.
*Last night we went to the theater.*

Liliana se **fue** de la casa.
*Liliana left home.*

**Exercise 4.** Complete the following sentences with the appropriate form and tense of the verb **andar, ir,** or **irse**.

1. Los exploradores _____ por aquí.
2. Mis padres _____ a Roma el mes pasado.
3. ¿Por dónde _____ los niños?
4. Este reloj no _____ bien.
5. Esta mañana _____ (ellos) por el bosque recogiendo setas.
6. ¡Es tarde! ¡_____! (nosotros)

## V. *Bajar*

In Spanish the verb **bajar** corresponds to the English verbs *to lower, to go down, to descend,* and *to download.*

### Example

Los intereses **han bajado** notablemente en los últimos meses.
*Interest rates have gone down noticeably in the last months.*

Vamos a **bajar** el piano lentamente.
*Let's lower the piano very slowly!*

Los buzos **bajaron** a las profundidades del océano.
*The divers descended to the depths of the ocean.*

Carlos **baja** muchos programas del internet.
*Carlos downloads a lot of software from the internet.*

**Exercise 5.** Complete the following sentences with the appropriate form of the verb **bajar.**

1. ¿Le _____ (tú) la temperatura al arroz, por favor?
2. Los estudiantes _____ las escaleras corriendo.
3. Por favor, _____ (ustedes) el volumen del radio.
4. Anoche, _____ (nosotros) varias fotos del internet.
5. Dante _____ a las profundidades del infierno.

## VI. *Convertirse en, Transformarse en*

In Spanish, the verbal expression **convertirse en** or **transformarse en** is used when a transformation is involved.

### Example

Después de años de felicidad, su matrimonio se **convirtió en** un infierno.
*After years of happiness, his marriage became a living hell.*

**Exercise 6.** Complete the following sentences with either the appropriate form of the verb **convertirse en** or **transformarse en.**

1. Doctor, lo que pasa es que mi marido después de casarse _____ un monstruo.
2. Todas las noches sueño que (él) _____ un perro con tres cabezas.
3. Con el tiempo _____ (yo, present perfect) en una mujer sin esperanzas.

## VII. *Cuidar, Cuidarse*

The verb **cuidar** followed by the prepositions **a** or **de** means *to care for* or *to take care of.* The reflexive form **cuidarse** means *to take care of oneself,* while **cuidarse de** means *to be careful of.*

### Example

La abuela **cuida a** los niños.
*The grandmother takes care of the children.*

Ella **cuida de** su apariencia.
*She takes care of her appearance.*

Gabriela trabaja mucho y no **se cuida** bien.
*Gabriela works too much and she doesn't take care of herself.*

Nosotros nos **cuidamos de** no enfermarnos.
*We take care not to get sick. (or) We are careful not to get sick.*

**Exercise 7.** Complete the following sentences with the appropriate form of the verb **cuidar** or **cuidarse.**

1. Jorge _____ de su salud.
2. ¡Fernando está loco! _____ su coche como si fuera su hijo.
3. Lucía _____ a su tía que está enferma.
4. Federico y Roberta comen mucho y no hacen ejercicio; parece que no se _____.

## VIII. *Dar*

The verb **dar**, *to give,* is used in numerous expressions.

- **Dar un paseo** (*to take a walk*)

  Los niños **dieron un paseo** por el parque.
  *The children took a walk in the park.*

- **Dar las gracias** (*to give thanks*)

  ¿Le **diste las gracias**?
  *Did you thank him?*

- **Darse cuenta** (*to realize something*)

  Cuando llegué a casa me **di cuenta** que había perdido las llaves.
  *When I arrived home, I realized I had lost my keys.*

- **Dar la bienvenida** (*to welcome someone*)

  Le **dimos la bienvenida** cuando llegó.
  *We welcomed him when he arrived.*

- **Dar de comer** (*to feed*)

  La madre le **da de comer** a su hijo.
  *The mother feeds her son.*

- **Dar un examen** (*to give an exam*)

  El profesor **dio el examen** final de español en la tarde.
  *The professor gave the Spanish final exam in the afternoon.*

- **Darse + noun** (impersonal sentences) (*to make + noun*)

  **Me da envidia.**
  *He makes me jealous.*

  **Me dan celos.**
  *It makes me jealous.*

  **Me da hambre.**
  *It makes me hungry.*

  **Me da pena.**
  *It makes me feel sorry.*

  **Me da tristeza.**
  *It makes me feel sad.*

  **Me da rabia.**
  *It makes me angry.*

- **Dar la gana** (*to want to*)

  ¡Hago lo que quiero porque me **da la gana**!
  *I do whatever I want because I want to!*

**Exercise 8.** Complete the following sentences with the appropriate form of the verb **dar.**

1. Me_____ pena pedirle su bicicleta prestada.
2. Él se fue porque le_____ susto ver a su madre.
3. Nosotros le _____ la mejor educación a nuestros hijos.
4. Nos _____ mucha pena no asistir a tu comida anoche.
5. No vinieron porque no les _____ la gana, ya que hubieran podido llegar un poco tarde.
6  Es que a Ana le _____ envidia de Victoria.
7. No te puedo ver porque a mi esposo le _____ celos desde la última vez que salimos juntos.
8. Cuando veo esa sopa me_____ más hambre.
9. A los hijos les _____ rabia cuando sus padres les prohiben algo.

## IX. *Dejar, Dejar de*

The verb **dejar** means *to leave*. When **dejar** is followed by the preposition **de**, it means *to stop doing something*.

### Example

Francisco **dejó** las llaves del carro adentro.
*Francisco left his car keys inside.*

Por favor **deje de** fastidiarme.
*Please stop bothering me.*

---

**TIP BOX**
The verb **salir** refers also to leaving when referring *to go out* or *to go away from* or *toward* a place.

### Example

¿A qué hora **sales** del trabajo?
*What time do you leave from work?*

¡No me digas! ¿**Sales** para Madrid?
*No kidding! Are you leaving for Madrid?*

---

**Exercise 9.** Complete the following dialogue with the appropriate form of the verb **dejar** or **dejar de.**

—He _____ quererte porque eres muy grosero. Anoche por ejemplo me _____ esperando en la entrada del teatro mientras estacionaba el carro.
—Mi amor, _____ pensar en tonterías y trata de componer las cosas.
—No querido, voy a _____ para siempre. ¡Yo también tengo dignidad!

## X. *Echar de Menos, Extrañar, Hacer Falta*

The expressions **echar de menos, extrañar, hacer falta,** all mean *to miss*.

### Example

Cuando viajo lejos **echo de menos** mi familia.
*When travelling far away, I miss my family.*

¿Acaso te **hago falta**?
*Do you mean you miss me?*

Sí, te **extraño** mucho.
*Yes, I miss you a lot.*

**Exercise 10.** Complete the following sentences with the appropriate form of the verb **echar de menos, extrañar** or **hacer falta**.

1. No me _____ el clima de Lima.
2. No _____ a su familia, será porque no los quiere.
3. Yo, personalmente, lo que más _____ son las tardes soleadas en el patio de mis abuelos.
4. Nosotros _____ las tertulias en el Café argentino del barrio Palermo.
5. Desde que vivimos en Toledo _____ las autopistas.
6. Siempre _____ (yo) los cuentos de mi abuelo desde cuando él murió.
7. A quien más _____ (yo) es a nuestro hijo menor.
8. Lo único que _____ (ellos) es la comida de mi país.

## XI. *Hacer, Hacerse*

The verb **hacer** means *to do*, in Spanish, but it is also used to talk about the weather.

### Example

Anoche **hicimos** toda la tarea de ciencia.
*Last night we did all of our science homework.*

Hoy **hace** sol.
*Today is sunny.*

Mañana **hará** buen tiempo.
*Tomorrow there will be nice weather.*

En el verano **hace** calor.
*Summer is hot.*

The pronominal form **hacerse** means *to become* or *to pretend*.

### Example

Con el pasar de los años la vida **se hace** más difícil.
*With the passing of years, life becomes more difficult.*

Julio **se hace** el que no me ve.
*Julio always pretends he doesn't see me.*

---

**TIP BOX**

To express the meaning of *to become* in Spanish, **volverse, ponerse** and **llegar a ser** are also used.

De ver tanta pobreza se <u>volvió</u> un líder de derechos humanos.
*Seeing so much poverty, he became a leader of human rights.*

La situación se <u>puso</u> difícil.
*The situation became difficult.*

Eurídice está muy orgullosa que su hijo <u>llegó a ser</u> presidente.
*Eurídice is very proud that her son became President.*

---

**Exercise 11.** Complete the following sentences with the appropriate form of the verbs **hacer, hacerse, ponerse, volverse, llegar a ser**.

1. Ayer, el gobierno _____ lo imposible para obtener la mayoría de los votos.
2. Me gusta cuando _____ calor.
3. Ojalá _____ buen tiempo durante el fin de semana.
4. En el invierno _____ mucho frío en Boston.
5. Una solución pacífica a la crisis política se _____ cada día más difícil.
6. María se _____ la muy interesante cada vez que hablo con ella.
7. Lucía se _____ una falda preciosa ayer.
8. La situación se _____ difícil.
9. Cuando seas grande _____ el mejor cantante de country.
10. Él siempre se _____ el que no sabe nada.
11. Nosotros _____ grandes amigos, si logramos superar nuestras diferencias.

## XII. *Jugar, Tocar*

- The verb **jugar** (*to play*) is used to mean the playing of a sport or a game. The verb **tocar** (*to play*) is used to mean the playing of an instrument.

---

**TIP BOX**

The verb tocar means also *to touch, to ring, to take your turn,* and *to need to.*

El geólogo <u>toca</u> la superficie de la roca.
*The geologist touched the surface of the rock.*

¡Alguien <u>toca</u> el timbre!
Someone is ringing the doorbell!

Te <u>toca</u> jugar a ti.
*It's your turn to play.*

Me <u>toca</u>* trabajar mañana temprano.
*I need to work tomorrow.*

* See Chapter 15, Special Constructions with Indirect Objects.

---

**Exercise 12.** Complete the following sentences with the appropriate form of the verb **jugar** or **tocar**.

1. ¿Cuántas veces me _____ decirte las misma cosas?
2. ¿Quieres _____ baloncesto?
3. ¡Lo que me estás diciendo de mi familia no me _____ porque sé que no es cierto!
4. Él es el que mejor_____ la tambora.
5. Ella _____ mejor tenis que ping-pong.
6. Creo que les _____ irse a la cama porque mañana _____ la final del campeonato.
7. A mí no me gusta _____ ajedrez.
8. A mí me _____ ir al trabajo todas las mañanas.
9. A ellos, lo que más les gusta es _____ la flauta.
10. ¡_____, te _____ a ti!

## XIII. *Llevar, Llevarse*

The verb **llevar** means *to take, to carry* and *to wear*. In its reflexive form **llevarse** means *to take*.

### Example

Abraham **lleva** a sus hijos todas las mañanas al colegio.
*Abraham takes his sons every morning to school.*

Estoy cansado de **llevar** la cruz.
*I am tired of carrying the [proverbial] cross.*

¡Cómo estás de guapa! ¡**Llevas** un vestido precioso!
*How gorgeous you are! You are wearing a wonderful dress!*

El ladrón se **llevó** la joyas.
*The thief took the jewelry.*

**Exercise 13.** Complete the following sentences with the appropriate form of the verbs **llevar, llevarse**.

1. El vendaval se _____los techos de las viviendas.
2. Me gusta Aníbal cuando _____ su camisa blanca.
3. ¿Me podrías_____ este sobre al correo?
4. Sólo Anita _____ nuestro noble apellido.
5 Los policías se _____al reo a la estación y luego lo liberaron.
6. El Señor de los Anillos se _____las ovaciones del público.
7. Mis padres _____ treinta años casados.
8. Los vecinos nos _____ a la escuela porque a mi papá se le averió el coche.
9. Nosotros nos_____muy bien desde que nos divorciamos.

## XIV. *Mover, Mudarse*

The verb **mover** means to move in the sense of changing the location of something, whereas **moverse** is used when the subject and the object that is moved are the same. However, to move from one place where you once lived to another, the verb **mudarse** is used instead.

### Example

¡**Mueve** la silla!
*Move the chair!*

¡No cabemos aquí! ¡**Muévete** un poco!
*We don't fit here! Move over a little bit!*

El año pasado **nos mudamos** tres veces.
*Last year we moved three times.*

**Exercise 14.** Complete the following sentences with the appropriate form of the verb **mover** or **mudarse.**

1. Mi hermano se _____ con su novia a un nuevo apartamento.
2. Yo también quiero ver televisión. ¿Podrías _____ un poco?
3. La tropa se _____ unos 1000 km. hacia atrás, evitando al enemigo.
4. Me enteré que compraron nueva casa. ¿Cuando se _____?
5. Pronto (nosotros) _____ a otro país.
6. Cuando me fui a sentar, alguien _____ la silla y por eso me fracturé la cadera.
7. ¿La tierra se _____ alrededor del sol, pero también hacia el sol?
8. No te _____ que te estoy poniendo alfileres, aun no acabo de medirte este vestido.

## XV. *Pedir, Preguntar*

The verbs **pedir** and **preguntar** both mean *to ask*. When requesting someone to do something, or to order in a restaurant, the verb **pedir** is used. When requesting information, the verb **preguntar** is used instead.

### Example

Julia me **pidió** que la acompañara a la fiesta.
*Julia asked me to go with her to the party.*

**Pedimos** una pizza enorme para todos.
*We asked for a large pizza for all of us.*

**Pregúntale** a Gabriel si tiene cerveza.
*Ask Gabriel if he has any beer.*

**Exercise 15.** Complete the following sentences with the appropriate form of the verb **pedir** or **preguntar.**

1. Te _____ que me des una explicación razonable de tu comportamiento.
2. Ustedes _____ demasiado y dan muy poco.
3. Ella me _____ dónde había estado anoche y tuve que mentir.
4. Amalia le _____ el divorcio a Joaquín.
5. Los sacerdotes no _____ nada, tú sólo vas y dices lo que quieres durante la confesión.
6. Te _____ que no me molestes más con tus preguntas.
7. Mis amigos _____ la cerveza y yo_____ la cuenta.
8. No me _____ (ellos) nada de mi pasado.
9. No te _____ que me contaras toda tu vida, sólo por qué no estudiaste la lección.

## XVI. *Perder, Perderse*

In Spanish the verb **perder** corresponds to the English verb *to lose*; however, in its pronominal form, **perderse** means *to get lost*.

### Example

> **Perdí** la paciencia contigo.
> *I lost my patience with you.*

> Ayer nos **perdimos** yendo a tu casa.
> *Yesterday, we got lost going to your home.*

---

## TIP BOX
Remember that the verb **perderse** may be used as a reflexive verb in special constructions with indirect objects. See Chapter 12.

Se me **perdieron** las llaves.
*I lost my keys.*

---

**Exercise 16.** Complete the following sentences with the appropriate form of the verb **perder** or **perderse.**

1. Lucía _____ el sentido de la realidad.
2. Todos en el pueblo _____ todo a causa de la guerra.
3. _____ todo lo que teníamos porque él apostaba en el casino y yo no lo sabía.
4. Rodrigo ___ _____ viniendo del trabajo.
5. Las ballenas ___ _____ cuando escuchan los sonares de los submarinos.
6. _____ todo vuestro dinero en la bolsa.
7. Ayer José _____ la billetera y sus documentos de identificación.
8. A Andrea ___ ____ _____ las llaves.
9. Por perezoso _____ su carrera como actor.

## XVII. *Prestar*

In Spanish, the verb **prestar** corresponds to the English verbs *to lend* and *to borrow*.

¡Devuélveme el libro que te **presté**!
*Give me back the book I lent you!*

Yo le pedí **prestado** el coche a María.
*I asked to borrow Maria's car.*

**Exercise 17.** Complete the following sentences with the appropriate form of the verb **prestar**.

1. No te voy a _____mis colores, porque tú les partes la punta siempre que te los _____.

2. ¿Me podrías _____ tu coche?
3. Si quieres yo te _____ mi abrigo para la fiesta.
4. Toma mi maleta, yo te la _____.
5. ¿Tú crees que el banco me _____ el dinero?

## XVIII. *Poner*

The verb **poner** means *to put* or *to place*. In its pronominal form it may mean *to start, to wear,* and *to become*.

### Example

Por favor, **ponga** música.
*Please, put on some music.*

El jefe los **puso** a todos en su sitio.
*The boss put all of them in their place.*

Cuando Helena supo la noticia, se **puso** a llorar.
*When Helena found out the news, she started to cry.*

María se **puso** la chaqueta.
*María put on her jacket.*

El jefe se **puso** furioso, pero a nosotros no nos importó.
*The boss became angry but we didn't care.*

---

**TIP BOX**

Remember that the verb **ponerse** may be used as a reflexive verb in special constructions with indirect objects. See Chapter 12.

Del susto, se me **pusieron** los pelos de punta.
*I was so scared, my hair stood on end.*

**Exercise 18.** Complete the following sentences with the appropriate form of the verb **poner** or **ponerse.**

1. No ___ _____ odioso porque te dejo hablando solo.
2. A Liliana ___ ___ _____ la piel roja cuando va a la playa.
3. Al oír sus palabras ___ _____ como una fiera y trató de morderlo.
4. ¡Te ves muy bien cuando ___ _____ el vestido rojo!
5. _____ en mi lugar y dime, tú, ¿qué harías?
6. Fue el fiscal Suárez quien logró _____ al gerente de la compañía en prisión.
7. No ___ _____ así, sólo te estoy diciendo que me voy por un año al Congo.
8. ¿_____ los sobres en el correo? Porque si no lo hiciste, ¡los _____mañana a primera hora!
9. El perro ___ _____ a ladrar sin parar hasta el amanecer.

## XIX. *Quedar, Quedarse*

The verb **quedar** means *to remain* or *to be located*. **Quedarse** means *to stay* but when followed by the preposition **en**, it means *to agree on something*.

- **Quedar** (*to remain*)

  ¿Cuánto tiempo **queda** para que termine la película?
  *How much time remains [is left] for the movie to end?*

- **Quedar** (*to be located*)

  ¿Dónde **queda** el teatro Colón?
  *Where is Colón Theater located?*

- **Quedar** (*to stay*)

  Es mejor que te **quedes** donde estás.
  *It is better for you to stay where you are.*

- **Quedar** (*to agree on something*)

  Sara y Felipe **quedaron** en ir juntos al cine.
  *Sara and Felipe agreed to go together to the movies.*

**Exercise 19.** Complete the following sentences with the appropriate form of the verb **quedar, quedar en,** or **quedarse**.

1. La estación de gasolina _____ a tres cuadras de aquí.
2. Fercho ___ _____ mudo cuando oyó la sentencia.
3. No olvides que _____ ___ pagar las bebidas.
4. ¡Este niñito no ___ _____ quieto un instante!
5. Hemos llegado tarde porque ___ _____ _____ dormidos.
6. La mujer del puerto ___ _____ esperando toda la vida y él nunca regresó.

7. No creo que ___ _____ a vivir en esta ciudad más de dos años.

8. ¡Mi amor! ¿Cuánto ___ _____ de dinero para este mes?

9. Todos _____ ___ encontrarnos en la puerta del teatro.

## XX. *Saber, Conocer*

The verbs **saber** and **conocer** both mean *to know*. **Saber** is used when we need to know a fact, a reason, or something related to professional knowledge. **Conocer** is used for knowing things, persons, and places.

- **Saber** (*to know facts, reasons, or professional knowledge*)

  Juliana **sabe** hacer una paella deliciosa.
  *Juliana knows how to make delicious paella.*

  Fernando es físico y por eso **sabe** matemáticas.
  *Fernando is a physicist, which is why he knows mathematics.*

- **Conocer** (*to know things, persons, or places*)

  Tu padre **conoce** un libro interesante.
  *Your father knows an interesting book.*

  Sara **conoce** al presidente.
  *Sara knows the president.*

  Lucrecia no **conoce** España.
  *Lucrecia doesn't know Spain.*

---

**TIP BOX**

The verb *saber* means also *to taste*. **Saber** followed by the preposition **a** means *to taste like*.

> Me fascinan los riñones al jerez. ¡**Saben** delicioso!
> *I love sherried kidneys. They taste delicious!*

> ¡Este trago **sabe a** fruta!
> *This food tastes fruity!*

---

**Exercise 20.** Complete the following sentences with either the verb **conocer** or the verb **saber**.

1. Samuel _____ Portugal pero no _____portugués.
2. Lo _____ desde que éramos niños y nunca he _____ quien es su padre.
3. Yo _____ a Stella pero no _____ a su familia.
4. Ellos _____lo que quieren, por eso son tan amables contigo.
5. Toda la geografía que _____ sólo la _____ por los libros.
6. Vamos a _____ el nuevo restaurante marroquí. Parece que la comida _____ delicioso.
7. Quisiera _____ las mezquitas de Sevilla.
8. Ese vino _____ ___ vinagre.
9. Perdóname, pero creo que no te _____ a ti mismo.

## XXI. *Servir, Servirse*

The verb **servir** means *to serve*, but it may also have other meanings, as follows.

- **Servir + para** (*to be useful*)

    Ese consejo no **sirve para** nada.
    *That advice is not useful at all.*

    No tires esa caja; me **sirve para** empacar mis cosas.
    *Don't throw away that box; I can use it to pack my things.*

- **Servir + de** (*to serve as*)

    Ese hombre le **sirve de** conductor.
    *This man serves him as his chauffeur.*

---

**TIP BOX**

- **Servirse de** (pronominal form) (*to make use of*)

    Él **se sirve** de sus empleados como si fueran esclavos.
    *He makes use of his employees as if they were slaves.*

---

Exercise 21. Complete the following sentences with the appropriate form of the verb **servir de**, **servir para**, or **servirse de**.

1. Haz el favor y _____ el café que está sobre la estufa.
2. Angela ____ _____ ____ los demás para obtener siempre lo que quiere.
3. Esos muchachos no estudian y no trabajan, no _____ ____ nada.
4. ¡Regálame ese cuadro! Me _____ ____ adornar la sala.
5. Vosotros ____ _____ ____ vuestros procesadores de texto, sólo para escribir tonterías.
6. Todos los domingos los niños de la escuela _____ ____ ayudantes en la ceremonia de la iglesia.
7. Los meseros que _____ en el restaurante Irlandés son muy informales, ¿no?
8. Me perdonas, pero esto que has escrito no _____ ____ el diario; tendrás que publicarlo en otra parte.
9. Tan caro este taladro y no _____ ____ nada.

## XXII. *Tener, Tener que, Tener Lugar*

The verb **tener** (*to have*) is used in many expressions that in English translate to the expression *to be*.

| tener hambre | tener fuerza | tener calor | tener cuidado | tener miedo | tener suerte |
|---|---|---|---|---|---|
| *to be hungry* | *to be strong* | *to be hot* | *to be careful* | *to be scared* | *to be lucky* |
| tener sed | tener éxito | tener frío | tener sueño | tener razón | tener ansias |
| *to be thirsty* | *to be successful* | *to be cold* | *to be sleepy* | *to be right* | *to be anxious* |

- **Tener que** (*to have to*)

  **Tienes que** salir inmediatamente.
  *You have to go immediately.*

- **Tener lugar** (*to take place*)

  El concierto **tendrá lugar** en el teatro Real.
  *The concert will take place at the Teatro Real.*

- **Tener + age** (*age concepts*)

  Rocío **tiene** veinticinco años.
  *Rocío is twenty-five years old.*

**Exercise 22.** Complete the following sentences with the appropriate form of the verb **tener**.

1. Lucía, no _____ más de quince años. Es todavía una niña.
2. La ceremonia _____ _____ en la capilla central de la universidad.
3. Mis padres _____ veinte años de casados.
4. Creo que ese perro _____ sólo dos años y es muy perezoso.
5. Seremos entonces cinco primos que _____ la misma edad.
6. Roberta _____ ____ salir de la oficina a las cinco si quiere llegar a tiempo al concierto.

## Review

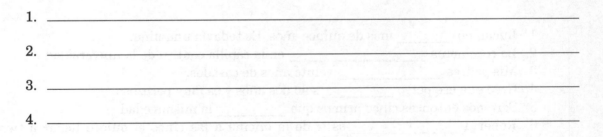

**Exercise 23.** Make a sentence for each frame of the illustration above, telling what Lucía does during her vacation. Use the appropriate expressions studied in this chapter.

1. _____

2. _____

3. _____

4. _____

# Chapter 17

# COMPARATIVES AND SUPERLATIVES

## I. Comparisons of Inequality

**a.** To indicate the idea of **superiority** or the quality of *more than*, the following structure is used in Spanish.

| más | + | noun adjective adverb | + | que |
|-----|---|-----------------------|---|-----|
| verb | + | más | + | que |

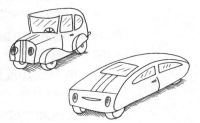

**Example**

David tiene **<u>más dinero que</u>** Sara.
*David has more money than Sara.*

Sara es **<u>más amable que</u>** David.
*Sara is kinder than David.*

Lucho corre **<u>más rápidamente que</u>** Luciano.
*Lucho runs faster than Luciano.*

Irene **<u>habla más que</u>** Teresa.
*Irene talks more than Teresa.*

**Exercise 1.** Complete the following exercises using comparatives of *more than*.

1. Normalmente yo _____ (tener / tiempo) mi esposa para estar en casa porque yo _____ (regresar / temprano) ella. Mi mujer trabaja todo el día. Yo, sólo trabajo por las mañanas.
2. El vino _____ (ser / caro) la cerveza.
3. Mario _____ (hacer deporte) yo, por eso él _____ (estar delgado) yo.

4. Carlos _____ (hablar español / lento) Sara, por eso le entiendo muy bien.

5. El nivel de vida de los países desarrollados _____(es/alto) el de los países subdesarrollados.

6. Las personas hoy día _____ (vivir/tiempo) las personas de antaño.

7. Federico es muy vanidoso, y _____(comprar/ropa) que su esposa.

8. Los franceses _____ (beber/vino) los americanos.

9. En el Caribe _____(hacer/calor) en Londres.

10. Ese coche _____ (andar/ rápido) esa moto.

**b.** To indicate the idea of **inferiority** or the quality of being ***less than***, the following structure is used in Spanish.

| menos | + | noun adjective adverb | + | que |
|-------|---|-----------------------|---|-----|
| verb  | + | menos                 | + | que |

**Example:**

Carlos tiene **<u>menos hambre que</u>** Lola.
*Carlos is less hungry than Lola.*

Liana es **<u>menos apasionada que</u>** Luisa.
*Liana is less passionate than Luisa.*

Lucía baila **<u>menos bien que</u>** Ana.
*Lucía dances less well than Ana.*

Irene **<u>come menos que</u>** Teresa.
*Irene eats less than Teresa.*

---

### TIP BOX

Note that when **más** or **menos** is followed by a number, the preposition **de** is used instead of **que**.

### Example

Hay **<u>más de dos millones y medio</u>** de argentinos sin trabajo.
*There are more than two and a half million Argentineans without jobs.*

In comparative sentences that are the result of a comparison of inequality, **de lo que** is used.

**Example**

Este examen es **más fácil de lo que** creía.
*This exam is easier that I thought.*

Esa camisa me costó **menos de lo que** me dijiste.
*That shirt cost me less that what you had told me.*

**Exercise 2.** Complete the following exercises using comparatives of *less than*.

1. Mi hermana Carmen _____ (ser / tímida) yo; por eso ella tiene muchos amigos.
2. Hoy estoy feliz porque _____ (tener / trabajo) yo pensaba.
3. La cena _____ (ser / cara) me dijiste.
4. Laura y Rosa _____ (ser / trabajador) Mónica. Ella siempre está en la oficina.
5. Roberto _____ (ser / divertido) Juan. Por eso yo prefiero salir con Juan los fines de semana.
6. José Alejandro _____ (tiene / entusiasmo) Lucía. Por eso, Lucía no quiere verlo más.
7. Carlos _____ (ser / amable) su esposa Carmen. Por eso, nos gusta más Carmen.
8. La vida _____ (ser / dura) uno se imagina.
9. Tomás _____(jugar / agresivamente al tenis) su hermano Luis.
10. Antes _____(haber / contaminación) ahora.

# II. Comparisons of Equality or Sameness

**a.** To indicate the idea of *equality or sameness,* the following structure is used in Spanish.

| tan | + | adjective<br>adverb | + | como |
|---|---|---|---|---|
| tanto<br>tanta<br>tantos<br>tantas | + | noun | + | como |
| verb | + | tanto | + | como |

### Example

La nieve es **tan blanca como** el azúcar.
*Snow is as white as sugar.*

Caminas **tan lento como** una tortuga.
*You walk as slowly as a turtle.*

Hay **tantas realidades como** puntos de vista.
*There are as many realities as there are points of view.*

Carlos **duerme tanto como** tú.
*Carlos sleeps as much as you do.*

**Exercise 3.** Complete the following exercises using comparisons of equality.

1. Alberto y Marcos son hermanos gemelos y tienen muchas cosas en común. Por ejemplo, Carlos _____ (ser / alto) Marcos, y Marcos _____ (ser / activo) Carlos. Carlos _____ (comer) Marcos, así que los dos hermanos tienen más o menos el mismo peso.
2. ¿Tu hermano _____ (ser / guapo) tú?
3. Yo no _____ (dormir) tú. Para mí es suficiente dormir siete horas.
4. Julio es bilingüe y yo también. Él _____ (hablar / lenguas) yo.
5. Marta _____ (trabajar / horas) su hermano José.
6. Todos ellos _____ (tener / urgencia) nosotros. Lo mejor es que nos apuremos.
7. Aunque no lo creas, el cerdo _____ (tener / grasa) el pollo.
8. No te preocupes que todo va a salir bien. Yo _____ (tener / fe en que habrá paz) tú.
9. Liliana _____ (comer) Pilar. Por eso, ambas se entienden muy bien.
10. Jorge _____ (bailar / bien) Lola. Ambos han ganado varios concursos de baile.

# III. Superlatives

**a.** To indicate the idea of ***comparison between persons or items***, the following structure is used in Spanish.

| el la los las | + | noun | + | más | + | adjective | + | de |
|---|---|---|---|---|---|---|---|---|

**Example**

> María es **la mujer más alta de** todas sus amigas.
> *María is the tallest woman of all her friends.*
>
> Diego es **el niño más inteligente de** la clase.
> *Diego is the smartest child in the class.*

**Exercise 4.** Complete the following exercises using superlatives.

1. Fabián dice que el café colombiano _____ (ser / rico) del mundo.
2. Para María las playas del Caribe _____ (ser / divertido).
3. Este es el hotel _____ (elegante) de la ciudad.
4. Dicen que Tokio es la ciudad _____ (caro) del mundo.
5. Las abuelas siempre piensan que sus nietos son _____ (inteligentes) del colegio.

# IV. Irregular Comparatives and Superlatives

**a.** The following are *irregular comparatives*.

| mejor(es) | peor(es) | mayor(es) | menor(es) |
|-----------|----------|-----------|-----------|
| *better* | *worse* | *older* | *younger* |
| *best* | *worst* | *higher* | *lower* |

**Example**

> Los españoles dicen que el vino español es **mejor** que el vino francés.
> *Spaniards say that wine from Spain is better than wine from France.*
>
> Sus ambiciones son **peores** de lo que me imaginaba.
> *His ambition is worse than what I had imagined.*
>
> Tus hermanas son **mayores** que tú.
> *Your sisters are older than you.*
>
> La abuela Laura es **menor** que su hermana Julieta.
> *Grandmother Laura is younger than her sister Julieta.*

**TIP BOX**

Note that when these irregular comparatives are used, the words **más** and **menos** are omitted.

Also note that **mayor** and **menor** are used when comparing age and nouns that can be measured, such as speed, height, and weight.

**Example**

Aquel avión está a **<u>mayor</u>** altura que aquel otro.
*This airplane is at a higher altitude than that other one.*

El sonido tiene **<u>menor</u>** velocidad que la luz.
*Sound is slower in speed than is light.*

**Exercise 5.** Complete the following exercises using irregular comparatives.

1. Pedro es una persona muy orgullosa. Él siempre piensa que _____ (ser / bueno) que los demás.
2. Este restaurante _____ (ser / malo) el restaurante italiano que hay al lado de casa.
3. Mariela _____ (ser / joven) que su esposo.
4. Mi prima Carmen _____ (ser / viejo) que yo.

**b.** The following are *irregular superlatives*.

| el, la, los, las mejor(es) | el, la, los, las peor(es) | el, la, los, las mayor(es) | el, la, los, las menor(es) |
|---|---|---|---|
| *the best* | *the worst* | *the oldest* *the highest* | *the youngest* *the lowest* |

**Example**

La carne argentina es **<u>la mejor</u>** del mundo.
*Argentinean meat is the best in the world.*

Tus modales son **<u>los peores</u>** que he conocido.
*Your manners are the worst I have ever seen.*

José es **<u>el mayor</u>** de los hermanos.
*José is the oldest of all the brothers.*

Tu hija es **<u>la menor</u>** de la clase.
*Your daughter is the youngest in the class.*

**Exercise 6.** Complete the following exercises using irregular superlatives.

1. Este _____ (*ser / bueno*) restaurante de la ciudad. Lo recomiendan en todas las guías.
2. Diego _____ (*ser / joven*) de sus hermanos.
3. El año pasado _____ (*tener / malo*) invierno en mucho tiempo.
4. Estoy pasando las_____ (*buenas*) vacaciones de mi vida.

# V. The Suffix *-ísimo*

The suffix **-ísimo,** added to an adjective, intensifies the meaning of the adjective. It is more or less equivalent to **muy** or *very*. Note that **ísimo**-intensified adjectives agree in number and gender with the noun they qualify.

| | |
|---|---|
| aburrido *bored* | aburridísimo *very bored* |
| bello *beautiful* | bellísimo *very beautiful* |
| bueno *good* | buenísimo *very good* |
| feo *ugly* | feísimo *very ugly* |
| guapo *handsome* | guapísimo *very handsome* |
| lindo *beautiful* | lindísimo *very beautiful* |
| pobre *poor* | pobrísimo *very poor* |
| rico *rich* | riquísimo *very rich* |
| simpático *nice* | simpatiquísimo *very nice* |

### Example

¡Esta comida está **buenísima**!
*This meal is very good!*

Ese perro es **feísimo**.
*That dog is very ugly.*

---

## TIP BOX

**Rules to add the suffix *-ísimo***

- For adjectives that end in vowels, drop the vowel and add a form of **-ísimo**.

**Example**

alto → altísimo
alta → altísima

- For adjectives that end in a consonant, simply add **-ísimo**.

**Example**

fácil → facilísimo
normal → normalísimo

- Adjectives that end in **-co** change the **c** to **qu** before adding **-ísimo**.

**Example**

loco → loquísimo
loca → loquísima

- Adjectives that end in **-go** change the **g** to **gu** before adding **-ísimo**.

**Example**

largo → larguísimo
larga → larguísima

- Adjectives that end in **-z+vowel** change the **z** to **c** before adding **-ísimo**.

**Example**

tenaz → tenacísimo
atroz → atrocísimo

**Exercise 7.** Complete the following exercises using the adjectives **bueno, malo, tarde, inteligente, interesante, difícil** with the suffix **-ísimo.**

1. Cristina tiene unas recetas _____ para preparar el pavo.
2. La última vez que fui al cine vi una película excelente, pero la que vimos ayer fue _____.
3. Esta mañana me levanté _____ porque no oí el despertador.
4. Me gusta mi profesor de historia porque es _____, y sus clases son _____.
5. La clase de español es fácil, pero las de alemán son _____.

## Review

**Exercise 8.** Answer using **más...que, menos...que, tan(to,tos,ta,tas)...como** as shown in the example below.

### Example

Lisette trabaja 20 horas diarias, José 30 horas diarias.
*Lisette trabaja menos que José.*

1. Julio bebe tres cervezas, Lola bebe dos.
   _____.

2. Javier gana 2000 euros, Liliana gana 3000 euros.
   _____.

3. Susana duerme 8 horas, Santiago 8.
   _____.

4. Sebastián tiene muchos amigos, Marta no tiene ninguno.
   _____.

5. Jorge corre muy rápido, Susana también corre igual de rápido.
   _____.

6. La altura de Luna es 1,70 mts, la altura de Jorge es 1,70 mts.
   _____.

**Exercise 9.** Study the picture below. Write complete sentences using superlatives as shown in the example.

Lola     Javier     María

### Example

*Lola es la más alta de las tres.*

1. Javier _____. (pequeña)
2. María _____. (pelo)
3. Javier _____. (viejo)
4. Lola _____. (joven)
5. María _____.(vestida)

**Exercise 10.** Write complete sentences as shown in the example below.

### Example

Alfredo es muy inteligente, pero Lucía *es más inteligente. Lucía es inteligentísima.*

1. Jorge es muy rico, pero Gabriel _____.
2. Julio es muy amable, pero Santiago _____.
3. Andrés es muy envidioso, pero Federico_____.
4. Melania es muy tacaña, pero Jonás _____.
5. Andrea es muy dramática, pero Claudia _____.
6. Sara es muy mala, pero María _____.
7. Liliana es muy aburrida, pero Germán _____.
8. Perión es muy valiente, pero Amadís _____.
9. Mario es muy guapo, pero Gabriela _____.
10. Kelly es muy nerviosa, pero Pedro _____.

# Chapter 18

# PREPOSITIONS

**P**repositions are words used to show the relationship of one word to another in a sentence. Prepositions usually indicate location, direction, or time.

The prepositions are **a** (*to*); **ante** (*before, in the presence of*); **bajo** (*under*); **con** (*with*); **contra** (*against*); **de** (*of, from*); **desde** (*from, since*); **durante** (*during*); **en** (*in, on*); **entre** (*between, among*); **excepto** (*except*); **hacia** (*toward*); **hasta** (*until, up to*); **para** (*for*); **por** (*for, by, through*); **según** (*according to*); **sin** (*without*); **sobre** (*upon, on, above, around*); **tras** (*behind*).

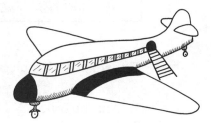

**Viaja por avión.**
(*He travels by airplane.*)

## A. The Preposition *a*

Study the following sentences.

> La familia Domínguez nos invitó **a** comer el domingo.
> *The Domínguez family invited us to eat over on Sunday.*

> ¡Mi amor, ven **a** mis brazos!
> *My love, come in to my arms.*

> Llegaremos mañana **a** las once de la noche.
> *We will arrive at eleven P.M.*

> Esa alfombra es de Tabriz y está hecho **a** mano.
> *That carpet is from Tabriz, and it is handmade.*

**Trabaja para gozar.**
(*He works in order to enjoy life.*)

---

**TIP BOX**

Remember that **al** is a Spanish contraction formed by the preposition **a** and the definite article **el**, and **del** is a contraction formed by the preposition **de** and the article **el**.

**Examples**

Julia va **al** museo del Prado.
*Julia goes to the Prado Museum.*

Aquel juguete es **del** niño.
*That toy belongs to that child.*

**TIP BOX**

Note that in Spanish, **a** is used before a direct object that refers to human beings or personalized things.

**Example:**

Tengo que llamar **a** Kelly.
*I need to call Kelly.*

¡Calla! ¡No llames **a** la muerte!
*Shut up! Don't call on Death!*

**Exercise 1.** Complete the following sentences with the preposition **a,** when required.

1. Anoche conocí ____ tu novio, ¡es muy guapo!
2. Mañana iré contigo ____ cenar, te lo prometo.
3. El otro día, me encontré ____ un anillo de oro en la calle.
4. Mi novia me invitó ____ Madrid.
5. Nos vemos ____ las ocho en el teatro.
6. Lucho me invitó ____ jugar billar.

# B. The Preposition *de*

- The preposition **de** is used to indicate possession.

**Example**

¿Te gustó la última novela **de** Vargas Llosa?
*Did you like the last novel by Vargas Llosa?*

Ese coche es **de** mi hermano.
*That is my brother's car.*

**Exercise 2.** Complete the following sentences with the preposition **de.**

1. Los libros son ____ la biblioteca.
2. La casa es ____ el banco, todavía no la hemos terminado de pagar.
3. Ese suéter es ____ tu hermano.
4. El aire y el agua es ____ todos.

- The preposition **de** is used to indicate origin, provenance, and cause.

## Example

Los geólogos llegaron **de** Italia.
*The geologists came from Italy.*

Hace una hora salieron **de** su casa y no han llegado.
*They left his home an hour ago and they haven't arrived.*

Clareta es **de** Italia, y tiene 18 años.
*Clareta is from Italy, and she is 18 years old.*

Rafael se enfermó **de** tanto comer comida grasa.
*Rafael got sick from eating greasy food.*

**Exercise 3.** Complete the following sentences with the preposition **de.**

1. Los invitados llegaron ____ Perú.
2. Las anchoas son ____ el mar adriático.
3. Mi profesora de francés es ____ Lyon.
4. Estamos cansados, venimos ____ la montaña.

- The preposition **de** is used to indicate the material from which something is made.

## Example

La silla es **de** madera.
*This chair is made of wood.*

**Exercise 4.** Complete the following sentences with the preposition **de.**

1. Los coches modernos son ____ plásticos.
2. Tú siempre estás pensando en castillos ____ arena.
3. Esas empanadas están deliciosas. Son ____ carne.
4. Me gusta el vino ____ La Rioja.

- The preposition **de** is used to indicate time.

## Example

¡Vámonos! ¡Son las cuatro **de** la mañana!
*Let's go! It's four in the morning!*

**Exercise 5.** Complete the following sentences with the preposition **de.**

1. ¡Apúrate! Tu novio llega a las tres ____ la tarde.
2. ¿Qué hora es? ¡Las tres ____ la mañana!
3. Dentro ____ un año iré a visitarte.
4. A las dos ____ la madrugada nació.

# C. The Preposition *en*

The preposition **en** is used to indicate place, direction, time, and manner.

### Example

El lápiz está **en** el escritorio.
*The pencil is on the desk.*

Susana entró **en** el almacén.
*Susana entered the shop.*

Jorge viajó a España **en** el verano.
*Jorge traveled to Spain in the summer.*

Lucho partió **en** avión.
*Lucho left [on a trip] on an airplane.*

**Exercise 6.** Complete the following sentences with the preposition **en.**

1. ¡Tráeme los libros! Están ____ la mesa.
2. Las golondrinas llegan ____ grupos de a miles.
3. Los osos duermen ____ el invierno.
4. La botella está ____ el piso.

# D. The Prepositions *para* and *por*

The use of **por** and **para** poses many difficulties, because both correspond to the English preposition *for* as well as the preposition *to*.

### a. *Para*

- To indicate destination and purpose, **para** is used as *for, to,* and *in order to*.

### Example

La próxima semana voy **para** Mérida.
*Next week I am going to Mérida.*

Esta olla es sólo **para** hervir el agua.
*This pot is [used] only for boiling water.*

**Exercise 7.** Complete the following sentences with the preposition **para.**

1.  Ese avión va ____ Europa.
2.  Las niñas están listas ____ partir.
3.  ____ poder jugar bien al fútbol hay que practicar.
4.  Esa llave no sirve ____ abrir esa puerta.

- To indicate time, **para** is used as *by*.

## Example

Terminaré este trabajo **para** mañana.
*I will finish this work by tomorrow.*

**Exercise 8.** Complete the following sentences with the preposition **para.**

1.  ____ el próximo año ya habrás terminado tu doctorado.
2.  La tarea es ____ mañana.
3.  Tenemos que tener listo el vestido ____ el jueves
4.  Lo siento, ya me comprometí ____ el próximo viernes.

### b. *Por*

- To indicate reason or motive, **por** is the equivalent of *because*.

## Example

Lo despidieron **por** inepto.
*He was fired because of his ineptitude.*

**Exercise 9.** Complete the following sentences with the preposition **por.**

1.  Ella hace cualquier cosa _____ dinero.
2.  Lo premiaron ____ su gran talento.
3.  ____ no estudiar, Diana vivió aburrida toda su vida.
4.  A vosotros os invitaron ____ cumplir con el protocolo.

- To introduce the agent in the passive voice, **por** is the equivalent of *by*.

## Example

Ese retrato fue pintado **por** Botero.
*That portrait was painted by Botero.*

**Exercise 10.** Complete the following sentences with the preposition **por.**

1. Esa catedral fue construida ____ Gaudí.
2. La imprenta fue inventada ____ Gutenberg.
3. La ley de la relatividad fue propuesta ____ Einstein.

- To indicate purpose, **por** is used in the espression **ir + por**, and is the equivalent of *going for something*.

## Example

Enrique fue **por** las llaves.
*Enrique went for the keys.*

**Exercise 11.** Complete the following sentences with the preposition **por.**

1. Vamos ____ aquel camino. Es más corto.
2. ¡María! Ve a la tienda ____ aceite, que se terminó.
3. Voy ____ el camino tropical.
4. Fueron ____ lana y salieron trasquilados.

- **Por** is used to indicate the means or manner by which something is done or accomplished.

## Example

El jefe llegó **por** avión.
*The boss arrived by plane.*

**Exercise 12.** Complete the following sentences with the preposition **por.**

1. Las ondas sonoras viajan ____ el aire.
2. Robert viajó ____ tierra.
3. El hombre viaja ____ aire, mar y tierra.
4. Todos los invitados llegaron ____ barco.

- **Por** is used to indicate substitution.

Yo trabajaré **por** ella.
*I will work in her place.*

**Exercise 13.** Complete the following sentences with the preposition **por.**

1. Juaco está enfermo. Liliana vendrá ____ él.
2. Rocío cambió su reloj ____ el vestido de flores.
3. Tomás y Helena reemplazaron su perro pastor alemán ____ un conejo.
4. Te cambio este coche ____ el tuyo.

# Review

**Exercise 14.** Complete the following paragraph with the appropriate preposition **a, de, en, por,** or **para** (use elisions if needed).

Eran las ocho ___ la noche, cuando Julio fue ___ comida al restaurante chino ___ el barrio. ___ el apartamento lo esperaba su novia Graciela. Como eran las once ___ la noche y Julio no llegaba, Graciela se acostó ___ el sofá ___ la sala ___ esperar. Graciela había conocido ___ Julio ___ suerte, una mañana ___ abril. Aquel día, Graciela había sido invitada ___ el señor Felipe Naranjo, dueño del periódico "El Vespertino", ___ que conociera su empresa. El señor Naranjo pensaba, ___ su imaginación, que Graciela sería la madre ___ sus hijos. Cuando Graciela llegó ___ las instalaciones ___ periódico, fue recibida ___ Felipe con un exquisito desayuno con panecillos hechos ___ harina ___ maíz. Felipe le habló ___ Graciela y le insinuó que si se casaba con él, ella sería tratada como una reina. Le propuso inclusive que ___ luna ___ miel la llevaría ___ su propio yate hasta su isla privada ___ el mar Caribe, y que luego viajarían ___ avión ___ París. Después del desayuno Felipe le presentó ___ los redactores ___ el periódico. Entre ellos estaba Julio, que había ido aquel día ___ reemplazar ___ Paco, uno ___ los periodistas ___ periódico, que ___ suerte ___ Julio se encontraba enfermo aquel día.

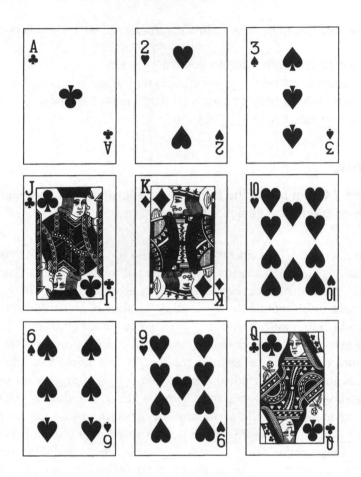

**Exercise 15.** According to the illustration, complete the following sentences using the appropriate prepositions.

1. El as ____ tréboles (A♣) está ____ la primera fila, junto ____ el dos ____ corazones (2♥) y el tres ____ picas (3♠).
2. El rey ____ diamantes (K♦) está ____ el valet ____ tréboles (J♣) y el 10 ____ corazones (10♥).
3. ____ el rey de diamantes (K♦) está el 2 ____ corazones (2♥).
4. ____ la derecha del rey ____ diamantes (K♦) está el 10 ____ corazones (10♥).
5. ____ el 10 ____ corazones (10♥) se encuentra la reina ____ tréboles (Q♣).

# ANSWER KEYS

## CHAPTER 1

### Exercise 1.

| | | | |
|---|---|---|---|
| 1. | fu/ria | muer/to | ra/bia |
| 2. | hue/vo | Dia/na | cui/da/do |
| 3. | tiem/po | ver/de | Juan |
| 4. | jue/go | a/gua | rí/o |
| 5. | via/ja | ca/rro/ña | gua/ri/da |
| 6. | ciu/dad | tre/gua | len/gua |
| 7. | puen/te | re/cuer/do | a/bue/lo |
| 8. | nie/ve | tie/mpo | reu/ma/tis/mo |
| 9. | viu/da | Lui/sa | vi/rue/la |
| 10. | pa/ñue/lo | a/za/lea | Eu/ro/pa |
| 11. | an/ti/guo | cuan/to | cua/dro |

### Exercise 2.

1. /**e**-rre-ko-n**e**-rre-si-g**a**-rro/
   /**e**-rre-ko-n**e**-rre-ba-rr**i**l/
   /rr**a**-pi-do-k**o**-rren-los-k**a**-rros/
   /kar-g**a**-dos-de-a-s**u**-ka-ral-fe-rro-ka-rr**i**l/

2. /tres-tr**i**s-tes-t**i**-gres-ko-m**i**-an-tr**i**-go/
   /en-tr**e**s-tr**i**s-tes-tr**a**s-tos-rre-pl**e**-tos-de-tr**i**-go/

3. /kom-p**a**-dre| k**o**m-pra-m**e**un-k**o**-ko/
   /kom-p**a**-dre| k**o**-ko-no-k**o**m-pro/
   /k**e**l-ke-p**o**-ko-k**o**-ko-k**o**-me/
   /p**o**-ko-k**o**-ko-k**o**m-pra/

4. /pa-bl**i**-to-kla-b**ou**n-kla-v**i**-to/
   /k**e**-kla-b**i**-to-kla-b**o**-pa-bl**i**-to/

5. /e-la-m**or**-es-**u**-na-lo-k**u**-ra/
   /ke-s**o**-l**oe**l-k**u**-ra-lo-k**u**-ra/
   /p**e**-r**oe**l-k**u**-ra-ke-lo-k**u**-ra/
   /ko-m**e**-t**eu**-na-gr**a**n-lo-k**u**-ra/

### Exercise 3.

/n**ue**s-tras-b**i**-das-son-los-rr**i**-os/
/ke-b**a**-na-d**ar**-en-la-m**ar**/
/k**e**s-el-mo-r**ir**/

/b**e**r-de-ke-te-k**ie**-ro-b**e**r-de/
/b**e**r-de-b**ien**-to| b**e**r-des-rr**a**-mas/

/el-b**a**r-ko-s**o**-bre-la-m**a**r/
/yel-ka-b**a**-yo-en-la-mon-t**a**-ña/

/hu-ben-t**u**d| di-b**i**-no-te-s**o**-ro/
/ya-te-b**a**s-p**a**-ra-no-bol-b**e**r/
/kuan-do-k**ie**-ro-yo-r**a**r| no-y**o**-ro/
/ya-b**e**-ses-y**o**-ro-sin-ke-r**e**r/

/la-mas-b**e**-ya-n**i**-ña/
/de-n**ue**s-tro-lu-g**a**r/
/oi-vi**u**-dai-s**o**-la/
/ya-y**e**r-por-ka-s**a**r/
/vi**e**n-do-ke-su-s**o**-jos/
/a-la-g**e**-rra-b**a**n/
/a-su-m**a**-dre-d**i**-se/
/kes-k**u**-č a-su-m**a**l/
/de-j**a**d-me-yo-r**a**r/
/a-o-r**i**-yas-del-m**a**r/

## Exercise 4.

1.  a/<u>ho</u>/ra        i/<u>de</u>/a       des/ha/<u>cer</u>    to-<u>a</u>-lla     <u>cuer</u>/da     ma/<u>es</u>/tro    ciu/<u>dad</u>
2.  a/<u>diós</u>        <u>cien</u>/cia     ins/pi/<u>rar</u>    du/<u>raz</u>/no     abs/<u>trac</u>/to   com/<u>ple</u>/to   des/truir
3.  re/cons/<u>truir</u>   cui/<u>da</u>/do    tem/<u>pra</u>/no    sep/<u>tiem</u>/bre   pe/<u>li</u>/gro    res/plan/<u>dor</u>   <u>lá</u>/piz
4.  em/pe/ra/<u>triz</u>   <u>ai</u>/re       Eu/<u>ge</u>/nia     ba/<u>úl</u>        <u>frí</u>/o        al/co/<u>hol</u>    lec/<u>ción</u>
5.  a/<u>zul</u>          <u>ca</u>/lle      Is/<u>lam</u>        des/pla/<u>zar</u>    in/flu/<u>ir</u>    le/<u>ón</u>        ce/re/<u>al</u>
6.  <u>bai</u>/le         <u>hé</u>/ro/e     mer/ca/<u>der</u>    fe/<u>liz</u>        pe/<u>lí</u>/cu/la   <u>tí</u>/tu/lo     gra/<u>má</u>/ti/ca

## Exercise 5.

1.  **jó**ven       re**loj**      **lá**piz      **án**gel      **dé**bil      ho**tel**      se**gún**
2.  a**mor**       **cé**lebre    ol**vi**do     pe**lí**cula   musul**mán**   **jó**venes    **án**geles
3.  direc**tor**   **ór**denes    **tí**tulo     **cré**dito    **tér**mino    ter**mi**no    **víc**tima
4.  infe**liz**    fe**liz**      ani**mal**     **ú**nico      mu**jer**      se**ñor**      sim**pá**tico
5.  **vír**genes   inte**rés**    es**tá**       **és**ta       gra**má**tica  pe**li**gro    ameri**ca**nos
6.  chime**ne**a   **sa**la       e**xa**men     e**xá**menes   ra**zón**      ra**zo**nes    **ár**bol
7.  aza**le**a     ta**re**a      mu**jer**      hipo**pó**tamo pa**pá**       an**ti**guo    **pa**pa

## Exercise 6.

1.  solo.
2.  té
3.  Te
4.  té
5.  ¿Cuánto, aquel
6.  Como, aún
7.  él
8.  Sólo, si
9.  Tú, sí
10. mas

# CHAPTER 2

### Exercise 1.

1. la nieta, la abuela
2. El hermano
3. el esposo
4. la suegra
5. la prima
6. el perro (la mascota)
7. la madre
8. el tío
9. la cuñada
10. la tía

### Exercise 2.

1. La hermana
2. La vecina
3. El amigo
4. La sobrina
5. El abuelo
6. La sicóloga
7. La gata
8. El perro
9. El tío
10. La prima

### Exercise 3.

1. El
2. El
3. La
4. El
5. La
6. la
7. El
8. La
9. El
10. La

### Exercise 4.

1. El patrón
2. La señora
3. El doctor
4. La rectora
5. El director
6. La embajadora

7.  El vendedor
8.  La conductora
9.  La exploradora
10. La administradora

**Exercise 5.**

1.  María, **la** estudiante, está contenta.
    José, **el** estudiante, está contento.

2.  Juan es **el** testigo del crimen.
    Marta es **la** testigo del crimen.

3.  El señor Rodríguez es **el** visitante más importante.
    La señora Rodríguez es **la** visitante más importante.

4.  **La** cliente es ami**ga** de mi padre.
    **El** cliente es ami**go** de mi padre.

5.  **El** guía es ami**go** de mi madre.
    **La** guía es ami**ga** de mi madre.

6.  **La** novelista es muy famos**a**.
    **El** novelista es muy famos**o**.

7.  **La** astronauta, Julia, se prepara para viajar a Marte.
    **El** astronauta, Carlos, se prepara para viajar a Marte.

8.  Teresa, **la** adolescente, juega para el equipo de fútbol de su escuela.
    Jorge, **el** adolescente, juega para el equipo de fútbol de su escuela.

9.  **La** cantante, Isabel, recibió muchos aplausos anoche en el concierto.
    **El** cantante, Romeo, recibió muchos aplausos anoche en el concierto.

**Exercise 6.**

1.  La
2.  La
3.  la
4.  Los
5.  Las
6.  los
7.  las
8.  la
9.  Los

**Exercise 7.**

**Across:**

1  nuera
4  caballero
6  princesa

8    actriz
10   baronesa
11   yerno
12   madre
13   mujer

**Down:**

2    reina
3    príncipe
4    caballo
5    rey
7    dama
9    padre
11   yegua

### Exercise 8.

1. **La** señora olvidó hacer **la** cama está mañana.
2. En **la** habitación está **el** computador, **la** silla, **el** televisor, **la** cama y **la** lámpara.
3. **La** ventana está cerrada y **el** clóset está abierto.
4. María compró **el** vestido en **el** almacén.
5. **El** tapete de la sala está sucio.
6. Mi abrigo negro está en **el** armario.

### Exercise 9.

1. la
2. el
3. la
4. el; la
5. el
6. la, la

### Exercise 10.

**el** acné
**la** actividad
**la** admiración
**el** afiche
**la** agresividad
**el** aljibe
**la** amabilidad
**la** ambición
**el** amplificador
**la** ansiedad
**el** antibiótico
**la** aptitud
**el** arco
**la** atracción

**el** baile
**el** banco
**el** barco
**la** bondad
**el** cable
**el** cacao
**el** café
**la** calefacción
**la** cantidad
**la** capacidad
**la** circulación
**la** ciudad
**la** claridad
**la** coalición
**el** coco
**la** composición
**el** cruce
**la** cruz
**la** decisión
**la** declaración
**la** depresión
**el** destornillador
**la** dirección
**el** domingo
**el** dulce
**la** educación
**el** electrodoméstico
**la** embarcación
**el** equipaje
**la** escasez
**la** estupidez
**la** evaluación
**la** habilidad
**el** humidificador
**la** infección
**la** liberación
**la** libertad
**la** luz
**la** madurez
**el** meteoro
**el** monitor
**la** nación
**la** nariz
**la** niñez
**la** operación
**la** pared
**la** pasión

**la** piedad
**la** prisión
**la** profesión
**la** propiedad
**la** publicidad
**el** reflector
**el** retrovisor
**la** revolución
**la** salud
**la** sed
**la** selección
**la** sencillez
**la** superstición
**el** tabaco
**la** televisión
**el** televisor
**la** tempestad
**la** tensión
**la** timidez
**el** tóxico
**el** tronco
**el** vapor
**la** vegetación
**la** versión
**la** virtud
**la** voz

**Exercise 11.**

María Sol utilizó **el teorema** de Pitágoras para resolver **el problema** de matemáticas. Ahora tiene que terminar la tarea de español. **El idioma** español es muy fácil.
La tarea de ciencias es más difícil. María Sol debe escribir un ensayo. **El tema** del ensayo es sobre **el clima** tropical. **El dilema** de María es escribir directamente el ensayo o hacer primero **el esquema.**

**Exercise 12.**

1. el mapa
2. el ataúd
3. el arroz
4. el lápiz
5. la avestruz
6. el ajedrez
7. el pez
8. el planeta
9. el tranvía

**Exercise 13.**

1. la mano
2. la llave
3. la calle
4. la carne
5. la nieve
6. la noche
7. la nube
8. la sangre
9. la sal

**Exercise 14.**

1. la fiebre
2. la foto
3. la nube
4. la llave
5. la mano

**Exercise 15.**

1. La modelo
2. El orden
3. El papa
4. La guía
5. La cura
6. La capital
7. La corte
8. El modelo
9. El policía, la orden
10. El corte
11. La papa
12. El guía

**Exercise 16.**

1. Los chocolates están sobre la mesa.
2. Las camas están sin tender.
3. Las casas están al norte de la ciudad.
4. Los tigres están en la jaula.
5. Los problemas están en los gobernantes.
6. Las tiendas están en el barrio.

**Exercise 17.**

1. **las** casas, **los** perros, **las** gatas
2. **los** dormitorios, **los** problemas, **las** manos
3. **el** teorema, **los** días, **las** motos

4. **las** noches, **la** luna, **la** Tierra
5. **los** sistemas, **el** viaje, **los** planetas
6. **los** mapas, **los** poemas, **los** programas

## Exercise 18.

1. Los hornos microondas son negros.
2. Las batidoras son verdes.
3. Los fregaderos son metálicos.
4. Las ollas son grandes.
5. Las cafeteras son eléctricas.
6. Las estufas son blancas.

## Exercise 19.

1. Los refrigeradores del hotel son blancos.
2. Los congeladores de mi casa son eficientes.
3. Los trenes son lentos.
4. Las leyes son obsoletas.
5. Los ataúdes son de madera.
6. Los sartenes son de hierro.

## Exercise 20.

1. El empleado está cansado.
2. El motor está encendido.
3. El rey está preso.
4. El actor está desesperado.
5. El maniquí está vestido elegantemente.
6. El pan está crujiente.

## Exercise 21.

Todos los días la abuela Rosario entra a **la sala** y mira **el cuadro** pintado por su hijo. Luego toma uno de **los libros** que están en **la estantería** al lado de la mesita y se sienta en **el sillón** próximo al sofá. Cuando hace frío, enciende **la calefacción** o prende **el fuego** en **la chimenea**. En **la mesita** coloca **la taza** de té. A la abuela Rosario le encantan **las flores** frescas.

## Exercise 22.

1. Las nueces
2. Los lápices
3. Los peces
4. Los pies
5. Los cafés
6. Los papás

**Exercise 23.**

1. **los**
2. **La**
3. **los**
4. **El**
5. **La**
6. **Las**

**Exercise 24.**

1. los microbuses
2. los compases
3. los gases
4. los meses
5. los corteses
6. los burgueses

**Exercise 25.**

1. la a<u>b</u>eja africana
   las a<u>b</u>ejas africanas

2. el <u>a</u>gua mineral
   las <u>a</u>guas minerales

3. el <u>á</u>guila calva
   las <u>á</u>guilas calvas

4. el <u>a</u>la del avión
   las <u>a</u>las del avión

5. la alca<u>p</u>arra en vinagre
   las alca<u>p</u>arras en vinagre

6. el <u>a</u>lma muerta
   las <u>a</u>lmas muertas

7. la al<u>men</u>dra tostada
   las al<u>men</u>dras tostadas

8. la almo<u>h</u>ada de plumas
   las almo<u>h</u>adas de plumas

9. el <u>a</u>rma de fuego
   las <u>a</u>rmas de fuego

10. la aza<u>lea</u> es una flor
    las aza<u>lea</u>s son unas flores

11. el <u>h</u>acha de piedra
    las <u>h</u>achas de piedra

12. la ham<u>br</u>una
    las ham<u>br</u>unas

**Exercise 26.**

1. **la**
2. **al**
3. **del**
4. **al**
5. **del, las**
6. **al**
7. **la**
8. **la**

**Exercise 27.**

1. unos problemas
2. una balanza
3. una decisión
4. un perfume
5. un hombre
6. un escritor
7. un idioma
8. una toalla
9. unas canciones
10. un príncipe
11. unas yeguas
12. unos leones

**Exercise 28.**

1. **un**
2. **una**
3. **un**
4. **una**
5. **un**
6. **unos**

**Exercise 29.**

1. **El, la**
2. **La**
3. **El**
4. **La, la**
5. **El**
6. **Las, la**

**Exercise 30.**

1. **El**
2. **La**
3. **El, el**
4. **La**
5. **El**
6. **Las, la**

**Exercise 31.**

1. Quiero beber vino de California.
2. Hay leche en el supermercado.
3. Rosario compra azúcar de caña.
4. No hay justicia en algunos países.
5. Sin tiempo, no podré terminar **el** ensayo de español.
6. Estudia matemáticas y física en la universidad.
7. Nosotros hablamos inglés.

**Exercise 32.**

1. **Una**
2. **Un**
3. **Una, una**
4. **un**
5. **un**
6. **Un, un**

**Exercise 33.**

1. **El** domingo pasado vimos **unos** globos en **el** parque del barrio.

2. **Un** niño encontró **un** guante en **la** puerta del teatro.

3. Necesitamos **una** libra de azúcar y **un** par de huevos para preparar **el** postre preferido de papá.

4. Juan tuvo que esperar **unos** minutos antes de entrar a **la** oficina de su jefe.

5. En **el** zoológico de la ciudad vimos **una** jirafa, **un** león, **un** elefante, **un** tigre y **unas** tortugas.

6. **El** animal preferido de todos fue **el** gorila.

**Exercise 34.**

**El** joven Javier, todos **los** días se levanta a **las** seis de **la** mañana. Se baña, se viste y bebe **una** taza de café con **una** galleta. Luego, se cepilla **los** dientes y toma **el** bus para ir a **la** universidad. **El** martes a **las** ocho de **la** mañana tiene clase de estadística. Javier es **el** mejor estudiante de la clase. **Una** vez a la semana juega fútbol con **unos** amigos que conoció en la universidad.

# Review

**Exercise 35.**

1. una señora triste
2. una mujer fiel
3. una esposa celosa
4. una oficial intrépida

5. una policía valiente
6. una gata negra
7. un reina déspota
8. una gobernadora popular

**Exercise 36.**

1. La señora Gómez es una artista famosa.
2. Lucía es una actriz famosa.
3. Martina es una campeona de tenis.
4. María es una cantante excepcional.

**Exercise 37.**

1. Tengo una perra valiente,
2. una yegua inteligente,
3. una gata divertida,
4. una ratona entrometida,
5. y una esposa desesperante.

**Exercise 38.**

1. John Glenn y Neil Armstrong son unos astronautas intrépidos.
2. Nicole Kidman y Tom Cruise son unos actores famosos.
3. Lance Armstrong y Robbie McEwen son unos ciclistas veloces.
4. Batistuta y Romario son unos futbolistas estupendos.

**Exercise 39.**

1. la, el, la
2. los, un
3. la, una
4. el, una
5. las, los
6. la, el

# CHAPTER 3

**Exercise 1.**

1. delgado
2. sucia
3. cara
4. largas
5. costosos
6. alta

**Exercise 2.**

1. d
2. f
3. e
4. a
5. b
6. c

**Exercise 3.**

1. español.
2. ecuatoriana.
3. americano.
4. suecos.
5. japoneses.
6. suizas.
7. inglesa.
8. franceses.
9. portuguesa.
10. boliviana.
11. alemanes
12. panameñas
13. salvadoreña
14. argentinas

**Exercise 4.**

1. importante
2. alegre
3. grande
4. interesante
5. rebelde
6. verde

**Exercise 5.**

1. homicidas
2. fuerte
3. insignificantes
4. inteligentes
5. excelente
6. reconfortante

**Exercise 6.**

1. atroz
2. cruel
3. gris

4. peor
5. joven
6. feliz

**Exercise 7.**

1. c
2. f
3. d
4. b
5. e
6. a

**Exercise 8.**

1. San
2. gran
3. grande
4. Santa
5. mal
6. malas

**Exercise 9.**

1. **El pobre** está sin trabajo.
2. **La joven** ganó el concurso de belleza.
3. **Los trabajadores** pidieron un aumento de salario.
4. **El alemán** viajó por Sudamérica.
5. **Las argentinas** son muy simpáticas.
6. **El negro** es mi preferido.

**Exercise 10.**

1. estas
2. Aquel
3. estos
4. esas
5. Este
6. estos

**Exercise 11.**

—Mamá, compremos **este** jabón.
—Vamos a comprar **aquel** jabón rosado, Gabriela. Es mi marca favorita.
—Pero no me gusta el perfume de **esa** marca de jabón, mamá.
—¿Qué te parece **este** jabón cremoso?
—Me gusta mucho más. ¿Ves **esas** flores?
—¡Qué lindas! Quedan perfectas en **aquel** jarrón que te regaló papá.

**Exercise 12.**

Estoy buscando **mi** mochila. Me voy de viaje con **mis** primos Arturo y Gonzalo. **Nuestra** tía Carmen y **su** esposo tienen una casa en el campo y vamos a visitarlos. Préstame **tu** auto y devuélveme **mis** maletas. Las voy a necesitar.

**Exercise 13.**

1. Así son, <u>tus</u> amigos. Esa es la pura verdad.
2. Dame <u>tu</u> teléfono. Te llamo mañana.
3. Lucía y Marta dejaron <u>sus</u> maletas en el hotel.
4. El panadero comienza <u>su</u> trabajo muy temprano.
5. Mi hermana y yo donamos <u>nuestra</u> ropa vieja a los pobres.
6. Pensad en la felicidad de <u>vuestras</u> familias.

**Exercise 14.**

1. Francisco me invitó a **la** finca **suya** el fin de semana.
2. Pero, yo prefiero quedarme en **la** casa **mía**.
3. Felipe, **el** novio **mío**, llega de Chile mañana.
4. Iremos a un bar el viernes en la noche con **unas** amigas **nuestras** de la universidad.
5. El sábado en la tarde iremos con **los** hijos **tuyos** a la playa.
6. Santiago perdió **los** libros **tuyos**.
7. Lola no puede abrir **el** coche **suyo** porque perdió **las** llaves **suyas**.
8. El futuro **del** país **vuestro** no es muy prometedor.

**Exercise 15.**

1. doscientos cuarenta y cinco coches
2. cuarenta y cinco televisores
3. mil doscientas ochenta y dos manzanas
4. ciento cuarenta y cinco mil setecientos sesenta y cinco personas
5. quinientos cincuenta y cuatro mil ochocientos noventa y ocho trabajadores
6. un millón doscientas ochenta y nueve mil novecientas ocho naranjas
7. doscientos nueve muchachos
8. doscientas veintinueve mil mujeres
9. ciento una niñas
10. quinientas noventa naranjas
11. veintiún balones
12. treinta y tres almacenes

**Exercise 16.**

1. 7,5 Kg.
2. $3.500
3. €1.300.000
4. 6,03 Kg.
5. $140.000.000.000

**Exercise 17.**

1. primer
2. tercera
3. primero, primer
4. tercer, cuarto
5. primeros
6. decimotercer

**Exercise 18.**

1. quinto
2. tercer
3. primer
4. sexto
5. cuarto
6. segundo

# Review

**Exercise 19.**

1. Marta es colombiana.
2. Mi tía es española.
3. Mi hermana es guapa.
4. Mi amiga está contenta.
5. Liliana es inteligente.

**Exercise 20.**

1. Un helicóptero eficiente y un avión **eficiente**.
2. Un jugo refrescante y una fruta **refrescante**.
3. Un amigo fiel y una compañera **fiel**.
4. Un actor famoso y una actriz **famosa**.
5. Un empleado perezoso y una empleada **perezosa**.
6. Un profesor exigente y una profesora **exigente**.

**Exercise 21.**

1. Hay doscientos mil soldados en Irak.
2. Tenemos tres mil seiscientos setenta y tres francos suizos.
3. José ganó quinientos setenta y ocho millones de pesos.
4. Ese toro pesa setecientos ochenta y siete kilos.
5. El premio mayor de la lotería es doscientos treinta y un millones quinientos treinta y siete mil dólares.

**Exercise 22.**

1. ese
2. esta
3. Estos
4. Esa
5. esa

**Exercise 23.**

1. **Estos** pantalones son **mis** pantalones. **Tus** pantalones están sobre la cama.
2. **Aquellos** muchachos están compitiendo con **sus** bicicletas.
3. **Esa** señora tiene **tus** libros de español.
4. ¿**Aquel** muchacho tiene **su** perro?
5. **Este** es **nuestro** amigo Marco.
6. **Esta** es **vuestra** casa, ¿verdad?

**Exercise 24.**

1. primeros
2. tercera
3. primer
4. quinto

# CHAPTER 4

**Exercise 1.**

1. llego
2. tememos
3. creen
4. viven
5. respondes
6. miran
7. insiste
8. comprende
9. necesitan
10. hablan

**Exercise 2.**

1. reconoce, reconozco
2. Venzo
3. Esparzo
4. desaparezco
5. introduzco

6. agradezco
7. Aborrezco
8. convenzo
9. Conduzco

**Exercise 3.**

1. recojo, exijo, protejo, acojo, restringes, finjo
2. escojo, dirijo, sumerjo

**Exercise 4.**

1. distingo
2. prosigo
3. sigo
4. extingo
5. yergo
6. consigo
7. persigo

**Exercise 5.**

1. distribuyes
2. concluyes
3. diluyen
4. destruyen
5. reconstruimos
6. obstruye
7. disminuís
8. recluye
9. sustituye
10. contribuyen

**Exercise 6.**

1. evalúan
2. ampliáis
3. enfría
4. sitúas
5. guía
6. perpetúa
7. insinuáis
8. devalúan
9. efectúan
10. continúa

Exercise 7.

Visita al psiquiatra

—Doctor, siempre temo cuando él **atraviesa** la calle y yo **pienso** que algo le va a pasar.

—¿Qué es lo que (tú) **sientes**?

—No sé Dr. Algo **gobierna** mis sentidos y (yo) **prefiero** alzarlo en mis brazos. Mis amigos me **recomiendan** comprar un cargador para bebés y (ellos) se **divierten** burlándose de mi. Y me preguntan con quién me **despierto** en las mañanas... Pero yo soy normal, sólo temo cuando (nosotros) **atravesamos** la calle...

—Por favor empieza de nuevo, es que (yo) **pierdo** el hilo con mucha facilidad. ¿Qué raza es tu perro?

Exercise 8.

1. viste
2. repite, consigue
3. corrige
4. mide
5. eliges
6. despedís
7. impedimos
8. sigues
9. persigue

Exercise 9.

1. adquieren
2. adquiere
3. inquiere
4. adquirís

Exercise 10.

1. vuelves
2. muere
3. resuelve
4. suenan
5. almorzamos
6. dormís
7. puede
8. huelo
9. recuerdan
10. devuelves

**Exercise 11.**

1. juegas
2. juego
3. juegan
4. juegan
5. juega

**Exercise 12.**

1. trae, traigo
2. dais, doy
3. dices, haces, digo, hago
4. viene, vengo
5. cabe, quepo
6. poneis, pongo
7. viene, vengo
8. ve, veo, ven
9. tengo, tienes
10. saben, sé
11. dicen, sabes, digo
12. Oigo, oyes
13. salgo, sales
14. vales, valgo

**Exercise 13.**

Me gustan los libros de caballerías porque **son** entretenidos. Por el contrario, los libros de gramática que (yo) **he** estudiado me aburren. Un libro de aventuras **es** siempre más divertido, y aún más, cuando **está** escrito con humor. Porque si vosotros **estáis** leyendo algo aburrido, **vais** directo a dormir. De todas maneras, recuerda que con voluntad y entusiasmo **es** más fácil aprender cualquier idioma.

**Exercise 14.** Using the present tense write about one day in Sonia's vacation.

1. Sonia se levanta.
2. Sonia se ducha.
3. Sonia se viste.
4. Sonia sale a caminar por la playa.
5. Sonia come en un restaurante.
6. Sonia va al museo.
7. Sonia conoce a un amigo.
8. Sonia sale a bailar.

**Exercise 15.**

Paco:—Hola, ¿Cómo te **llamas**?

Pilar:—Me **llamo** Pilar.

Paco:—Yo me **llamo** Paco. ¿Qué **haces**? ¿**Trabajas** o **estudias**?

Pilar:—**Trabajo** en una librería. ¿Y tú, qué **haces**?

Paco:—**Estudio** administración de empresas. ¿Quieres una cerveza?

Pilar:—¡Vale!

Paco:—Esta noche **vamos** a ir con unos amigos a un concierto de música de Senegal.
      ¿**Quieres** venir?

Pilar:—¡Estupendo!

Paco:—Entonces, nos **vemos** en el Teatro Real a las ocho en punto.

Pilar:—De acuerdo. Hasta entonces.

Paco:—Chao.

# Review

**Exercise 16.**

Marta y Carlos **son** novios. Ambos **asisten** a la Universidad Nacional y **estudian** biología. En un mes **van** a graduarse, y por eso Marta **busca** un trabajo urgentemente. **Viven** juntos porque no **pueden** estar separados un minuto. Los viernes **juegan** tenis por la tarde y por la noche **bailan** salsa. Los sábados, Marta **duerme** hasta las ocho de la mañana, se **viste** y **corre** siete kilómetros. Cuando Carlos **decide** ir con ella, siempre le dice: "Marta, esta vez sí te **venzo**", pero la verdad es que nunca la **vence**. Cuando ella lo **socorre,** Carlos le **contesta**: "Mi amor te lo **agradezco**". Yo les **confieso** algo: "Carlos **es** un flojo" y Marta siempre lo **protege**. Yo lo **conozco** desde hace dos años. A Marta le **reconozco** su ternura. Pero, también le **exijo** prudencia. Ese hombre **es** un vividor. **Persigue** a las muchachas dulces y las **hace** sentir diosas. Pero luego, cuando **adquiere** confianza, se **muda** a su apartamento. Allí, **almuerza, come** y **duerme** y no **trae** nada, sólo **distribuye** sonrisas y palabras bonitas, y una las **oye** como venidas del cielo. Luego que una se **ha** ilusionado, **tiene** la desfachatez de decir que algo extraño le **sucede** y dice: "Mi pasión se **enfría**, lo **siento** corazón pero me **voy**". Cuando **dice** aquello, no **cabe** la menor duda que **es** porque **ha** visto otra mujer. Lo **digo** yo, que lo **he** vivido en carne propia.

**Exercise 17.**

1. amó
2. aprendí
3. abrió, encontró
4. bailaron
5. corrí
6. asististe
7. socorrí
8. decidisteis

9. caminó
10. emprendió
11. escribieron
12. alisté
13. insistió
14. compraste
15. comió
16. hablé

**Exercise 18.**

1. La verdad es que nosotros no **comprendimos** nada.

2. Miguel Induráin **subió** los Pirineos en el Tour de Francia en primer lugar.

3. Otra vez Andrew **llegó** tarde a clase.

4. Martín Lutero **vivió** entre 1483 y 1546.

5. ¡La última semana de clase mi profesor **miró** los ejercicios de todo el curso!

6. Andrea le **respondió** muy mal al jefe.

7. Yo siempre le estoy agradecido, porque cuando **necesité** dinero, ella me lo **prestó**.

8. Todos **temimos** el terremoto.

9. Exactamente un año después del exilio en Elba, Napoleón **retornó** a Francia en febrero de 1815.

10. Ellos **vendieron** todo antes de partir.

11. Darwin y Wallace **trabajaron** independiente y simultáneamente para elaborar la teoría de la evolución.

12. Pedro y su esposa **viajaron** en avión a Bruselas.

13. Los padres de mis primos les **permitieron** muchas cosas a sus hijos.

14. Lucho **envió** sus cartas por correo rápido.

15. Sócrates **bebió** una infusión de cicuta antes de morir.

16. Los estudiantes **recibieron** sus calificaciones el lunes.

**Exercise 19.**

1. ubicaron
2. toqué
3. supliqué
4. secaron
5. sacó
6. publicó
7. pesqué
8. fabricasteis
9. explicó
10. empacaron
11. duplicó

12. dediqué
13. busqué
14. ataqué
15. calificaron
16. Coloqué

## Exercise 20.

1. apagó
2. arriesgamos
3. cargué
4. Colgué
5. encargó
6. fumigué
7. jugamos
8. llegaste
9. pagó
10. regué

## Exercise 21.

1. apaciguó
2. atestiguó
3. averigüé
4. desaguó
5. fragüé
6. santiguó

## Exercise 22.

1. abrazó
2. adelgazaron
3. Alcancé
4. almorzamos
5. alzamos
6. analicé
7. cazaron
8. cruzaron
9. destrozaron
10. empezaste
11. encabezó
12. lancé
13. organizaste
14. reemplazó
15. memorizaron
16. localizasteis
17. tranquilizó
18. tropezó

**Exercise 23.**

1. corroyó
2. cayó
3. poseyó
4. royeron
5. recayeron
6. creí
7. proveyó

**Exercise 24.**

1. oyó
2. atribuyó
3. concluyó
4. reconstruyeron
5. destruyeron
6. disminuyó
7. distribuyó
8. incluiste
9. influisteis
10. sustituyó

**Exercise 25.**

1. consintieron
2. divirtió
3. mentimos
4. prefirió
5. recomendó
6. sintieron
7. sugerimos

**Exercise 26.**

1. consiguió
2. corrigió
3. despidió
4. eligió
5. impidió
6. midió
7. persiguió
8. rieron
9. repitieron
10. siguió
11. sonreísteis
12. vestimos

**Exercise 27.**

1. durmió
2. murieron
3. durmieron
4. murieron

**Exercise 28.**

1. Carlos le **dio** las gracias al taxista.
2. María y José le **dieron** un regalo de cumpleaños a su hijo.
3. Tú **contribuiste** con dinero para proteger el medio ambiente.
4. Nosotros le **dimos** la bienvenida al astronauta.
5. Yo **di** lo mejor de mí.

**Exercise 29.**

1. anduvimos
2. estuvo
3. tuvieron
4. viniste
5. cupiste
6. dijeron
7. Hubo
8. produjeron
9. redujeron
10. pudieron
11. traje
12. retrajo
13. pusieron
14. supimos
15. hice
16. quisiste

**Exercise 30.**

1. incluyó
2. retiraste
3. repetí
4. pagamos
5. influyó
6. explicaron
7. destrocé
8. caminamos
9. temí
10. rió
11. reduje
12. llegaron
13. fabricaron

14. decidimos
15. cruzaron

**Exercise 31.**

1. sugirió
2. socorrieron
3. proveyó
4. pescamos
5. persiguió
6. necesité
7. jugamos
8. Hubo
9. distribuyeron
10. cazó
11. sentimos
12. respondió
13. publicó
14. midió
15. fumigué
16. disminuyen

**Exercise 32.**

1. abrazó
2. pudieron
3. emprendiste
4. empezó
5. empacamos
6. anduve
7. ubicaste
8. oyeron
9. durmieron
10. consiguió
11. comprendieron
12. apagó
13. amó

**Exercise 33.**

1. *El abuelo Marco nació el 21 de mayo de 1920,*
2. se casó el 5 de junio de 1941.
3. El 7 de marzo de 1942 tuvo un hijo.
4. El 23 de julio de 1945 se graduó de la escuela de arquitectura.
5. El 8 de mayo de 1950 se accidentó y fue internado en el hospital.
6. El 3 de agosto de 1955 ganó un concurso de arquitectura.
7. El 5 de mayo de 1969 arrestaron a su hijo.
8. El 3 de abril de 1970 fue al matrimonio de su hijo.

**Exercise 34.**

1. recogía
2. hacía
3. almorzabas
4. protegían
5. insistíais
6. escribía
7. decidíamos
8. asistían
9. vendía
10. temían
11. respondía
12. creían
13. comprendía
14. buscaba
15. bailaba
16. tenían
17. dormía

**Exercise 35.**

1. iba
2. íbamos
3. erais
4. era
5. veíamos
6. eran
7. iban
8. eran
9. iba
10. veía
11. era
12. veías
13. era

**Exercise 36.**

Ahora recuerdo que cuando **estábamos** en la escuela secundaria, para poder ir de paseo **organizábamos** rifas. En los paseos, muchos de mis compañeros **bebían** aguardiente a escondidas y les **enviaban** serenatas a sus prometidas sin el consentimiento de sus padres. En casa, nuestros padres eran muy estrictos. Todos los días **comíamos** en una mesa diferente a la de los adultos. Allí, en esa mesa exclusiva para nosotros los niños, nos **divertíamos** monstruosamente, especialmente con mis primos que todos los años, **venían** en las vacaciones a visitarnos. Después de comer, durante el verano todas las tardes **íbamos** a la playa y **jugábamos** voleibol. A veces **caminábamos** por la montaña y nos **escondíamos** de mi hermano menor.

**Exercise 37.**

1. Ricardo tiene dos novias, **pero antes tenía sólo una.**

2. Adriana canta rock, **pero antes cantaba tango.**

3. Alberto y Daniel escriben para el diario más importante del país, **pero antes escribían para el diario local.**

4. Mi madre sonríe sólo de vez en cuando, **pero antes sonreía todo el tiempo.**

5. Lucrecia no duerme mucho, **pero antes dormía muchas horas.**

6. Ahora nunca miento, **pero antes mentía todo el tiempo.**

7. Rosa corre tres kilómetros, **pero antes corría diez kilómetros.**

8. Mi padre no tiene mucho dinero, **pero antes tenía mucho.**

9. Hoy, mi madre no posee nada, **pero antes poseía una fortuna.**

**Exercise 38.**

1. Mi perra **era** grande y blanca y **era** muy juguetona.
2. Mi profesora **tenía** el cabello negro y **era** muy estricta.
3. Los niños **eran** muy inquietos y **tenían** mucha energía.
4. María y Josefa **eran** altas y bondadosas, y además **tenían** mucha paciencia.
5. Rosa **era** muy simpática y se **vestía** muy elegante.
6. Fernando **era** guapo, **tenía** los ojos negros y el cabello oscuro. Además **era** inteligente.

**Exercise 39.**

Julia **se sentía** agobiada cuando nuestra madre la **reprendía**. A ninguno nos **gustaba** estudiar. La escuela nos **aburría** y **llorábamos** desconsoladamente todos los lunes cuando **íbamos** camino a la escuela. **Mirábamos** a los pescadores y al mar con nostalgia. **Pensábamos** que la libertad era lanzar piedras desde el acantilado. Julia además siempre **sentía** miedo cuando **entraba** a la clase de latín. Muchas veces para no ir a la escuela **decía** que **estaba** enferma y que **tenía** náuseas. Pero mamá nunca le **creía**.

**Exercise 40.**

1. Mis padres **pensaban** que **era** un perezoso.
2. Yo **creía** que **tenía** una enfermedad grave.
3. Mi hermana **estaba** segura de mi lealtad.
4. Raúl nos **aseguraba** que **tenía** un secreto.
5. Andrea **pensaba** que yo nunca **tenía** la razón, y **era** cierto.
6. Yo no **reconocía** que me **equivocaba**.
7. Clemente **insinuaba** que yo **perdía** todo.
8. Yo **insistía** en ser astronauta.
9. Ellas siempre **averiguaban** dónde **era** la fiesta.

**Exercise 41.**

1. hacía
2. miraban
3. vivíamos
4. trabajaba
5. recogía
6. encendían
7. aparcaba
8. rezabas
9. leía
10. vendían

**Exercise 42.**

1. era
2. hacía
3. Llovía, había
4. seguía, nevaba
5. Hacía
6. estaba, hacía
7. Era
8. había
9. corría

**Exercise 43.** Cuando la madre llegó:

1. Un niño pintaba en la pared de la sala.
2. El otro niño rompía los libros de arte.
3. El padre bebía cerveza.
4. El padre también miraba televisión.

**Exercise 44.**

**Past Imperfect**

**Era** alrededor de las ocho de la mañana
Afuera, **había** miles de personas gritando
**Era** un día de verano
el cielo **estaba** completamente azul
Todos, en la calle, **iban** vestidos con
disfraces de variados colores
(todos) **cantaban**
(todos) **bailaban** como locos
Todos nos **miraban** de manera extraña.
No **había** duda
**teníamos** cara de turistas.

**Simple Preterit**

**oímos** gritos en la calle.
Marta y yo nos **levantamos**
nos **asomamos** a la ventana
—Ya **comenzó** el Carnaval—
le **dije** a Marta.
Nos **vestimos** rápidamente
**tomamos** la cámara
**salimos** a la calle.

**Exercise 45.** Put the following text in the past.

El Bogotazo

El señor Torres **era** un hombre maduro, casado con una mujer que **trabajaba** en la oficina de correos. El 9 de abril de 1948, se **encontraba** bebiendo una cerveza en el Café Royal, sobre la calle Séptima. De repente, **escuchó** una multitud de hombres armados que **venían** enfurecidos de todas partes, con palos y machetes. Como no **tuvo** tiempo suficiente para levantarse y salir corriendo, **decidió** refugiarse en el bar. Desde la ventana **vio** cómo hombres enfurecidos **destruían** y **saqueaban** todo lo que **estaba** a su alrededor. Toda el centro de la ciudad de Bogotá **estaba** en llamas. El señor Torres **pasó** la noche en el bar y sólo al día siguiente **logró** salir. Se **dirigió** a su casa, preocupado por su mujer. No **sabía** si **estaba** viva. Aunque **había** muertos por todas partes, el señor Torres **encontró** a su mujer sana y salva.

**Exercise 46.**

*Answers may vary*

1. Porque hacía mucho calor.
2. Porque no funcionaba bien.
3. Porque no tenía tu número de teléfono y no pude llamarte.
4. Porque estaba cansado.
5. Porque estaba enfermo y no tenía ganas de trabajar.

**Exercise 47.**

1. En la sala de espera del aeropuerto, hay un hombre que está tocando la guitarra.
2. Un hombre calvo está leyendo el periódico.
3. Un mendigo está durmiendo en una silla.
4. Una mujer está comprando un pasaje de avión.

**Exercise 48.**

1. estoy encendiendo
2. estamos despidiendo
3. está lloviendo
4. estás alistando
5. está apareciendo
6. estás escribiendo
7. Estoy leyendo
8. está asistiendo
9. Estoy comprando
10. estás comiendo

**Exercise 49.**

1. Durante el otoño, las hojas **estuvieron cayendo** sobre el jardín.
2. El año pasado, Tomás **estuvo escribiendo** sus memorias.

3. Anoche, Nicolás **estuvo alistando** todo su equipaje.

4. Ayer, nosotros **estuvimos mirando** su última obra de teatro pero no nos gustó.

5. Ayer en la tarde el profesor **estuvo corrigiendo** las partes mal escritas de las composiciones.

6. ¿Por qué ayer **estuvieron recogiendo** las uvas si aún no estaban maduras?

7. ¡Durante toda la comida **estuviste sonriendo** con el esposo de tu amiga!

8. Nos duelen las piernas porque **estuvimos caminando** ayer toda la tarde.

9. ¿Cómo se llamaba esa muchacha con la que **estuviste viviendo** en Bruselas?

10. Los niños están cansados, toda la tarde **estuvieron subiendo** los muros de los vecinos.

**Exercise 50.**

1. estaban bebiendo
2. estaba vendiendo
3. estaba buscando
4. estaban bailando
5. estaban viajando
6. estaba oyendo
7. estabas leyendo
8. estábamos asistiendo
9. estaban construyendo

**Exercise 51.**

1. escribirá
2. alistaré
3. leeremos
4. insistirá
5. comprará
6. comerá
7. permitirán
8. enviará
9. beberás
10. recibirás

**Exercise 52.**

1. cabrán
2. habré
3. sabrás
4. cabrá
5. podremos
6. habrá
7. querrán
8. habremos
9. sabrán

**Exercise 53.**

1. compondrás
2. tendremos
3. saldrán
4. pondrá
5. valdrá
6. sobresaldréis
7. entretendremos
8. vendrá
9. equivaldrá
10. intervendrán

**Exercise 54.**

1. dirán
2. harás
3. contradiré
4. dirás
5. desharán
6. diremos
7. reharán
8. hará
9. satisfará
10. rehará

**Exercise 55.**

1. A las 4:45 P.M. los niños harán sus tareas.
2. A las 5:45 P.M. los niños jugarán en la computadora.
3. A las 6:30 P.M. los niños comerán.
4. A las 8:00 P.M. los niños verán televisión.

**Exercise 56.**

1. Ahora no tengo bastante dinero, pero el próximo año tendré bastante.
2. Ahora no hablo muy bien español, pero el próximo año hablaré muy bien.
3. Ahora trabajo en Estados Unidos, pero el próximo año trabajaré en España.
4. Ahora no hago mucho ejercicio, pero el próximo año haré mucho.
5. Ahora te obedezco en todo, pero el próximo año no te obedeceré más.
6. Ahora soy muy responsable, pero el próximo año no lo seré.

**Exercise 57.**

—Todos las Nochebuenas vamos a la Misa de Gallo, ¿**irás** este año?
—No lo sé porque el párroco está enfermo y no sabemos si la **celebrará**.

—He oído que ganaste la lotería. ¿Qué **harás** con todo ese dinero?
—Me voy a Ibiza, **compraré** un carro nuevo y el resto se lo **regalaré** a los pobres.

—¿Cuándo **irás** al odontólogo?

—La semana entrante y también **visitaré** a mi psicólogo.

—Son la cinco de la tarde y el bus no pasa. ¿Crees que **pasará** pronto?

—No lo sé, pero de seguro que **dejará** la estación a las 5:30 así que **estará** acá a las 5:35 a más tardar.

—Vete ahora, que en un momento **llegará** mi padre y nos **sorprenderá**.

—Espero que pronto me **presentarás** a tu familia como tu novio oficial.

—Nosotros **organizaremos** la venta de las boletas y tú **prestarás** tu casa para la rifa. ¿Qué dices?

—Esta bien, ¿pero yo cuánto **ganaré**?


## Exercise 58.

—¿Quién crees que **ganará** las elecciones para el cargo de alcalde?

—No sé, pero dicen que Guerra de seguro **tratará** de hacer trampa.

—En el futuro cercano todo lo que haces y dices lo **sabrá** el gobierno.

—¿Dijiste lo **sabrá?** Hace tiempo ya lo saben.

—Ayer un virus atacó el internet a nivel mundial. ¿Cómo sabremos que esto no se **producirá** de nuevo?

—Creo que eso nadie lo **garantizará**.


## Exercise 59.

1. Estarán enfermo.
2. Estarán jugando fútbol.
3. Estaremos viendo televisión.
4. Estaré en la corte.
5. Estarás en un embotellamiento de tráfico.
6. Estará hablando con sus amigos.
7. Estaréis escuchando música.


## Exercise 60.

1. Las golondrinas **van a salir** con el sol.
2. El precio de la carne **va a aumentar**.
3. Las computadoras **van a ser** más baratas en unos años.
4. **Voy a tener** una entrevista para un nuevo empleo el próximo mes.
5. Tú **vas a emprender** un largo viaje.
6. Tus planes **van a ser** exitosos.
7. Esta historia **va a tomar** un rumbo impredecible.
8. Dos grandes editoriales españolas se **van a fusionar** en el transcurso de este año.
9. Si todo sale bien **vamos a comprar** un yate en abril.

**Exercise 61.**

1. Antes de gritar, Julio debería razonar.
2. Antes de salir a jugar, deberían comer.
3. Antes de comenzar un nuevo proyecto, deberíamos terminar este.
4. Antes de precipitarte, deberías calmarte.
5. Antes de lanzar al país a la guerra, el presidente debería reflexionar un poco más.
6. Antes de subir la montaña, deberíais preparar el equipo.
7. Antes de comprar una casa, debería comprar un coche.
8. Antes de comer, deberías lavarte las manos.

**Exercise 62.**

1. —Yo, que usted no iría *or* Yo, que tú no iría.
2. —Yo, que ustedes no invertiría *or* Yo, que vosotros, no invertiría.
3. —Yo, que usted no me retiraría *or* Yo, que tú no me retiraría.
4. —Yo, que usted no me saldría *or* Yo, que tú no me saldría.
5. —Yo, que ustedes no me los pondría *or* Yo, que vosotros, no me los pondría.
6. —Yo, que usted no saldría *or* Yo, que tú no saldría.

**Exercise 63.**

1. Nos gustaría tener más tiempo libre.
2. Le gustaría conocer más gente.
3. Me gustaría vivir en Granada.
4. Les gustaría salir más a menudo por la noche.
5. Os gustaría ir con más frecuencia a cine.
6. Nos gustaría tener más libertad.

**Exercise 64.**

1. ¿Me podría usted traer pan, por favor?
2. Por favor, ¿me podría usted traer un vaso de agua?
3. ¿Podría usted traerme una garrafa de vino?
4. ¿Me podría traer usted una paella? Por favor.
5. Por favor, ¿podría usted traerme flan de postre?
6. ¿Me podría usted traer la cuenta, por favor?

**Exercise 65.**

1. —De entrada, ¿me podría usted traer un plato de jamón y lomo ibérico, por favor?
2. —De carne, ¿me podría usted traer un solomillo al oporto con setas, por favor?
3. —De postre, ¿me podría usted traer una cuajada de leche de oveja con miel, por favor?
4. —Para beber, ¿me podría usted traer una botella de vino, por favor?

**Exercise 66.**

1.  —Quisiera azúcar *or* Quisiera miel.
2.  —Quisiera una tostada *or* Quisiera un panecillo.
3.  —Quisiéramos agua *or* Quisiéramos jugo de naranja.
4.  —Quisiera huevos fritos *or* Quisiera huevos revueltos.
5.  —Quisiéramos fruta o Quisiéramos helado.
6.  —Quisiéramos pagar en efectivo *or* Quisiéramos pagar con tarjeta de crédito.

**Exercise 67.**

1.  —Que recogerían el niño en la guardería.
2.  —Que retiraría la demanda.
3.  —Que aprobarían la ley.
4.  —Que iría a la guerra.
5.  —Que protestarían hasta el final.
6.  —Que los metería a la cárcel.

**Exercise 68.**

1.  Estaría enferma.
2.  Estaría discutiendo de política.
3.  Estaría escuchando un concierto.
4.  Estaría hablando por teléfono.
5.  Estaría en una reunión muy importante.
6.  Estaría redactando la composición.
7.  Estaría visitando su médico.

# CHAPTER 5

**Exercise 1.**

1.  Leer
2.  Hacer
3.  Bailar
4.  beber
5.  ir
6.  Correr
7.  Comer
8.  Caminar
9.  Dormir
10. Conducir

**Exercise 2.**

1.  **Quiero pasear** en el parque.
2.  **Quiero nadar** con frecuencia para sentirme bien.
3.  **Quiero cortar** el césped del jardín durante el fin de semana.

4. **Quiero ir** al cine porque estrenan una película interesante.
5. **Quiero leer** una novela antes de dormirme.
6. **Quiero ir** a un concierto de jazz con mis amigos.

## Exercise 3.

1. Observaré preparar esta receta.
2. Escuché la orquesta ensayar para el concierto.
3. Oí a un chico pedir auxilio en la calle.
4. ¿Ves salir el sol desde tu habitación?
5. Miramos los niños patinar sobre el hielo.
6. ¿Escuchaste el guitarrista dar un concierto?
7. Sentiste a tu hermano cerrar la puerta.*
8. Contemplaremos a Óscar hacer una escultura.*
9. Vi a Patricia entrar en correos.*
10. Oyes sonar el teléfono.

* Note that the personal **a** is needed in these sentences.

## Exercise 4.

1. Al graduarme, viajé a Chile.
2. Al abrir la puerta, escuché a alguien hablar dentro de la casa.
3. Al leer el libro, aprendí mucho sobre la cultura azteca.
4. Al ver las noticias, nos enteramos de que nevaría mañana.
5. Al hablar con Laura por teléfono, me dijo que no estabas.
6. Al salir del museo, nos encontramos a Pepe.
7. Al hacer la compra, descubriste que habías olvidado el dinero.
8. Al abrir el mapa, supe dónde estaba.
9. Al tomar un café, mi hermano entró en la cocina.
10. Al manejar al trabajo, escuchaba las noticias por la radio.

## Exercise 5.

1. plantando
2. comiendo
3. dando
4. construyendo
5. durmiendo
6. leyendo

## Exercise 6.

1. Viviendo en Madrid conocí a Pepe.
2. Haciendo ejercicio, te sentirás mejor.
3. Viajando a Guatemala aprendí a cocinar tamales.
4. Viendo el partido de tenis, llamaron a la puerta.
5. Leyendo el periódico, estarás informado.
6. Entrando a la oficina, me dijeron que había una reunión importante.

**Exercise 7.**

1. salido
2. entrenado
3. llevado
4. divertido
5. trabajado
6. decidido
7. abierto
8. preferido
9. dicho
10. mandado

**Exercise 8.**

1. escritos
2. firmado
3. puesta, preparada
4. encontradas
5. construida
6. elegido
7. cerrada
8. rescatados
9. tomada
10. resuelto

**Exercise 9.**

1. borrado
2. pintado
3. usados
4. tenido
5. ido
6. preocupado
7. hecho
8. conocido
9. construida
10. corrido

# Review

**Exercise 10.**

1. abierto        abriendo
2. absuelto       absolviendo
3. amado          amando
4. bebido         bebiendo
5. comido         comiendo

6. cubierto        cubriendo
7. dicho           diciendo
8. descubierto     descubriendo
9. encubierto      encubriendo
10. escrito        escribiendo
11. estado         estando
12. hablado        hablando
13. hecho          haciendo
14. jugado         jugando
15. leído          leyendo
16. muerto         muriendo
17. pedido         pidiendo
18. podrido        pudriendo
19. puesto         poniendo
20. reunido        reuniendo
21. roto           rompiendo
22. satisfecho     satisfaciendo
23. servido        sirviendo
24. venido         viniendo
25. vuelto         volviendo

**Exercise 11.**

Claudia está **comiendo** con Rebeca. Ambas **discuten** sobre la situación política mundial. El profesor de Historia ha **convencido** a Claudia que estamos **viviendo** un momento muy importante en la Historia. Rebeca está **sorprendida**, para ella todo sigue igual. Trabaja mucho y está **cansada**. Lo único que quiere es **descansar** y **ver** televisión. Claudia por el contrario está **preocupada** y **enojada** con la indiferencia de Rebeca. Claudia ha **escrito** varios correos electrónicos a sus amigos que están **viviendo** fuera del país para **saber** qué piensan.

# CHAPTER 6

**Exercise 1.**

1. He caminado
2. ha escrito
3. ha leído
4. hemos comprado
5. han comido
6. hemos permitido
7. Habéis bebido
8. He insistido
9. has conseguido
10. ha enviado

**Exercise 2.**

1. he escrito
2. has dicho
3. he vuelto
4. hemos muerto
5. han frito
6. han leído
7. has visto
8. han descubierto
9. han abierto
10. han cubierto

**Exercise 3.**

1. —No, todavía no he ido.
2. —Sí, ya la limpié.
3. —Sí, ya comí.
4. —No, todavía no lo he conocido.
5. —No, todavía no los he hecho.
6. —No, todavía no lo he terminado.
7. —Sí, ya los grabé.
8. —Sí, ya los hizo.
9. —No, todavía no lo han terminado.
10. —No, todavía no se ha ido.

**Exercise 4.**

1. había abierto
2. habías bailado
3. había estudiado
4. había venido
5. habían vivido
6. habíamos roto
7. habían comido
8. había visitado
9. había llegado
10. habían muerto

**Exercise 5.**

1. —¿Ya **viste** la última película de Penélope?
   —¿Cuál? ¿Una en que **hizo** el papel de monja?
   —¡No! Esa ya la **había hecho** antes de venir a Hollywood.

2. —Cuando Martín **entró** a la casa, ya Andrea **había hecho** sus maletas y se disponía a partir.
   —¿Y él qué **hizo**?
   —Le pidió la llave del buzón del correo, pero ella le dijo que ya la **había dejado** encima de la nevera con una carta para él.

3.  —¡La última vez que te vi aún no **habías dejado** los pantalones cortos! ¡Y mira ya hasta te **ha salido** bigote!

    —Sí es verdad, la última vez que la **vi** fue cuando **vino** a visitar a mi padre. Ud. recientemente **ha publicado** su primer libro, ¿verdad?

**Exercise 6.**

1.  habré terminado
2.  te habrás casado; habrás tenido
3.  habrá estudiado
4.  habrán realizado
5.  habremos hecho
6.  habré comenzado
7.  habrás ido
8.  habré oído
9.  habré llegado
10. habremos partido

**Exercise 7.**

1.  Los asesinos se habrán llevado el cadáver.
2.  La policía habrá perdido la pista de los delincuentes.
3.  Un testigo habrá estado en el lugar del crimen.
4.  El testigo lo habrá visto todo.
5.  La policía habrá entrevistado al testigo.
6.  El testigo habrá sido uno de los asesinos.

**Exercise 8.**

1.  Probablemente el perro habrá comido basura.
2.  Probablemente habrá recorrido la ciudad con otros perros.
3.  Probablemente habrá entrado a un restaurante a comer.
4.  Probablemente habrá mordido un policía.
5.  Probablemente habrá jugado con los niños en el parque.
6.  Probablemente se habrá bañado en el lago.

**Exercise 9.**

1.  Aquel día nosotros habríamos comido, pero no teníamos hambre.
2.  Esa noche me habría acostado, pero no tenía sueño.
3.  Aquella mañana te habría besado, pero no te conocía lo suficiente.
4.  Esa tarde habría jugado contigo al fútbol, pero no tenía el balón.
5.  Aquel año habría estudiado, pero no tuve dinero para pagar la matrícula.
6.  Aquella noche te habría dicho la verdad, pero no tuve la valentía de decírtela.
7.  Ese día me habría quedado contigo en casa, pero no tenía tiempo.
8.  Jorge y Tomás habrían ido a la fiesta, pero tenían que estudiar para un examen.
9.  Ellos habrían construido la casa, pero no tenían los medios.
10. Lucía me habría saludado, pero seguro que no me vio.

**Exercise 10.**

1. Marcela ya habría probado las albóndigas en casa de su abuela.

2. El señor Rodríguez ya habría muerto cuando llegó al hospital.

3. Mi madre ya habría llamado cuando yo llegué a casa.

4. Roberto ya habría salido del trabajo cuando yo lo llamé.

5. Filomena y su hija ya habrían hecho las maletas cuando llegó el taxi.

6. El presidente ya habría tomado la decisión de ir a la guerra cuando asumió la presidencia.

7. Lucía ya habría pensado abandonar a su esposo cuando se marchó.

# CHAPTER 7

**Exercise 1.**

1. Lucía se cepilla el cabello.
2. Los niños se toman la leche.
3. Tú te cortas cuando cocinas.
4. El bebé se levanta temprano.
5. Yo me levanto tarde.
6. Fernando se arregla para salir.
7. Nosotros nos duchamos con agua caliente.
8. Ustedes se miran en el espejo.

**Exercise 2.** Write six reflexive sentences describing one day in Jorge's life.

*Jorge se levanta a las seis de la mañana.*

1. Jorge se afeita a las seis y media de la mañana.

2. Jorge se baña a las seis y cuarenta y cinco de la mañana.

3. Jorge se viste a las siete de la mañana.

4. Jorge se pone su sombrero y se despide de su esposa a las siete y cuarenta y cinco de la mañana.

5. Jorge se sube al autobús a las ocho de la mañana.

**Exercise 3.**

1. se turnan
2. se reúnen
3. se besan
4. se abrazan
5. se miran
6. se estrellan

**Exercise 4.**

1. buscan
2. necesitan
3. venden
4. alquila
5. reparan
6. cocinan
7. preparan

**Exercise 5.**

1. Se cortan las patatas y la cebolla en rodajas.

2. Se les añade un poco de sal a las patatas.

3. Se sofríen en aceite a fuego lento.

4. Una vez cocinadas, se sacan las patatas del aceite.

5. Aparte en un recipiente, se baten los huevos.

6. Se añaden las patatas a los huevos.

7. A fuego alto en una sartén, con una gota de aceite, se colocan las patatas y los huevos.

8. Se le da la vuelta a la tortilla y se cocina a fuego bajo por cuatro minutos.

9. Se sirve la tortilla en un plato y se come.

**Exercise 6.**

1. espera
2. encierra
3. preocupa
4. ocupa
5. habla
6. dice
7. sabe
8. prefiere
9. construye
10. permite

# CHAPTER 8

**Exercise 1.**

1. Él
2. Ellas
3. Nosotros
4. Tú
5. Ellos

**Exercise 2.**

1. nosotros
2. tú
3. yo
4. ellas
5. nosotros
6. ella
7. ellos
8. vosotros

**Exercise 3.**

1. usted *or* ustedes
2. ella
3. ellos
4. tú
5. Yo
6. nosotros
7. él
8. ellas

**Exercise 4.**

1. lo
2. La
3. Las
4. La
5. comprar**los**
6. la
7. Ábre**la**

**Exercise 5.**

1. En la reunión el presidente **lo** discutió.
2. La multitud **los** aprobó.
3. **Las** leí.
4. **Los** estoy buscando.
5. No **la** conozco.
6. Los científicos **la** encontraron.
7. Gabriela **las** vende en la feria.

**Exercise 6.**

1. le
2. le
3. Nos
4. te
5. Os
6. les
7. me

**Exercise 7.**

1. a mí
2. a ti
3. a él
4. a ustedes
5. a ellos
6. a nosotros
7. a ella

**Exercise 8.**

1. Quiero que **se la** entregues.
2. **La** llamamos esta mañana.
3. Los obreros **lo** cerraron durante el fin de semana.
4. No **la** esperes más.
5. Es una lástima que **lo** hayamos perdido.
6. Los González **las** invitaron a cenar.
7. Búsca**la** en esta libreta.

**Exercise 9.**

—¡Qué desorden hay en este cuarto! ¿Has visto mis zapatos?
—No **los** he visto. ¿Dónde los dejaste?
—Dentro de una caja blanca. ¿**La** viste por aquí?
—Sí. **La** dejé sobre el escritorio.
—No veo el escritorio. ¿Dónde **lo** pusiste?
—**Lo** saqué a la calle para que alguien se lo lleve.
—¡No puede ser! ¿Desocupaste los cajones?
—Ni **lo** miré. ¿Tenías algo dentro?
—Mi colección de postales. ¿Cómo voy a recuperar**las?**
—Estaba bromeando. Aquí están tus postales. **Las** guardé en este sobre.
—Casi **me** matas del susto. Me alegro de que no **las** hayas perdido.

**Exercise 10.**

1. Sí, es suyo.
   No, no es suyo.

2. Sí, son nuestras.
   No, no son nuestras.

3. Sí, son suyos
   No, no son suyos

4. Sí, es mía.
   No, no es mía.

5. Sí, son nuestros.
   No, no son nuestros.

6. Sí, es suya.
   No, no es suya.

7. Sí, es suya.
   No, no es suya.

8. Sí, es mío.
   No, no es mío.

**Exercise 11.**

1. mío
2. vuestra
3. nuestro
4. suya
5. tuya
6. tuyo, mío
7. nuestra
8. míos
9. suyas
10. suya

**Exercise 12.**

1. mía
2. nuestra
3. tuyo, mío
4. vuestros, nuestros
5. suyo, mío

**Exercise 13.**

1. aquellas
2. Esto
3. esa
4. este
5. esos
6. Éste
7. ese
8. Aquel
9. Eso
10. aquella

**Exercise 14.**

1. el teléfono
2. un amigo
3. la música
4. las personas
5. el regalo
6. una pena
7. las situaciones

8. los rumores
9. el barco
10. los estudiantes

**Exercise 15.**

1. Las flores que están en el jarrón son de muchos colores.
2. Julián le regaló a Claudia un collar de perlas que costó mucho dinero.
3. Presentamos el examen de química que fue muy fácil, el lunes pasado.
4. La niña llevaba una muñeca que perdió en su carrito.
5. Quiero que me devuelvas el dinero que te presté la semana pasada.
6. Vimos una película de horror que se llama "La pesadilla".
7. Enviamos las invitaciones que no llegaron a tiempo por correo.
8. Silvia tiene una casa en la playa que es muy valiosa.
9. Encontré unos libros que eran de Gustavo en el parque.
10. El camino que lleva a la laguna está lleno de baches.

**Exercise 16.**

1. que
2. a quien
3. quien
4. quienes
5. a quien
6. a quienes
7. que
8. que
9. que
10. que

**Exercise 17.**

1. con quien
2. con quien
3. para quien
4. por quien
5. de quienes
6. a quien

**Exercise 18.**

1. El barco, **que** había zarpado minutos antes, se esfumó entre la niebla.

2. Con este anillo, **que** es una prueba de nuestro pacto, sellemos el trato.

3. Los saltamontes **que** se habían escondido entre la hierba, formaron una nube sobre la granja.

4. El hidrógeno y el oxígeno, **el cual** tiene un peso molecular de 16, son los dos componentes del agua.

5. Las gerentes, **que** se habían reunido para discutir la reunión, tomaron una decisión importante.

6. El cielo, **que** se veía desde mi ventana, se estaba tornando gris.

## Exercise 19.

1. **Lo que** me preguntó **fue** si quería salir con él.
2. **Lo que** nos sentíamos **fue** estar muy cansados de viajar a caballo.
3. **Lo que** perdimos **fue** el tren por haber salido tarde.
4. **Lo que** me asustó **fue** cuando el teléfono timbró.
5. **Lo que** me sorprendió **fue** no haberte visto en la fiesta.
6. **Lo que** le pedí **fue** que se casara conmigo.

## Exercise 20.

1. lo que *or* lo cual
2. lo que *or* lo cual
3. lo que *or* lo cual
4. lo que *or* lo cual
5. lo que *or* lo cual
6. lo que *or* lo cual

## Exercise 21.

1. cuya
2. cuyos
3. cuyas
4. cuyo
5. cuyas
6. cuyos

## Exercise 22.

1. Sí, me asombré de ellos.
2. Sí, soñé contigo.
3. Sí, hablé con ella.
4. Según él, se necesita...
5. Sí, están preocupados por ella.
6. Sí, vas a tener que ir sin mí.

## Exercise 23.

—Esta es mi silla. Papá la compró para **mí** (me) el año pasado.

—¿Para **ti** (you)? Creo que te equivocas. Yo estaba con **él** (him) ese día.

—Si te sientas en ella no vuelvo a hablar **contigo** (you) nunca más.

—Tú no puedes pasar ni un día sin hablar **conmigo** (me), hermanita.

—Tienes razón. Soy tan charlatana como tú.

## Review

**Exercise 24.**

Fernando:—Hola Clarita y Laura.

Clara y Laura:—Hola Fernando.

Fernando:—Quiero que vengan a la fiesta de inauguración de mi apartamento la próxima semana.

Laura:—¿**Nos** vas invitar a **nosotras**?

Fernando:—¡Sí, a **ustedes**!

Laura:—Muchas gracias. Y, ¿cómo está tu novia?

Fernando:—¡Uhm! No se... ¿Y tu novio Clarita?

Clara: ¿El **mío**? **Yo** no tengo novio.

Laura: ¿Cómo está tu familia?

Fernando—Muy bien, gracias. ¿Y la **tuya**?

Laura:—La verdad, no muy bien. A mi padre **lo** despidieron del trabajo ayer.

Clara: Y recién ha comprado un apartamento.

Laura:—Sí, **lo** compró hace justo una semana.

Fernando:—Quisiera conocer**lo**.

Laura: ¡**Te** invito la próxima semana!

Clara:—¿Vieron la última película con Penélope Cruz?

Fernando:—No, no **la** he visto. De todas maneras no me gusta **ella** como actriz.

Clara: —¡Laura! Olvidé mi bolso en la cafetería. Hasta luego.

Fernando:—¡Espera!

Clara: ¡**Nos** vemos otro día!

Laura:—¡**Le** advertí que no **la** olvidara!

Fernando—¿Por qué no **le** dijiste que esperara un momento?

Laura:—Mejor así, así podemos estar solos. Anoche soñé con**tigo.**

Fernando:—¿**Conmigo**?

Fernando:—¡Oh! ¡Qué suerte tengo!

Laura:—¿Por qué?

Fernando:—Allí hay un letrero **que** dice: "**Se** reparan relojes". Y debo llevar el **mío** a que **lo** reparen.

Laura:—¡Déja**me** ver**lo,** que **yo te** acompaño!

Fernando:—No es necesario. Gracias. ¡Bueno...! **Nos** vemos otro día.

Laura:—¿Cuándo es la fiesta?

Fernando:—¿Cuál fiesta?

Laura:—¡**Aquella** a **la** que **nos** invitaste a Clara y **a mí**! ¡Idiota!

Fernando:—¡Espera Laura, no **te** enojes...! "¡A las mujeres no **las** entiende nadie!"

# CHAPTER 9

**Exercise 1.**

1. El profesor habla **rápidamente.**
2. Los gallos pelean **violentamente.**
3. El pianista toca **suavemente.**
4. El jefe habla con sus empleados **cortésmente.**

5. El niño respondió a su maestro **inteligentemente.**
6. El padre juega con su hijo **cariñosamente.**

**Exercise 2.**

1. El cantante canta estupendamente.
2. María simplemente desea invitarte a la fiesta.
3. Los niños juegan alegremente.
4. La obra de teatro fue absolutamente fantástica.
5. Los estudiantes protestan enérgicamente.
6. La profesora habla suavemente.

**Exercise 3.**

1. largamente
2. sinceramente
3. alegremente
4. absolutamente
5. discretamente
6. secretamente
7. rápidamente
8. frecuentemente
9. enormemente
10. gentilmente
11. locamente

**Exercise 4.**

1. Aquel hombre está <u>como</u> <u>loco</u>.
2. No me siento <u>bien</u>.
3. Quiero que vengas <u>pronto</u>.
4. Los caracoles se desplazan <u>despacio</u>.
5. Ese muchacho está <u>pálido</u>; anda <u>muy</u> <u>mal</u> de salud.
6. No es fácil trabajar <u>así</u>.

**Exercise 5.**

1. Tus amigos vendrán **pronto**.
2. A nosotros nos gusta caminar **despacio**.
3. Rosalba se siente **mal** por lo que te dijo anoche.
4. No me gusta que me hables **así**.
5. No te preocupes, que estamos **bien**.
6. Lo hice **como** me indicaste.

**Exercise 6.**

1. Hay <u>apenas</u> <u>cinco</u> naranjas en la mesa.
2. Hay <u>muy</u> <u>poca</u> gente en el parque.
3. Tú comes <u>muy</u> <u>poco</u>, menos de 400 calorías diarias.

4. Tengo <u>demasiados</u> amigos en la universidad.

5. ¡<u>Cuán</u> <u>contento</u> me siento hoy!

6. A nosotros nos gustan <u>más</u> las verduras frescas que la carne.

7. Casi pierdo el examen de física; estaba <u>bastante</u> <u>difícil</u>.

8. Me siento <u>algo</u> <u>enfermo</u> y también un <u>poco</u> <u>cansado</u>.

9. No hay <u>nada</u> que me guste; <u>sólo</u> dormir.

10. Hay <u>tanto</u> por aprender que es <u>mejor</u> no dormir <u>tanto</u>.

### Exercise 7.

1. <u>Anteayer</u> estuvimos en la casa de <u>mis</u> tíos. <u>Nunca</u> antes había estado en la casa de ellos.

2. <u>Antes</u>, <u>cuando</u> niña, <u>siempre</u> jugaba en el parque. En <u>aquel</u> entonces tenía ocho años.

3. <u>Anoche</u>, <u>aún</u> <u>después</u> de visitarte seguía extrañándote.

4. <u>Ayer</u> amanecí <u>contento</u>; <u>hoy</u> no lo estoy.

5. <u>Mañana</u> iremos a la playa en la mañana y <u>luego</u>, <u>tarde</u> en la noche, iremos a bailar.

6. <u>Hoy</u> <u>todavía</u> me siento un <u>poco</u> enfermo; <u>ahora</u> no podré salir contigo.

7. <u>Luego</u> te invito a <u>mi</u> casa; <u>ahora</u> vamos a comer un helado.

8. No he ido <u>jamás</u> a <u>aquel</u> restaurante. ¿Vamos?

9. <u>Todavía</u> tengo un <u>poco</u> de dinero; yo te invito.

10. <u>Mientras</u> comíamos llegó Lucía con su <u>estúpido</u> novio.

11. <u>Ya</u> es hora de partir, es <u>muy</u> <u>tarde</u>.

### Exercise 8.

1. <u>Cerca</u> de <u>tu</u> casa hay un edificio <u>grande</u>.

2. <u>Allá</u>, a lo <u>lejos</u> veo un pájaro <u>enorme</u>.

3. <u>Abajo</u> está el sótano <u>oscuro</u> y <u>frío</u> y <u>arriba</u> el ático.

4. Ven <u>acá</u>, a <u>mi</u> lado, <u>donde</u> pueda verte.

5. La Tierra gira <u>alrededor</u> del Sol.

6. Las manzanas <u>rojas</u> están <u>encima</u> de la mesa.

7. <u>Detrás</u> de <u>mi</u> casa hay un parque muy <u>lindo</u>.

8. ¡Eres muy <u>desordenado</u>! Busca <u>tus</u> medias <u>debajo</u> de la cama.

9. <u>Delante</u> de nosotros hay un coche <u>sospechoso</u>.

10. ¡No dejes la leche <u>fresca</u> <u>fuera</u> de la nevera!

11. <u>Cuando</u> oigo las noticias de la guerra siento una tristeza <u>inmensa</u> <u>dentro</u> de mí.

### Exercise 9.

1. Mi hijo se aprendió la poesía **de memoria**.

2. María le respondió a su madre **de mala gana**.

3. Los presos fueron encarcelados **en el exterior**.

4. Todos corren **a prisa** para llegar a tiempo.

5. **Al fin**, descubrió que ya no era un niño.

6. Todos los empleados hicieron su trabajo **en vano**.

# CHAPTER 10

**Exercise 1.**

**Part A.**

1. Yo <u>bail</u>o.
2. Yo <u>camin</u>o.
3. Yo <u>cocin</u>o.
4. Yo <u>compart</u>o.
5. Yo <u>viv</u>o.
6. Yo <u>ve</u>o.
7. Yo <u>pong</u>o.
8. Yo <u>hag</u>o.

**Part B.**

1. <u>bailes</u>
2. <u>camine</u>
3. <u>cocine</u>
4. <u>comparta</u>
5. <u>vivamos</u>
6. <u>vea</u>
7. <u>ponga</u>
8. <u>haga</u>

**Exercise 2.**

1. duermas
2. vayáis
3. pague
4. empiecen
5. cierre
6. sepamos
7. agregue
8. desagüe
9. refreguéis
10. vayas
11. busque
12. almuercen
13. dé
14. ruegues
15. apacigüe
16. entregues

**Exercise 3.**

1. Es importante que lleguen puntuales a la clase.
2. Es necesario que corrijan los ejercicios.

3. Es bueno que repasen con regularidad.
4. Es necesario que escriban los trabajos en procesador de texto.
5. Es aconsejable que lean con cuidado el programa.
6. Es esencial que participen en las actividades comunes.
7. Es importante que estudien con anticipación los temas que se van a ver en clase.
8. Es recomendable que hagan preguntas para aclarar dudas.
9. Es importante que participen en los trabajos en equipo.
10. Es esencial que practiquen antes y después de clase.

## Exercise 4.

1. Quiero que **vayas** al banco.
2. Quiero que **prepares** la ropa.
3. Quiero que te **despidas** de tu hermana.
4. Quiero que **recojas** los billetes de avión.
5. Quiero que **hagas** la reserva del hotel.
6. Quiero que **riegues** las plantas.
7. Quiero que **lleves** el perro a casa de tu primo.
8. Quiero que **canceles** la entrega del periódico.
9. Quiero que **avises** en la oficina de correos que estaremos de vacaciones.
10. Quiero que **empaques** las vitaminas y los medicamentos.

## Exercise 5.

1. No creo que los políticos **digan** siempre la verdad.
2. Dudo que el presidente no **cobre** suficiente dinero.
3. Es posible que los ciudadanos no **paguemos** muchos impuestos.
4. No creo que los programas de televisión **sean** muy educativos.
5. No estoy seguro que **seas** el mejor trabajador de tu empresa.
6. No creo que los vinos alemanes **sean** los mejores.
7. No es verdad que el fútbol americano **sea** el deporte más inofensivo.
8. No pienso que el precio de la gasolina **haya estado** estable en los últimos diez años.
9. No es cierto que sólo los niños **deban** usar protector solar.
10. No es cierto que la pizza **sea** un alimento con bajo contenido de grasas.

## Exercise 6.

1. No creo que sea sano tomar el sol.
2. Es posible que te encuentres con tu ex-novio.
3. No es posible que te guste ir a un lugar con tanta gente.
4. Es evidente que tienes ganas de ver a Federico, tu ex-novio.
5. Es posible que prefiera quedarme solo en casa.
6. Creo que estoy celoso de Federico.
7. Creo que no tengo traje de baño.
8. Me parece que va a llover esta tarde.
9. Prefiero que nos quedemos en casa.
10. Quizá podamos ir mañana.

### Exercise 7.

1. Me encanta que seas sincero.
2. Me maravilla que seas honrado.
3. Me molesta que seas de mal genio.
4. Es terrible que seas desordenado.
5. Es una pena que seas olvidadizo.
6. Es una desgracia que seas imprudente.
7. Es estupendo que seas comprensivo.
8. Es lamentable que seas entrometido.
9. Es maravilloso que seas divertido.
10. Es bueno que seas muy inteligente.

### Exercise 8.

1. Es una suerte que haya escrito.
2. Es el colmo que me ladre.
3. Es una desgracia que no tenga trabajo.
4. Es increíble que seas tan irresponsable.

### Exercise 9.

1. Busco un amigo que sea sincero.
2. Busco un amigo que tenga tiempo para mí.
3. Busco un amigo que le guste hablar y reír.
4. Busco un amigo que trabaje poco.
5. Busco un amigo que goce la vida.
6. Busco un amigo que sepa bailar.
7. Busco un amigo que le guste leer.
8. Busco un amigo que no sea celoso.
9. Busco un amigo que sea chistoso.
10. Busco un amigo que sea muy inteligente.

### Exercise 10.

1. Ella busca un hombre que sea guapo.
2. Ella busca un hombre que sea chistoso.
3. Ella busca un hombre que sea rico.
4. Ella busca un hombre que sea inteligente.

5–8. Ella se casa con un hombre que no es guapo y que es calvo, serio, y pobre.

### Exercise 11.

1. Necesitamos un apartamento que tenga una sala grande.
2. Queremos un apartamento que esté bien ubicado.
3. Buscamos un apartamento que tenga una cocina moderna.
4. Queremos un apartamento que tenga vista al mar.
5. Necesitamos un apartamento que tenga una sala amplia.
6. Buscamos un apartamento que tenga garaje.

7. Queremos un apartamento que tenga portero.
8. Necesitamos un apartamento que no sea costoso.
9. Buscamos un apartamento que esté en un último piso.
10. Queremos un apartamento que sea claro.

**Exercise 12.**

Sonia y Javier tienen un apartamento en Houston que cuesta mucho dinero. Ambos quieren una vida más divertida y aspiran vender el apartamento que tienen en Estados Unidos y comprar uno en España. Sonia quiere que el apartamento esté ubicado en la ciudad de Granada. Javier está de acuerdo, pero además quiere que el apartamento quede en el Albaicín, el antiguo barrio moro. Sonia desea que tenga vista a la Sierra Nevada y a la Alhambra. Javier, también quiere que el apartamento no sea ruidoso y tenga garaje.

**Exercise 13.**

1. Tal vez trabaje durante el verano.
2. Quizás vaya a México este verano.
3. A lo mejor tenga que estudiar para los exámenes de doctorado.
4. Probablemente visite a mi familia en España.
5. Quizás tenga suerte y puedas venir a visitarme.
6. Tal vez compre una casa este verano.
7. Quizás juegue la final de la copa de fútbol.
8. Tal vez consiga un perro.
9. Probablemente conduzca a Montreal.
10. A lo mejor vaya al festival de cine en agosto.

**Exercise 14.**

1. Después de que termine mis estudios.
2. Hasta que aparezca Luis.
3. En cuanto tenga tiempo.
4. Después de que Jorge tuvo que retirarse del juego.
5. Luego que nos despedimos.
6. Cuando hayan comido.
7. Tan pronto como sean las siete en punto.
8. Cuando lo repare el técnico.
9. Mientras estaba comiendo.
10. En cuanto esté seca.

**Exercise 15.**

1. Cuando pinten la casa nueva.
2. Después de que leímos el periódico.
3. Cuando se derrita la nieve.
4. Antes de que oscurezca.
5. Tan pronto como comience la primavera.
6. En cuanto tuvo una entrevista con el jefe.

7.  Cuando cumpla 21 años.
8.  Mientras dormía.
9.  En cuanto encontremos las llaves del auto.
10. Hasta que se acabe el mundo.

**Exercise 16.**

1.  pueda
2.  venden
3.  caminemos
4.  haya
5.  podamos
6.  termina
7.  pueda
8.  quieran
9.  vaya
10. vimos

**Exercise 17.**

1.  dijeron
2.  había imaginado
3.  indicó
4.  prometí
5.  sucedieron
6.  expliqué
7.  son
8.  ocurrió
9.  pronosticó
10. habían planeado

**Exercise 18.**

1.  cambie
2.  espere
3.  vea
4.  dejen
5.  llegues
6.  pueda
7.  arregle
8.  comas
9.  note
10. digas

**Exercise 19.**

1.  llegaste
2.  están

3.  necesitaba
4.  llegaste
5.  saben
6.  es
7.  viniste
8.  tienes
9.  es
10. tengo

### Exercise 20.

1.  enterasen
2.  avise
3.  lleguemos
4.  váyase
5.  caigan
6.  estén
7.  puedan
8.  aprenda
9.  pierda
10. tienes

### Exercise 21.

1.  —¡Obvio, para que pueda entrar!
2.  —¡Obvio, para que traiga cerveza!
3.  —¡Obvio, para que llegue temprano!
4.  —¡Obvio, para que tengamos donde sentarnos!
5.  —¡Obvio, para que no tengamos hambre después!
6.  —¡Obvio, para que esté limpio para cuando lleguen los invitados!

### Exercise 22.

1.  tengas
2.  inscribas
3.  advertimos
4.  quieran
5.  vimos
6.  acostó

### Exercise 23.

1.  Ellos <u>incluy</u>eron
2.  Ellos <u>retirar</u>on
3.  Ellos <u>repitier</u>on
4.  Ellos <u>pagar</u>on
5.  Ellos <u>influy</u>eron
6.  Ellos <u>explicar</u>on

7. Ellos <u>destrozar</u>on
8. Ellos <u>caminar</u>on
9. Ellos <u>temier</u>on
10. Ellos <u>rier</u>on
11. Ellos <u>redujer</u>on
12. Ellos <u>produjer</u>on
13. Ellos <u>llegar</u>on
14. Ellos <u>fabricar</u>on
15. Ellos <u>decidier</u>on
16. Ellos <u>cruzar</u>on

**Exercise 24.**

1. incluyera
2. retiráramos
3. repitiera
4. pagaran
5. influyera
6. explicaras
7. destrozaras
8. caminara
9. temiera
10. riera
11. redujera
12. produjera
13. llegaras
14. fabricáramos
15. decidiera
16. cruzara

**Exercise 25.**

1. Era importante que ustedes prepararan la tienda de campaña.
2. Era esencial que consiguieran combustible para la estufa portátil.
3. Era necesario que María trajera un botiquín.
4. Era importante que hicieran un mapa del recorrido
5. Era clave que averiguaran cómo llegar al sitio del campamento.
6. Ere necesario que compraran repelente de insectos.

**Exercise 26.**

*Yo quisiera que fuera más grande...*

tuviera suficiente luz.
la cocina fuera moderna,
el color de las paredes no fuera triste.
tuviera clósets para guardar la ropa,
hubiera restaurantes cerca.

**Exercise 27.**

1. Nosotros no pensábamos que vinieras.
2. Los ingenieros no creían que el terreno se hundiera.
3. La policía dudaba que se produjera un atentado.
4. Mi madre no estaba segura que yo viniera a ayudarla.
5. El juez no creía que el testigo estuviera diciendo la verdad.
6. Quizá si nosotros llevaramos mucho dinero podríamos comprar el anillo.

**Exercise 28.**

1. Marisela temía que se le mojará el cabello.
2. Yo me preocupé de que el dinero se perdiera.
3. ¡Qué miedo que hubiera una avalancha!
4. Me alegré que fuéramos juntos a la fiesta
5. Me preocupó que el gato no comiera.
6. La anciana se emocionó que nosotros viniéramos de visita.

**Exercise 29.**

1. Necesitaba un coche que fuera de color amarillo.
2. Necesitaba un coche que tuviera cuatro puertas.
3. Necesitaba un coche que marchara rápido.
4. Necesitaba un coche que frenara bien.
5. Necesitaba un coche que estuviera entre los diez mejores.
6. Necesitaba un coche que no fuera muy costoso.

**Exercise 30.**

1. regresara
2. llegaran
3. fueran
4. sintieras
5. escribiera
6. fuera
7. necesitara
8. vieran
9. viviera
10. terminara

**Exercise 31.**

1. escondiera
2. pudiera
3. hubiera
4. hubiera
5. pudieran

**Exercise 32.**

1. quisieran
2. tuviera
3. indicara
4. fuera

**Exercise 33.**

1. fueran
2. probáramos
3. quisiéramos
4. anduvieran

**Exercise 34.**

1. conservara
2. mojara
3. quedaran
4. deslumbrara
5. alternaran
6. cumplieran

**Exercise 35.**

1. quisiera
2. supiera
3. pagáramos
4. vistiera
5. bajaran

**Exercise 36.**

1. hayas perdido
2. haya subido
3. hayamos encontrado
4. haya cerrado
5. hayan visto
6. hayan demostrado

**Exercise 37.**

1. No creo que Luis te **haya prestado** la motocicleta.
2. ¡Es un milagro que Martín **haya llegado** sano y salvo!
3. Es posible que la tía Magdalena **haya vendido** su colección de sombreros.
4. No se sabe si Nubia **se haya ido** en el tren de las cuatro.
5. ¡Qué bueno que **hayamos conseguido** todos los disfraces para la obra!
6. No es cierto que **me haya sentido** solo.

**Exercise 38.**

1. hubieras venido
2. hubieran podido
3. hubieras escrito
4. hubieran reconciliado
5. hubiéramos cantado
6. hubiera sido

**Exercise 39.**

1. Ojalá hubiéramos tenido suerte en el concurso.
2. Era imposible que hubiera terminado de escribir el libro a tiempo.
3. Ojalá hubiéramos ganado el campeonato de fútbol.
4. Ojalá hubieras venido a mi graduación.
5. Ojalá nos hubiera escrito a menudo.
6. Sin la ayuda del viento, es posible que la casa no se hubiera quemado.

# CHAPTER 11

**Exercise 1.**

1. c
2. f
3. b
4. d
5. e
6. a

**Exercise 2.**

1. iremos
2. concentro
3. burlaban
4. llegan
5. sales
6. animo
7. pongo
8. escribiré
9. empujes

**Exercise 3.**

Si conduces ebrio, te accidentarás, si te accidentas, irás al hospital, si vas al hospital, no podrás trabajar, si no puedes trabajar, no tendrás dinero para las vacaciones, si no tienes dinero para las vacaciones, no podrás ir a Grecia, si no puedes ir a Grecia te aburrirás.

**Exercise 4.**

1. *Si el ladrón pasa con los dos lingotes de oro, se caerá al vacío.*
2. Si el ladrón pasa con un lingote sus cómplices lo golpearán.
3. Si el ladrón larga los lingotes de oro sus cómplices no lo perdonarán.
4. Si el ladrón no atraviesa el puente la policía lo arrestará.
5. Pero, si el ladrón baja 5 kg de peso corriendo, logrará cruzar.

**Exercise 5.**

1. compraría
2. irías
3. ayudaría
4. tuviera
5. dijeras
6. saludaríamos
7. trabajaría
8. intentara, lograría
9. entenderías
10. cometerías
11. llegaras
12. fabricáramos
13. decidiera

**Exercise 6.**

1. Si invitara a Carmen a comer, la llevaría a un restaurante elegante.
2. Si tuviera dinero, viajaría a Grecia.
3. Si hiciera una fiesta, invitaría a Carmen.
4. Si cambiara de carro, compraría un Alfa Romeo.
5. Si fuera viernes, iría a cine.

**Exercise 7.**

1. habríamos venido
2. hubiera detenido
3. habría tenido
4. habría tenido
5. hubieran llegado
6. habría pasado
7. hubiera estado
8. habría quedado
9. habría despertado
10. hubiera cargado

**Exercise 8.**

1. —Si hubieras tenido una semana de vacaciones, ¿qué habrías hecho?
   —Habría ido a España.

2. —Si hubieras tenido la oportunidad de escoger un coche, ¿qué habrías hecho?
   —Habría escogido un Peugeot.

3. —Si hubieras perdido el examen, ¿qué habrías hecho?
   —Me habría retirado de la universidad.

4. —Si Carmen te hubiera abandonado, ¿qué habrías hecho?
   —Me habría puesto a llorar.

5. —Si hubieras tenido una hija, ¿qué habrías hecho?
   —La habría llamado Gabriela.

6. —Si se hubiera incendiado tu casa, ¿qué habrías hecho?
   —Habría llamado a los bomberos.

7. —Si hubieras tenido que salir del país, ¿qué habrías hecho?
   —Habría ido a Italia.

8. —Si hubieras ido a cine, ¿qué habrías hecho?
   —Habría visto la película sueca.

9. —Si te hubiera dado su teléfono, ¿qué habrías hecho?
   —La habría llamado.

10. —Si te hubiera invitado, ¿qué habrías hecho?
    —Te habría llevado un regalo.

**Exercise 9.**

1. hubiera olvidado
2. tuviera
3. estuviera empujando
4. tuviera
5. hubieran derretido
6. fuéramos
7. estuviera
8. supiera
9. conocieras
10. fuera

**Exercise 10.**

1. —Como si no me conociera.
2. —Como si tuviera quince años.
3. —Como si fuera un cohete.
4. —Como si fueran unos ángeles.
5. —Como si estuviera muerto de risa.
6. —Como si fuera nuevo.
7. —Como si tuviera una papa en la boca.
8. —Como si tuviera una pata de palo.
9. —Como si fuera un perro.
10. —Como si fueran marranos.

# CHAPTER 12

**Exercise 1.**

1. Sí, empáquela.
   No, no la empaque.

2. Sí, llámala mañana.
   No, no la llames mañana.

3. Sí, subámonos.
   No, no nos subamos.

4. Sí, pódalos todos.
   No, no los podes todos.

5. Sí, córtemelo.
   No, no me lo corte.

6. Sí, llénelo.
   No, no lo llene.

7. Sí, dígala.
   No, no la diga.

8. Sí, cuéntemelo.
   No, no me lo cuente.

9. Sí, apáguelas.
   No, no las apague.

10. Sí, siéntese.
    No, no se siente.

**Exercise 2.**

1. Escoja un título breve.
2. Incluya el nombre del autor.
3. Mencione el tema del cuento.
4. Haga una lista de vocabulario nuevo.
5. Envíe dibujos o fotografías que ilustren el cuento.
6. Prepare tres originales en sobres diferentes.
7. Ponga los sobres al correo.
8. Espere con paciencia la respuesta del comité de publicación.

**Exercise 3.**

1. Sí, préstamelo.
   No, no me lo prestes.

2. Sí, mézclala.
   No, no la mezcles.

3. Sí, llámala.
   No, no la llames.

4. Sí, búscame.
   No, no me busques.

5. Sí, escríbela.
   No, no la escribas.

6. Sí, págame lo que me debes.
   No, no me pagues lo que me debes.

7. Sí, llévalas.
   No, no las lleves.

8. Sí, anótala.
   No, no la anotes.

9. Sí, prepárala.
   No, no la prepares.

10. Sí, inténtalo.
    No, no lo intentes.

## Exercise 4.

1. Saca a pasear al perro.
2. Levanta tu ropa del piso.
3. Tiende la cama antes de salir de casa.
4. Trae el periódico.
5. Aspira la alfombra de la sala.
6. Ayuda a tu papá a cortar el césped.
7. Saca las compras del auto.
8. Recoge tus libros.
9. Pon gasolina al auto.
10. Llega temprano esta noche.

## Exercise 5.

1. Juega hasta que oscurezca.
   No juegues hasta que oscurezca.
   Jugad hasta que oscurezca.
   No juguéis hasta que oscurezca.

2. Ven a almorzar con nosotros.
   No vengas a almorzar con nosotros.
   Venid a almorzar con nosotros.
   No vengáis a almorzar con nosotros.

3. Sueña con el futuro.
   No sueñes con el futuro.
   Soñad con el futuro.
   No soñéis con el futuro.

4. Perdona la interrupción.
   No perdones la interrupción.
   Perdonad la interrupción.
   No perdonéis la interrupción.

5. Olvida los disgustos que hemos tenido.
No olvides los disgustos que hemos tenido.
Olvidad los disgustos que hemos tenido.
No olvidéis los disgustos que hemos tenido.

6. Haz un diseño del mobiliario.
No hagas un diseño del mobiliario.
Haced un diseño del mobiliario.
No hagáis un diseño del mobiliario.

7. Di sólo lo estrictamente necesario.
No digas sólo lo estrictamente necesario.
Decid sólo lo estrictamente necesario.
No digáis sólo lo estrictamente necesario.

8. Come todo lo que te sirvan.
No comas todo lo que te sirvan.
Comed todo lo que os sirvan.
No comáis todo lo que os sirvan.

9. Vete de inmediato.
No te vayas de inmediato.
Id de inmediato.
No os vayáis de inmediato.

10. Entiende la gravedad de la situación.
No entiendas la gravedad de la situación.
Entended la gravedad de la situación.
No entendáis la gravedad de la situación.

**Exercise 6.**

1. No te cortes el cabello.
2. No salgáis tan tarde.
3. No empujes.
4. No sea ingenuo.
5. No toquen esos cuadros
6. No penséis en cosas tristes.
7. No olvides tus promesas.
8. No cierre los ojos.

**Exercise 7.**

1. Compremos esa marca de jabón.
2. Vamos a jugar al parque.
3. No hablemos de política.
4. Gritemos.
5. Vamos a la cafetería.
6. Mandemos la carta a Julia.
7. Vamos a bailar.

8. No nos vayamos de aquí.
9. No vayamos al cine.
10. Vamos a la playa.

# CHAPTER 13

### Exercise 1.

1. nada
2. nada
3. nadie
4. algunos
5. ninguna
6. ningún

### Exercise 2.

1. nadie
2. nada
3. nunca
4. ninguna
5. nunca
6. también
7. tampoco

### Exercise 3.

1. Cuál
2. qué
3. qué
4. qué
5. qué
6. cuál
7. cuáles
8. cuál
9. qué
10. qué
11. cuál
12. qué
13. cuál
14. cuál
15. qué
16. cuál
17. qué
18. cuál
19. qué
20. cuáles

# CHAPTER 14

### Exercise 1.

1. es
2. son
3. es
4. es
5. es
6. Son
7. es
8. es
9. son
10. son
11. es
12. es

### Exercise 2.

1. está
2. estamos
3. están
4. estás
5. está
6. está
7. está
8. está
9. estamos
10. está
11. está
12. están

### Exercise 3.

1. es
2. es
3. es
4. están
5. son
6. es
7. estamos
8. están
9. están
10. están
11. estoy
12. está
13. está

## Review

**Exercise 4.**

| La madre | El padre | El adolescente | El bebé |
|---|---|---|---|
| 1. La madre está de mal humor. | 1. El padre está contento. | 1. El adolescente está parado tocando la guitarra. | 1. El bebé es muy pequeño. |
| 2. Está ocupada. | 2. Él está sentado leyendo el periódico. | 2. Él es alto y flaco. | 2. Él está en la cuna. |
| 3. Ella es alta. | 3. Él es bajo y calvo. | 3. Él es un artista. | 3. Él está llorando. |
| 4. Está en la cocina | 4. Él también es gordo. | 4. Él está cantando. | 4. El bebé tiene un año. |

**Exercise 5.**

Alberto:—¡Hola! ¿Cómo te llamas?

Lola:—Me llamo Lola.

Alberto:—¿De dónde eres?

Lola:—Soy de España. ¿Y tú, cómo te llamas?

Alberto:—Yo me llamo Alberto y soy argentino.

Lola:—¿Qué haces?

Alberto:—Soy matemático.

Lola:—¡Eres matemático!

Alberto:—Sí, la verdad que es una profesión inútil pero divertida.

Lola:—Sabes, hoy estoy un poco aburrida. Te invito a una cerveza.

Alberto:—¡Genial! Vamos al bar "La Casita de Piedra", es buenísimo.

Lola:—¿Cuál? ¿El bar que está en la calle Bolívar?

Alberto:—Sí, es un bar tranquilo y además podemos oír tangos.

Lola:—¿Te gustan los tangos? Eres un poco pasado de moda, ¿no te parece?

Alberto:—Quizás. Y dime una cosa, ¿tú que haces?

Lola:—Yo soy estudiante de administración de empresas.

Alberto:—¿Dónde estudias?

Lola:—En el Instituto de Negocios y Finanzas.

Alberto:—¿Dónde está ese instituto?

Lola:—Está en la avenida Las Américas.

Alberto:—¡Ah! ¡Ya sé cuál es! ¡Qué tal si vamos al bar!

Lola:—¡Vale! Vamos que me estoy muriendo de sed.

# CHAPTER 15

**Exercise 1.**

1. A Pedro y José les corresponde lavar la ropa.
2. A nosotros nos conviene no gastar tanto dinero.
3. Daniel tiene tanta hambre que le cabría un pollo entero.
4. A Jorge le extraña que María no haya vuelto.
5. A vosotros os basta una comida al día.
6. ¿A ti te apetece una bebida?
7. Me alegra que vengas pronto.

8. ¿A vosotros os atrae ese hombre?
9. A nosotros nos agrada tu visita.
10. A Pedro le apasiona la literatura.
11. A nosotros ese perro nos costó un ojo de la cara.

**Exercise 2.**

1. nos encanta
2. le hace falta
3. le fascinan
4. nos toca
5. le sobra
6. les molesta
7. os quedan
8. me interesa
9. nos importa
10. le gusta
11. te fastidia

**Exercise 3.**

1. Al señor se le cayó su copa encima de la señora.
2. A la señora se le perdió algo.
3. A la señora se le quemó la comida.
4. Al señor se le rompió el florero.

**Exercise 4.**

1. A Julio se le perdió su perro.
2. A Pablo y Marcela se les perdió su anillo de matrimonio.
3. A Andrea se le rompieron los platos.
4. A Santiago se le cayó el armario.
5. A vosotros se os perdieron las llaves del carro.
6. A Clemente y a mí se nos olvidaron los pasaportes en la casa.
7. A Federico se le quemaron las tostadas del desayuno.
8. A Teresa se le rompió el florero.
9. A ellos se les perdió la maleta en el aeropuerto.
10. Al niño se le cayó la pelota.

**Exercise 5.**

1. A Juan se le cayó el vaso.
2. A ti se te quemó la carne.
3. A nosotros se nos rompieron los platos.
4. A vosotros se os perdieron las llaves.
5. A ellos se les olvidaron los libros.
6. A mí se me quemó la casa.
7. A nosotros se nos olvidó el dinero.

8. A Pedro se le perdió la billetera.
9. A ustedes se les olvidó pagar las cuentas.
10. A Lucía se le cayó el niño.

# CHAPTER 16

### Exercise 1.

1. acabó de
2. acabé
3. acabé por
4. acabó
5. acabaron
6. acabaron de
7. acabó de
8. acabó

### Exercise 2.

1. Siempre me acordaré de aquellos años dichosos.
2. El abuelo no se acuerda de nada; ha perdido la memoria.
3. Las tortugas se acuerdan del lugar donde nacieron durante toda su vida.
4. El niño no se acordó que tenía que hacer los deberes.
5. El otro día mientras comíamos nos acordamos de ti con alegría.

### Exercise 3.

1. ahorran
2. salvaste
3. ahorramos
4. ahorramos
5. salvar

### Exercise 4.

1. andan
2. fueron
3. andan
4. anda
5. anduvieron
6. Vámonos

### Exercise 5.

1. bajas
2. bajan
3. bajen
4. bajamos
5. bajó

**Exercise 6.**

1. se convirtió *or* se transformó
2. se convierte *or* se transforma
3. me he convertido *or* me he transformado

**Exercise 7.**

1. cuida
2. Cuida
3. cuida
4. cuidan

**Exercise 8.**

1. da
2. dio
3. dimos
4. dio
5. dio
6. da
7. dan
8. da
9. da

**Exercise 9.**

—He **dejado de** quererte porque eres muy grosero. Anoche por ejemplo me **dejaste** esperando en la entrada del teatro mientras estacionaba el carro.

—Mi amor, **deja de** pensar en tonterías y trata de componer las cosas.

—No querido, voy a **dejarte** para siempre. ¡Yo también tengo dignidad!

**Exercise 10.**

1. hace falta
2. echa de menos *or* extraña *or* le hace falta
3. echo de menos *or* extraño *or* me hace falta
4. echamos de menos *or* extrañamos *or* nos hacen falta
5. echamos de menos *or* extrañamos *or* nos hacen falta
6. echo de menos *or* extraño *or* me hacen falta
7. echo de menos *or* extraño
8. echan de menos *or* extrañan *or* les hace falta

**Exercise 11.**

1. hizo
2. hace

3.  haga
4.  hace
5.  hace
6.  hace
7.  puso
8.  puso
9.  llegarás a ser
10. hace
11. llegaremos a ser

## Exercise 12.

1.  toca
2.  jugar
3.  toca
4.  toca
5.  juega
6.  toca, juegan
7.  jugar
8.  toca
9.  tocar
10. juega, toca

## Exercise 13.

1.  llevó
2.  lleva
3.  llevar
4.  lleva
5.  llevaron
6.  llevó
7.  llevan
8.  llevan
9.  llevamos

## Exercise 14.

1.  mudó
2.  moverte
3.  movió
4.  mudan
5.  nos mudaremos
6.  había movido
7.  mueve
8.  muevas

## Exercise 15.

1. pido
2. piden
3. preguntó
4. pidió
5. preguntan
6. pido
7. piden, pido
8. preguntaron
9. pedí

## Exercise 16.

1. perdió
2. perdieron
3. Perdimos
4. se perdió
5. se pierden
6. Perdisteis
7. perdió
8. se le perdieron
9. perdió

## Exercise 17.

1. prestar, presto
2. prestar
3. presto
4. presto
5. prestará

## Exercise 18.

1. te pongas
2. se le pone
3. se puso
4. te pones
5. Ponte
6. poner
7. te pongas
8. Pusiste, pongo
9. se puso

## Exercise 19.

1. queda
2. se quedó
3. quedaste en

4. se queda
5. nos hemos quedado
6. se quedó
7. se quede
8. nos queda
9. quedamos en

**Exercise 20.**

1. conoce, sabe
2. conozco, sabido
3. conozco, conozco
4. saben
5. sé, conozco
6. conocer, sabe
7. conocer
8. sabe a
9. conoces

**Exercise 21.**

1. sirve
2. se sirve de
3. sirven para
4. sirve para
5. os servís de
6. sirven de
7. sirven
8. sirve para
9. sirve para

**Exercise 22.**

1. tiene
2. tuvo lugar
3. tienen
4. tiene
5. tenemos
6. tiene que

# Review

**Exercise 23.**

1. Lucía cuida sus plantas.
2. Lucía le da de comer a su gato.
3. Lucía da un paseo por la playa.
4. Lucía juega tenis.

# CHAPTER 17

**Exercise 1.**

1. Normalmente yo tengo **más tiempo que** mi esposa para estar en casa porque yo regreso **más temprano que** ella. Mi mujer trabaja todo el día. Yo, sólo trabajo por las mañanas.

2. El vino es **más caro que** la cerveza.

3. Mario **hace más deporte que** yo, por eso él **está más delgado que** yo.

4. Carlos **habla español más lento que** Sara, por eso le entiendo muy bien.

5. El nivel de vida de los países desarrollados **es más alto que** el de los países subdesarrollados.

6. Las personas hoy día viven **más tiempo que** las personas de antaño.

7. Federico es muy vanidoso, y **compra más ropa** que su esposa.

8. Los franceses **beben más vino que** los americanos.

9. En el Caribe **hace más calor que** en Londres.

10. Ese coche **anda más rápido que** esa moto.

**Exercise 2.**

1. Mi hermana Carmen **es menos tímida que** yo; por eso ella tiene muchos amigos.

2. Hoy estoy feliz porque **tengo menos trabajo de lo que** yo pensaba.

3. La cena **fue menos cara de lo que** me dijiste.

4. Laura y Rosa **son menos trabajadoras que** Mónica. Ella siempre está en la oficina.

5. Roberto **es menos divertido que** Juan. Por eso yo prefiero salir con Juan los fines de semana.

6. José Alejandro **tiene menos entusiasmo que** Lucía. Por eso, Lucía no quiere verlo más.

7. Carlos **es menos amable que** su esposa Carmen. Por eso, nos gusta más Carmen.

8. La vida **es menos dura de lo que** uno se imagina.

9. Tomás **juega menos agresivamente al tenis que** su hermano Luis.

10. Antes **había menos contaminación que** ahora.

**Exercise 3.**

1. Alberto y Marcos son hermanos gemelos y tienen muchas cosas en común. Por ejemplo, Carlos **es tan alto como** Marcos, y Marcos **es tan activo como** Carlos. Carlos **come tanto como** Marcos, así que los dos hermanos tienen más o menos el mismo peso.

2. ¿Tu hermano **es tan guapo como** tú?

3. Yo no **duermo tanto como** tú. Para mí, es suficiente dormir siete horas.

4. Julio es bilingüe y yo también. Él **habla tantas lenguas como** yo.

5. Marta **trabaja tantas horas como** su hermano José.

6. Todos ellos **tienen tanta urgencia como** nosotros. Lo mejor es que nos apuremos.

7. Aunque no lo creas, el cerdo **tiene tanta grasa como** el pollo.

8. No te preocupes que todo va a salir bien. Yo **tengo tanta fe en que habrá paz como** tú.

9. Liliana **come tanto como** Pilar. Por eso, ambas se entienden muy bien.

10. Jorge **baila tan bien como** Lola. Ambos han ganado varios concursos de baile.

## Exercise 4.

1. Fabián dice que el café colombiano **es el más rico** del mundo.
2. Para María las playas del Caribe **son las más divertidas**.
3. Este es el hotel **más elegante de** la ciudad.
4. Dicen que Tokio es la ciudad **más cara del** mundo.
5. Las abuelas siempre piensan que sus nietos son **los más inteligentes del** colegio.

## Exercise 5.

1. Pedro es una persona muy orgullosa. Él siempre piensa que **es mejor que** los demás.
2. Este restaurante **es peor que** el restaurante italiano que hay al lado de casa.
3. Mariela **es menor** que su esposo.
4. Mi prima Carmen **es mayor** que yo.

## Exercise 6.

1. Este **es el mejor** restaurante de la ciudad. Lo recomiendan en todas las guías.
2. Diego **es el menor** de sus hermanos.
3. El año pasado **tuvimos el peor** invierno en mucho tiempo.
4. Estoy pasando las **mejores** vacaciones de mi vida.

## Exercise 7.

1. Cristina tiene unas recetas **buenísimas** para preparar el pavo.
2. La última vez que fui al cine vi una película excelente, pero la que vimos ayer fue **malísima**.
3. Esta mañana me levanté **tardísimo** porque no oí el despertador.
4. Me gusta mi profesor de historia porque es **inteligentísimo**, y sus clases son **interesantísimas.**
5. La clase de español es fácil, pero las de alemán son **dificilísimas**.

# Review

## Exercise 8.

1. Julio bebe más cervezas que Lola.
2. Javier gana menos euros que Liliana.

3. Susana duerme tantas horas como Santiago.
4. Sebastián tiene más amigos que Marta.
5. Jorge corre tan rápido como Susana.
6. Luna es tan alta como Jorge.

### Exercise 9.

1. Javier es el más pequeño de los tres.
2. María es la que tiene más pelo de los tres.
3. Javier es el mayor de los tres.
4. Lola es la más joven de los tres.
5. María es la mejor vestida de los tres.

### Exercise 10.

1. Jorge es muy rico, pero Gabriel es más rico. Gabriel es riquísimo.
2. Julio es muy amable, pero Santiago es más amable. Santiago es amabilísimo.
3. Andrés es muy envidioso, pero Federico es más envidioso. Federico es envidiosísimo.
4. Melania es muy tacaña, pero Jonás es más tacaño. Jonás es tacañísimo.
5. Andrea es muy dramática, pero Claudia es más dramática. Claudia es dramatiquísima.
6. Sara es muy mala, pero María es peor. María es malísima.
7. Liliana es muy aburrida, pero Germán es más aburrido. Germán es aburridísimo.
8. Perión es muy valiente, pero Amadís es más valiente. Amadís es valientísimo.
9. Mario es muy guapo, pero Gabriela es más guapa. Gabriela es guapísima.
10. Kelly es muy nerviosa, pero Pedro es más nervioso. Pedro es nerviosísimo.

# CHAPTER 18

### Exercise 1.

1. Anoche conocí **a** tu novio, ¡es muy guapo!
2. Mañana iré contigo **a** cenar, te lo prometo.
3. El otro día, me encontré un anillo de oro en la calle.
4. Mi novia me invitó **a** Madrid.
5. Nos vemos **a** las ocho en el teatro.
6. Lucho me invitó **a** jugar billar.

### Exercise 2.

1. Los libros son **de** la biblioteca.
2. La casa es **del** banco, todavía no la hemos terminado de pagar.
3. Ese suéter es **de** tu hermano.
4. El aire y el agua es **de** todos.

### Exercise 3.

1. Los invitados llegaron **de** Perú.
2. Las anchoas son **del** mar Adriático.
3. Mi profesora de francés es **de** Lyon.
4. Estamos cansados, venimos **de** la montaña.

### Exercise 4.

1. Los coches modernos son **de** plásticos.
2. Tu siempre estás pensando en castillos **de** arena.
3. Esas empanadas están deliciosas. Son **de** carne.
4. Me gusta el vino **de** La Rioja.

### Exercise 5.

1. ¡Apúrate! Tu novio llega a las tres **de** la tarde.
2. ¿Qué hora es? ¡Las tres **de** la mañana!
3. Dentro **de** un año iré a visitarte.
4. A las dos **de** la madrugada nació.

### Exercise 6.

1. ¡Tráeme los libros! Están **en** la mesa.
2. Las golondrinas llegan **en** grupos de a miles.
3. Los osos duermen **en** el invierno.
4. La botella está **en** el piso.

### Exercise 7.

1. Ese avión va **para** Europa.
2. Las niñas están listas **para** partir.
3. **Para** poder jugar bien al fútbol hay que practicar.
4. Esa llave no sirve **para** abrir esa puerta.

### Exercise 8.

1. **Para** el próximo año ya habrás terminado tu doctorado.
2. La tarea es **para** mañana.
3. Tenemos que tener listo el vestido **para** el jueves.
4. Lo siento, ya me comprometí **para** el próximo viernes.

### Exercise 9.

1. Ella hace cualquier cosa **por** dinero.
2. Lo premiaron **por** su gran talento.
3. **Por** no estudiar, Diana vivió aburrida toda su vida.
4. A vosotros os invitaron **por** cumplir con el protocolo.

### Exercise 10.

1. Esa catedral fue construida **por** Gaudí.
2. La imprenta fue inventada **por** Gutenberg.
3. La ley de la relatividad fue propuesta **por** Einstein.

### Exercise 11.

1. Vamos **por** aquel camino. Es más corto.
2. ¡María! Ve a la tienda **por** aceite, que se terminó.
3. Voy **por** el camino tropical.
4. Fueron **por** lana y salieron trasquilados.

### Exercise 12.

1. Las ondas sonoras viajan **por** el aire.
2. Robert viajó **por** tierra.
3. El hombre viaja **por** aire, mar y tierra.
4. Todos los invitados llegaron **por** barco.

### Exercise 13.

1. Juaco está enfermo. Liliana vendrá **por** él.
2. Rocío cambió su reloj **por** el vestido de flores.
3. Tomás y Helena reemplazaron su perro pastor alemán **por** un conejo.
4. Te cambio este coche **por** el tuyo.

### Exercise 14.

Eran las ocho **de** la noche, cuando Julio fue **por** comida al restaurante chino **del** barrio. **En** el apartamento lo esperaba su novia Graciela. Como eran las once **de** la noche y Julio no llegaba, Graciela se acostó **en** el sofá **de** la sala **a** esperar. Graciela había conocido **a** Julio **por** suerte, una mañana **de** abril. Aquel día, Graciela había sido invitada **por** el señor Felipe Naranjo, dueño del periódico "El Vespertino", **para** que conociera su empresa. El señor Naranjo pensaba, **en** su imaginación, que Graciela sería la madre **de** sus hijos. Cuando Graciela llegó **a** las instalaciones **del** periódico, fue recibida **por** Felipe con un exquisito desayuno con panecillos hechos **de** harina **de** maíz. Felipe le habló **a** Graciela y le insinuó que si se casaba con él, ella sería tratada como una reina. Le propuso inclusive que **de** luna **de** miel la llevaría **en** su propio yate hasta su isla privada **en** el mar Caribe, y que luego viajarían **por** avión **a** París. Después del desayuno Felipe le presentó **a** los redactores **del** periódico. Entre ellos estaba Julio, que había ido aquel día **para** reemplazar **a** Paco, uno **de** los periodistas **del** periódico, que **por** suerte **para** Julio se encontraba enfermo aquel día.

**Exercise 15.** According to the illustration complete the following sentences, using the appropriate prepositions.

1. El as **de** tréboles (A♣) está **en** la primera fila, junto **con** el dos **de** corazones (2♥) y el tres **de** picas (3♠).

2. El rey **de** diamantes (K♦) está **entre** el valet **de** tréboles (J♣) y el 10 **de** corazones (10♥).

3. **Sobre** el rey de diamantes (K♦) está el 2 **de** corazones (2♥).

4. **A** la derecha del rey **de** diamantes (K♦) está el 10 **de** corazones (10♥).

5. **Bajo** el 10 **de** corazones (10♥) se encuentra la reina **de** tréboles (Q♣).

# SPANISH-ENGLISH GLOSSARY

This vocabulary includes the words used in this book. (Some exceptions are ordinal and cardinal numbers, and proper nouns.) Each word is followed by its grammatical function and its corresponding English definition. The definition is limited to the context in which the word is used in this book. Nouns, adjectives, and participles appear in masculine form. If the word is both masculine and feminine, it is so noted. The following abbreviations are used.

| | | | | |
|---|---|---|---|---|
| *adj.* | adjective | | *inv.* | invariable |
| *adj. dem.* | demonstrative adjective | | *loc. adv.* | adverbial locution |
| *adv.* | adverb | | *m.* | masculine |
| *dem. pron.* | demonstrative pronoun | | *n.* | noun |
| *def. art.* | definite article | | *part.* | participle |
| *indef. art.* | indefinite article | | *pers. pron.* | subject pronoun |
| *f.* | feminine | | *poss. adj.* | possessive adjective |
| *g.* | gerund | | *poss. pron.* | possessive pronoun |
| *ind. pron.* | indefinite pronoun | | *prep.* | preposition |
| *interj.* | interjection | | *sup. adj.* | superlative adjective |
| *interr. pron.* | interrogative pronoun | | *v.* | verb |

## A

| | |
|---|---|
| ¡Ah! *(interj.)* | Oh! |
| a *(prep.)* | to |
| a menudo *(loc. adv.)* | often |
| abandonado *(adj.)* | abandoned |
| abandonar *(v.)* | to abandon |
| abdominales *(n., m.)* | sit-ups |
| abeja *(n., f.)* | bee |
| abierto *(part.)* | open |
| abogado *(n.)* | lawyer |
| abonar *(v.)* | to certify |
| abrazar *(v.)* | to embrace |
| abrazarse *(v.)* | to be embraced |
| abrazo *(n., m.)* | hug |
| abrigo *(n., m.)* | coat |
| abril *(n., m.)* | April |
| abrir *(v.)* | to open |
| absoluto *(adj.)* | absolute |
| absolver *(v.)* | to absolve |
| absolviendo *(g.)* | absolving |
| abstener *(v.)* | to abstain |
| abstracto *(adj.)* | abstract |
| absuelto *(adj.)* | acquitted |
| abuela *(n., f.)* | grandmother |
| abuelita *(n., f.)* | granny |
| abuelo *(n., m.)* | grandfather |

| | |
|---|---|
| aburridísimo *(adj.)* | extremely bored |
| aburrido *(adj.)* | bored |
| aburrir *(v.)* | to bore |
| aburrirse *(v.)* | to be bored |
| acá *(adv.)* | here |
| acabar *(v.)* | to finish |
| acabarse *(v.)* | to be finished |
| acampando *(g.)* | camping |
| acantilado *(n., m.)* | cliff |
| acaso *(adv.)* | perhaps |
| accidentarse *(v.)* | to have an accident |
| accidente *(n., m.)* | accident |
| aceite *(n., m.)* | oil |
| acerca *(adv.)* | about |
| acercar *(v.)* | to approach |
| ácido *(adj.)* | acid |
| aclarar *(v.)* | to clarify |
| acné *(n., m.)* | acne |
| acoger *(v.)* | to receive |
| acompañar *(v.)* | to accompany |
| aconsejable *(adj., m./f.)* | advisable |
| aconsejar *(v.)* | to advise |
| acordado *(adj.)* | agreed |
| acordar *(v.)* | to agree |
| acordarse *(v.)* | to be agreed |
| acostarse *(v.)* | to go to bed |
| actividad *(n., f.)* | activity |

| | |
|---|---|
| activo *(adj.)* | active |
| acto *(n., m.)* | act |
| actor *(n., m.)* | actor |
| actriz *(n., f.)* | actress |
| actualmente *(adv.)* | at present |
| actuar *(v.)* | to act |
| acudir *(v.)* | to respond |
| acuerdo *(n., m.)* | agreement |
| acumulado *(adj.)* | accumulated |
| acusado *(n., m.)* | defendant |
| acusar *(v.)* | to accuse |
| adelantado *(adj.)* | advanced |
| adelante *(adv.)* | ahead |
| adelgazar *(v.)* | to lose weight |
| además *(adv.)* | besides |
| adentro *(adv.)* | inside |
| adiós *(n., m.)* | good-bye |
| administración *(n., f.)* | administration |
| administrador *(n., m.)* | administrator |
| admiración *(n., f.)* | admiration |
| admirador *(n., m.)* | admirer |
| admirar *(v.)* | to admire |
| adolescente *(n., m./f.)* | adolescent |
| adonde *(adv.)* | where |
| adorado *(part.)* | worshipped |
| adornar *(v.)* | to adorn |
| adquirir *(v.)* | to acquire |
| adulto *(n., m.)* | adult |
| advertir *(v.)* | to notify |
| aeropuerto *(n., m.)* | airport |
| afeitarse *(pron. v.)* | to shave |
| afiche *(n., m.)* | poster |
| afición *(n., f.)* | hobby |
| afortunadamente *(adv.)* | fortunately |
| africano *(adj.)* | African |
| afuera *(adv.)* | outside |
| agente *(n., m.)* | agent |
| agobiado *(adj.)* | burdened |
| agosto *(n., m.)* | August |
| agradar *(v.)* | to please |
| agradecer *(v.)* | to thank |
| agradecido *(adj.)* | thankful |
| agregar *(v.)* | to add |
| agresividad *(n., f.)* | aggressiveness |
| agricultura *(n., f.)* | agriculture |
| agua *(n., m. if sing., f. if pl.)* | water |
| aguacero *(n., m.)* | heavy rain |
| aguardiente *(n., m.)* | schnapps |
| águila *(n., m. if sing., f. if pl.)* | eagle |
| ahí *(adv.)* | there |
| ahora *(adv.)* | now |
| ahorrado *(part.)* | saved |
| ahorrar *(v.)* | to save |
| aire *(n., m.)* | air |
| ajedrez *(n., m.)* | chess |
| al (a+el) *(prep. + def. art., m. sing.)* | to the |
| ala *(n., m. if sing., f. if pl.)* | wing |
| alacena *(n., f.)* | pantry cupboard |
| alberca *(n., f.)* | swimming pool |
| albóndiga *(n., f.)* | meatball |
| alcalde *(n., m.)* | mayor |
| alcanzar *(v.)* | to reach |
| alcaparra *(n., f.)* | caper |
| alcoba *(n., f.)* | bedroom |
| alcohol *(n., m.)* | alcohol |
| alegrar *(v.)* | to cheer |
| alegre *(adj., inv.)* | happy |
| alegría *(n., f.)* | happiness |
| alemán *(adj.)* | German |
| alfabético *(adj.)* | alphabetical |
| alfiler *(n., m.)* | pin |
| alfombra *(n., f.)* | carpet |
| algo *(adv.)* | something |
| alguien *(ind. pron., m./f.)* | someone |
| algún *(ind. adj.)* | some |
| aliento *(n., m.)* | breath |
| alimento *(n., m.)* | food |
| alistando *(g.)* | getting ready |
| alistar *(v.)* | to prepare |
| aljibe *(n., m.)* | well |
| allá a lo lejos *(adv.)* | way off in the distance |
| allí *(adv.)* | there |
| alma *(n., m. if sing., f. if pl.)* | soul |
| almacén *(n., m.)* | store |
| almendra *(n., f.)* | almond |
| almohada *(n., f.)* | pillow |
| almorzar *(v.)* | to have lunch |
| alquilar *(v.)* | to rent |
| alquiler *(n., m.)* | rent |
| alrededor *(adv.)* | around |
| alternar *(v.)* | to alternate |
| altísimo *(sup. adj.)* | highest |
| alto *(adj.)* | high |
| altura *(n., f.)* | height |
| alzar *(v.)* | to raise |
| amabilidad *(n., f.)* | amiability |
| amabilísimo *(sup. adj.)* | extremely kind |
| amable *(adj., inv.)* | kind |
| amado *(part.)* | beloved |
| amanecer *(v.)* | to wake up |
| amar *(v.)* | to love |
| amarillo *(adj.)* | yellow |
| ambición *(n., f.)* | ambition |
| ambicioso *(adj.)* | ambitious |
| ambiente *(n., m.)* | environment |
| ambos *(adj. pl.)* | both |
| ameno *(adj.)* | pleasant |
| americano *(adj.)* | American |
| amigo *(n., m.)* | friend |
| amistad *(n., f.)* | friendship |
| amor *(n., m.)* | love |
| amortiguador *(n., m.)* | shock absorber |
| ampliar *(v.)* | to expand |
| amplificador *(n., m.)* | amplifier |
| amplio *(adj.)* | extensive |

| | | | |
|---|---|---|---|
| añadidura (por) *(n., f.)* | in addition | arena *(n., f.)* | sand |
| añadir *(v.)* | to add | argentino *(adj.)* | Argentinean |
| analizar *(v.)* | to analyze | argumento *(n., m.)* | argument |
| anchoa *(n., f.)* | anchovy | arma *(n., m.* if sing., *f.* if pl.*)* | arm |
| anciano *(n., m.)* | elderly man | armado *(adj.)* | armed |
| andar *(v.)* | to walk | armario *(n., m.)* | cabinet |
| ángel *(n., m.)* | angel | armonía *(n., f.)* | harmony |
| anillo *(n., m.)* | ring | arqueólogo *(n., m.)* | archaeologist |
| ánima *(n., m.* if sing., *f.* if pl.*)* | soul | arquitectura *(n., f.)* | architecture |
| animado *(adj.)* | animated | arrancar *(v.)* | to start |
| animal *(n., m.)* | animal | arrastrar *(v.)* | to drag |
| animarse *(v.)* | to encourage oneself | arreglar *(v.)* | to fix |
| año *(n., m.)* | year | arreglarse *(v.)* | to get oneself ready |
| anoche *(adv.)* | last night | arrestar *(v.)* | to arrest |
| anotar *(v.)* | to write down | arriba *(adv.)* | above; up |
| ansiedad *(n., f.)* | anxiety | arriesgar *(v.)* | to risk |
| antaño *(adv.)* | long ago | arroz *(n., m.)* | rice |
| anteayer *(adv.)* | the day before yesterday | arruinado *(adj.)* | ruined |
| antes *(adv.)* | before | arte *(n. m.)* | art |
| antibiótico *(n., m.)* | antibiotic | artista *(n., m./f.)* | artist |
| anticipación *(n., f.)* | anticipation | asaltante *(n., m./f.)* | assailant |
| antiguo *(adj.)* | old | asegurar *(v.)* | to assure; to ensure; |
| antipático *(adj.)* | unpleasant | | to insure |
| anunciar *(v.)* | to announce | asesinar *(v.)* | to murder |
| anzuelo *(n., m.)* | fishhook | asesinato *(n., m.)* | murder |
| apaciguar *(v.)* | to appease | asesino *(n., m.)* | murderer |
| apagar *(v.)* | to put out | así *(adv.)* | thus |
| apagón *(n., m.)* | blackout | asistencia *(n., f.)* | aid |
| aparcar *(v.)* | to park | asistir *(v.)* | to attend |
| aparecer *(v.)* | to appear | asomarse *(pron. v.)* | to appear oneself |
| aparecido *(part.)* | appeared | asombrarse *(pron. v.)* | to be amazed |
| apariencias engañan (las) *(idiom.)* | appearances can be deceptive | aspirando *(g.)* | aspiring |
| | | aspirar *(v.)* | to aspire |
| apartamento *(n., m.)* | apartment | aspirina *(n., f.)* | aspirin |
| aparte *(adv.)* | aside | asqueroso *(adj.)* | filthy |
| apasionar *(v.)* | to be passionate about something | astronauta *(n., m./f.)* | astronaut |
| | | astucia *(n., f.)* | cunning |
| apellido *(n., m.)* | surname | asustar *(v.)* | to frighten |
| apenado *(adj.)* | sorry | atacar *(v.)* | to attack |
| apenas *(adv.)* | barely | ataúd *(n., m.)* | coffin |
| apetecer *(v.)* | to desire | atención *(n., f.)* | attention |
| aplauso *(n., m.)* | applause | atender *(v.)* | to attend |
| aplicado *(adj.)* | applied | atentado *(n., m.)* | attack |
| apostar *(v.)* | to bet | atestiguar *(v.)* | to testify |
| apoyo *(n., m.)* | support | atleta *(n., inv.)* | athlete |
| aprender *(v.)* | to learn | atracción *(n., f.)* | attraction |
| aprisa *(adv.)* | hurriedly | atraer *(v.)* | to attract |
| aprobar *(v.)* | to approve | atrapar *(v.)* | to trap |
| aptitud *(n., f.)* | aptitude | atrás *(adv.)* | behind |
| apunte *(n., m.)* | annotation | atravesar *(v.)* | to cross |
| apurarse *(pron v.)* | to hurry oneself | atreverse *(pron. v.)* | to dare oneself |
| aquel *(adj. dem. m.)* | that | atribuir *(v.)* | to attribute |
| aquí *(adv.)* | here | atroz *(adj., inv.)* | atrocious |
| arar *(v.)* | to plough | aumentar *(v.)* | to enlarge; to increase |
| árbol *(n., m.)* | tree | aumento *(n., m.)* | increase |
| archivo *(n., m.)* | file | aún *(adv.)* | still |
| arco *(n., m.)* | arch | aun *(conj.)* | even |
| ardilla *(n., f.)* | squirrel | aunque *(conj.)* | although |

| | |
|---|---|
| auto *(n., m.)* | car |
| autobús *(n., m.)* | bus |
| automático *(adj.)* | automatic |
| autónomo *(adj.)* | autonomous |
| autopista *(n., f.)* | freeway |
| autor *(n., m.)* | author |
| auxilio *(n., m.)* | help |
| avalancha *(n., f.)* | avalanche |
| avenida *(n., f.)* | avenue |
| aventura *(n., f.)* | adventure |
| averiar *(v.)* | to damage |
| averiguar *(v.)* | to find out |
| avestruz *(n., m.)* | ostrich |
| avión *(n., m.)* | airplane |
| avisar *(v.)* | to notify |
| ayer *(adv.)* | yesterday |
| ayuda *(n., f.)* | aid |
| ayudado *(part.)* | helped |
| ayudante *(n., m.)* | assistant |
| ayudar *(v.)* | to help |
| azalea *(n., f.)* | azalea |
| azteca *(adj., m./f.)* | Aztec |
| azúcar *(n., m.)* | sugar |
| azul *(adj., m./f.)* | blue |

# B

| | |
|---|---|
| bache *(n., m.)* | pothole |
| bailando *(g.)* | dancing |
| bailar *(v.)* | to dance |
| baile *(n., m.)* | dance |
| bajar *(v.)* | to descend; to download; to bring down |
| bajo *(adj.)* | short, lower |
| bajo *(adv.)* | low |
| bajo *(prep.)* | under |
| balanza *(n., f.)* | scale |
| balcón *(n., m.)* | balcony |
| ballena *(n., f.)* | whale |
| balón *(n., m.)* | ball |
| baloncesto *(n., m.)* | basketball |
| bañando *(g.)* | bathing |
| bañar *(v.)* | to bathe |
| banco *(n., m.)* | bank |
| bandido *(n., m.)* | bandit |
| bañera *(n., f.)* | bathtub |
| baño *(n., m.)* | bath |
| bar *(n., m.)* | bar |
| baratija *(n., f.)* | trifle |
| barato *(adj.)* | cheap |
| barco *(n., m.)* | ship |
| barón *(n., m.)* | baron |
| baronesa *(n., f.)* | baroness |
| barrio *(n., m.)* | neighborhood |
| bastante *(adj., m./f.)* | enough |
| bastar *(v.)* | to suffice |
| basura *(n., f.)* | trash |

| | |
|---|---|
| batería *(n., f.)* | battery |
| batidora *(n., f.)* | electric mixer |
| batir *(v.)* | to beat |
| baúl *(n., m.)* | trunk |
| bebé *(n., m./f.)* | baby |
| beber *(v.)* | to drink |
| bebida *(n., f.)* | beverage |
| bebido *(part.)* | drunk |
| bebiendo *(g.)* | drinking |
| belleza *(n., f.)* | beauty |
| bellísimo *(sup. adj.)* | most beautiful |
| bello *(adj.)* | beautiful |
| bendito *(adj.)* | blessed |
| besarse *(pron. v.)* | to kiss |
| biberón *(n., m.)* | baby bottle |
| Biblia *(n., f.)* | Bible |
| biblioteca *(n., f.)* | library |
| bibliotecaria *(n., f.)* | librarian |
| bicicleta *(n., f.)* | bicycle |
| bien *(adj., m./f.)* | well |
| bien *(adv.)* | well |
| bienestar *(n., m.)* | welfare |
| bienvenida *(n., f.)* | welcome |
| bigote *(n., m.)* | mustache |
| bilingüe *(adj.)* | bilingual |
| billar *(n., m.)* | billiards |
| billete *(n., m.)* | bill |
| billetera *(n., f.)* | wallet |
| biología *(n., f.)* | biology |
| blanco *(adj.)* | white |
| boca *(n., f.)* | mouth |
| boda *(n., f.)* | wedding |
| bohío *(n., m.)* | hut |
| bola *(n., f.)* | ball |
| boleto *(n., m.)* | ticket |
| boliviano *(adj.)* | Bolivian |
| bolsa *(n., f.)* | stock market |
| bolsillo *(n., m.)* | pocket |
| bolso *(n., m.)* | bag |
| bombero *(n., m./f.)* | fireman |
| bondad *(n., f.)* | kindness |
| bondadoso *(adj.)* | kind |
| bonito *(adj.)* | pretty |
| bordado *(n., m.)* | embroidered |
| borrado *(part.)* | erased |
| borrar *(v.)* | to erase |
| bosque *(n., m.)* | forest |
| bota *(n., f.)* | boot |
| bote *(n., m.)* | boat |
| botella *(n., f.)* | bottle |
| botiquín *(n., m.)* | first aid kit |
| brazo *(n., m.)* | arm |
| breve *(adj., m./f.)* | brief |
| británico *(adj.)* | British |
| bromeando *(g.)* | joking |
| buen *(adj.)* | good |
| buenísimo *(sup. adj.)* | excellent |
| bueno *(adj.)* | good |

burgués *(n., m.)* — bourgeois; middle class
burlarse *(v.)* — to mock oneself
bus *(n., m.)* — bus
buscando *(g.)* — seeking
buscar *(v.)* — to seek
buzón *(n., m.)* — mailbox

# C

caballería *(n., f.)* — cavalry
caballero *(n., m.)* — gentleman
caballo *(n., m.)* — horse
cabaña *(n., f.)* — cabin
cabello *(n., m.)* — hair (head, human)
caber *(v.)* — to fit
cabeza *(n., f.)* — head
cable *(n., m.)* — cable
cacao *(n., m.)* — cocoa; chocolate; cacao
cada *(adj., inv.)* — each
cadáver *(n., m.)* — cadaver; corpse
cadera *(n., f.)* — hip
caer *(v.)* — to fall
caerse *(pron. v.)* — to fall oneself
café *(n., m.)* — coffee; coffee shop
cafetera *(n., f.)* — coffee pot
cafetería *(n., f.)* — cafeteria
caída *(n., f.)* — fall
caído *(part.)* — fallen
caja *(n., f.)* — box
cajero *(n., m.)* — cashier
cajón *(n., m.)* — drawer
calculadora *(n., f.)* — calculator
calefacción *(n., f.)* — heater; heating
calentamiento *(n., m.)* — warm-up
calidad *(n., f.)* — quality
cálido *(adj.)* — warm
calificación *(n., f.)* — assessment; evaluation
calificar *(v.)* — to rate; to class
cáliz *(n., m.)* — chalice
calle *(n., f.)* — street
calma *(n., f.)* — calm
calmarse *(pron. v.)* — to calm oneself
calor *(n., m.)* — heat
caloría *(n., f.)* — calory
calva *(n., f.)* — bald head
calvo *(adj.)* — bald
cama *(n., f.)* — bed
cámara *(n., f.)* — chamber; camera
camarada *(n., m./f.)* — comrade
cambiar *(v.)* — to change
cambio *(n., m.)* — change
caminando *(g.)* — walking
caminar *(v.)* — to walk
camino *(n., m.)* — road
camión *(n., m.)* — truck
camisa *(n., f.)* — shirt
campamento *(n., m.)* — camp

campana *(n., f.)* — bell
campaña *(n., f.)* — campaign
campeón *(n., m.)* — champion
campeonato *(n., m.)* — championship
campesino *(n., m.)* — peasant
campo *(n., m.)* — field
caña *(n., f.)* — cane; fishing rod
canasta *(n., f.)* — basket
cancelar *(v.)* — to cancel
cáncer *(n., m.)* — cancer
canción *(n., f.)* — song
cansado *(adj.)* — tired
cantando *(g.)* — singing
cantante *(n., m./f.)* — singer
cantar *(v.)* — to sing
cantidad *(n., f.)* — quantity
caótico *(adj.)* — chaotic
capacidad *(n., f.)* — capacity
capaz *(adj., m./f.)* — capable; able
capilla *(n., f.)* — chapel
capital *(n., f.)* — capital (city)
capital *(n., m.)* — capital (money)
capricho *(n., m.)* — whim
captura *(n., f.)* — capture
cara *(n., f.)* — face
caro *(adj.)* — expensive
caracol *(n., m.)* — snail
cárcel *(n., f.)* — jail
cargador de bebé *(n., m.)* — baby carrier
cargar *(v.)* — to charge, to carry
cargo *(n., m.)* — post
  See also *hacerse cargo de*
caridad *(n., f.)* — charity
cariño *(n., m.)* — affection
carnaval *(n., m.)* — carnival
carne *(n., f.)* — meat
caro *(adj.)* — expensive
carpintero *(n., m.)* — carpenter
carrera *(n., f.)* — career; race
carrito *(n., m.)* — little cart
carro *(n., m.)* — car
carta *(n., f.)* — letter
cartero *(n., m.)* — mailman
casa *(n., f.)* — house
casado *(adj.)* — married
casarse *(pron. v.)* — to get married
casi *(adv.)* — almost
casino *(n., m.)* — casino
casita *(n., f.)* — little house
caso *(n., m.)* — See *hacer caso*
castigar *(v.)* — to punish
castigo *(n., m.)* — punishment
castillo *(n., m.)* — castle
catedral *(n., f.)* — cathedral
causa *(n., f.)* — cause
cava *(n., f.)* — wine cellar
caverna *(n., f.)* — cavern
cayendo *(g.)* — falling

| | |
|---|---|
| caza (n., f.) | hunt |
| cazador (n., m.) | hunter |
| cazar (v.) | to hunt |
| cebolla (n., f.) | onion |
| cebra (n., f.) | zebra |
| celebración (n., f.) | celebration |
| celebrar (v.) | to celebrate |
| célebre (adj., m./f.) | famous |
| celos (n., m.) | jealousy |
| celoso (n., m.) | jealous |
| cena (n., f.) | supper |
| cenar (v.) | to have dinner |
| centímetro (n., m.) | centimeter |
| central (adj., inv.) | central |
| centro (n., m.) | center |
| cepillarse (pron. v.) | to brush |
| cerca (adv.) | nearby |
| cercano (adj.) | close |
| cercar (v.) | to surround |
| cerdo (n., m.) | pig; pork |
| cereal (n., m.) | cereal |
| cerebro (n., m.) | brain |
| ceremonia (n., f.) | ceremony |
| cerrado (adj.) | closed |
| cerrar (v.) | to close |
| cerveza (n., f.) | beer |
| césped (n., m.) | lawn |
| chaqueta (n., f.) | jacket |
| charlatán (n., m.) | charlatan |
| cheque (n., m.) | check |
| chica (n., f.) | girl |
| chico (n., m.) | boy |
| chimenea (n., f.) | chimney |
| chimpancé (n., m.) | chimpanzee |
| chino (adj.) | Chinese |
| chiquillo (n., m.) | kid |
| chistoso (adj.) | funny |
| chocante (adj., m./f.) | shocking |
| chocar (v.) | to collide |
| chocolate (n., m.) | chocolate |
| ciclismo (n., m.) | cycling |
| ciclista (n., f.) | biker |
| cicuta (n., f.) | hemlock |
| ciegamente (adv.) | blindly |
| cielo (n., m.) | sky |
| ciencia (n., f.) | science |
| científico (n., m.) | scientist |
| científico (adj.) | scientific |
| cierto (adj.) | certain |
| cifra (n., f.) | figure |
| cine (n., m.) | movies |
| circulación (n., f.) | traffic; circulation |
| circular (v.) | to circulate |
| ciudad (n., f.) | city |
| ciudadano (n., m.) | citizen |
| claridad (n., f.) | clarity |
| claro (adj.) | clear |
| clase (n., f.) | class |
| clemencia (n., f.) | clemency |
| cliente (n., m./f.) | client |
| clima (n., m.) | climate |
| coalición (n., f.) | coalition |
| cobrar (v.) | to charge |
| cocer (v.) | to cook |
| coche (n., m.) | car |
| cocina (n., f.) | kitchen |
| cocinado (adj.) | cooked |
| cocinar (v.) | to cook |
| cocinero (n., m.) | cook |
| coco (n., m.) | coconut |
| cohete (n., m.) | rocket |
| colección (n., f.) | collection |
| colegio (n., m.) | school |
| colgar (v.) | to hang |
| colina (n., f.) | hill |
| collar (n., m.) | necklace |
| colmo | See Es el colmo. |
| colocar (v.) | to place |
| colombiano (adj.) | Colombian |
| color (n., m.) | color |
| combustible (n., m.) | combustible; flammable |
| comenzar (v.) | to begin |
| comer (v.) | to eat |
| comercial (adj., m./f.) | commercial |
| comestible (adj., m./f.) | edible |
| cometer (v.) | to commit |
| comida (n., f.) | food |
| comido (part.) | eaten |
| comiendo (g.) | eating |
| comité (n., m.) | committee |
| como (adv.) | how |
| cómo (adv.) | how? |
| como (prep.) | as |
| compañero (n., m.) | companion |
| compañía (n., f.) | company |
| compartir (v.) | to share |
| compás (n., m.) | compass |
| competencia (n., f.) | competence |
| compitiendo (g.) | competing |
| completamente (adv.) | completely |
| completar (v.) | to complete |
| completo (adj.) | complete |
| complicar (v.) | to complicate |
| cómplice (n., m.) | accomplice |
| complot (n., m.) | conspiracy |
| componente (n., m.) | component |
| componer (v.) | to compose |
| comportamiento (n., m.) | behavior |
| composición (n., f.) | composition |
| compra (n., f.) | purchase |
| comprado (part.) | bought |
| comprar (v.) | to buy |
| comprender (v.) | to understand |
| comprensible (adj., inv.) | understandable |
| comprensivo (adj.) | comprehensive |
| comprometer (v.) | to commit |

| | |
|---|---|
| computador *(n., m.)* | computer |
| computadora *(n., f.)* | computer |
| común *(adj., m./f.)* | common |
| con *(prep.)* | with |
| concentrar *(v.)* | to concentrate |
| concentrarse *(pron. v.)* | to concentrate oneself |
| concepto *(n., m.)* | concept |
| concierto *(n., m.)* | concert |
| concluir *(v.)* | to conclude |
| concurso *(n., m.)* | contest |
| condenar *(v.)* | to condemn |
| conducir *(v.)* | to drive |
| conductor *(n., m.)* | driver; chauffeur |
| conectar *(v.)* | to connect |
| conejito *(n., m.)* | little rabbit |
| conejo *(n., m.)* | rabbit |
| conferencia *(n., f.)* | conference |
| confesar *(v.)* | to confess |
| confesión *(n., f.)* | confession |
| confianza *(n., f.)* | confidence |
| confiar *(v.)* | to confide; to trust |
| congelador *(n., m.)* | freezer |
| conmigo *(pers. pron.)* | with me |
| conocer *(v.)* | to know |
| conocido *(part.)* | known |
| conocimiento *(n., m.)* | knowledge |
| conquistar *(v.)* | to conquer |
| consecuencia *(n., f.)* | consequence |
| conseguir *(v.)* | to obtain |
| consejo *(n., m.)* | counsel |
| consentimiento *(n., m.)* | consent |
| consentir *(v.)* | to spoil; to allow |
| conservarse *(pron. v.)* | to conserve oneself |
| constante *(adj., m./f.)* | constant |
| construido *(part.)* | constructed; built |
| construir *(v.)* | to build |
| consultorio *(n., m.)* | doctor's office |
| consumir *(v.)* | to consume |
| consumo *(n., m.)* | consumption |
| contagioso *(adj.)* | contagious |
| contaminación *(n., f.)* | contamination |
| contar *(v.)* | to count |
| contemplar *(v.)* | to contemplate |
| contener *(v.)* | to contain |
| contenido *(n., m.)* | content |
| contento *(adj.)* | content; happy |
| contestar *(v.)* | to answer |
| contigo *(pers. pron.)* | with you |
| continuar *(v.)* | to continue |
| contra *(prep.)* | against |
| contradecir *(v.)* | to contradict |
| contraer *(v.)* | to contract |
| contrario *(n., m.)* | contrary |
| contravenir *(v.)* | to contravene |
| contribuir *(v.)* | to contribute |
| contrincante *(n., m.)* | opponent |
| convencer *(v.)* | to convince |
| convencido *(part.)* | convinced |
| convenir *(v.)* | to agree |
| convertido *(part.)* | converted |
| convertirse *(pron. v.)* | to became or change into |
| copa *(n., f.)* | cup; glass (wine) |
| corazón *(n., m.)* | heart |
| cordillera *(n., f.)* | mountain range |
| corredor *(n., m.)* | hall |
| corregir *(v.)* | to correct |
| correo *(n., m.)* | mail |
| correo electrónico *(n., m.)* | e-mail |
| correos *(n., m.)* | post office |
| correr *(v.)* | to run |
| correspondencia *(n., f.)* | correspondence; mail |
| corresponder *(v.)* | to correspond |
| corrido | moved |
| corriendo *(g.)* | running |
| corroer *(v.)* | to corrode |
| cortar *(v.)* | to cut |
| cortarse *(pron. v.)* | to be cut; to cut oneself |
| corte *(n., f.)* | court |
| corte *(n., m.)* | cut |
| cortés *(adj., m./f.)* | courteous |
| cortesía *(n., f.)* | courtesy |
| cortina *(n., f.)* | curtain |
| corto *(adj.)* | short |
| cosa *(n., f.)* | thing |
| cosecha *(n., f.)* | crop; harvest |
| costa *(n., f.)* | coast |
| costo *(n., m.)* | cost |
| costar *(v.)* | to cost |
| costoso *(adj.)* | costly |
| cotidiano *(adj.)* | quotidian; routine |
| crear *(v.)* | to create |
| creciendo *(g.)* | growing |
| crédito *(n., m.)* | credit |
| creer *(v.)* | to believe |
| crema *(n., f.)* | cream |
| cremoso *(adj.)* | creamy |
| criar *(v.)* | to raise; to rear children or animals |
| crimen *(n., m.)* | crime |
| crisis *(n., f.)* | crisis |
| cristal *(n., m.)* | crystal |
| cruce *(n., m.)* | crossing |
| cruel *(adj., m./f.)* | cruel |
| crujiente *(adj.)* | crusty |
| cruz *(n., f.)* | cross |
| cruzar *(v.)* | to cross |
| cuadra *(n., f.)* | block (city) |
| cuadro *(n., m.)* | picture |
| cuajada *(n., f.)* | farm cheese |
| cual *(indef. pron. sing.)* | which |
| cuál *(interr. pron. sing.)* | which? |
| cualquier *(indef. adj.)* | any |
| cuando *(adv.)* | when |
| cuándo *(adv.)* | when? |
| cuanto *(adv.)* | as much as |
| cuánto *(pron., interr.)* | how much? |

| | |
|---|---|
| cuarto (n., m.) | room |
| cubierto (part.) | covered |
| cubriendo (g.) | covering |
| cubrir (v.) | to cover |
| cucharadita (n., f.) | teaspoon |
| cuenta (n., f.), | account |
| See also darse cuenta | |
| cuento (n., m.) | story |
| cuerda (n., f.) | cord |
| cuerdo (adj.) | sane |
| cuero (n., m) | leather |
| cuidado (n., m.) | care |
| cuidar (v.) | to take care of |
| cuidarse (pron. v.) | to be taken care of |
| cultivar (v.) | to cultivate |
| cultura (n., f.) | culture |
| cumpleaños (n., m.) | birthday |
| cumplido (part.) | compliment |
| cumplir (v.) | to comply; to have a birthday |
| cuñado (n., m.) | brother-in-law |
| cuota (n., f.) | quota; payment |
| cura (n., f.) | cure |
| cura (n., m.) | priest |
| curiosidad (n., f.) | curiosity |
| curioso (n., m.) | curious |
| curso (n., m.) | course |
| cuyo (relative pron.) | whose |

# D

| | |
|---|---|
| dama (n., f.) | lady |
| damnificado (n., m.) | flood victim |
| dando (g.) | giving |
| dar (v.) | to give |
| dar la vuelta (v.) | to flip; to turn around |
| darse cuenta (v.) | to realize |
| dato (n., m.) | datum; fact |
| de (prep.) | of |
| de modo que (loc. adv.) | so that |
| de pura (loc. adv.) | excessively |
| de repente (loc. adv.) | suddenly |
| de veras (loc. adv.) | truly |
| deber (v.) | to owe |
| deberes (n., m.) | homework; chores |
| débil (adj. m./f.) | weak |
| decidir (v.) | to decide |
| decir (v.) | to say |
| decisión (n., f.) | decision |
| declaración (n., f.) | declaration; statement |
| dedicado (adj.) | dedicated |
| dedicar (v.) | to dedicate |
| dedo (n., m.) | finger |
| dejando (g.) | leaving |
| dejar (v.) | to leave |
| del (de + el) (prep. + def. art.) | of the |
| delante de (adv.) | in front of |

| | |
|---|---|
| delegado (n., m.) | delegate |
| delgado (adj.) | thin |
| delicado (adj.) | delicate |
| delicioso (adj.) | delicious |
| delincuente (n., m.) | delinquent; offender |
| demanda (n., f.) | demand |
| demás (adj., inv., pl.) | others |
| demasiado (adj.) | too much |
| demostrar (v.) | to show |
| dentro (adv.) | inside |
| departamento (n., m.) | department |
| deponer (v.) | to depose |
| deporte (n., m.) | sport |
| depresión (n., f.) | depression |
| deprisa (adv.) | quickly; fast |
| derecha (n., f.) | right |
| derretirse (pron. v.) | to melt oneself |
| derrumbar (v.) | to bring down |
| desaguar (v.) | to drain |
| desamparado (adj.) | abandoned |
| desaparecer (v.) | to disappear |
| desapercibido (adj.) | unnoticed |
| desarrollado (adj.) | developed |
| desayuno (n., m.) | breakfast |
| descansar (v.) | to rest |
| descanso (n., m.) | rest |
| descargar (v.) | to discharge |
| descendiente (n., m.) | descendant |
| descomponer (v.) | to break down |
| desconcertante (adj.) | disconcerting |
| descongelar (v.) | to defrost |
| desconsoladamente (adv.) | hopelessly |
| descubierto (adj.) | discovered |
| descubriendo (g.) | discovering |
| descubrir (v.) | to discover |
| desde (adv.) | since |
| desear (v.) | to desire |
| desesperado (adj.) | desperate |
| desesperante (adj., m./f.) | maddening; infuriating |
| desfachatez (n., f.) | shamelessness; insolence |
| desgano (n., m.) | reluctance |
| desgracia (n., f.) | misfortune |
| deshacer (v.) | to undo |
| deslumbrar (v.) | to dazzle |
| desobediente (adj., m./f.) | disobedient |
| desocupar (v.) | to empty |
| desorden (n., m.) | disorder |
| desordenado (adj.) | disorderly |
| despacio (adv.) | slowly |
| despedir (v.) | to fire from a job |
| despedirse (pron. v.) | to say good-bye |
| desperdicio (n., m.) | waste; remains |
| despertador (n., m.) | alarm clock |
| despertar (v.) | to awake |
| despierto (adj.) | awake |
| despilfarrar (v.) | to squander |
| desplazar (v.) | to displace |
| déspota (adj. m./f.) | despot |

| | |
|---|---|
| después *(adv.)* | later |
| destornillador *(n., m.)* | screwdriver |
| destripador *(n., m.)* | ripper (as in Jack the Ripper) |
| destrozar *(v.)* | to wreck; to smash |
| destruido *(adj.)* | destroyed |
| destruir *(v.)* | to destroy |
| detective *(n., m.)* | detective |
| detener *(v.)* | to stop |
| detenerse *(pron. v.)* | to stop oneself |
| detenido *(n., m.)* | detained |
| deterioro *(n., m.)* | deterioration |
| determinar *(v.)* | to determine |
| detrás *(adv.)* | behind |
| deuda *(n., f.)* | debt |
| deudor *(n., m.)* | debtor |
| devaluar *(v.)* | to devalue |
| devolver *(v.)* | to return |
| día *(n., m.)* | day |
| diabetes *(adj., f.)* | diabetes |
| diario *(adj.)* | daily |
| diario *(n., m.)* | newspaper |
| dibujo *(n., m.)* | drawing |
| dicho *(part.)* | said |
| dichoso *(adj.)* | happy |
| diciendo *(g.)* | saying |
| diente *(n., m.)* | tooth |
| diferencia *(n., f.)* | difference |
| diferente *(adj., m./f.)* | different |
| difícil *(adj., m./f.)* | difficult |
| dificilísimo *(sup. adj.)* | most difficult |
| dignidad *(n., f.)* | dignity |
| dilema *(n., m.)* | dilemma |
| diluir *(v.)* | to dilute |
| dinero *(n., m.)* | money |
| dinosaurio *(n., m.)* | dinosaur |
| dios *(n., m.)* | god |
| dirección *(n., f.)* | direction |
| directamente *(adv.)* | directly |
| directo *(adj.)* | direct |
| director *(n., m.)* | director |
| dirigente *(n., f./m.)* | leader |
| dirigir *(v.)* | to direct |
| disciplina *(n., f.)* | discipline |
| disco *(n., m.)* | record; disk |
| discoteca *(n., f.)* | discotheque |
| discreto *(adj.)* | discreet |
| discutiendo *(g.)* | arguing; discussing |
| discutir *(v.)* | to argue; to discuss |
| diseñador *(n., m.)* | designer |
| diseño *(n., m.)* | design |
| disfraz *(n., m.)* | disguise |
| disgusto *(n., m.)* | displeasure |
| disimular *(v.)* | to pretend |
| disminuir *(v.)* | to diminish |
| disponer *(v.)* | to arrange |
| dispuesto *(adj.)* | ready; available for |
| distinguir *(v.)* | to distinguish |
| distinto *(adj.)* | distinct; different |
| distraído *(adj.)* | distracted; absentminded |
| distribuir *(v.)* | to distribute |
| divagación *(n., f.)* | digression |
| divertido *(adj.)* | amusing |
| divertir *(v.)* | to entertain |
| divertirse *(pron. v.)* | to entertain oneself |
| divisa *(n., f.)* | currency |
| divorciarse *(pron. v.)* | to be divorced |
| divorcio *(n., m.)* | divorce |
| doctor *(n., m.)* | doctor |
| documental *(n., m.)* | documentary |
| documento *(n., m.)* | document |
| dólar *(n., m.)* | dollar |
| doler *(v.)* | to hurt |
| dolor *(v.)* | pain |
| domingo *(n., m.)* | Sunday |
| donar *(v.)* | to donate |
| donde *(adv.)* | where |
| dónde *(adv.)* | where? |
| dormido *(part.)* | asleep |
| dormir *(v.)* | to sleep |
| dormitorio *(n., m.)* | bedroom |
| dragón *(n., m.)* | dragon |
| dramático *(adj.)* | dramatic |
| dramatiquísimo *(sup. adj.)* | most dramatic |
| droga *(n., f.)* | drug |
| ducha *(n., f.)* | shower |
| ducharse *(pron. v.)* | to shower |
| duda *(n., f.)* | doubt |
| dudar *(v.)* | to doubt |
| dueño *(n., m.)* | owner |
| dulce *(adj., m./f.)* | sweet |
| dulces *(n., m.)* | sweets; candy |
| dulzura *(n., f.)* | sweetness |
| duplicar *(v.)* | to duplicate |
| durante *(adv.)* | during |
| durazno *(n., m.)* | peach |
| durmiendo *(g.)* | sleeping |
| duro *(adj.)* | hard |

# E

| | |
|---|---|
| ebrio *(n., m.)* | drunk |
| echar de menos *(v.)* | to miss |
| ecologista *(n., m./f.)* | ecologist |
| económico *(adj.)* | economic |
| ecuatoriano *(adj.)* | Ecuadorian |
| edad *(n., f.)* | age |
| edificio *(n., m.)* | building |
| editorial *(n., f.)* | publishing house |
| educación *(n., f.)* | education |
| educar *(v.)* | to educate |
| educativo *(n., m.)* | educational |
| efectivo (en) *(adj.)* | in cash |
| efectuar *(v.)* | to carry out; to perform |
| eficiente *(adj., m./f.)* | efficient |

| | |
|---|---|
| egoísmo (n., m.) | selfishness |
| ejercicio (n., m.) | exercise |
| ejército (n., m.) | army |
| el (def. art., m., sing.) | the |
| él (pers. pron., m., sing.) | he |
| elaborar (v.) | to elaborate; to make; to devise |
| elecciones (n., m.) | elections |
| eléctrico (adj.) | electric |
| electrodoméstico (n., m.) | appliance |
| electrónico (adj.) | electronic |
| See also correo electrónico | |
| elefante (n., m.) | elephant |
| elegante (adj., m./f.) | elegant |
| elegantemente (adv.) | elegantly |
| elegido (part.) | elected |
| elegir (v.) | to elect |
| eliminatorias (n., f.) | playoffs |
| ella (pers. pron., f., sing.) | she |
| ellas (pers. pron., f., pl.) | they |
| ellos (pers. pron., m., pl.) | they |
| embajador (n., m.) | ambassador |
| embarcación (n., f.) | boat |
| embargo (n., m.) | embargo |
| emborracharse (pron. v.) | to get drunk |
| embotellamiento (n., m.) | traffic jam |
| emocionarse (pron. v.) | to become emotional; to be moved by something |
| empacar (v.) | to pack |
| empanada (n., f.) | turnover |
| empaque (n., m.) | package |
| emparedado (n., m.) | sandwich |
| empeño (n., m.) | effort |
| emperatriz (n., f.) | empress |
| empezar (v.) | to begin |
| empleado (n., m.) | employee |
| empleo (n., m.) | employment |
| emprender (v.) | to undertake |
| empresa (n., f.) | business |
| empujando (g.) | pushing |
| empujar (v.) | to push |
| en (prep.) | in |
| enamorado (adj.) | in love |
| enamorar (v.) | to court |
| encabezar (v.) | to head |
| encantar (v.) | to like |
| encarcelado (adj.) | imprisoned |
| encargar (v.) | to entrust |
| encender (v.) | to light; to turn on |
| encendido (adj.) | on; lighted |
| encendiendo (g.) | lighting |
| encerrado (adj.) | enclosed |
| encerrar (v.) | to enclose |
| encima (adv.) | on top |
| encoger (v.) | to shrink |
| encontrado (part.) | found |
| encontrar (v.) | to find |
| encontrarse (pron. v.) | to find oneself |
| encubierto (part.) | concealed |
| encubrir (v.) | to conceal |
| enderezar (v.) | to straighten |
| enemigo (n., m.) | enemy |
| energía (n., f.) | energy |
| enérgico (adj.) | energetic |
| enfermarse (pron. v.) | to become ill |
| enfermedad (n., f.) | illness |
| enfermo (adj.) | sick |
| enfermo (n., m.) | sick person |
| enfriar (v.) | to chill |
| enfriarse (v.) | to become chilled |
| enfurecido (adj.) | enraged |
| engañar (v.) | to deceive |
| engaño (n., m.) | deceit |
| engordarse (pron. v.) | to become fat |
| enojado (adj.) | angry |
| enojarse (pron. v.) | to become angry |
| enorme (adj., m./f.) | enormous |
| enormemente (adv.) | enormously |
| ensayar (v.) | to practice |
| ensayo (n., m.) | attempt; trial |
| enseñar (v.) | to teach |
| entender (v.) | to understand |
| enterarse (v.) | to become informed |
| entero (adj.) | entire |
| entierro (n., m.) | burial |
| entonces (adv.) | then |
| entrada (n., f.) | entrance |
| entrando (g.) | entering |
| entrante (adj., m./f.) | coming |
| entrar (v.) | to enter |
| entre (prep.) | between |
| entrega (n., f.) | delivery |
| entregar (v.) | to deliver |
| entrenado (part.) | trained |
| entrenadora (n., f.) | trainer; coach |
| entrenar (v.) | to train; to coach |
| entretener (v.) | to entertain |
| entretenido (adj.) | entertained |
| entrevista (n., f.) | interview |
| entrevistado (part.) | interviewed |
| entristecerse (pron. v.) | to become sad |
| entrometido (adj.) | meddlesome |
| entusiasmo (n., m.) | enthusiasm |
| enviar (v.) | to send |
| envidia (n., f.) | envy |
| envidioso (adj.) | envious |
| equipaje (n., m.) | luggage |
| equipo (n., m.) | team |
| equivaler (v.) | to equal |
| equivocado (adj.) | wrong |
| equivocarse (pron. v.) | to be mistaken |
| erguir (v.) | to straighten up |
| error (n., m.) | error |
| Es el colmo. (idiom.) | You really take the cake. |
| esa (adj. dem.; pron., f.) | that; that one; that thing |

esas *(adj. dem.; pron., f., pl.)* those; those ones; those things
escaleras *(n., f., pl.)* stairs
escasear *(v.)* to become scarce
escasez *(n., f.)* shortage
escoger *(v.)* to choose
escolar *(adj.)* school-related
esconderse *(pron. v.)* to hide
escondido *(part.)* hidden
escondite *(n., m.)* hideout
escribiendo *(g.)* writing
escribir *(v.)* to write
escrito *(adj.)* written
escrito *(part.)* written
escritor *(n., m.)* writer
escritorio *(n., m.)* desk
escuchado *(part.)* listened
escuchando *(g.)* listening
escuchar *(v.)* to listen
escuela *(n., f.)* school
escultura *(n., f.)* sculpture
ese *(adj. dem.; pron., m.)* that; that one; that thing
esencial *(adj., m./f.)* essential
esfuerzo *(n., m.)* effort
esfumarse *(pron. v.)* to be faded
eso *(pron. neut., m.)* that
esos *(adj. dem.; pron., m., pl.)* those; those ones; those things
espacial *(adj., m./f.)* spatial; related to outer space
espacio *(n., m.)* space
espacioso *(adj.)* spacious
espalda *(n., f.)* back
español *(adj.)* Spanish
español *(n., m.)* Spanish language
esparcir *(v.)* to spread
especial *(adj., m./f.)* special
especialmente *(adv.)* especially
especies *(n., f.)* species
espectáculo *(n., m.)* spectacle
espectador *(n., m.)* spectator
espejo *(n., m.)* mirror
esperando *(g.)* expecting
esperanza *(n., f.)* hope
esperar *(v.)* to expect
espía *(n., m./f.)* spy
espiritual *(adj., m./f.)* spiritual
esposa *(n., f.)* wife
esposas *(n., f., pl.)* handcuffs
esposo *(n., m.)* husband
esquema *(n., m.)* plan; scheme
esquiar *(v.)* to ski
esquimal *(n., m.)* Eskimo
esquina *(n., f.)* corner
esta *(adj. dem.; pron., f.)* this; this one; this thing
estabilizar *(v.)* to stabilize
estable *(adj., m./f.)* stable
establecer *(v.)* to establish

estación *(n., f.)* station
estacionar *(v.)* to park
estadística *(n., f.)* statistics
estado *(n., m.)* state
　　See *golpe de estado*
estado *(part.)* state
estantería *(n., f.)* bookcase
estar *(v.)* to be
estas *(adj. dem.; pron., f.)* these; these ones; these things
este *(adj. dem.; pron., m.)* this; this one; this thing
esto *(pron. neut., m.)* this
estos *(adj. dem.; pron., m.)* these; these ones; these things
estrella *(n., f.)* star
estrellarse *(pron. v.)* to crash
estrenar *(v.)* to premiere
estrictamente *(adv.)* strictly
estricto *(adj.)* strict
estudiado *(part.)* studied
estudiando *(g.)* studying
estudiante *(n., m./f.)* student
estudiar *(v.)* to study
estudios *(n., m.)* studies
estufa *(n., f.)* stove
estupendo *(adj.)* stupendous
estupidez *(n., f.)* stupidity
euro *(n., m.)* euro (currency)
europeo *(adj.)* European
evaluación *(n., f.)* evaluation
evaluar *(v.)* to evaluate
evidencia *(n., f.)* evidence
evidente *(adj., m./f.)* evident
evitando *(g.)* avoiding
evitar *(v.)* to avoid
evolución *(n., f.)* evolution
exactamente *(adv.)* exactly
exacto *(adj.)* exact
examen *(n., m.)* exam
examinar *(v.)* to examine
excederse *(pron. v.)* to exceed
excelente *(adj., m./f.)* excellent
excepcional *(adj., m./f.)* exceptional
exclusivo *(adj.)* exclusive
exigente *(adj., m./f.)* demanding
exigir *(v.)* to demand; to require
exilio *(n., m.)* exile
existir *(v.)* to exist
éxito *(n., m.)* success
exitoso *(adj.)* successful
expandirse *(pron. v.)* to be expanded
experiencia *(n., f.)* experience
experimento *(n., m.)* experiment
explicación *(n., f.)* explanation
explicar *(v.)* to explain
explorador *(n., m.)* explorer
exquisito *(adj.)* exquisite
exterior *(n., m.)* exterior

| | |
|---|---|
| exterminar (v.) | to exterminate |
| externo (adj.) | external |
| extinción (n., f.) | extinction |
| extinguir (v.) | to extinguish |
| extrañar (v.) | to miss |
| extraño (adj.) | strange |
| extraordinario (adj.) | extraordinary |
| extraterrestre (n., m.) | extraterrestrial |
| extraviarse (pron. v.) | to become lost; to lose one's way |

## F

| | |
|---|---|
| fabricar (v.) | to manufacture |
| fabuloso (adj.) | fabulous |
| fácil (adj., inv.) | easy |
| facilidad (n., f.) | facility |
| factura (n., f.) | invoice |
| facturar (v.) | to invoice; to bill |
| falda (n., f.) | skirt |
| falso (adj.) | false |
| falta (n., m.) | fault |
| fama (n., f.) | fame |
| familia (n., f.) | family |
| famoso (adj.) | famous |
| fantástico (adj.) | fantastic |
| fascinar (v.) | to fascinate |
| fastidiar (v.) | to bother |
| favor (n., m.) | favor |
| favorito (adj.) | favorite |
| fe (n., f.) | faith |
| febrero (n., m.) | February |
| fecha (n., f.) | date |
| felicidad (n., f.) | happiness |
| felicitar (v.) | to congratulate |
| feliz (adj., inv.) | happy |
| felpa (n., f.) | felt |
| fenicio (n.) | Phoenician |
| feo (adj.) | ugly |
| feria (n., f.) | fair |
| ferrocarril (n., m.) | railroad |
| festival (n., m.) | festival |
| ficción (n., f.) | fiction |
| fiebre (n., f.) | fever |
| fiel (adj., inv.) | faithful |
| fiera (n., f.) | wild animal |
| fiesta (n., f.) | festival |
| fila (n., f.) | row |
| filmoteca (n., f.) | film library |
| filosofía (n., f.) | philosophy |
| fin (n., m.) | end |
| final (n., m.) | final |
| finalmente (adv.) | finally |
| financiero (adj.) | financial |
| finanzas (n., f., pl.) | finances |
| finca (n., f.) | farm |
| fingir (v.) | to pretend |

| | |
|---|---|
| finlandés (adj.) | Finnish |
| firmar (v.) | to sign |
| firme (adj., m./f.) | firm |
| fiscal (n., m.) | fiscal |
| física (n., f.) | physics |
| flan (n., m.) | custard |
| flauta (n., f.) | flute |
| flojo (adj.) | weak |
| flor (n., f.) | flower |
| florero (n., m.) | flower pot |
| foca (n., f.) | seal |
| forma (n., f.) | shape, form |
| fórmula (n., f.) | formula |
| fortuna (n., f.) | fortune |
| foto (n., f.) | photograph |
| fotocopiar (v.) | to photocopy |
| fotografía (n., f.) | photography |
| fotográfico (adj.) | photographic |
| fotógrafo (n., m.) | photographer |
| fraguar (v.) | to forge |
| francés (adj.) | French |
| franco suizo (n., m.) | Swiss franc |
| frecuencia (n., f.) | frequency |
| frecuente (adj.) | frequent |
| fregadero (n., m.) | sink |
| freír (v.) | to fry |
| frescos (adj.) | fresh |
| frío (n., m.) | cold |
| frito (adj.) | fried |
| fruta (n., f.) | fruit |
| fuego (n., m.) | fire |
| fuente (n., f.) | source |
| fuera de (adv.) | out from |
| fuerte (adj., inv.) | strong |
| fuerza (n., f.) | force |
| fugaz (adj., inv.) | fleeting |
| fumar (v.) | to smoke |
| fumigar (v.) | to fumigate |
| funcionar (v.) | to function |
| fundador (n., m.) | founder |
| fundamental (adj., inv.) | fundamental |
| furia (n., f.) | furious |
| fusionar (v.) | to fuse |
| fútbol (n., m.) | soccer |
| futbolista (n., m./f.) | soccer player |
| futuro (n., m.) | future |

## G

| | |
|---|---|
| galleta (n., f.) | cookie; cracker |
| gallo (n., m.) | rooster |
| galón (n., m.) | gallon |
| ganado (n., m.) | cattle |
| ganado (part.) | won |
| ganando (g.) | winning |
| ganar (v.) | to win |
| gana (n., f.) | desire |

| | |
|---|---|
| ganso *(n., m.)* | goose |
| garaje *(n., m.)* | garage |
| garantizar *(v.)* | to guarantee |
| garganta *(n., f.)* | throat |
| garrafa *(n., f.)* | bottle |
| gas *(n., m.)* | gas |
| gasolina *(n., f.)* | gasoline |
| gastar *(v.)* | to spend |
| gasto *(n., m.)* | expense |
| gato *(n., m.)* | cat |
| gaveta *(n., f.)* | drawer |
| gaviota *(n., f.)* | seagull |
| gemelos *(n., m.)* | twins |
| genial *(adj., m./f.)* | genial |
| genio *(n., m./f.)* | genius |
| gente *(n., f.)* | people |
| gentil *(adj., m./f.)* | genteel |
| geografía *(n., f.)* | geography |
| gerente *(n., m.)* | manager |
| gimnasio *(n., m.)* | gymnasium |
| gitano *(n., m.)* | gypsy |
| global *(adj., m./f.)* | global |
| globo *(n., m.)* | globe |
| gobernador *(n., m.)* | governor |
| gobernante *(n., m.)* | ruler |
| gobernar *(v.)* | to govern |
| gobierno *(n., m.)* | government |
| golondrina *(n., f.)* | swallow (bird) |
| golpe *(n., m.)* | strike |
| golpe de estado *(n., m.)* | coup d'état; military overthrow |
| gordo *(adj.)* | fat |
| gorila *(n., m.)* | gorilla |
| gota *(n., f.)* | drop |
| gozar *(v.)* | to enjoy |
| grabar *(v.)* | to record |
| gracias *(n., f.)* | thanks |
| gracioso *(adj.)* | funny |
| grado *(n., m.)* | degree |
| graduarse *(pron. v.)* | to graduate from |
| gramática *(n., f.)* | grammar |
| gran *(adj., m./f.)* | great |
| grande *(adj., m./f.)* | large |
| grandemente *(adv.)* | largely |
| granja *(n., f.)* | farm |
| granjero *(n., m.)* | farmer |
| grano *(n., m.)* | grain |
| grasa *(n., f.)* | grease |
| grasas *(n., f.)* | fatty foods |
| grave *(adj., m./f.)* | serious |
| gravedad *(n., f.)* | gravity |
| grillo *(n., m.)* | cricket |
| gris *(adj., m./f.)* | gray |
| gritando *(g.)* | yelling; screaming |
| gritar *(v.)* | to yell; to scream |
| grito *(n., m.)* | yell; scream |
| grosero *(adj.)* | impolite |
| grupo *(n., m.)* | group |

| | |
|---|---|
| guante *(n., m.)* | glove |
| guapísimo *(sup. adj.)* | very handsome |
| guapo *(adj.)* | handsome |
| guardado *(part.)* | kept |
| guardar *(v.)* | to keep |
| guardería *(n., f.)* | preschool |
| guarecerse *(pron. v.)* | to shelter oneself |
| guarida *(n., f.)* | den; lair |
| guerra *(n., f.)* | war |
| guía *(n., f.)* | guidebook |
| guía *(n., m.)* | guide |
| guiar *(v.)* | to guide |
| guitarra *(n., f.)* | guitar |
| guitarrista *(n., m./f.)* | guitarist |
| gustado *(part.)* | liked |
| gustar *(v.)* | to like; to please |
| gusto *(n., m.)* | taste |
| gustosamente *(adv.)* | gladly |

# H

| | |
|---|---|
| haber *(v.)* | to have |
| habilidad *(n., f.)* | ability |
| habitación *(n., f.)* | room |
| habitante *(n., m./f.)* | inhabitant |
| hablando *(g.)* | speaking |
| hablar *(v.)* | to speak |
| hacer *(v.)* | to do; to make |
| hacer caso *(idiom.)* | to obey |
| hacerse *(pron. v.)* | to pretend to be |
| hacerse cargo de *(idiom.)* | to take charge of |
| hacha *(n., m. if sing., f. if pl.)* | ax |
| hacia *(prep.)* | toward |
| haciendo *(g.)* | doing |
| hambre *(n., m. if sing., f. if pl.)* | hunger |
| hambruna *(n., f.)* | famine |
| harina *(n., f.)* | flour |
| hasta *(prep.)* | to |
| hay See also *haber* | there is; there are |
| hecho *(adj.)* | made |
| hecho *(n., m.)* | fact |
| hecho *(part.)* | made |
| helado *(n., m.)* | ice cream |
| helicóptero *(n., m.)* | helicopter |
| herencia *(n., f.)* | inheritance |
| herido *(adj.)* | injured; wounded |
| herir *(v.)* | to wound |
| hermana *(n., f.)* | sister |
| hermanita *(n., f.)* | little sister |
| hermano *(n., m.)* | brother |
| hermosamente *(adv.)* | beautifully |
| hermoso *(adj.)* | beautiful |
| héroe *(n., m.)* | hero |
| hidrógeno *(n., m.)* | hydrogen |
| hielo *(n., m.)* | ice |
| hierba *(n., f.)* | herb |
| hierro *(n., m.)* | iron |

| | |
|---|---|
| hija *(n., f.)* | daughter |
| hijo *(n., m.)* | son |
| hilo *(n., m.)* | thread |
| hinchar *(v.)* | to swell |
| hindú *(adj.)* | Hindu |
| hipócrita *(adj., m./f.)* | hypocritical |
| hipopótamo *(n., m.)* | hippopotamus |
| historia *(n., f.)* | history |
| historiador *(n., m.)* | historian |
| hoja *(n., f.)* | leaf |
| Hola. *(interj.)* | Hello. |
| hombre *(n., m.)* | man |
| hombro *(n., m.)* | shoulder |
| homicida *(n., m./f.)* | murderer |
| honrado *(adj.)* | honest |
| hora *(n., f.)* | hour |
| hormiga *(n., f.)* | ant |
| horno *(n., m.)* | oven |
| horno microondas *(n., m.)* | microwave oven |
| horrible *(adj., m./f.)* | horrible |
| horror *(n., m.)* | horror |
| hospital *(n., m.)* | hospital |
| hospitalario *(adj.)* | hospitable |
| hotel *(n., m.)* | hotel |
| hoy *(adv.)* | today |
| hueco *(n., m.)* | hole; hollow |
| huella *(n., f.)* | print; track |
| huerta *(n., f.)* | orchard |
| hueso *(n., m.)* | bone |
| huésped *(n., m./f.)* | guest |
| huevo *(n., m.)* | egg |
| humano *(n., m.)* | human |
| húmedo *(adj.)* | humid |
| humidificador *(n., m.)* | humidifier |
| humor *(n., m.)* | humor |
| hundirse *(pron. v.)* | to sink |

# I

| | |
|---|---|
| idea *(n., f.)* | idea |
| identificación *(n., f.)* | identification |
| idioma *(n., m.)* | language |
| idiota *(n., m./f.)* | idiot |
| iglesia *(n., f.)* | church |
| igual *(adj., m./f.)* | equal |
| ilusionado *(adj.)* | hopeful |
| imagen *(n., f.)* | image |
| imaginación *(n., f.)* | imagination |
| imaginado *(part.)* | imagined |
| imaginarse *(pron. v.)* | to imagine |
| impedir *(v.)* | to impede |
| imperio *(n., m.)* | empire |
| imponer *(v.)* | to impose |
| importante *(adj., m./f.)* | important |
| importar *(v.)* | to import |
| imposible *(adj., m./f.)* | impossible |
| impredecible *(adj., m./f.)* | unpredictable |

| | |
|---|---|
| imprenta *(n., f.)* | press |
| imprudente *(adj., m./f.)* | imprudent |
| impuesto *(n., m.)* | tax |
| impulso *(n., m.)* | impulse |
| inauguración *(n., f.)* | inauguration |
| inca *(n., m.)* | Inca |
| incendiado *(part.)* | burned |
| incendiarse *(v.)* | to catch fire |
| incendio *(n., m.)* | fire |
| inclinado *(adj.)* | inclined |
| incluir *(v.)* | to include |
| inclusive *(adv.)* | inclusive |
| inconstitucional *(adj., m./f.)* | unconstitutional |
| increíble *(adj., m./f.)* | incredible |
| independiente *(adj., m./f.)* | independent |
| indicar *(v.)* | to indicate |
| indígena *(n., inv.)* | indigenous; native |
| indispensable *(adj., m./f.)* | essential |
| infarto *(n., m.)* | heart attack |
| infección *(n., f.)* | infection |
| infeliz *(adj., m./f.)* | unhappy |
| infierno *(n., m.)* | hell |
| inflamado *(adj.)* | inflamed |
| influir *(v.)* | to influence |
| informado *(adj.)* | informed; reported |
| informal *(adj., m./f.)* | informal |
| infusión *(n., f.)* | infusion |
| ingeniero *(n., m./f.)* | engineer |
| ingenuo *(adj.)* | naive; ingenuous |
| inglés *(n., m.)* | English |
| inglés *(adj.)* | Englishman |
| ingrediente *(n., m.)* | ingredient |
| iniciar *(v.)* | to initiate |
| inmediatamente *(adv.)* | immediately |
| inmediato (de) *(loc. adv.)* | immediate |
| inmenso *(adj.)* | huge |
| inocencia *(n., f.)* | innocence |
| inofensivo *(adj.)* | inoffensive |
| inoportuno *(adj.)* | inopportune |
| inquieto *(adj.)* | restless |
| inquirir *(v.)* | to inquire |
| inscribirse *(pron. v.)* | to register oneself |
| insecto *(n., m.)* | insect |
| inseparable *(adj., m./f.)* | inseparable |
| insignificante *(adj., m./f.)* | insignificant |
| insinuar *(v.)* | to insinuate |
| insistido *(part.)* | insisted |
| insistir *(v.)* | to insist |
| insomnio *(n., m.)* | insomnia |
| inspirar *(v.)* | to inspire |
| instalación *(n., f.)* | installation |
| instante *(n., m.)* | instant |
| instituto *(n., m.)* | institute |
| instrumento *(n., m.)* | instrument |
| inteligente *(adj., m./f.)* | intelligent |
| inteligentísimo *(sup. adj.)* | very intelligent |
| intentar *(v.)* | to try; to attempt |
| interés *(n., m.)* | interest |

interesante *(adj., m./f.)* — interesting
interesar *(v.)* — to interest
internado *(adj.)* — inmate; boarder
interrupción *(n., f.)* — interruption
intervenir *(v.)* — to intervene
intrépido *(adj.)* — intrepid
intriga *(adj.)* — intrigue
introducir *(v.)* — to introduce
inundado *(part.)* — flooded
inundarse *(pron. v.)* — to flood
inútil *(adj., m./f.)* — useless
inventado *(adj.)* — invented
inversionista *(n., inv.)* — investor
invertir *(v.)* — to invest
investigación *(n., f.)* — investigation; research
invierno *(n., m.)* — winter
invitación *(adj.)* — invitation
invitado *(n., m.)* — guest
invitar *(v.)* — to invite
ir *(v.)* — to go
irlandés *(adj.)* — Irish
irse *(pron. v.)* — to be gone
isla *(n., f.)* — island
italiano *(adj.)* — Italian
izquierda *(n., f.)* — left

## J

jabalí *(n., m.)* — boar
jabón *(n., m.)* — soap
jamás *(adv.)* — never
japonés *(adj.)* — Japanese
jardín *(n., m.)* — garden
jardinería *(n., f.)* — gardening
jarrón *(n., m.)* — vase
jaula *(n., f.)* — cage
jefe *(n., m.)* — chief
jirafa *(n., f.)* — giraffe
jornada *(n., f.)* — day
joven *(adj., m./f.)* — young
joven *(n., m.)* — young one
joya *(n., f.)* — jewel
juego *(n., m.)* — game
jueves *(n., m.)* — Thursday
juez *(n., m.)* — judge
jugador *(n., m.)* — player
jugando *(g.)* — playing
jugar *(v.)* — to play
jugarse la vida *(pron. v.)* — to risk one's life
jugo *(n., m.)* — juice
juguete *(n., m.)* — toy
juguetón *(adj.)* — playful
juicio *(n., m.)* — judgment
julio *(n., m.)* — July
junio *(n., m.)* — June
junto *(adv.)* — close to

junto *(adj.)* — together
jurado *(n., m.)* — jury
justicia *(n., f.)* — justice
justo *(adj.)* — just

## K

kilo *(n., m.)* — kilogram
kilómetro *(n., m.)* — kilometer

## L

la *(def. art., f. sing.)* — the
labor *(n., f.)* — labor
lado *(n., m.)* — side
ladrar *(v.)* — to bark
ladrón *(n., m.)* — thief
lago *(n., m.)* — lake
laguna *(n., f.)* — pond
lamentable *(adj., m./f.)* — lamentable
lámpara *(n., f.)* — lamp
lana *(n., f.)* — wool
langosta *(n., f.)* — lobster
lanzar *(v.)* — to throw
lápiz *(n., m.)* — pencil
largo *(adj.)* — long
larguísimo *(sup. adj.)* — very long
las *(def. art., f., pl.)* — the
lástima *(n., f.)* — pity
lastimar *(v.)* — to injure
lata *(n., f.)* — tin can
latín *(n., m.)* — Latin
latinoamericano *(adj.)* — Latin American
lavabo *(n., m.)* — washroom
lavadora *(n., f.)* — washing machine
lavaplatos *(n., m.)* — dishwasher
lavar *(v.)* — to wash
lavarse *(pron. v.)* — to wash oneself
le *(obj. pron.)* — it
leal *(adj., m./f.)* — loyal
lealtad *(n., f.)* — loyalty
lección *(n., f.)* — lesson
leche *(n., f.)* — milk
leer *(v.)* — to read
lejos *(adv.)* — distant; far away
lengua *(n., f.)* — tongue
lengua *(n., f.)* — language
lentamente *(adv.)* — slowly
lento *(adj.)* — slow
león *(n., m.)* — lion
les *(obj. pron.)* — them
letrero *(n., m.)* — sign
levantar *(v.)* — to wake; to lift; to raise
levantarse *(pron. v.)* — to wake up
ley *(n., f.)* — law

| | |
|---|---|
| leyendo *(g.)* | reading |
| libanés *(adj.)* | Lebanese |
| liberación *(n., f.)* | liberation |
| liberar *(v.)* | to free |
| libertad *(n., f.)* | liberty |
| libertador *(adj.)* | liberator |
| libra *(n., f.)* | pound |
| libre *(adj., m./f.)* | free |
| librería *(n., f.)* | bookstore |
| libreta *(n., f.)* | notebook |
| libro *(n., m.)* | book |
| licuar *(v.)* | to blend |
| liebre *(n., f.)* | hare |
| limpiar *(v.)* | to clean |
| limpio *(adj.)* | clean |
| lindísimo *(sup. adj.)* | very pretty |
| lindo *(adj.)* | pretty |
| linterna *(n., f.)* | flashlight; lantern |
| lista *(n., f.)* | list |
| listo *(adj.)* | ready |
| literatura *(n., f.)* | literature |
| llamado *(part.)* | called |
| llamar *(v.)* | to call |
| llamarse *(pron. v.)* | to be called |
| llanto *(n., m.)* | wail; cry |
| llave *(n., f.)* | key |
| llegado *(part., adj.)* | arrived |
| llegar *(v.)* | to arrive |
| llenarse *(pron. v.)* | to be filled |
| lleno *(adj.)* | full |
| llevar *(v.)* | to carry |
| llorando *(g.)* | crying |
| llorar *(v.)* | to cry |
| llover *(v.)* | to rain |
| lluvia *(n., f.)* | rain |
| lo *(obj. pron.)* | it |
| lobo *(n., m.)* | wolf |
| local *(adj., m./f.)* | local |
| localizado *(adj.)* | located |
| localizar *(v.)* | to locate |
| loco *(adj.)* | crazy |
| lodo *(n., m.)* | mud |
| lograr *(v.)* | to achieve |
| loquísimo *(sup. adj.)* | very crazy |
| los *(ind. art., m., pl.)* | the |
| lotería *(n., f.)* | lottery |
| loza *(n., f.)* | dishware; china |
| luchar *(v.)* | to fight |
| lucir *(v.)* | to display; to wear; to shine |
| luego *(adv.)* | then |
| lugar *(n., m.)* | place |
| luminoso *(adj.)* | luminous |
| luna *(n., f.)* | moon |
| lunes *(n., m.)* | Monday |
| luz *(n., f.)* | light |

# M

| | |
|---|---|
| machete *(n., m.)* | machete |
| madera *(n., f.)* | wood |
| madre *(n., f.)* | mother |
| madriguera *(n., f.)* | burrow |
| madrugada *(n., f.)* | early morning |
| madurez *(n., f.)* | maturity |
| maduro *(adj.)* | mature |
| maestro *(n., m.)* | master; teacher |
| mafia *(n., f.)* | mafia |
| maíz *(n., m.)* | corn |
| mal *(n., m.)* | evil |
| maleta *(n., f.)* | suitcase |
| malo *(adj.)* | bad |
| maltratado *(part.)* | mistreated |
| mamá *(n., f.)* | mom |
| mamífero *(n., m.)* | mammal |
| mamut *(n., m.)* | mammoth |
| mañana *(adv.)* | morning |
| mañana *(n., f.)* | tomorrow |
| manantial *(n., m.)* | spring |
| mandar *(v.)* | to send |
| manejar *(v.)* | to drive |
| manera *(n., f.)* | way; manner |
| manifestación *(n., f.)* | demonstration |
| manifestante *(n., m.)* | demonstrator |
| maniquí *(n., m./f.)* | mannequin; model |
| mano *(n., f.)* | hand |
| mansión *(n., f.)* | mansion |
| mantener *(v.)* | to maintain |
| manzana *(n., f.)* | apple |
| mapa *(n., m.)* | map |
| máquina *(n., f.)* | machine |
| mar *(n., m.)* | sea |
| maratón *(n., f.)* | marathon |
| maravilla *(n., f.)* | marvel; wonder |
| maravillar *(v.)* | to amaze |
| maravilloso *(adj.)* | marvelous |
| marca *(n., f.)* | label; brand |
| marcha *(n., f.)* | march |
| marchar *(v.)* | to walk; to go; to march |
| marco *(n., m.)* | frame; framework |
| marido *(n., m.)* | husband |
| marinero *(n., m.)* | sailor |
| marisco *(n., m.)* | shellfish |
| marrano *(n., m.)* | pig |
| marrón *(adj., m./f.)* | brown |
| marroquí *(adj., m./f.)* | Moroccan |
| Marte *(pers. n., m.)* | Mars |
| martes *(n., m.)* | Tuesday |
| marzo *(n., m.)* | March |
| más *(adv.)* | more |
| mas *(prep.)* | but |
| mascota *(n., f.)* | mascot; pet |
| matar *(v.)* | to kill |
| mata *(n., f.)* | plant |
| matemáticas *(n., f.)* | mathematics |

| | |
|---|---|
| matemático *(n., m.)* | mathematician |
| matrícula *(n., f.)* | registration |
| matrimonio *(n., m.)* | marriage |
| mayo *(n., m.)* | May |
| mayor *(adj., m./f.)* | greater |
| mayoría *(n., f.)* | majority |
| me *(obj. pron.)* | me |
| medalla *(n., f.)* | medal |
| media *(n., f.)* | sock |
| medicamento *(n., m.)* | medication |
| medicina *(n., f.)* | medicine |
| médico *(n., m.)* | physician |
| medio *(adj.)* | half |
| medio ambiente *(n., m.)* | environment |
| medioevo *(n., m.)* | Middle Ages |
| medios *(n., m.)* | means |
| medir *(v.)* | to measure |
| mejor *(adj., m./f.)* | better |
| mejorado *(part.)* | improved |
| memorándum *(n., m.)* | memorandum |
| memoria *(n., f.)* | memory |
| memorizar *(v.)* | to memorize |
| mencionar *(v.)* | to mention |
| menor *(adj., m./f.)* | smaller |
| menos *(adv.)* | less |
| mensaje *(n., m.)* | message |
| mensual *(adj., m./f.)* | monthly |
| mentir *(v.)* | to lie |
| menú *(n., m.)* | menu |
| menudo | See *a menudo* |
| mercader *(n., m./f.)* | merchant |
| mercado *(n., m.)* | market |
| mercancía *(n., f.)* | merchandise |
| mero *(n., m.)* | grouper |
| mes *(n., m.)* | month |
| mesa *(n., f.)* | table |
| mesero *(n., m.)* | waiter |
| mesita *(n., f.)* | little table |
| meta *(n., f.)* | goal |
| metal *(n., m.)* | metal |
| metálico *(adj.)* | metallic |
| meteorito *(n., m.)* | meteorite |
| meteoro *(n., m.)* | meteor |
| meter *(v.)* | to insert |
| metro *(n., m.)* | meter |
| mezclar *(v.)* | to mix |
| mezquita *(n., f.)* | mosque |
| mi *(poss. adj., sing.)* | my |
| mí *(poss. pron.)* | me |
| mía *(poss. pron. & adj., f., sing.)* | mine |
| mías *(poss. pron. & adj., f., pl.)* | mine |
| microbús *(n., m.)* | bus |
| microondas | microwave |
| See also *horno microondas* | |
| miedo *(n., m.)* | fear |
| miel *(n., f.)* | honey |
| mientras *(adv.)* | while |

| | |
|---|---|
| milagro *(n., m.)* | miracle |
| mina *(n., f.)* | mine |
| mineral *(n., m.)* | mineral |
| ministro *(n., m.)* | minister |
| minuciosamente *(adv.)* | meticulously |
| minuto *(n., m.)* | minute |
| mío *(poss. pron. & adj., m., sing.)* | mine |
| míos *(poss. pron. & adj., m., pl.)* | mine |
| mirada *(n., f.)* | look |
| mirando *(g.)* | looking |
| mirar *(v.)* | to look |
| mirarse *(pron. v.)* | to look at oneself |
| mis *(poss. adj., pl.)* | my |
| misa *(n., f.)* | mass |
| miserable *(adj., m./f.)* | miserable |
| misión *(n., f.)* | mission |
| misionero *(n., m.)* | missionary |
| mismo *(adj.)* | same |
| mobiliario *(n., m.)* | furniture |
| mochila *(n., f.)* | backpack |
| moda *(n., f.)* | fashion |
| modelo *(n., m.)* | model |
| moderno *(adj.)* | modern |
| modista *(n., f.)* | seamstress |
| modo | See *de modo que* |
| mojarse *(pron. v.)* | to get wet |
| molecular *(adj.)* | molecular |
| molestar *(v.)* | to bother |
| momento *(n., m.)* | moment |
| moneda *(n., f.)* | currency; coin |
| monitor *(n., m.)* | monitor |
| monja *(n., f.)* | nun |
| monopolio *(n., m.)* | monopoly |
| monstruo *(n., m.)* | monster |
| monstruosamente *(adv.)* | monstrously |
| montaña *(n., f.)* | mountain |
| monumento *(n., m.)* | monument |
| morder *(v.)* | to bite |
| mordido *(part.)* | bitten |
| morir *(v.)* | to die |
| moro *(n., m.)* | Moor |
| mostrar *(v.)* | to show |
| moto *(n., f.)* | motorcycle |
| motocicleta *(n., f.)* | motorcycle |
| motor *(n., m.)* | motor |
| mover *(v.)* | to move |
| moverse *(pron. v.)* | to be moved |
| muchacha *(n., f.)* | teenage girl |
| muchacho *(n., m.)* | teenage boy |
| mucho *(adj.)* | many |
| mudarse *(v.)* | to move |
| mudo *(adj.)* | mute |
| See also *quedarse mudo* | |
| muerte *(n., f.)* | death |
| muerto *(adj.)* | dead |
| muerto *(part.)* | dead |

| | |
|---|---|
| muestra (n., f.) | sample |
| mujer (n., f.) | woman |
| multitud (n., f.) | multitude |
| mundial (adj.) | world |
| mundo (n., m.) | world |
| muñeca (n., f.) | doll |
| muriendo (g.) | dying |
| muro (n., m.) | wall |
| museo (n., m.) | museum |
| música (n., f.) | music |
| músico (n., m.) | musician |
| musulmán (adj.) | Muslim |
| muy (adv.) | very |

# N

| | |
|---|---|
| nacer (v.) | to be born |
| nacido (adj.) | born |
| nacimiento (n., m.) | birth |
| nación (n., f.) | nation |
| nacional (adj.) | national |
| nada (loc. adv.) como si ~ | like nothing |
| nada (loc. adv.) para ~ | for nothing |
| nada (pron. indef.) | nothing |
| nadar (v.) | to swim |
| nadie (pron. indef.) | nobody |
| naranja (n., f.) | orange |
| naranjo (n., m.) | orange tree |
| narcótico (n., m.) | narcotic |
| nariz (n., f.) | nose |
| natural (adj., m./f.) | natural |
| naufragio (n., m.) | shipwreck |
| náusea (n., f.) | nausea |
| navegar (v.) | to navigate; to sail |
| Navidad (n., f.) | Christmas |
| necesario (adj.) | necessary |
| necesitado (part.) | needed |
| necesitar (v.) | to need |
| necio (adj.) | irritating; bothersome |
| negocio (n., m.) | business |
| negro (adj.) | black |
| nervioso (adj.) | nervous |
| nevada (n., f.) | snowstorm |
| nevar (v.) | to snow |
| nevera (n., f.) | refrigerator |
| ni (conj.) | neither |
| niebla (n., f.) | fog |
| nieto (n., m.) | grandchild |
| nieve (n., f.) | snow |
| niña (n., f.) | girl |
| niñez (n., f.) | childhood |
| ningún (indef. adj.) | no |
| ninguna (indef. adj. & pron., f.) | none |
| ninguno (indef. adj. & pron., m.) | none |
| niñito (n., m.) | little boy |
| niño (n., m.) | boy |

| | |
|---|---|
| nivel (n., m.) | level |
| noble (adj., m./f.) | noble; stoic; humane |
| noche (n., f.) | night |
| nombre (n., m.) | name |
| norma (n., f.) | norm |
| normal (adj., m./f.) | normal |
| normalmente (adv.) | normally |
| norte (n., m.) | north |
| nos (pers. pron.) | us |
| nosotras (pers. pron., f.) | we |
| nosotros (pers. pron., m.) | we |
| nostalgia (n., f.) | nostalgia |
| nota (n., f.) | note |
| notar (v.) | to note |
| noticia (n., f.) | news |
| novela (n., f.) | fiction |
| novelista (n., n./f.) | novelist |
| novia (n., f.) | girlfriend; bride |
| novio (n., m.) | boyfriend; groom |
| novios (n., m.) | bride and groom |
| nube (n., f.) | cloud |
| nublado (adj.) | cloudy |
| nuera (n., f.) | daughter-in-law |
| nuestra (poss. pron. & adj., f., sing.) | ours |
| nuestras (poss. pron. & adj., f., pl.) | ours |
| nuestro (poss. pron. & adj., m., sing.) | ours |
| nuestros (poss. pron. & adj., m., pl.) | ours |
| nuevo (adj.) | new |
| nuez (n., f.) | nut |
| número (n., m.) | number |
| nunca (adv.) | never |

# O

| | |
|---|---|
| ¡Oh! (interj.) | Oh! |
| obedecer (v.) | to obey |
| objeto (n., m.) | object |
| obra (n., f.) | work |
| obrero (n., m.) | worker |
| observar (v.) | to observe |
| obsoleto (adj.) | obsolete |
| obstruir (v.) | to obstruct; to block |
| obtener (v.) | to obtain |
| obvio (adj.) | obvious |
| occidental (adj., inv.) | western |
| ocupado (adj.) | occupied |
| ocupar (v.) | to occupy |
| ocurrido (part.) | occurred |
| ocurrir (v.) | to occur |
| odioso (adj.) | odious; hateful |
| odontólogo (n., m.) | dentist |
| ofender (v.) | to offend |
| oficial (n., m./f.) | officer |
| oficial (adj., m./f.) | official |

| | | | |
|---|---|---|---|
| oficina *(n., f.)* | office | panadero *(n., m.)* | baker |
| oído *(part.)* | heard | panameño *(adj.)* | Panamanian |
| oír *(v.)* | to hear | panecillo *(n., m.)* | bun |
| Ojalá *(interj.)* | I hope that… | pantalón *(n., m.)* | pant |
| ojo *(n., m.)* | eye | pantanoso *(adj.)* | marshy |
| ola *(n., f.)* | wave | pañuelo *(n., m.)* | handkerchief |
| oler *(v.)* | to smell | papa *(n., f.)* | potato |
| olla *(n., f.)* | pot | Papa *(n., m.)* | Pope |
| olvidadizo *(adj.)* | forgetful | papá *(n., m.)* | dad |
| olvidado *(adj.)* | forgotten | papel *(n., m.)* | paper |
| olvidado *(part.)* | forgotten | paquete *(n., m.)* | package |
| olvidar *(v.)* | to forget | par *(n., m.)* | pair |
| onda *(n., f.)* | wave | para *(prep.)* | for |
| operación *(n., f.)* | operation | paraguas *(n., m.)* | umbrella |
| opinar *(v.)* | to have an opinion; to think; to believe | parar *(v.)* | to stop |
| | | parcela *(n., f.)* | parcel of land |
| oponer *(v.)* | to oppose | parecer *(v.)* | to seem |
| oportunidad *(n., f.)* | opportunity | pared *(n., f.)* | wall |
| oprimir *(v.)* | to oppress | parque *(n., m.)* | park |
| oración *(n., f.)* | prayer | parqueadero *(n., m.)* | parking lot |
| orden *(n., f.)* | order | párroco *(n., m.)* | clergyman |
| organizar *(v.)* | to organize | parte *(n., f.)* | part |
| orgullo *(n., m.)* | pride | participar *(v.)* | to participate |
| orgulloso *(adj.)* | proud | partida *(n., f.)* | start (race) |
| original *(adj., m./f.)* | original | partido *(n., m.)* | party (political) |
| ornitólogo *(n., m.)* | ornithologist | partido *(part.)* | left |
| oro *(n., m.)* | gold | partir *(v.)* | to leave |
| orquesta *(n., f.)* | orchestra | pasado *(adj.)* | past |
| os *(pers. pron.)* | you | pasado *(part.)* | passed |
| oscurecer *(v.)* | to get dark | pasaje *(n., m.)* | ticket |
| oscuro *(adj.)* | dark | pasando *(g.)* | passing |
| osito *(n., m.)* | teddy bear | pasaporte *(n., m.)* | passport |
| oso *(n., m.)* | bear | pasar *(v.)* | to pass |
| otoño *(n., m.)* | autumn | paseando *(g.)* | wandering |
| otro *(adj.)* | another | pasear *(v.)* | to promenade |
| ovación *(n., f.)* | ovation | paseo *(n., m.)* | walkway; promenade |
| oveja | sheep | pasillo *(n., m.)* | hall; walkway |
| oxígeno *(n., m.)* | oxygen | pasión *(n., f.)* | passion |
| | | paso *(n., m.)* | step |
| | | pastel *(n., m.)* | pie |
| | | pastelero *(n., m.)* | pastry cook |
| **P** | | pastor *(n., m.)* | shepherd |
| | | pata *(n., f.)* | leg (animal or furniture) |
| paciencia *(n., f.)* | patience | patata *(n., f.)* | potato |
| paciente *(n., m.)* | patient | patinar *(v.)* | to skate |
| pacífico *(adj.)* | peaceful | patio *(n., m.)* | patio |
| padre *(n., m.)* | father | patrón *(n., m.)* | boss |
| paella *(n., f.)* | traditional Spanish rice dish | pavo *(n., m.)* | turkey |
| | | paz *(n., f.)* | peace |
| pagar *(v.)* | to pay | peatón *(n., m.)* | pedestrian |
| página *(n., f.)* | page | pedido *(part.)* | asked |
| país *(n., m.)* | country | pedir *(v.)* | to ask |
| pájaro *(n., m.)* | bird | peinado *(part.)* | combed |
| palabra *(n., f.)* | word | peinarse *(pron. v.)* | to comb |
| pálido *(adj.)* | pale | pelear *(v.)* | to fight |
| palo *(n., m.)* | stick | película *(n., f.)* | movie |
| paloma *(n., f.)* | dove | peligro *(n., m.)* | danger |
| pan *(n., m.)* | bread | peligroso *(adj.)* | dangerous |
| panadería *(n., f.)* | bakery | | |

| | |
|---|---|
| pelo (n., m.) | hair |
| pelota (n., f.) | ball |
| pena (n., f.) | grief |
| pensado (part.) | thought |
| pensando (g.) | thinking |
| pensar (v.) | to think |
| pensionarse (pron. v.) | to be retired |
| peor (adj. inv.) | worse |
| pequeño (adj.) | small |
| perder (v.) | to lose |
| perderse (v.) | to get lost |
| pérdida (n., f.) | loss |
| perdido (adj.) | lost |
| perdido (part.) | lost |
| perdiendo (g.) | losing |
| perdonar (v.) | to forgive |
| perezoso (adj.) | lazy |
| perfecto (adj.) | perfect |
| perfume (n., m.) | perfume |
| perico (n., m.) | parrot |
| periódico (n., m.) | newspaper |
| perla (n., f.) | pearl |
| permitido (part.) | allowed |
| permitir (v.) | to permit; to allow |
| pero (conj.) | but |
| perpetuar (v.) | to perpetuate |
| perro (n., m.) | dog |
| perseguir (v.) | to pursue |
| persona (n., f.) | person |
| personalmente (adv.) | personally |
| pertinaz (adj., m./f.) | obstinate |
| pesadilla (n., f.) | nightmare |
| pesado (adj.) | heavy |
| pesar (v.) See a pesar que | to weigh |
| pescado (n., m.) | fish |
| pescar (v.) | to fish |
| peseta (n., f.) | old Spanish currency |
| peso (n., m.) | currency in some Latin American countries |
| peso (n., m.) | weight |
| petróleo (n., m.) | petroleum; oil |
| pez (n., m.) | fish |
| pianista (n., m./f.) | pianist |
| piano (n., m.) | piano |
| pie (n., m.) | foot |
| piedad (n., f.) | pity |
| piedra (n., f.) | stone |
| piedrita (n., f.) | pebble |
| piel (n., f.) | skin |
| pierna (n., f.) | leg |
| piloto (n., m./f.) | pilot |
| pino (n., m.) | pine |
| pintado (adj.) | painted |
| pintar (v.) | to paint |
| pintor (n., m.) | painter |
| pintura (n., f.) | painting; paint |
| pisar (v.) | to step |
| piscina (n., f.) | pool |
| piso (n., m.) | apartment; floor |
| pista (n., f.) | clue |
| pistacho (n., m.) | pistachio |
| pizza (n., f.) | pizza |
| plan (n., m.) | plan |
| planear (v.) | to plan |
| planeta (n., m.) | planet |
| planta (n., f.) | plant; factory |
| plantar (v.) | to plant |
| plástico (n., m.) | plastic |
| plata (n., f.) | silver |
| plátano (n., m.) | plantain |
| platino (n., m.) | platinum |
| plato (n., m.) | dish |
| playa (n., f.) | beach |
| plaza (n., f.) | plaza |
| plazo (n., m.) | time limit |
| plomero (n., m.) | plumber |
| pluma (n., f.) | feather |
| población (n., f.) | population |
| poblar (v.) | to populate |
| pobre (adj., m./f.) | poor |
| poco (adj.) | little |
| podadora (n., f.) | lawn mower |
| poder (v.) | to be able |
| podido (part.) | been able |
| podrido (part.) | rotten |
| podrirse (v.) | to rot |
| poema (n., m.) | poem |
| poesía (n., f.) | poetry |
| poeta (n., m./f.) | poet |
| policía (n., f.) | police |
| policía (n., m./f.) | police officer |
| política (n., f.) | politics |
| político (n., m.) | politician |
| pollo (n., m.) | chicken |
| Polo Norte (n., m.) | North Pole |
| poner (v.) | to put; to place |
| ponerse (v.) | to place oneself |
| poniendo (g.) | placing; putting |
| popular (adj., m./f.) | popular |
| popularización (n., f.) | popularization |
| por (prep.) | by |
| por qué (adv. loc.) | why |
| porque (conj.) | because |
| porqué (n., m.) | reason |
| portarse (pron. v.) | to behave oneself |
| portátil (adj., m./f.) | portable |
| portería (n., f.) | entrance |
| portero (n., m.) | doorman |
| portugués (adj.) | Portuguese |
| portugués (n., m.) | Portuguese language |
| poseer (v.) | to possess |
| posesionarse (v.) | to take possession |
| posibilidad (n., f.) | possibility |
| posible (adj., m./f.) | possible |
| postal (n., f.) | postcard |
| poste (n., m.) | post |

| | |
|---|---|
| postre *(n., m.)* | dessert |
| practicar *(v.)* | to practice |
| prado *(n., m.)* | meadow; field |
| precio *(n., m.)* | price |
| precioso *(adj.)* | precious |
| precipitarse *(pron. v.)* | to make a false start |
| preciso *(adj.)* | exact |
| preferido *(adj.)* | preferred |
| preferir *(v.)* | to prefer |
| pregunta *(n., f.)* | question |
| preguntar *(v.)* | to ask |
| premiar *(v.)* | to reward |
| premio *(n., m.)* | prize |
| prender *(v.)* | to light |
| preocupado *(adj.)* | worried |
| preocupar *(v.)* | to worry |
| preocuparse *(pron. v.)* | to be worried |
| preparar *(v.)* | to prepare |
| presentación *(n., f.)* | presentation |
| presentar *(v.)* | to present |
| presidencial *(adj., inv.)* | presidential |
| presidente *(n., m.)* | president |
| preso *(n., m.)* | prisoner |
| prestado *(adj.)* | loaned; lent |
| prestar *(v.)* | to lend |
| prestigio *(n., m.)* | prestige |
| presuponer *(v.)* | to presuppose; to assume |
| pretérito *(n., m.)* | past |
| prevaler *(v.)* | to prevail |
| prevenir *(v.)* | to prevent |
| prima *(n., f.)* | cousin |
| primavera *(n., f.)* | spring |
| primero *(adj.)* | first |
| primo *(n., m.)* | cousin |
| princesa *(n., f.)* | princess |
| principal *(adj., m./f.)* | main |
| principio *(n., m.)* | beginning; principle |
| prisa *(adv.)* | hurry |
| prisión *(n., f.)* | prison |
| privado *(adj.)* | private |
| probablemente *(adv.)* | probably |
| probado *(part.)* | tried; tested |
| probar *(v.)* | to try; to test |
| problema *(n., m.)* | problem |
| procesador *(n., m.)* | processor |
| procesión *(n., f.)* | procession |
| producir *(v.)* | to produce |
| producirse *(v.)* | to be produced |
| producto *(n., m.)* | product |
| profesión *(n., f.)* | profession |
| profesor *(n., m.)* | professor; teacher |
| profundamente *(adv.)* | profoundly; deeply |
| profundidad *(n., f.)* | depth |
| programa *(n., m.)* | program |
| prohibido *(adj.)* | prohibited |
| prohibir *(v.)* | to prohibit |
| prolongar *(v.)* | to prolong |
| promesa *(n., f.)* | promise; pledge |
| prometedor *(adj.)* | promising |
| prometer *(v.)* | to promise |
| prometido *(adj.)* | promised |
| promocionar *(v.)* | to promote |
| pronosticar *(v.)* | to prognosticate; to foretell |
| pronto *(adv.)* | fast; rapidly |
| propiedad *(n., f.)* | property |
| propina *(n., f.)* | tip |
| propio *(adj.)* | one's own |
| proponer *(v.)* | to propose |
| propuesta *(n., f.)* | proposal |
| proseguir *(v.)* | to continue |
| protector *(n., m.)* | protector |
| proteger *(v.)* | to protect |
| protestar *(v.)* | to protest |
| protocolo *(n., m.)* | protocol |
| proveer *(v.)* | to provide |
| próximo *(adj.)* | next; near |
| proyecto *(n., m.)* | project |
| prudencia *(n., f.)* | prudence; caution |
| prueba *(n., f.)* | test |
| psicólogo *(n., m.)* | psychologist |
| psiquiatra *(n., m./f.)* | psychiatrist |
| publicación *(n., f.)* | publication |
| publicado *(part.)* | published |
| publicar *(v.)* | to publish |
| publicidad *(n., f.)* | publicity; advertising |
| público *(n., m.)* | public |
| pueblo *(n., m.)* | town |
| puente *(n., m.)* | bridge |
| puerta *(n., f.)* | door |
| puerto *(n., m.)* | harbor |
| pues *(conj.)* | therefore |
| puesto que *(loc. conj.)* | since |
| punta *(n., f.)* | point; tip |
| punto *(n., m.)* | point |
| puntual *(adj., m./f.)* | punctual |
| pura | See *de pura* |
| puro *(adj.)* | pure |

# Q

| | |
|---|---|
| que *(indef. pron.)* | that |
| qué *(interr. pron.)* | what |
| quedar *(v.)* | to remain |
| quedarse *(pron. v.)* | to stay |
| quedarse mudo *(idiom.)* | to be left speechless |
| quejarse *(v.)* | to complain |
| quemarse *(pron. v.)* | to burn oneself |
| querer *(v.)* | to want |
| querido *(part.)* | wanted |
| queriendo *(g.)* | wanting |
| queso *(n., m.)* | cheese |
| quien *(indef. pron., sing.)* | who |
| quién *(interr. pron., sing.)* | who |

| | |
|---|---|
| quienes *(indef. pron., pl.)* | who |
| quiénes *(interr. pron., pl.)* | who |
| quieto *(adj., m.)* | quiet |
| química *(n., f.)* | chemistry |
| quizá(s) *(adv.)* | perhaps |

# R

| | |
|---|---|
| rabia *(n., f.)* | rage; anger |
| radicar *(v.)* | to be rooted |
| radio *(n., f.)* | radio station |
| radio *(n., m.)* | radio set |
| raíz *(n., f.)* | root |
| rama *(n., f.)* | branch |
| rana *(n., f.)* | frog |
| rápidamente *(adv.)* | quickly |
| rapidez *(n., f.)* | rapidity |
| rápido *(adj.)* | quick |
| ratito *(n., m.)* | in a short while |
| rato *(n., m.)* | while |
| ratón *(n., m.)* | mouse |
| ratoncito *(n., m.)* | little mouse |
| raza *(n., f.)* | breed; race |
| razón *(n., f.)* | reason |
| razonable *(adj., m./f.)* | reasonable |
| razonar *(v.)* | to reason |
| reaccionar *(v.)* | to react |
| real *(adj., m./f.)* | real |
| realidad *(n., f.)* | reality |
| realizar *(v.)* | to carry out, to do |
| realmente *(adv.)* | really |
| reanudado *(part.)* | resumed |
| rebelde *(n., inv.)* | rebel; dissenter |
| recaer sobre *(v.)* | to fall on |
| receta *(n., f.)* | prescription; recipe |
| recibir *(v.)* | to receive |
| recién *(adv.)* | recent |
| recientemente *(adv.)* | recently |
| recipiente *(n., m.)* | recipient; container |
| recluir *(v.)* | to imprison |
| recoger *(v.)* | to collect |
| recogiendo *(g.)* | collecting |
| recomendable *(adj., m./f.)* | recommendable; advisable |
| recomendar *(v.)* | to recommend |
| reconciliado *(part.)* | reconciled |
| reconciliar *(v.)* | to reconcile |
| reconfortante *(adj., m./f.)* | comforting |
| reconocer *(v.)* | to recognize |
| reconstruir *(v.)* | to reconstruct |
| recordar *(v.)* | to remember |
| recorrer *(v.)* | to travel around |
| recorrido *(n., m.)* | distance traveled; run |
| recostado *(adj.)* estar ~ | to be lying down |
| rector *(n., m.)* | principal (school) |
| recuperar *(v.)* | to recuperate; to recover |
| redactando *(g.)* | editing; writing |

| | |
|---|---|
| redactor *(n., m.)* | editor; journalist; writer |
| reducir *(v.)* | to reduce |
| reemplazar *(v.)* | to replace |
| reflector *(n., m.)* | reflector |
| reflexionar *(v.)* | to reflect; to think |
| refregar *(v.)* | to scrub |
| refrescante *(adj., m./f.)* | refreshing |
| refrigerador *(n., m.)* | refrigerator |
| refugiarse *(v.)* | to find refuge |
| regalar *(v.)* | to give; to present |
| regalo *(n., m.)* | gift |
| regar *(v.)* | to water |
| región *(n., f.)* | region |
| regresar *(v.)* | to return |
| regularidad *(n., f.)* | regularity |
| regularmente *(adv.)* | regularly |
| rehacer *(v.)* | to redo |
| reina *(n., f.)* | queen |
| reír *(v.)* | to laugh |
| relatividad *(n., f.)* | relativity |
| reloj *(n., m.)* | clock; watch |
| remedio *(n., m.)* | remedy |
| remolacha *(n., f.)* | beet |
| renunciar *(v.)* | to resign |
| reo *(n., m.)* | prisoner; inmate |
| reparar *(v.)* | to repair |
| reparto *(n., m.)* | cast |
| repasar *(v.)* | to review |
| repelente de insectos *(n., m.)* | insect repellent |
| repente | See *de repente* |
| repetir *(v.)* | to repeat |
| reportaje *(n., m.)* | report |
| reposo *(n., m.)* | repose; tranquillity |
| reprender *(v.)* | to scold |
| reputación *(n., f.)* | reputation |
| requisito *(n., m.)* | requirement |
| resbalarse *(pron. v.)* | to slip |
| rescatar *(v.)* | to rescue |
| reserva *(n., f.)* | reservation |
| resolver *(v.)* | to solve |
| respetar *(v.)* | to observe; to respect |
| resplandor *(n., m.)* | brightness |
| responder *(v.)* | to respond |
| respondido *(part.)* | responded |
| responsabilidad *(n., f.)* | responsibility |
| responsable *(adj., m./f.)* | responsible |
| respuesta *(n., f.)* | answer |
| restaurante *(n., m.)* | restaurant |
| resto *(n., m.)* | remainder |
| restringir *(v.)* | to restrict |
| resumir *(v.)* | to summarize |
| retener *(v.)* | to retain |
| retirado *(part.)* | withdrawn |
| retirando *(g.)* | withdrawing |
| retirar *(v.)* | to retire; to withdraw |
| retirarse *(pron. v.)* | to leave; to go away |
| retorcer *(v.)* | to twist |
| retornar *(v.)* | to return |

retraerse *(pron. v.)* — to isolate oneself
retroceder *(v.)* — to back up; to go back
retrovisor *(n., m.)* — rearview mirror
reumatismo *(n., m.)* — rheumatism
reunido *(part.)* — met
reuniendo *(g.)* — gathering
reunión *(n., f.)* — meeting
reunir *(v.)* — to gather
reunirse *(v.)* — to meet
revelador *(n., m.)* — developer
revisar *(v.)* — to revise
revista *(n., f.)* — magazine
revolución *(n., f.)* — revolution
revólver *(n., m.)* — revolver
revolver *(v.)* — to stir
revuelto *(adj.)* — scrambled; mixed-up
rey *(n., m.)* — king
rezar *(v.)* — to pray
riachuelo *(n., m.)* — brook; stream
rico *(adj.)* — wealthy; rich
riesgo *(n., m.)* — risk
rifa *(n., f.)* — lottery
río *(n., m.)* — river
riquísimo *(sup. adj.)* — extremely wealthy; very rich
risa *(n., f.)* — laughter
rival *(n., m.)* — rival
robar *(v.)* — to rob; to steal
rodaja *(n., f.)* — slice
rodeado *(adj.)* — surrounded
roer *(v.)* — to gnaw
rogar *(v.)* — to beg; to pray
rojo *(adj.)* — red
romano *(adj.)* — Roman
romántico *(adj.)* — romantic
romper *(v.)* — to break
romperse *(v.)* — to be broken
rompiendo *(g.)* — breaking
ropa *(n., f.)* — clothes
rostro *(n., m.)* — face
roto *(adj.)* — broken
rubio *(adj.)* — blond
rueda *(n., f.)* — wheel
ruido *(n., m.)* — noise
ruidoso *(adj.)* — noisy
rumbo *(n., m.)* — course
rumor *(n., m.)* — rumor
ruta *(n., f.)* — route

# S

sábado *(n., m.)* — Saturday
saber *(v.)* — to know
sabido *(part.)* — known
sabiduría *(n., f.)* — wisdom
sacar *(v.)* — to remove
sacerdote *(n., m.)* — priest

sacrificio *(n., m.)* — sacrifice
sagrado *(adj.)* — sacred
sal *(n., f.)* — salt
sala *(n., f.)* — living room
salario *(n., m.)* — salary
salida *(n., f.)* — exit
salido *(part.)* — left
salir *(v.)* — to leave
salón *(n., m.)* — classroom
salsa *(n., f.)* — sauce
saltamontes *(n., m.)* — grasshopper
salud *(n., f.)* — health
saludado *(part.)* — greeted
saludar *(v.)* — to greet
salvadoreño *(adj.)* — Salvadorean
salvar *(v.)* — to save
salvo *(adv.)* — safe
san *(adj.)* — saint
sanar *(v.)* — to heal
sangre *(n., f.)* — blood
sano *(adj.)* — healthy
santiguar *(v.)* — to bless
santo *(adj.)* — saint
sapo *(n., m.)* — toad
sartén *(n., f.)* — frying pan
satisfacer *(v.)* — to satisfy
satisfecho *(adj.)* — satisfied
se *(pron.)* — itself
secar *(v.)* — to dry
secretario *(n., m.)* — secretary
secreto *(n., m.)* — secret
sector *(n., m.)* — sector
secundaria *(n., f.)* la escuela ~ — high school; secondary school
sed *(n., f.)* — thirst
seda *(n., f.)* — silk
seguir *(v.)* — to continue; to follow
según *(prep.)* — according to
seguro *(adj.)* — sure
selección *(n., f.)* — selection
seleccionado *(part.)* — selected
seleccionar *(v.)* — to select
sellar *(v.)* — to seal
selva *(n., f.)* — jungle
semáforo *(n., m.)* — signal; traffic light
semana *(n., f.)* — week
sembrar *(v.)* — to sow
semilla *(n., f.)* — seed
seña *(n., f.)* — sign
senador *(n., m.)* — senator
sencillez *(n., f.)* — simplicity
señor *(n., m.)* — Mr.; mister
señora *(n., f.)* — Mrs.; missus
señorita *(n., f.)* — Miss; young lady
sentar *(v.)* — to sit down
sentencia *(n., f.)* — sentence
sentido *(part.)* — felt
sentido *(n., m.)* — sense

| | | | |
|---|---|---|---|
| sentir (v.) | to feel | solo (adj.) | alone |
| sentirse (v.) | to be felt | sólo (adv.) | only |
| separado (adj.) | separated | soltero (adj.) | single (man) |
| separarse (pron. v.) | to be separated | solución (n., f.) | solution |
| septiembre (n., m.) | September | sombrero (n., m.) | hat |
| ser (v.) | to be | sonambulismo (n., m.) | sleepwalking |
| serenata (n., f.) | serenade | sonando (g.) | sounding; ringing |
| serio (adj.) | serious | sonar (n., m.) | sonar |
| servicio (n., m.) | service | sonar (v.) | to sound |
| servido (part.) | served | soñar (v.) | to dream |
| servir (v.) | to serve | sonido (n., m.) | sound |
| servirse de (v.) | to use | sonora (adj.) onda~ | sound wave |
| seta (n., f.) | mushroom | sonreír (v.) | to smile |
| sí (adv.) | yes | sonrisa (n., f.) | smile |
| si (conj.) | if | sopa (n., f.) | soup |
| sí (pers. pron.) | me | sopor (n., m.) | torpor |
| sicólogo (n., m.) | psychologist | sor (n., f.) | sister (addressing a nun) |
| sido (part.) | been | sorprender (v.) | to surprise |
| siembra (n., f.) | sowing | sorprenderse (pron. v.) | to be surprised |
| siempre (adv.) | always | sorprendido (adj.) | surprised |
| siendo (g.) | being | sorpresa (n., f.) | surprise |
| sierra (n., f.) | mountain range; saw | sospechoso (n., m.) | suspicious |
| siglo (n., m.) | century | sostener (v.) | to maintain |
| siguiente (adj., m./f.) | following | sótano (n., m.) | basement |
| silencio (n., m.) | silence | su (pos. adj.) | its |
| silla (n., f.) | chair | suave (adj., m./f.) | soft; smooth |
| sillón (n., m.) | armchair | suavidad (n., f.) | softness; smoothness |
| simpático (adj.) | nice; cute | subdesarrollado (adj.) | underdeveloped |
| simple (adj., m./f.) | simple | subido (part.) | risen |
| simultáneamente (adv.) | simultaneously | subir (v.) | to rise |
| sin (prep.) | without | subirse (pron. v.) | to be risen |
| sincero (adj.) | sincere | submarino (n., m.) | submarine |
| sinfonía (n., f.) | symphony | submarino (adj.) | underwater |
| sino (conj.) | but | suceder (v.) | to happen |
| síntesis (n., f.) | synthesis | sucio (adj.) | dirty |
| síntoma (n., m.) | symptom | sucursal (n., f.) | branch office |
| sirviendo (g.) | serving | sueco (adj.) | Swedish |
| sistema (n., m.) | system | suegra (n., f.) | mother-in-law |
| sitio (n., m.) | place | suegro (n., m.) | father-in-law |
| situación (n., f.) | situation | sueldo (n., m.) | salary |
| situar (v.) | to situate | suelo (n., m.) | floor |
| sobrar (v.) | to exceed; to be left over | sueño (n., m.) | dream |
| sobre (n., m.) | envelope | suerte (n., f.) | luck |
| sobre (prep.) | on | suficiente (adj., m./f.) | sufficient |
| sobresalir (v.) | to excel | sufrir (v.) | to suffer |
| sobrevenir (v.) | to happen unexpectedly | sugerir (v.) | to suggest |
| sobrina (n., f.) | niece | suizo (adj.) | Swiss |
| sobrino (n., m.) | nephew | sumergir (v.) | to submerge |
| social (adj., m/f.) | social | superar (v.) | to surpass; to transcend |
| socio (n., f.) | partner; associate | supermercado (n., m.) | supermarket |
| socorrer (v.) | to help | superstición (n., f.) | superstition |
| sofá (n., m.) | sofa | suplicar (v.) | to beg |
| sofreír (v.) | to fry | suponer (v.) | to suppose |
| sol (n., m.) | sun | sur (n., m.) | south |
| solar (adj.) | solar | sus (pos. adj.) | their |
| soldado (n., m.) | soldier | suscripción (n., f.) | subscription |
| soleado (adj.) | sunny | sustituir (v.) | to substitute |
| solicitud (n., f.) | request | susto (n., m.) | scare |

| | |
|---|---|
| sutil *(adj., m./f.)* | subtle |
| suya *(poss. pron. & adj., f., sing.)* | hers; yours |
| suyas *(poss. pron. & adj., f., pl.)* | theirs; yours |
| suyo *(poss. pron. & adj., m., sing.)* | his; yours |
| suyos *(poss. pron. & adj., m., pl.)* | theirs; yours |

# T

| | |
|---|---|
| tabaco *(n., m.)* | tobacco |
| tablero *(n., m.)* | blackboard |
| tacañísimo *(sup. adj.)* | extremely tightwad |
| tacaño *(adj.)* | tightwad |
| tal *(adj., m./f.)* | such |
| taladro *(n., m.)* | drill |
| talento *(n., m.)* | talent |
| tamal *(n., m.)* | corn dish |
| también *(adv.)* | also |
| tambor *(n., m.)* | drum |
| tampoco *(adv.)* | neither |
| tan *(adv.)* | so |
| tango *(n., m.)* | tango |
| tanque *(n., m.)* | tank |
| tanto *(adj.)* | so much |
| tanto *(adv.)* | so much |
| tapete *(n., m.)* | rug |
| tapiz *(n., m.)* | tapestry |
| tardar *(v.)* | to delay |
| tarde *(adv.)* | late |
| tarde *(n., f.)* | afternoon |
| tarea *(n., f.)* | task; homework |
| tarjeta *(n., f.)* | card |
| taxi *(n., m.)* | taxi |
| taxista *(n., m./f.)* | cabdriver |
| taza *(n., f.)* | cup |
| té *(n., m.)* | tea |
| te *(pers. pron.)* | you |
| teatro *(n., m.)* | theater |
| techo *(n., m.)* | ceiling; roof |
| tele *(n., f.)* | television |
| telefónico *(adj.)* | telephonic |
| teléfono *(n., m.)* | telephone |
| televisión *(n., f.)* | television |
| televisor *(n., m.)* | television set |
| tema *(n., m.)* | topic |
| temer *(v.)* | to fear |
| temperatura *(n., f.)* | temperature |
| tempestad *(n., f.)* | storm |
| temporada *(n., f.)* | season |
| temprano *(adv.)* | early |
| tender *(v.)* ~ la cama | to make the bed |
| tener *(v.)* | to have |
| tenido *(part.)* | had |
| tenis *(n., m.)* | tennis |
| tensión *(n., f.)* | tension |
| tenue *(adj., m./f.)* | tenuous; weak |
| teorema *(n., m.)* | theorem |
| teoría *(n., f.)* | theory |
| terminado *(part.)* | finished |
| terminar *(v.)* | to finish |
| término *(n., m.)* | term |
| ternura *(n., f.)* | tenderness |
| terremoto *(n., m.)* | earthquake |
| terreno *(n., m.)* | land; terrain |
| terrible *(adj., m./f.)* | terrible |
| territorio *(n., m.)* | territory |
| tertulia *(n., f.)* | social gathering |
| tesis *(n., f.)* | thesis |
| testigo *(n., m.)* | witness |
| ti *(pers. pron.)* | you |
| tía *(n., f.)* | aunt |
| tiempo *(n., m.)* | time |
| tienda *(n., f.)* | store |
| tierra *(n., f.)* | earth; land |
| tigre *(n., m.)* | tiger |
| timbrar *(v.)* | to stamp |
| timidez *(n., f.)* | shyness |
| tío *(n., m.)* | uncle |
| tirar *(v.)* | to throw |
| tiritar *(v.)* | to shiver |
| toalla *(n., f.)* | towel |
| tocando *(g.)* | playing (instrument) |
| tocar *(v.)* | to play (instrument) |
| todavía *(adv.)* | still |
| todo *(adj.)* | all |
| tomado *(part.)* | taken |
| tomar *(v.)* | to take |
| tomarse *(v.)* | to be taken |
| tomate *(n., m.)* | tomato |
| tontería *(n., f.)* | foolishness |
| tormenta *(n., f.)* | storm |
| tornando *(g.)* | becoming |
| toro *(n., m.)* | bull |
| torre *(n., f.)* | tower |
| torrencial *(adj., m./f.)* | torrential |
| torrencialmente *(adv.)* | tempestuously |
| torta *(n., f.)* | pastry; tart |
| tortilla *(n., f.)* | tortilla |
| tortuga *(n., f.)* | tortoise |
| tostada *(n., f.)* | toast |
| trabajador *(n., m.)* | worker |
| trabajando *(g.)* | working |
| trabajar *(v.)* | to work |
| trabajo *(n., m.)* | work |
| traer *(v.)* | to bring |
| tráfico *(n., m.)* | traffic |
| traje *(n., m.)* | suit |
| trampa *(n., f.)* | trap |
| tranquilizar *(v.)* | to calm down |
| tranquilo *(adj.)* | calm; tranquil |
| transbordador *(n., m.)* | shuttle |
| transcurso *(n., m.)* | course |

| | |
|---|---|
| transformarse *(v.)* | to be transformed |
| transitar *(v.)* | to transit |
| transmisión *(n., f.)* | transmission; broadcast |
| transparente *(adj., m./f.)* | transparent |
| tranvía *(n., m.)* | trolley |
| tras *(prep.)* | after |
| trasquilado *(adj.)* | sheared |
| trasto *(n., m.)* | stuff |
| tratado *(adj.)* | treated |
| tratar *(v.)* | to try; to treat |
| trato *(n., m.)* | deal |
| tren *(n., m.)* | train |
| trigo *(n., m.)* | wheat |
| triste *(adj., m./f.)* | sad |
| tristeza *(n., f.)* | sadness |
| tronco *(n., m.)* | trunk |
| tropa *(n., f.)* | troop |
| tropezado *(part.)* | tripped |
| tropezar *(v.)* | to trip |
| tropical *(adj., m./f.)* | tropical |
| trópico *(n., m.)* | tropics |
| truco *(n., m.)* | trick |
| tú *(pers. pron.)* | you |
| tu *(poss. adj.)* | your |
| tubería *(n., f.)* | plumbing |
| tumba *(n., f.)* | tomb |
| túnel *(n., m.)* | tunnel |
| turista *(n., m./f.)* | tourist |
| turístico *(adj.)* lugares ~ | tourist places |
| turnarse *(v.)* | to take turns |
| tus *(poss. adj.)* | your |
| tuya *(poss. pron. & adj., f., sing.)* | yours; of yours |
| tuyas *(poss. pron. & adj., f., pl.)* | yours; of yours |
| tuyo *(poss. pron. & adj., m., sing.)* | yours; of yours |
| tuyos *(poss. pron. & adj., m., pl.)* | yours; of yours |

## U

| | |
|---|---|
| ubicar *(v.)* | to locate |
| último *(adj.)* | last |
| un *(ind. art.)* | a |
| una *(ind. art.)* | a |
| unas *(ind. art., f.)* | some |
| único *(adj.)* | unique |
| unido *(adj.)* | united |
| universidad *(n., f.)* | university |
| unos *(ind. art., m.)* | some |
| urgencia *(n., f.)* | urgency |
| urgente *(adj., m./f.)* | urgent |
| urgentemente *(adv.)* | urgently |
| usado *(adj.)* | used |
| usado *(part.)* | used |
| usar *(v.)* | to use |

| | |
|---|---|
| uso *(n., m.)* | use; usage |
| usted *(pers. pron., sing.)* | you |
| ustedes *(pers. pron., pl.)* | you |
| utilizando *(g.)* | using |
| utilizar *(v.)* | to use |
| uva *(n., f.)* | grape |

## V

| | |
|---|---|
| ¡Vale! *(interj.)* | OK! |
| vaca *(n., f.)* | cow |
| vacaciones *(n., f.)* | holidays |
| vacío *(adj.)* | empty |
| vacuna *(n., f.)* | vaccine |
| valentía *(n., f.)* | courage |
| valer *(v.)* | to be worth |
| valiente *(adj., m./f.)* | brave |
| valentísimo *(sup. adj.)* | extremely brave |
| valioso *(adj.)* | valuable |
| valor *(n., m.)* | value |
| vanidoso *(adj.)* | vain |
| vapor *(n., m.)* | vapor |
| variado *(adj.)* | varied |
| varios *(adj.)* | several |
| vaso *(n., m.)* | glass (cup) |
| vasto *(adj.)* | vast |
| vecino *(n., m.)* | neighbor |
| vegetación *(n., f.)* | vegetation |
| vela *(n., f.)* | sail |
| velada *(n., f.)* | party |
| velocidad *(n., f.)* | speed; velocity |
| veloz *(adj., m./f.)* | fast |
| venado *(n., m.)* | deer |
| vencer *(v.)* | to vanquish |
| vendaval *(n., m.)* | gale |
| vendedor *(n., m.)* | salesman |
| vendedora *(n., f.)* | saleswoman |
| vender *(v.)* | to sell |
| vendido *(adj.)* | sold |
| venido *(part.)* | come |
| venir *(v.)* | to come |
| venta *(n., f.)* | sale |
| ventana *(n., f.)* | window |
| ver *(v.)* | to see |
| verano *(n., m.)* | summer |
| verbo *(n., m.)* | verb |
| verdad *(n., f.)* | truth |
| verde *(adj., m./f.)* | green |
| verdura | green (vegetable) |
| veredicto *(n., m.)* | verdict |
| verídico *(adj.)* | truthful |
| verse *(pron. v.)* | to see oneself |
| versión *(n., f.)* | version |
| verso *(n., m.)* | verse |
| vespertino *(adj.)* | vespertine; evening |
| vestido *(adj.)* | dressed |
| vestido *(n., m.)* | dress |

| | | | |
|---|---|---|---|
| vestir *(v.)* | to dress | viviendo *(g.)* | living |
| vestirse *(v.)* | to dress oneself | vivir *(v.)* | to live |
| vez *(n., f.)* | time | vivo *(adj.)* | alive |
| vía *(n., f.)* | way | vocabulario *(n., m.)* | vocabulary |
| viajado *(part.)* | traveled | volador *(adj.)* | flying |
| viajar *(v.)* | to travel | volar *(v.)* | to fly |
| viaje *(n., m.)* | trip | voleibol *(n., m.)* | volleyball |
| vicepresidencia *(n., f.)* | vice-presidency | volumen *(n., m.)* | volume |
| víctima *(n., f.)* | victim | voluntad *(n., f.)* | will |
| vida *(n., f.)* | life | volver *(v.)* | to return |
| vidrio *(n., m.)* | glass | volverse *(pron. v.)* | to become |
| viejito *(n., m.)* | elderly man (affectionate) | vosotras *(pers. pron., f., pl.)* | you |
| | | vosotros *(pers. pron., m., pl.)* | you |
| viejo *(adj.)* | old | voto *(n., m.)* | vote |
| viendo *(g.)* | seeing | voz *(n., f.)* | voice |
| viento *(n., m.)* | wind | vuelta See also *dar la vuelta* | turn |
| viernes *(n., m.)* | Friday | vuelto *(part.)* | returned |
| vigilante *(n., m./f.)* | security guard | vuestra *(poss. pron., f., sing.)* | yours |
| vinagre *(n., m.)* | vinegar | vuestras *(poss. pron., f., pl.)* | yours |
| viniendo *(g.)* | coming | vuestro *(poss. pron., m., sing.)* | yours |
| vino *(n., m.)* | wine | vuestros *(poss. pron., m., pl.)* | yours |
| violencia *(n., f.)* | violence | | |
| violonchelo *(n., m.)* | violoncello | | |
| virgen *(n., f.)* | virgin | | |
| virtud *(n., f.)* | virtue | | |
| viruela *(n., f.)* | smallpox | | |

## Y

| | |
|---|---|
| ya *(adv.)* | already |
| yate *(n., m.)* | yacht |
| yegua *(n., f.)* | mare |
| yerno *(n., m.)* | son-in-law |
| yo *(pers. pron.)* | I |

| | |
|---|---|
| virus *(n., m.)* | virus |
| visita *(n., f.)* | visit |
| visitado *(part.)* | visited |
| visitando *(g.)* | visiting |
| visitante *(n., m.)* | visitor |
| visitar *(v.)* | to visit |
| vista *(n., f.)* | view |
| visto *(part.)* | seen |
| vitamina *(n., f.)* | vitamin |
| viuda *(n., f.)* | widow |
| víveres *(n., m.)* | provisions |
| vivido *(part.)* | lived |
| vividor *(n., m.)* | freeloader |
| vivienda *(n., f.)* | dwelling |

## Z

| | |
|---|---|
| zapato *(n., m.)* | shoe |
| zarpado *(part.)* | sailed |
| zarpar *(v.)* | to sail |
| zoológico *(n., m.)* | zoo |
| zurcir *(v.)* | to darn |

# MOVE TO THE HEAD OF YOUR CLASS
# THE EASY WAY!

Barron's presents THE EASY WAY SERIES—specially prepared by top educators, it maximizes effective learning while minimizing the time and effort it takes to raise your grades, brush up on the basics, and build your confidence. Comprehensive and full of clear review examples, **THE EASY WAY SERIES** is your best bet for better grades, quickly!

| | |
|---|---|
| 0-7641-1976-1 | **Accounting the Easy Way, 4th Ed.**—$14.95, Can. $21.95 |
| 0-7641-1972-9 | **Algebra the Easy Way, 4th Ed.**—$13.95, Can. $19.50 |
| 0-7641-1973-7 | **American History the Easy Way, 3rd Ed.**—$14.95, Can. $21.00 |
| 0-7641-0299-0 | **American Sign Language the Easy Way**—$14.95, Can. $21.00 |
| 0-8120-9134-5 | **Anatomy and Physiology the Easy Way**—$14.95, Can. $19.95 |
| 0-8120-9410-7 | **Arithmetic the Easy Way, 3rd Ed.**—$14.95, Can. $21.95 |
| 0-7641-1358-5 | **Biology the Easy Way, 3rd Ed.**—$14.95, Can. $21.95 |
| 0-7641-1079-9 | **Bookkeeping the Easy Way, 3rd Ed.**—$14.95, Can. $21.00 |
| 0-8120-4760-5 | **Business Law the Easy Way**—$14.95, Can. $21.00 |
| 0-7641-0314-8 | **Business Letters the Easy Way, 3rd Ed.**—$13.95, Can. $19.50 |
| 0-7641-1359-3 | **Business Math the Easy Way, 3rd Ed.**—$14.95, Can. $21.00 |
| 0-8120-9141-8 | **Calculus the Easy Way, 3rd Ed.**—$13.95, Can. $19.50 |
| 0-7641-1978-8 | **Chemistry the Easy Way, 4th Ed.**—$14.95, Can. $21.95 |
| 0-7641-0659-7 | **Chinese the Easy Way**—$14.95, Can. $21.00 |
| 0-7641-2146-4 | **Earth Science The Easy Way**—$14.95, Can. $21.95 |
| 0-7641-1981-8 | **Electronics the Easy Way, 4th Ed.**—$14.95, Can. $21.00 |
| 0-7641-1975-3 | **English the Easy Way, 4th Ed.**—$13.95, Can. $19.50 |
| 0-8120-9505-7 | **French the Easy Way, 3rd Ed.**—$14.95, Can. $21.00 |
| 0-7641-0110-2 | **Geometry the Easy Way, 3rd Ed.**—$14.95, Can. $21.00 |
| 0-8120-9145-0 | **German the Easy Way, 2nd Ed.**—$14.95, Can. $21.00 |
| 0-7641-1989-3 | **Grammar the Easy Way**—$14.95, Can. $21.00 |
| 0-8120-9146-9 | **Italian the Easy Way, 2nd Ed.**—$13.95, Can. $19.50 |
| 0-8120-9627-4 | **Japanese the Easy Way**—$14.95, Can. $21.00 |
| 0-7641-0752-6 | **Java™ Programming the Easy Way**—$18.95, Can. $25.50 |
| 0-7641-2011-5 | **Math the Easy Way, 4th Ed.**—$13.95, Can. $19.50 |
| 0-7641-1871-4 | **Math Word Problems the Easy Way**—$14.95, Can. $21.00 |
| 0-8120-9601-0 | **Microeconomics the Easy Way**—$14.95, Can. $21.00 |
| 0-7641-0236-2 | **Physics the Easy Way, 3rd Ed.**—$14.95, Can. $21.00 |
| 0-7641-2263-0 | **Spanish Grammar**—$14.95, Can. $21.00 |
| 0-7641-1974-5 | **Spanish the Easy Way, 3rd Ed.**—$13.95, Can. $19.50 |
| 0-8120-9852-8 | **Speed Reading the Easy Way**—$14.95, Can. $21.95 |
| 0-8120-9143-4 | **Spelling the Easy Way, 3rd Ed.**—$13.95, Can. $19.50 |
| 0-8120-9392-5 | **Statistics the Easy Way, 3rd Ed.**—$14.95, Can. $21.00 |
| 0-7641-1360-7 | **Trigonometry the Easy Way, 3rd Ed.**—$14.95, Can. $21.00 |
| 0-8120-9147-7 | **Typing the Easy Way, 3rd Ed.**—$19.95, Can. $28.95 |
| 0-8120-9765-3 | **World History the Easy Way, Vol. One**—$15.95, Can. $22.50 |
| 0-8120-9766-1 | **World History the Easy Way, Vol. Two**—$14.95, Can. $21.00 |
| 0-7641-1206-6 | **Writing the Easy Way, 3rd Ed.**—$14.95, Can. $21.00 |

**Barron's Educational Series, Inc.**
250 Wireless Boulevard • Hauppauge, New York 11788
**In Canada:** Georgetown Book Warehouse • 34 Armstrong Avenue, Georgetown, Ontario L7G 4R9
www.barronseduc.com                                    $ = U.S. Dollars   Can. $ = Canadian Dollars

Prices subject to change without notice. Books may be purchased at your local bookstore, or by mail from Barron's. Enclose check or money order for total amount plus sales tax where applicable and 18% for postage and handling (minimum charge $5.95 U.S. and Canada). All books are paperback editions.

(#45) R 9/03

# Helpful Guides for Mastering a Foreign Language

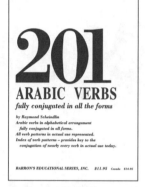

## 2001 Idiom Series

Indispensable resources, these completely bilingual dictionaries in four major European languages present the most frequently used idiomatic words and phrases to help students avoid stilted expression when writing in their newly acquired language. Each book includes illustrative sentences. Each feature is easy to locate and designed with clarity in mind.

**2001 French and English Idioms, 2nd**
0-8120-9024-1   $14.95, Can $19.95

**2001 German and English Idioms**
0-8120-9009-8   $16.95, Can $23.95

**2001 Italian and English Idioms**
0-8120-9030-6   $15.95, Can $22.50

**2001 Japanese and English Idioms**
0-8120-9433-6   $16.95, Can $23.95

**2001 Russian and English Idioms**
0-8120-9532-4   $18.95, Can $26.50

**2001 Spanish and English Idioms**
0-8120-9028-4   $14.95, Can $21.00

## 201 Verb Series

The most commonly used verbs are presented alphabetically and in all their forms, one to a page, in each of the many foreign languages listed here. Features of this series include discussions of participles, punctuation guides, listings of compounds, the phrases and expressions often used with each verb, plus much more!

**201 Arabic Verbs**
0-8120-0547-3   $13.95, Can $17.95

**201 Dutch Verbs**
0-8120-0738-7   $13.95, Can $19.95

**201 Modern Greek Verbs**
0-8120-0475-2   $11.95, Can $15.95

**201 Swedish Verbs**
0-8120-0528-7   $15.95, Can $23.50

**201 Turkish Verbs**
0-8120-2034-0   $14.95, Can $21.00

## 501 Verb Series

Here is a series to help the foreign language student successfully approach verbs and all their details. Complete conjugations of the verbs are arranged one verb to a page in alphabetical order. Verb forms are printed in boldface type in two columns, and common idioms using the applicable verbs are listed at the bottom of the page in each volume.

**501 English Verbs**
0-7641-0304-0   $14.95, Can $19.95
**501 French Verbs, 4th**
0-7641-2429-3   $14.95, Can $21.95
**501 German Verbs, 3rd**
0-7641-0284-2   $18.95, Can $27.50
**501 Hebrew Verbs**
0-8120-9468-9   $16.95, Can $21.95
**501 Italian Verbs**
0-7641-1348-8   $14.95, Can $21.00
**501 Japanese Verbs, 2nd**
0-7641-0285-0   $16.95, Can $23.95
**501 Latin Verbs**
0-8120-9050-9   $16.95, Can $23.95
**501 Portuguese Verbs**
0-8120-9034-9   $16.95, Can $23.95
**501 Russian Verbs**
0-7641-1349-6   $14.95, Can $21.00
**501 Spanish Verbs, 4th**
0-7641-2428-5   $14.95, Can $21.00

Books may be purchased at your bookstore, or by mail from Barron's. Enclose check or money order for total amount plus sales tax where applicable and add 18% for postage and handling (minimum charge $5.95). All books are paperback editions. Prices subject to change without notice.

**Visit our website at: www.barronseduc.com**

**Barron's Educational Series, Inc.** • 250 Wireless Boulevard, Hauppauge, NY 11788
**In Canada:** Georgetown Book Warehouse, 34 Armstrong Avenue, Georgetown, Ont. L7G 4R9

(#33) R 9/03

# THE "INSTANT" FOREIGN LANGUAGE PROGRAM FOR TRAVELERS.

If you're planning a trip abroad, these concise little guides will teach you enough of the language to "get by." You'll pick up the most useful expressions for everyday situations like ordering a meal and asking directions. Tips on pronunciation and grammar are included.

For that extra touch of finesse, try the set of two cassettes available with each booklet. They feature real-life conversations and include timed pauses for your responses.

*Each book: $4.95–$5.95 if sold separately.*
*Book-cassette pack: $18.95–$19.95*

**BARRON'S EDUCATIONAL SERIES**
250 Wireless Boulevard
Hauppauge, New York 11788
**Visit us at our website: www.barronseduc.com**

Please send me the following:

| | BOOK:<br>U.S. Price | BOOK-Cassette Pack:<br>U.S. Price |
|---|---|---|
| GETTING BY IN ARABIC | ☐ $4.95 (0-8120-2720-5) | ☐ $18.95 (0-8120-7357-6) |
| GETTING BY IN CHINESE, 2nd | | ☐ $19.95 (0-8120-8450-0) |
| GETTING BY IN FRENCH, 2nd | | ☐ $18.95 (0-8120-8440-3) |
| GETTING BY IN GERMAN, 2nd | | ☐ $18.95 (0-8120-8441-1) |
| GETTING BY IN HEBREW | ☐ $5.95 (0-8120-2662-4) | ☐ $19.95 (0-8120-7151-4) |
| GETTING BY IN ITALIAN, 2nd | | ☐ $18.95 (0-8120-8444-6) |
| GETTING BY IN JAPANESE, 2nd | | ☐ $18.95 (0-8120-8449-7) |
| GETTING BY IN PORTUGUESE, 2nd | | ☐ $18.95 (0-8120-8447-0) |
| GETTING BY IN RUSSIAN, 2nd | | ☐ $18.95 (0-8120-8448-9) |
| GETTING BY IN SPANISH, 2nd | | ☐ $18.95 (0-8120-8445-4) |
| GETTING BY IN TURKISH | | ☐ $18.95 (0-8120-8454-3) |

Include sales tax and 18% handling charges (minimum charge $5.95).
Return within 30 days if not satisfied for full refund.
Prices subject to change without notice.
I enclose $ _____ check or money order in total payment.
Please bill my
☐ American Express  ☐ Visa  ☐ MasterCard

Acct. #: _____  Exp.: __/__/

Signature: _____

Name: _____

Address: _____

City: _____

State: _____  Zip: _____

Phone: _____

(#68) R 9/03